Gérald Antoine, Louis Beirnaert, François Bovon,

Jacques Leenhardt, Paul Ricoeur, Grégoire Rouiller,

Philibert Secretan, Christophe Senft, Yves Tissot

EXEGESIS

Problems of Method and Exercises in Reading (Genesis 22 and Luke 15)

Studies published under the direction of

François Bovon and Grégoire Rouiller

Translated by

Donald G. Miller

THE PICKWICK PRESS

Pittsburgh, Pennsylvania

1978

Library of Congress Cataloging in Publication Data

Main entry under title:

Exegesis : problems of method and exercises in reading (Genesis 22 and Luke 15)

(Pittsburgh theological monograph series ; 21)
Bibliography: p.
1. Bible--Hermeneutics--Addresses, essays, lectures. 2. Bible. O.T. Genesis XXII, 1-19--Criticism, interpretation, etc.--Addresses, essays, lectures. 3. Bible. N.T. Luke XV, 11-32--Criticism, interpretation, etc.--Addresses, essays, lectures. I. Antoine, Gérald. II. Bovon, François. III. Rouiller, Grégoire. IV. Miller, Donald G. V. Series.

Library of Congress Cataloging in Publication Data

BS476.E9413　　220.6　　78-27622
ISBN 0-915138-25-5

THE PICKWICK PRESS
5001 Baum Boulevard
Pittsburgh, PA 15213

PITTSBURGH THEOLOGICAL MONOGRAPH SERIES

Dikran Y. Hadidian

General Editor

21

EXEGESIS

Problems of Method and Exercises in Reading (Genesis 22 and Luke 15)

OTHER BOOKS IN THE SERIES

Rhetorical Criticism; essays in honor of James Muilenberg. Edited by Jared J. Jackson and Martin Kessler. 1974.

Structural Analysis and Biblical Exegesis; interpretational essays by R. Barthes, F. Bovan, F. J. Leenhardt, R. Martin-Achard, J. Starobinski. Translated by Alfred M. Johnson, Jr. 1974.

Semiology and Parables; exploration of the possibilities offered by structuralism for exegesis. Papers of the Vanderbilt University conference, May 15-17, 1975. Edited by Daniel Patte. 1976.

The New Testament and Structuralism; a collection of essays edited and translated by Alfred M. Johnson, Jr. 1976.

Bridge Between the Testaments; reappraisal of Judaism from Exile to the birth of Christianity. By Donald E. Gowan. 1976.

Scripture in History and Theology; essays in honor of J. Coert Rylaarsdam. Edited by Arthur L. Merrill and Thomas W. Overholt. 1977.

The Hellenistic Mystery Religions by Richard Reitzenstein. Translated by John E. Steely. 1978.

Jesus Christ and the Faith; a collection of studies by Philippe H. Menoud, 1905-1973. With an appreciation of Jean-Louis Leuba and a preface by Oscar Cullman. Translated by Eunice M. Paul. 1978.

Exegesis; problems of method and exercises in reading (Genesis 22 and Luke 15). Studies published under the direction of François Bovon and Grégoire Rouiller. Translated by Donald G. Miller. 1978.

Signs and Parables: Semiotics and Gospels Text, with a study by Jacques Geninasca and postface by Algirdas Julien Gremas. Translated by Gary Phillips. 1978.

Candid Questions Concerning Gospel Form Criticism; a methodological sketch of fundamental problematics of form and redaction criticism. By Erhardt Güttgemanns. Translated by William G. Doty. 1979.

CONTENTS

PREFACE

The studies reassembled in this volume were presented in the framework of teaching in the third cycle organized by the Faculties of Theology of the Universities of Fribourg, Geneva, Lausanne and Neuchâtel during the winter of 1972-1973.

The authors of these studies are:

GÉRALD ANTOINE, stylist, University of Paris III.

LOUIS BEIRNAERT, S.J., psychoanalyst, director of a center for psychology, Paris.

FRANÇOIS BOVON, New Testament exegete, Faculty of Theology, University of Geneva.

JACQUES LEENHARDT, sociology of literature, Practical School of Higher Studies, Paris.

PAUL RICOEUR, philosopher, Universities of Paris X and Chicago.

GRÉGOIRE ROUILLER, exegete, Faculty of Theology, University of Fribourg.

PHILIBERT SECRETAN, philosopher, Faculty of Theology, University of Fribourg.

CHRISTOPHE SENFT, New Testament exegete, Faculty of Theology, University of Lausanne.

YVES TISSOT, doctoral candidate in Patristics, Faculty of Theology, University of Neuchâtel.

Messrs François Bovon and Grégoire Rouiller who were responsible for this instruction have also secured the publication of these works. They have kept to that which a large public could attend, with the aid of two fundamental biblical texts, the sacrifice of Isaac and the parable of the prodigal son, to the birth of critical exegesis, to the present dialogue which it maintains with certain of the human sciences and to the recalling of the patristic documents. This program could not be exhausted in one volume. The authors have preferred to attempt a series of significant soundings.

LIST OF ABBREVIATIONS

ATD	Altes Testament Deutsch.
BH	Biblia Hebraica.
Bib	Biblica.
BJ	The Holy Bible translated into French under the direction of the École Biblique.
BLE	Bulletin de littérature ecclésiastique.
BThB	Bulletin de théologie biblique.
CBQ	The Catholic Biblical Quarterly.
CC	Corpus Christianorum, Series latina.
DBS	Dictionnaire de la Bible, Supplément.
DeutR	Deuteronomium Rabba.
E	Elohist.
EThR	Les Etudes théologiques et religieuses.
EvTh	Evangelische Theologie.
ExR	Exodus Rabba.
GCS	Die Grieschichen Christlichen Schrifsteller der ersten Jahrhunderte.
ICC	The International Critical Commentary.
J	Jahvist.
JBL	The Journal of Biblical Literature.
JTS	The Journal of Theological Studies.
LevR	Leviticus Rabba.
MT	Massoretic text.
N.F.	Neue Folge.
NRTh	Nouvelle Revue Théologique.
n.s.	new series
NT	Novum Testamentum.
NTD	Neues Testament Deutsch.
NTS	New Testament Studies.
PG	J. P. Migne, Patrologiae crusus completus. Series Graeca.
PL	J. P. Migne, Patrologiae cursus completus. Series Latina.
Pléiade	La Bible, l'Ancien Testament, Bibliothèque de la Pléiade.
PLS	A. Hamman and M. L. Guillaumin, J. P. Migne, Patrologiae Latinae Supplementum.
R	Redactor.
RB	Revue Biblique.
R^E	Redactor of the elohist source.
R^D	Redactor of the deuteronomic source.
R^{JE}	Redactor who reunited the sources J and E.
RechSR	Recherches de Science Religieuse.

REJ	Revue des Etudes Juives.
RevSR	Revue des Sciences Religieuses.
RGG	Die Religion in Geschichte und Gegenwart. Handwörterbuch für Theologie und Religionswissenschaft.
RSPhTh	Revue des Sciences Philosophiques et Théologiques.
RThom	Revue Thomiste.
RThPh	Revue de Théologie et de Philosophie.
SAT	Die Schriften des Alten Testaments.
SC	Sources Chrétiennes.
ScotJTh	The Scottish Journal of Theology.
ThLZ	Theologische Literaturzeitung.
ThRu	Theologische Rundschau.
ThZ	Theologische Zeitschrift.
TJ I	Targum Pseudo-Jonathan (Yerushalmi I).
TU	Texte und Untersuchungen.
v.	verse.
VD	Verbum Domini.
VT	Vetus Testamentum.
ZNW	Zeitschrift für die Neutestamentliche Wissenschaft.
ZThK	Zeitschrift für Theologie und Kirche.
ZwTh	Zeitschrift für wissenschaftliche Theologie.

INTRODUCTION

Let us state precisely the subject of this book and indicate by that the goal which we have set for ourselves: to review the principal ways of approaching a biblical text. The object of our principal preoccupation, then, will be the scriptural text. Some today rightly propose to read the text first in itself, understood for itself, apart from all reference to an author, to a history or to a reader. At certain times this will also be our method of proceeding.

Our investigation, however, will involve interposing, by the text, the reader and his tools, that is to say, the biblical scholar and the principal methods of exegesis. For, as readers of the Bible, we hope (is not this the hope of all readers) to have access to the text and, through it, to the meaning. A reflection on our status as readers will impose itself therefore, as it will prove necessary an investigation of the most appropriate methods. The image of roads shows that diverse ways of access are possible and that each one reveals an aspect of the landscape. A text does not have a single door nor a single key.

In spite of its inner coherence and its own functioning, an isolated text remains incomprehensible. To take or to retake life, it must be associated with other realities, that is to say, reinserted into diverse contexts: language, history and consciousness.

Taking up again the saussurian opposition between language [*lángue*] (system) and the word [*parole*] (event),[1] we must certainly distinguish a Greek text from the Greek language in general. He does not oppose the view that the text is inseparable from the language in which it is written.

There is no access to this event of language which a text is, without knowledge of the linguistic system, of the language, then, in which it is shaped but outside of which it also arises.

From another standpoint, language contains some constitutive elements of a particular type, words which have a double face: that of the signifier and that of the signified. With the signified aspect of a word, we proceed from the side of semantics. It is not possible to understand the parable of the prodigal son, for example, without knowing what the concept of father or son represents. Furthermore, if we draw near to the father of the son, we are going to imagine diverse significant associations, which are met again in other texts, of which our memory is quite abundant. These associations help in understanding the universal importance of some part of the text.

To understand a text is to learn to situate it in its double relation to language: a) first, to a linguistic system which permits it to function, b) afterwards, to semantic units of which our text, like a kaleidoscope, is a temporary fixation. Resorting to an image, we could say that each semantic unit of a text or each signifying association resembles the fixed bibliography of a catalogue: it manifests and conceals at the same time a richness which is scarcely foreseeable.

The second level is that of history. In fact, this level is scarcely different from the preceding since a text is only comparable to another text and history is accessible under a "verbal" form only, usually written. To situate a text in its relations with history, as we will attempt to do, is in reality to associate it with other texts. Let us, nevertheless, retain the notion of history, knowing full well that history is never the presence of *bruta facta*, but that of a discourse on some facts whose reality is not verifiable in the manner of often repeatable natural phenomena.

In fact, there exist at least two bonds between the text and history. There is, first, the relation which all writing maintains with the referent, to know the reality aimed at by the totality of the things signified. This reality is not always historical: it can be aesthetic, as in the case of a work of art (the parables and the legends of the Bible have an aesthetic aspect); it can be also metahistorical (when it is a question of the intervention of God in the life of men). In the Bible, however, it is most often historical. In fact, loaded with information, the referent is constituted in history.

Someone has remarked, however, that the load of information in a text can be inversely proportionate to its semantic importance: the more the exact details of the assassination of Kennedy are told, the more the meaning of this historic event is lessened. It is necessary, nevertheless, to ask if there is still any meaning when no information is transmitted. In the New Testament, the resurrection has so much more meaning because the stories give us little information on the unfolding of the resurrection. But would not this meaning disappear at one stroke, with the swiftness of the air which leaves a pricked balloon, if the event of the resurrection gave way? However that may be, to read a text is also to put it in relation to what it relates.

A text has still other ties with history. Like men, texts are born and die. Like men, they are historic. The Gnostic phrase "Who were we? What have we become? Where were we? Where have we been cast? Toward what end do we hasten? Whence are we redeemed? What is generation and regeneration?",[2] can be applied to a text as well as to man. To know the origins of a man is certainly not yet to understand him; but it is already to situate him and to begin to know him. In determining the genesis of a text, then in discovering its *Sitz im Leben*, we will learn in what milieu, like a living being, it feels itself at ease.

From this second relation with history, we pass to the third level which we have discerned, that of consciousness. Certain structuralists refuse to consider history (the referent) other than as one code among others. They also exclude the subject, in our case the author of the text. For our part, following Jean Starobinski,[3] we consider that, whatever may be our interest in the text in itself, we always arrive at the moment when the text, as an object of analysis, loses this finality and becomes a mediator of meaning and a critical subject between the consciousness of the one who reads and the consciousness of the one who writes.

These considerations are theoretical: supported by certain contemporary analyses which, by their method of explanation, seek to determine the functioning of texts, they also re-echo the preoccupations of modern hermeneutics which, by an effort at comprehension, attempt to re-establish a living contact between author and reader. Our hope would be fulfilled if the distinction of W. Dilthey[4] between explanation and comprehension could be surpassed.[5]

In fact, the exegete has preoccupations which are often very modest, but nevertheless urgent. What textual form must be retained (textual criticism)? What limits should be put on the text (literary criticism)? What literal meaning should be given to it (exegesis)?

The book before you begins in an empirical manner: it will give first the exegesis of two textual witnesses (Genesis 22:1-19 and Luke 15:11-32) in the customary manner: following the historical-critical method utilized by almost all contemporary exegetes. Certainly, in the beginning, certain elements will be laid aside to be taken up later in the presentation of some great teachers of the 19th century or in the confrontation with the human sciences. Strictly speaking, the exegesis of our texts will only be provisionally accomplished at the end of the work. Nevertheless, we wish to depart from what is done, from what we do daily as exegetes. In following this route, we will reflect on the work in the act of accomplishing it. From the outset, as a presupposition, methodological suspicion will weigh heavily on our attempt.

This suspicion will quickly become an inquiry. From where did the historical-critical method come? What was the influence of the Enlightenment and especially of the 19th century on our manner of work? What role did Ferdinand Christian Baur play and of what usefulness were his historical researches in the formation of our discipline? What place did Julius Wellhausen have? Finally, what function did Hermann Gunkel fill with his *religionsgeschichtlich* and literary preoccupation?[6]

We will establish the fact that exegesis has, up until now, followed numerous ways: it has taken the way of theology in the beginning, that of philology since the Renaissance and that of history since the 19th century. Why has it not assumed other ways: that of literary criticism, of psychoanalysis or of the sociology of literature?

For difficult excursions, it is prudent to engage a guide. We have done that in the second stage of our research. For each of these fields, little known by exegetes, we have invited a specialist: Mr. Gérald Antoine, renowned stylist, who expounds, by some very concrete but at the same time religious examples, the part which one can, that is to say, which one ought to take from the linguistic and stylistic methods of approach; Father Louis Beirnaert, S.J., a psychoanalyst, who broaches the difficult problem of the application to literary texts of certain categories of psychoanalysis designed for direct and oral contact between the patient and the analyst: he sees in the parable of Luke 15: 11-32 a witness to the choice of unquenched desire; finally, Mr. Jacques Leenhardt, whose sociological works on Robbe-Grillet,[7] inspired by Lucien Goldmann, have shaken some citadels of traditional literary criticism. Each one invited to write furnishes some methodological information on the discipline which he represents and attempts to apply his method of reading to the textual witnesses which we have submitted to him.[8]

Mr. Philibert Secretan, who joined us during the second stage of our research, stresses this meeting between biblical exegesis and the human sciences. After that, the Geneva philosopher, Mr. Paul Ricoeur, attempts a provisional synthesis. In a letter which preceded his coming, he formulated his intention thus: "The title of my contribution could be biblical exegesis and hermeneutics. The theme would be the double connection of exegesis with hermeneutics: as a special hermeneutic in relation to a general hermeneutic, as kerygmatic hermeneutic in relation to a hermeneutic considered as a canon."[9]

The third stage, only broached in this volume, poses the following question: Do these new ways permit us to understand the biblical texts better? Or to understand them simply in a different sense? What progress or what difference is there between the exegeses proposed so far in this work and the Christian interpretation of the centuries preceding the appearance of the critical consciousness? Some Fathers of the Church, as witnesses, will then be called to appear at the bar.

As the bibliography placed at the end of this volume will attest, our effort is entered in the framework of a methodological inquiry undertaken today in numerous countries.

FRANÇOIS BOVON

NOTES

1. Cf. F. de Saussure, *Cours de linguistique générale* (published by Ch. Bally and A. Sechehaye with the collaboration of A. Riedlinger), Paris, 1916; critical edition prepared by T. de Mauro, Paris, 1973, pp. 36-39 [Eng. tr., *Course in General Linguistics*, tr. by Wade Baskin, New York, 1966].

2. Cited by Clement of Alexandria in his *Extraits de Théodote*, 78, 2. Cf. F. Sagnard, *Clément d'Alexandrie, Extraits de Théodote, texte grec, traduction et notes*, Sources chrétiennes 23, Paris, 1948, pp. 202-203.

3. "In my view, the risk of escapism into an *ahistorical* formalism can be avoided as soon as one questions the objective structures (the text in all its formal complexity) as the product of a structurizing conscious. A return to the idea of *intention* here becomes necessary, but it must be made clear that here it is only a question of an intention immanent to the unfolding of the structures and pages of the texts, and not of an anterior intention." J. Starobinski, "Consideration on the Present State of Literary Criticism," *Diogenes*, 74 (April-June, 1971), p. 83.

4. Cf. W. Dilthey, *Le Monde de l'Esprit*, I [*Die geistige welt*, I], Paris, 1947, p. 200; R. Marlé, *Introduction to Hermeneutics*, New York, 1967; P. Ricoeur, *Les incidences théologiques des recherches actuelles concernant le langage*, Paris, n.d., pp. 23-27.

5. Cf. P. Ricoeur, "Qu'est-ce qu'un texte? Expliquer et comprendre," in *Hermeneutik und Dialektik, Aufsätze II, Hans-Georg Gadamer zum 70. Geburtstag*, Tübingen, 1970, pp. 181-200.

6. For lack of time, we have not been able to study the Anglo-Saxon, French, Dutch and Scandinavian contributions to the biblical studies of the 19th century. We refer the reader to S. Neill, *The Interpretation of the New Testament, 1861-1961*, London, 1964.

7. Cf. J. Leenhardt, *Lecture politique du roman. La Jalousie d'Alain Robbe-Grillet*, Paris, 1973. (One should note particularly the important methodological introduction.)

8. Being more familiar with the social situation of the 17th century than with that of the 1st century, J. Leen-

hardt has applied his method to a sermon of Massillon on the parable of the prodigal son. In this sermon, Massillon preaches precisely on the biblical text of Luke 15.

9. Letter of July 18, 1972.

PART ONE

First Reading of the Texts of Reference

Genesis 22:1-19

Luke 15:11-32

GRÉGOIRE ROUILLER

The Sacrifice of Isaac

FRANÇOIS BOVON

The Parable of the Prodigal Son

THE SACRIFICE OF ISAAC
(Genesis 22:1-19)

by Grégoire Rouiller

FIRST READING

We turn now to a first reading of Genesis 22:1-19. This approach does not propose to repeat what is found in the commentaries, nor to champion any particular method of interpretation. Our remarks are intended to sketch the present state of classic research with regard to this pericope.

I. ELEMENTS OF READING

The text of Genesis 22 is excellent and its translation poses no major problems. Hence, the following remarks will be sufficient: In verse 1, it is preferable to accept the simple reading: "and he said to him, 'Abraham.'" The repetition springs without doubt from an assimilation with verse 11. In verse 13, in spite of the remark of R. Kilian,[1] we prefer the reading "a ram" rather than "behind him was a ram". The confusion between *resh* and *daleth* is so very natural. In verse 14, the correction proposed by Kittel's BH and followed by the JB appears to us fruitless. The MT offers two acceptable meanings: "On the mount of the Lord it shall be provided" or "On the mount of the Lord he (that is to say, the Lord) will be seen (or will appear)." Lastly, in verse 16 it is preferable to follow the MT, which the JB, by following certain versions in adding ממני, has not done.

On the whole, the translation by E. Dhorme (Pleiade) is quite correct.

The compactness of the literary unity makes its reading easy. Indeed, the expression "after these things" confirms the connection with that which precedes and appears as an editorial remark announcing the beginning of a development. Likewise, the geographical note in verse 19, with its inclusive tone, certainly concludes our unit. The repetition of the formula "Now after these things" in verse 20 confirms the fact that this is the beginning of a new unit.

We need not, however, believe that our pericope is monolithic. We may easily propose a division of our text:

A. 1-12: A trial succeeds
- 1-2: Introduction and command
- 3-10: Execution of the command
- 11-12: Divine acceptance

B. 13-14: A sacrifice which confirms

C. 15-19: Benediction and promise. Conclusion.

As to the documentary allotment of our verses, there is large agreement in attributing verses 1-12 to the Elohist. The divine name "Elohim", the assumed nocturnal revelation, the intervention of the angel, some psychological traits and a certain theological spiritualization point in this direction.[2] This Elohist redaction has without doubt undergone some changes in verses 2, 11 and 12.

Likewise, verses 13-14, and verse 19 as a conclusion, are sometimes attributed to E (but not without modifications). But what is the type of editorial deletion that occurs between verses 1-12 and 13-14? We are tempted to believe that this is important.

Verses 15-18 are acknowledged as secondary by most critics. Opinions differ when it comes to assigning their source: vestiges of a narrative, J, R^{JE}, R^{D}, R^{E}. The analysis of Kilian presents the opinions on the problem. His opinion which sees here an addition of a post-Elohist editor is quite probable.[3] We recognize then a late rereading (post-Elohist or not), made at a time when the traditions were largely mixed.

READING OF THE TEXT

Vs. 1. The formula of transition and introduction, "after these events", is found as well in texts attributed to J as to E (15:1; 22:20; 39:7; 41:1). It is, from all evidence, editorial. Hence, it is important in throwing light on the thought of the Elohistic editor. Indeed, we are warned: Abraham's sacrifice must not be isolated from the whole of his action, which finds its zenith in our text. After this supreme testing, Abraham can die, having buried Sarah and assured the marriage of his son. This observation puts us on guard against the tendency of numerous commentaries which systematically devalue the editorial verses or expressions. It is important to state precisely what one is seeking: the primary elements of a text or those which contribute to an understanding of its meaning.

"Elohim tempted":[4] The meaning of this rather frequently used verb (36 times in the piel) is clear: נסה signifies to institute a trial in order to obtain a clarification. In every case, it underlines the idea of an event, of something which happens, of the raising of a doubt. Thus a trial should indicate the ease of handling an armor (I Sam. 17:39), the confirming of a reputed wisdom (I Kings 10:1// II Chron. 9:1), the hidden meaning of suspicious deportment (Dan. 1:12, 14), the legitimacy of a quest (Eccles. 2:1, 7:23).

Nevertheless, the verb has chiefly a theological usage. We may therefore state that, from the standpoint of geography, it is a preferred term in relation to desert events; that, from the literary standpoint, it is found especially in the sequence E - D of the deuteronomic texts. If we take the point of view of a particular case, such as that of Gideon (Judges 6:39), the verb characterizes above all Israel's negative attitude with respect to God, and God's positive attitude with respect to Israel or a member of the people of Israel.

The term appears to be important in the relations between God and His people. The action of God which reveals Him as redeemer precedes the reaction of the people. To put God to test, after having experienced his benefits, is equivalent to refusing Him confidence, despising Him, disobeying Him, and finally not believing (Numbers 14:22; Exodus 17:2, 7; Psalm 78:18, 41, 56; 106:14); it is to mistrust God, as in Genesis 3. One understands why Deuteronomy 6:16 should prohibit it, and why the transgressor is guilty of a violation of the first and fundamental commandment.

On the contrary, God does no harm to man in putting him to the test. By definition man is weak, changeable, unstable and in need of development. This is his grandeur, and the peril of his liberty. Thus to understand the anthropological importance of testing appears to us essential for the correct interpretation of the text.[5]

Here the term "tempt" opens the way to the essential choice on the part of a man. The decisive importance of this act of freedom will appear in the raising of the stakes: the only son. To reduce the sense of the verb to a "pretense" seems to me considerably to weaken the importance of the testing[6] and the meaning of the text. Besides, we should not forget the exemplary significance of the action of Abraham, which forbids the weakening of the dimension of a serious option for him.[7]

The style of opening the dialogue is customary and ancient (27:1; 31:11; 46:2; Ex. 3:4; I Sam. 3:5, 6, 8, 16).

Vs. 2. With sublime literary skill the accent is clearly placed on the son, the only and beloved son, this Isaac of promise. All the terms of the verse, both those which picture the son and those which convey the order given, mutually reinforce and underline the gravity of the step awaited. "Take, I pray you" (33:11; I Sam. 9:3; 17:17): the expression often denotes haste and urgency;[8] "and go": this expression is already found in 12:1. Moreover, stylistically these two verses have a curious resemblance. In both cases we have a detailed description of what Abraham must leave: land, home, father's house (12:1), only son, the one whom you love, Isaac (22:2). In both cases, there is a similarly undefined goal to attain: "Go...to the land that I will show you" (12:1); "go to the land...of which I shall tell you" (22:2). Are these similarities purely accidental? We believe rather that the Elohist did not wish to isolate the episode of Genesis 22 from the entire career of Abraham. It is indeed a venture in response to a continuing call--the call of Abraham, the man of fresh starts, the man of faith, the "pilgrim, on account of the promises".

"Of Moriah."[9] Since J. Wellhausen and H. Gunkel, all those who have undertaken the study of this word have not pierced its enigma. One may hold, as do many studies, that the word is probably secondary; that because of its presence in II Chronicles 3:1 it should perhaps be related to the location of the temple, and that it is in every way consonant with the later liturgy.[10] I would add that in 12:1, after the word "land" we already meet the verb "to see", or "to show", and that this is what the Vulgate (*in terram visionis*) and Symacchus (τῆς ὀπτασίας) read here. The remainder of the entire story abounds in plays on words and assonances on the Hebrew verbs ראה and ירא, abandoning an etiological interpretation which in the course of the tradition was no longer perceived as essential.

"Offer him...as a burnt offering."[11] The term "burnt offering" is used not less than six times in a few verses. The hiphil of the verb not only indicates the act of "lifting up" a victim on the altar but especially, in a sacrificial context, the act of making a victim totally "disappear" into the presence of God, reducing it to vapor. Thus the burnt offering, probably borrowed from the Canaanites, was felt to be the most perfect of the sacrifices and was progressively used at the time of the various feasts. The substance of the temptation thus takes on its total meaning: the victim is supreme, the beloved son; also the sacrifice, the entire passing of the victim into the presence of God. Also, the force of the term and the meaning of such a sacrifice have been grasped by F. Josèphe in his observations on the life of Abraham. In the solemn declaration which Abraham addresses to his son, once he is bound on the altar, he recognizes both what had been his desire as a father and the primacy of the will of God. He even goes so far as to extol the privileged lot of Isaac who, having been born in a miraculous fashion, is not returned to God by an ordinary death (through illness, war, or some other natural cause), but in the midst of prayers and sacrificial rites, goes to be preserved in his presence.[12]

Vs. 3. This verse indicates that the command came by night (E?). All the commentators have brought to light the beauty of the story. On our part, we simply wish to underline its paradoxical character: the prolixity of verbs on the one hand (no less than six are necessary to lose nothing of the film of the action), but, on the other hand, the sharpness of the story: nothing distracts from the goal.

There is not one psychological notation. There must be no distance, nor any earthly consideration, between the will of God and that of Abraham. It is already a New Covenant moment existing before the letter of that Covenant, when the law of the Lord becomes one with the heart of Abraham (cf. Jer. 31: 33).

Vs. 4. What is the significance of the mention of the "third day"?[13] Is it merely fortuitous? Or is it a preciseness that allows the calculation of the distance traversed from the presumed point of departure, Beer-sheba? Or, does it underline the liturgical and even paschal flavor of the passage, in connection with the mention of "place" (מקום) and in reference to Ex. 5:3; 8:23? For our part, without excluding other nuances, we respond especially to the remarks of J. Jeremias:[14]

> It is necessary here to proceed from two negative linguistic remarks. First, it is a linguistic characteristic of Hebrew and Aramaic that in ordinary usage they lack a word which corresponds exactly to "time" in the sense of duration; they speak of "days" in place of "time" as duration (cf. Mt. 2:1; 11:12; 23:30; 28:20; Lk. 1:5; 4:25; Acts 7: 45, and frequently). Still more important is the fact that Hebrew and Aramaic do not even possess an ordinary equivalent for "several", "some", "a couple". The Old Testament sought to supply the place of these by saying very simply, in place of "some time", or "a few days", *iamim* (Gen. 24:55; 40:4; Neh. 1:4; Isa. 65:20; Dan. 8: 27), or better *iom o iomaim* (Exod. 21:21; "a day or two"), or still better *iamim ekhadim* (Isa. 22:13, cited in I Cor. 15:32--"Let us eat and drink, for tomorrow we die"--Judg. 20:28, also 30; Prov. 3:28; Matt. 6:30, and parallels; Luke 12:28); and once *iamim mispar* (Num. 9:20: "days", that is to say, "a small number"). Nevertheless, it is "three days" which is used most frequently in the construct case, *chelocheth iamim*

> (Ex. 3:18; 15:22; Num. 10:33; Josh. 1:11; 2: 16, 22; II Sam. 24:13 and parallels; I Chron. 21:12; Jon. 3:3), or indeed in the absolute case, *chelochah iamim* (I Sam. 30:12; Jon. 2: 1; with inversion, I Chron. 20:25). Corresponding with this, the temporal expression "the third day" does not at all necessarily designate the third day of the calendar, but it has chiefly and in a preponderant fashion the vague signification of "a few days after", "in a little time", "soon" (II Kings 20:5, 8; Hos. 6:2). All these expressions are relative indications, that is to say that the context must show each time whether a short or a long period of time is intended.

Here, the expression indicates equally that Abraham has done nothing else since the hearing of the order, but also that the accomplishment of it demands a pilgrimage of a certain importance. The dialogue between Abraham and his son will make the duration of this pilgrimage very poignant.

Vs. 5. The writer does not wish to raise a conflict between the servants and Abraham. We have here rather a beautiful example of dramatic duality.[15] It is an instance, at the principal moment of the narrative, of separating the protagonists from the mass, in order the better to place them in the light, and to dismiss those who should not gain undue attention. The verb designating the liturgical act to be carried out is vague (it can designate the total homage of the one who prostrates himself). This vagueness corresponds well with the moment of the narrative.

Vs. 6. Is it necessary to conjecture a design in the distribution of functions, Isaac carrying the wood, Abraham the fire and the knife? The suggestion of H. Gunkel seems to be too psychological,[16] that of the Rabbis' precocious.[17] We prefer to be bound by the extreme literary tension of the story where everything is necessary and points toward the end. Thus, in Isaac carrying the wood we see the holocaust beforehand, in Abraham with the fire and the knife, the sacrificial action is in some fashion anticipated. The insistence on their journey "together" leads in the same direction.

Vss. 7-8. "The narrator has tears in his eyes," H. Gunkel tells us. We will return later to the importance of this dialogue. What makes these verses poignantly beautiful is the position of the reader (with his knowledge) in relation to the characters. Isaac is ignorant, and his question is set in relief by this ignorance. Abraham knows, but his reply contains no false note. The testing is found in the full unfolding of the story; it is not a question of distorting the unfolding by a premature response. "God will provide." This is not a refusal to respond. Abraham does not go toward a future already made and preformed. The reply then is suited to each one: to Isaac as well as to Abraham, on whose part it takes a limitless valor of confidence, to the narrator as well as to the reader.

We observe the repetition, in the forces of an inclusion, of the phrase "they went both of them together". The dialogue enclosed by the repetition of this phrase is thus presented as a sort of lyric barrier holding the total attention of the reader on the sacrificial ascent.

Vss. 9-10. The sacrifice of perfect obedience can be performed only at the place designated by God. The narrator nevertheless feels the need of repeating that for us. Ritual and technical terms are multiplied here. The same is also true for the verbs of action. The two symmetrical series of verbs of action of verse 3 on the one hand, and of verses 9-10 on the other, separated by the journey and the dialogue which underline its length, are of a somber beauty. Abraham arranges the wood as the ritual requires in Lev. 1:7; I Kings 18:33; Num. 23:4; he binds Isaac. The verb "to bind" (עקד), even if in verse 9 we have its only attested use in Hebrew, in its proper meaning is nonetheless of great importance in Aramaic and in the Jewish liturgical tradition. Father Le Déaut says of this:[18] the root צקד is very frequent in Aramaic, whether speaking of the sacrifice of Isaac, or describing the manner of binding the lambs for the burnt offering (Num. 28); the tradition specifies that the method of binding signified by צקד is, not the two front feet together, nor the two back feet, but "a hand and a foot, in the manner in which Isaac was bound" (then each front foot corresponded with the back foot)...Further, in the strictly cultic sense, the word צקד has evolved toward the meaning "to bow one's self to the earth, to prostrate one's self, to adore" (as if one drew hands and feet together to bind them!). This secondary religious meaning is not to be neglected in an examination of the Aqéda.

The verb "to slay", "to cut the throat", is frequently used in a sacrificial context. Cf. Lev. 1:5; Ex. 12:6, 21; 29:11, 26, etc.

An interpretation of the whole chapter should not overlook the liturgical coloration of these verses, their quality of ceremonial reporting, whose close examination underlines the intensity and permits no digression.

Vss. 11-12. The presence of the angel (cf. 16:10; 21:17), and the repetition of the name Abraham, are perhaps works of the hand of the Elohist. The urgency is equally underlined. The commentators do not sufficiently bring to light the force of the "now" as a necessary anthropomorphism. The knowledge is experimental, it is founded on the free act, once it is carried out. The anthropological importance of this becomes considerable.

"You fear God.":[19] With regard to this verse we may note the following points:

The formula is rather rare in the singular (Job 1:1, 1:8,

2:3; with Yahweh, Ps. 25:12; 128:1, 4). Here it facilitates the assonances with the verb "to see". Further, this quasi-substantive participle takes on the value of a definition. This corresponds well with its place at the apex of the narrative. Tested, Abraham behaves as a true believer, in "fearing God".

There is no trace here of numinous fear. It is a case rather of a customary attitude, of a response to an indubitable Presence who has previously revealed himself as the All. To fear God is to accept a situation of total dependence, in a climate of obedience and of confidence. It is to permit no idol (though it should be his beloved son) to arise in the presence of such a God.

For the Elohist, fear clearly indicated this attitude of faith and of love which finds, in varied circumstances, an adequate response: the respect for the wife of Abraham by Abimelech (Gen. 20:11-18), the respect for life on the part of the midwives in Egypt (Ex. 1:17, 21).[20] Is it necessary to call this response an attitude of a covenant partner [*partenaire d'alliance*]? L. Derousseaux believes so.[21] This is acceptable if one gives the term "covenant" its ordinary meaning, without wishing to discover here a too precise terminology. Abraham carries out completely what Deuteronomy will later develop in its observations on the first commandment.

Vss. 13-14. From a literary standpoint one unit is complete after verse 12. One may conjecture a background of varied connections for our two verses. With one place of worship where animal and not human victims are offered? With a folk tale (Canaanite?) which justifies the substitution of a ram for the first-born? With a polemic against the sacrifice of infants? Research on the history of the tradition only results in hypotheses.[22]

On the other hand, however, there is no doubt that these verses are related to a wholly later liturgical and sacrificial practice (cf. *infra*).

Vs. 14. Without taking up the discussion growing out of different types of etiological phrases,[23] we rather favor the opinion of R. Kilian. The verse seems to be retouched. Although verse 14a is in its rightful place and possesses excellent parallels (Gen. 28:19; Judg. 15:17; 2:5; 1:17), verse 14b is likely added.[24] The modification of the divine name (vss. 11 and 14) is due to the intervention of an epoch when the sanctuary known under the name of "El (or Elohim) sees (or provides)" no longer exists.[25]

Vss. 15-18. These are generally held to be secondary. The reasons for attributing them to J are very weak. Herewith simply a few remarks: This second intervention of the angel gives the impression of a repetition and denotes a rereading. The expression "by myself I have sworn" belongs neither to J nor to E. In Genesis 32:12 it is plainly secondary. It is similar to the formula "oracle of Yahweh", which is prophetic.

The promises again take up well-known ancient elements: the stars (15:5; 26:4; Ex. 32:13; Deut. 1:10; 10:22; 28:62);[26] the sand of the sea (32:13); the gate of the enemies (24:60).[27]

Vs. 19. We see here chiefly a good literary conclusion. The narrative is completed.

II. JEWISH EXEGESIS

In most commentaries Jewish exegesis, considered late and inexact, is simply ignored. We think that this occasions an impoverishment of the reading, all the more that a series of solidly serious recent studies permits us to attain tangible results very quickly. We should like to set this forth briefly.[28]

The reading of the Palestinian Targum, in the recension given us in the Neophyti Targum, furnishes us with the essential ideas of this exegesis which will be sufficient to present.[29]

Genesis 22:1-19, according to Neophyti

1 After these events, it happened that Yahweh[30] tested Abraham with the tenth temptation and said to him: "Abraham!" Abraham replied in the language of the sanctuary and Abraham said to him: "Here am I."

2 He said: "Take then your son, your only son whom you love, Isaac, and go to the country of Mount Moriah[31] and there offer him as a sacrifice on one of the mountains which I will tell you."

3 Abraham arose early in the morning, saddled the ass, took with him two of his servants and his son Isaac. Then he split the wood[32] for the sacrifice, arose and went toward the place which Yahweh[33] had told him.

4 The third day, Abraham raised his eyes and saw the place afar off.

5 And Abraham (said)[34] to his servants:[35] "Remain here with the ass while I and the boy[36] go yonder; we will pray and return to you.

6 Abraham took the wood for the sacrifice, placed it on his son Isaac, took in his hand the fire and the knife and both of them went together, with one perfect heart.[37]

7 And Isaac spoke to his father Abraham and said to him: "My father!" He said, "Here am I, my son!" He said: "Here is the fire and the wood. But where is the lamb for the sacrifice?"

8 Abraham said: "Before Yahweh a lamb[38] for the sacrifice will be prepared for him. If not, you are the lamb for the sacrifice." And both of them went together with a perfect heart.[39]

9 They arrived at the place of which God had told him and there Abraham built the altar. He arranged the wood, bound his son Isaac and placed him on the altar upon the wood.

10 Then Abraham raised the hand and took the knife to sacrifice his son Isaac. Isaac began to speak and said to Abraham, his father: "My father, bind me well so that I do not make[40] any kicks[41] of a sort that your offering be rendered invalid and that I be[42] precipitated[43] into the pit of perdition in the world to come." The eyes of Abraham were (fixed) on the eyes of Isaac and the eyes of Isaac were turned toward the angels on high.[44] Abraham did not see them. At that moment a voice descended from the heavens which said: "Come, see two unique[45] (persons) in my universe.[46] The one sacrifices and the other is sacrificed: he who sacrifices does not hesitate[47] and he who is sacrificed bends the neck."

11 But the angel of Yahweh called him (from above) from the heavens and said: "Abraham! Abraham!"[48] He said: "Here am I!"

12 He said: "Do not extend your hand against the boy[49] and do not do anything to him, for now I know that you fear Yahweh and that you have not refused me your only son."

13 Abraham raised his eyes and saw that there was a ram among the trees, (held)[50] by his horns. Abraham went and took the ram and offered it as a sacrifice in the place[51] of his son.

14 Then Abraham worshipped and invoked the name of the Word of Yahweh, and said: "I pray you, by your mercy[52] (literally: by the mercy before you), Yahweh! All things are manifest and known before you. There has not been any division in my heart from the first moment when you told me to sacrifice my son Isaac, to reduce him to dust and ashes before you. But immediately I arose early in the morning and quickly carried out your words, with joy, and performed your commandment.[53] And now, when[54] your sons find themselves in a time of distress, remember the *aqēdah* of their father Isaac and hear the voice of their supplication. Hear them and deliver them from all tribulation. For the generations to come will say: On the mountain of the sanctuary of Yahweh where Abraham offered his son Isaac, on this mountain the Glory of the Shekinah of Yahweh appeared to him.

15 The angel of Yahweh called Abraham (from above) from the heavens, a second time,

16 and said to him: "I have sworn by the name of his Word--says Yahweh--because[55] you have done this and have not refused your son, your only son.

17 I will overwhelm you with blessings and will multiply your sons as the stars of heaven and as the sand of the seashore and your sons will inherit the ramparts of their enemies.

18 Because you have obeyed the voice of his Word, in your descendants will all the nations of the earth be blessed."

19 Then Abraham came back[56] to his servants. They arose and left together for Beersheba and Abraham dwelt at Beersheba.[57]

This page allows us to grasp how difficult it is to distinguish between the Targum and the Midrash.[58] It gives us a translation and also the traditional interpretation of the text, especially at verse 14, which should be nearer to the Jewish cultic practice. But can we affirm that the claim mentioned by D. Macho--"the Targum demands that the Midrash...be limited"--is here respected?

Let us deduce the following remarks:

Vs. 1. The marginal gloss frequently introduces the *Memra* of Yahweh (vss. 1, 3, 8, 14, 15). *Memra* is indeed revealer and saviour, as D. Munoz has established, and is the mark of a liturgical reading.[59] It is the case of the *tenth temptation*, then of the supreme temptation.[60] This confirms the importance of our text in the narrative of Abraham. Abraham responds in the "language of the sanctuary". The expression may also be translated "holy language". Just as we come across at the same time the expressions for the Spirit: *ruah qudsha* and *ruah bet-qudsha*, we find also *lishan qudsha* and *lishan bet-qudsha*.[61]

These expressions clearly mark the *Sitz im Kultus* of our chapter in the Jewish tradition.

Vs. 2. The love for the son is indicated by a more visceral verb than in the Hebrew. Besides, the bond with the Temple explicitly established by the gloss will be considerably developed in the *midrash.*

Vs. 6. "with a perfect heart": the term שלמה, whole, upright, just, often takes on a liturgical and even a sacrificial coloration.

Vs. 8. We have here a fine example of the "divine passive" which permits the avoidance of the name of God as subject. The exegetical process utilized here by the Targum is not uncommon. It plays on the possibilities of the consonants:

> Yahweh will provide the lamb for the burnt offering, my son!
>
> Yahweh will provide! As for the lamb for the burnt offering, (it is) my son![62]

Vs. 10. The ritual dread of Isaac is largely developed, founded on Levitical perspectives (Lev. 1:3; 3:1-6; 22:21-22) likewise developed by the *Halakha.*

With the mention of the vision, we are at the starting point of a development which will involve many variants.[63] Isaac, at the inclination of the various recensions, will see the celestial world, the angels, the throne of God, the glory of God, or even the *Shekinah.* Some have even spoken of a literary genre, that of the *Deute-Vision,*[64] which will ordinarily include a preamble to the vision (dreaming, eyes turned towards, open heavens), the vision itself (angels, Glory, chariot of God), a preamble to the hearing (one hears a voice, the *bat quol* coming from heaven), finally the words which reveal the person.[65]

The term "unique" (or "righteous" according to other recensions), and the celestial acknowledgement likewise place us not far from Genesis 15:6.

Vs. 14. The etiological motif disappears. A long development involving all sorts of variations in the Rabbinic literature exalting the exemplary quality of Abraham, accords an equal, and even sometimes predominant, place to Isaac. The excellence of both is presented as a guarantee of salvation for future generations.

The Midrash will develop many details of the text (sometimes attributing the temptation to Satan, relating it to the temptation of Job; justifying the leaving of the servants with the ass by their not having known how to gaze properly on the cloud on the mount...), but few important elements are introduced. The following points will serve our purpose:

--The third day is understood, in the light of several parallel passages (Hos. 6:2; Gen. 42:18; Ex. 19:16; Josh. 2:16; Jon. 2:1; Esd. 8:32; Esther 5:1), as the culminating point of a crisis and a solemn testing, issuing often in a liberation-resurrection.

--The vision is often associated with the cloud, in dependence on Targum Pseudo-Jonathan I: "he sees the cloud of Glory smoking on the mountain and recognizes it from afar." Sometimes it is discerned only at the moment of sacrifice. In every way the connection with Sinai, and especially with the Temple, is established.

--The prayer of Abraham will be equally drawn out. The sacrifice will take on more and more an expiatory importance.[66]

As is the custom, the liturgical texts reinforce all the traits encountered. One may read the major texts in the work of R. Le Déaut.[67] The bond becomes more and more strong between the *aqēdah* and the Passover.[68] Thus Ex. R. 12:2: "This is the month when the Israelites were freed from Egypt and when they will be free....This is the month

Isaac was born and was bound (on the altar) and this is the month that Jacob received the blessings from his father."

Little by little the bond was established between the *aqêdah* and all sacrifice offered in the Temple, notably the two daily sacrifices: "At the moment when Abraham bound his son Isaac, God chose two lambs. Why this? Because at the hour when the Israelites offer the daily sacrifice on the altar and read the verse: On the north side of the altar! ...God remembers the acceptance of Isaac and that not only for the collective or individual salvation of Israel, but more for the heathen." Lv. R. 1:11.

Doubtless many problems remain concerning the rereading of Abraham's sacrifice, notably the importance to be given to the expiatory value of the *aqêdah*.[69] Did the *aqêdah* encounter the theme of Isaiah 53 before the Christian era? Were the *aqêdah*, the paschal lamb, and the Servant, blended before the New Testament?[70]

Conclusion

We believe that an interpretation of Genesis 22 cannot ignore the following points:

--The episode of Genesis 22 has become a multiple point of reference in Jewish life.

--The life of Abraham here reaches its fullness.

--The obedience of Israel, in every epoch, finds here a model of epic stature.

--One may insist on faith, on righteousness, on obedience, on the fear of God: but always it is a question of contemplating a pregnant and total attitude, the image of the father who had found the exact response to the questioning of God.[71]

--The person of Isaac takes on more and more importance,

not to the detriment of Abraham, but as his worthy son, the one who is the precursor of Sinai, the lamb, the Servant, the Christ.

--The mutual penetration between the moral attitude of Abraham (and of Isaac) before God, and the liturgy, becomes more and more strongly expressed. The act of Abraham offers the model of all sacrifice, of all liturgical prayer.

--The salvation of Isaac also becomes the model and the precursor of all liberations, of all resurrections.

III. REMARKS AND QUESTIONS CONCERNING THE HISTORY OF THE TRADITION

1. An initial remark thrusts itself in: the fullness of the editorial work makes all research on the stages of the tradition difficult. It is also important, if we wish to avoid reductionist readings, to pose many questions to the text.[72]

2. Genesis 22 betrays some strong ancient attachments with a *sacred place*, perhaps a sanctuary. The name of this sanctuary, as well as the cultic customs which were practiced there seem to have been in relation to the verb ראה (vs. 2; especially vss. 14a and 14b, but also, according to H. Gunkel, vss. 8, 12, 13). From this come certain etiological traces. But how should they be interpreted? We believe that many questions cannot be answered with certainty. What was the name of the sanctuary? Did they originally sacrifice infants there? Or rams? Was the idea of redemption connected with the original practices? Is the element recognized by C. Westermann as *Rettung des zum Opfer bestimmten Sohnes* primitive? Was this sanctuary the goal of a pilgrimage?

3. If we refer to analogous instances of patriarchal

actions, there are serious reasons for thinking that this sanctuary was not, from its founding, in relation with the clans of the Patriarchs. It likely had its own life in Canaanite territory.

4. Some ancient elements (historic, cultic, narrative) have encountered (when and under what form?) the traditions concerning the clan of Abraham. We think that this was well before the installation of the tribes in Palestine. There is reason for believing that it was at this stage of the tradition that the narrative received its essential ideas.

5. We believe, nevertheless, that the part played by the Elohist is very important. It is likely that we owe to him the placing of the episode at the summit of the life of Abraham, its character as a testing, its quality of unveiling a pattern of behavior in the fear of God,[73] the significant strictness of the sequence "God-man-faith-sacrifice-divine verification."

6. An editor with a "syncretistic" tendency has prepared the subsequent Jewish exegesis--in a cultic direction (Moriah), especially if one attributes to him the rehandling of verses 13-14; in a perspective of the history of salvation by the integration of the promises (vss. 15-18).

7. Finally, we believe that the theological dimension must be brought to light in a true interpretation of the text. For this one will take into account the coloration given by the Elohist, the rereading due to the final Redactor (or Redactors), and even[74] the position of our text as the "pylon" of a "network": cf. I Sam. 15; Deut. 26; II Kings 4; Job 1:1...without forgetting certain texts of the New Testament.

NOTES

1. "Es besteht somit keinerlei Veranlassung, 'ahar (= hinten) in 'ahad (= einer, ein einzelner) abzuändern, wie es oft geschieht und auch in vielen Textzeugen belegt ist" (R. Kilian, *op. cit.*, p. 57, n. 14). We have been able to consult: *Compte rendu préliminaire et provisoire sur le travail d'analyse textuelle de l'Ancien Testament hébreu*, London, 1973.

2. M. Noth, *A History of Pentateuchal Traditions*. Englewood Cliff, N.J., 1972, p. 110, n. 316.

3. R. Kilian, *op. cit.*, p. 27-31.

4. L. Derousseaux, *La crainte de Dieu dans l'Ancien Testament*. Paris, 1970, p. 176ff.

5. This anthropological dimension is underlined on several occasions by C. Tresmontant, *La métaphysique du Christianisme et la naissance de la philosophie chrétienne*. Paris, 1961, pp. 45-54, especially chapter 8, pp. 650-691. "There is first the time of the creation by which being is proposed, lifted up, with its possibility of consciousness and reflection, and freedom. Then the time when the being thus created consented to his own creation, assumed and appropriated to himself the creative act, accepted it freely. But this creative act is not only a circumstance. It is a call; an invitation", p. 651.

6. This is what G. von Rad says: "The reader is told in advance, however, that the story concerns a temptation given by God, a demand which God did not intend to take seriously." *Genesis: A Commentary*. Philadelphia, 1961, p. 234.

7. Driver, in his commentary on *Deuteronomy* (ICC, 1895) has well grasped the importance of this verb: "*nissah* is a neutral word, and means to *test* or *prove* a person, to see *whether* he will act in a particular way (Ex. 16:4; Jud. 2:22; 3:4), or *whether* the character he bears is well established (I K. 10:1). God thus *proves* a person, or *puts* him *to the test*, to see if his fidelity or affection is sincere", p. 95.

8. One senses this haste and urgency, for example, in II Kings 5:15 or in Jonah 4:3.

9. Besides P. Zerafa, *op. cit.*, one should read the excellent notice in the Hebrew dictionary of Zorell and the study of R. Kilian, *op. cit.*, pp. 31ff. But the observations of M. Noth remain effective: "Moriah in this combination seems to be an appelative, whose meaning, however, is unknown." *A History of Pentateuchal Tradition*, p. 114, n. 326. It is the same for the localization: "All ancient and modern conjectures concerning the setting of this scene are completely uncertain." *Ibid.*, p. 126.

10. R. Le Déaut profusely demonstrates this.

11. On the question one may consult R. Rendtorff, R. de Vaux, L. Lyonnet, L. Sabourin, *op. cit.*, p. 123, 169.

12. Josephus, *Antiquities of the Jews*, I, 13, par. 2-4.

13. Cf. H. Reventlow, *op. cit.*, pp. 56-57.

14. J. Jeremias, *op. cit.*, p. 192.

15. A procedure which will be extensively utilized by an evangelist like Matthew: two characters face each other, Jesus and the one who must be saved, then the entourage must be kept in the background.

16. "Der Knabe trägt die schwere Last, der Vater das Gefährlichere: Messer und Feuer", *op. cit.*, p. 237.

17. According to which it is not necessary that Isaac be wounded and thus render the sacrifice ritually impossible. Cf. the text of Neophyti.

18. R. Le Déaut, *op. cit.*, pp. 137-138. On the verb and substantive one will consult the dictionary of Lévy which furnishes numerous references.

19. Studies on fear have multiplied in recent years: those of S. Plath, I. Becker, L. Derousseaux are worthy of note. Add to them the study of H. P. Stäbli in Jenni-Westermann, *Theologisches Handwörterbuch zum alten Testament*, München, 1971, col. 765-778.

20. H. W. Wolff has clearly demonstrated that for the Elohist fear goes beyond a moral attitude in the narrow sense: "Das hervorragende Thema des Elohisten ist die Gottesfurcht", *op. cit.*, p. 67.

21. "Finally the Elohist employs the root ירא in a new sense which appears to us to be intermediary between the first two, the 'sacred' and the 'moral' meanings, to describe what ought to be the attitude of the covenant", *op. cit.*, p. 180. L. Derousseaux seems to us, differently from J. Becker, to understand precisely the term 'moral' in a sufficiently restrictive sense.

22. One will read some interesting pages of A. George, *op. cit.*, pp. 104-105, on this problem. But especially the studies of J. Henninger and H. Cazelles, "Premiers-nés (en ethnologie et dans l'Ancien Testament)", *DBS* VIII, col. 461-491. These articles were published in 1968-1969.

23. As H. Reventlow does, who leans on the study of J. Fichter and who recognizes in verse 14 a form of etiology utilized ordinarily for place names, and Kilian who contests, with good reason we believe, the conclusions of Reventlow. Cf. Reventlow, *op. cit.*, pp. 26-31; R. Kilian, *op. cit.*, pp. 37ff.

24. Was it introduced by the redactor who has modified verse 2? R. Kilian thinks so. That is possible.

25. Cf. R. Kilian, *op. cit.*, p. 48.

26. Cf. N. Lohfink, *Die Landverheissung als Eid*, Stuttgart, 1967, p. 53.

27. The comparison of the entire passage with Gen. 26:1-7 and 32:13 made by R. Kilian is instructive.

28. Studies of R. Le Déaut, A. Jaubert, M. McNamara, R. Rendtorff, L. Sabourin, G. Vermès.

29. We have henceforth the excellent edition of A. Diez Macho, *Neophyti I: Targum palestinense, I, Genesis*, Madrid-Barcelona, 1968.

30. M (marginal gloss): "The Word of Yahweh."

31. M: "...where the Temple is built."

32. M: "and he cut."

33. M: "the Word (of Yahweh)."

34. Lacking in the text.

35. M: "to his two servants."

36. M: "the child."

37. M: "with a quiet heart (= tranquil)."

38. M: "the Word of Yahweh will prepare the lamb himself..."

39. M: "with a quiet heart."

40. M: "...(for fear that) at the hour of my suffering we do not struggle and cause confusion and that our offering be found invalid and that we not be in debt to you, between the hands of the heavens (= God). The eyes of Isaac..."

41: Literally: "so that we should not give..."

42. Literally: "...that we be."

43. Literally: pushed = thrown.

44. M: "Isaac saw them..."

45. = righteous.

46. Probably: "in the universe."

47. M: "has no regard" (does not spare - חוס).

48. M: "Abraham replied in the language of the sanctuary and said..."

49. M: "against the child."

50. Lacking in the text. Given by M.

51. M: "instead of."

52. M: "You are, Yahweh, the one who sees and who does not see. All..."

53: M: "...your commandment and observed your order."

54. M: "I pray you, by your mercy, Yahweh God. When the sons of Isaac enter into the time of anguish (<ἀνάγκη = by force, necessity), you will recall in their favor the *aqêdah* of Isaac, their father. You will forgive them and pardon their sins and will deliver them from all anguish. For the generations to come should arise to say: On the mountain of the sanctuary of Yahweh, Abraham offered..."

55: M: "thus."

56. M: "returned."

57. M: "and they traveled together toward Beersheba." We always interpret this: "the wells of Sheba".

58. On the Neophyti and the Palestinian Targum in general one can consult the studies of R. Le Déaut, notably the *Introduction à la littérature targumique*, Rome, 1966, and the excellent state of the question by A. Diez Macho, "Le Targum palestinien," *RevSR* 47 (1073), pp. 169-231.

On the distinction between Targum and Midrash see: R. Le Déaut, "...we know nothing exact on the relations between midrash and targum, in the ancient epoch; both were transmitted orally for a long time and seem to be a blending of the earliest written appearances of each," *Bib.* 48 (1967) (review of J. A. Fitzmyer, *The Genesis Apocryphon of Qumran Cave 1*). The same author takes up the problem two years later: "A propos d'une définition du *midrash*," *Bib.* 50 (1969), pp. 395-413; finally, above all in his article: "Un phénomène spontané de l'herméneutique juive ancienne le targumisme," *Bib.* 52 (1971), pp. 505-525. Comparing the *targum* and the *midrash*, R. Le Déaut writes: "The exegesis [in the targum] is also very clear, although the midrashim already present some techniques of extreme subtlety. Indeed, the genre of the version imposes certain limits and some demands for clarity which then permit us to see clearly the hermeneutical tendencies brought into play. If targumism is midrashic by nature, what characterizes it is the frugality of riches which demand respect for the text and the limits which that imposes on the paraphrase," *art. cit.*, pp. 508-509.

P. Grelot expresses himself in a very prudent manner in distinguishing *targum* and *midrash*: "...the question seems to me very complex, and I do not know whether one can succeed in defining the *targum* and the *midrash* in a very precise fashion, radically to distinguish them one from the other," *RB* 77 (1970), p. 232.

A. Diez Macho, in the article cited, appears to stand very close to the position of R. Le Déaut, simply insisting more on the traditional side of the *targum*: "In conclusion: the *targum* is not opposed to the *midrash* as a method of ancient exegesis among the Jews; on the contrary, the *targum* should give the meaning of the Scripture, the simple meaning or *peshat* and the midrashic meaning, reached by the techniques of *derash*, provided that it be a meaning accepted at the *bet ha-midrash* and at the Synagogue. Only the *targum* demands that the *midrash* should be subordinated to the 'translation' of the text and that it should be limited," *op. cit.*, p. 175. On the same question one should read the complements of A. Paul, "Littérature intertestamentaire," *Rech SR*, 60 (1972), pp. 438-442.

59. Munoz D. in A. Diez Macho, *Neophyti I*, vol. III, Madrid-Barcelona, 1971, pp. 75ff. It has been noted that I Q Gn Ap. never substitutes the *Memra* for the Tetragrammaton, a sign of its more erudite utilization. Cf. R. Le Déaut, *Bib.* 48 (1967), pp. 142-143.

60. One will find numerous references to the temptations of Abraham in L. Ginsberg, *The Legends of the Jews*, 7 vols., Philadelphia, 1925 (see the Index under "Abraham" and "temptation"). The text of the Pirke Aboth, 5.3 is equally significant: "With ten temptations was Abraham our father tempted, and he stood steadfast in them all, to show how great was the love of Abraham our father." The same text mentions the ten words by which the world was created; the ten generations from Adam to Noah; the ten signs effected for the fathers in Egypt; the ten signs on the sea; the ten temptations of the Israelites with respect to God; the ten signs wrought by the fathers in the Temple; finally, the ten things which were created on the eve of the Sabbath, to which certain ones add "the ram of Abraham, our father".

61. Cf. A. Diez Macho, *op. cit.*, p. 206 and the authors cited in note 165.

62. Cf. R. Le Déaut, *La nuit pascale*, p. 159.

63. R. Le Déaut, *La nuit pascale*, pp. 140-142.

64. F. Lentzen-Deis, *Die Taufe nach den Synoptikern*, Frankfurt am Main, 1970. Cited by Diez Macho, *op. cit.*, p. 204.

65. The context could well be apocalyptic, as in Mark 1:9-11.

66. Cf. A. Jaubert, *op. cit.*, pp. 381f. The merit of Abraham will, moreover, be utilized diversely. Thus *Mekhilta* on the Exodus will say: "R. Banna: it is by the merit of the good deed which Abraham did, that I will split the sea for them: Gen. 22:3" (he split the wood for the sacrifice). On Exod. 14:15. Likewise: "R. Yosé of Galilee: when the Israelites reached the sea, Mount Moriah was already uprooted from its place; the bond of Isaac disposed as if it were placed on the altar and Abraham as when he raised his hand to sacrifive him (Gen. 22:10)." On Exod. 14:15.

67. Le Déaut, *La nuit pascale*, ch. III.

68. The Book of Jubilees, 17:15, already locates the sacrifice of Abraham on the date of Easter. The same text attributes the temptation to the instigation of prince Mastéma. Chapter 18 will be a law for Israel to celebrate this feast.

69. A. Jaubert indicates with what nuances this expiatory value must be interpreted, *op. cit.*, p. 382. The study of G. Vermès on this point remains essential (along with the review of P. Grelot, *Bib.* 42 (1061), p. 458).

70. A. Jaubert cites some studies on these problems, *op. cit.*, p. 382, note 35.

71. The Sifra on Deuteronomy 10 testifies to this: "As long as our father Abraham had not come into the world, so to speak, the Holy One, b. s. was king only in heaven (Gen. 24:7); but from the time that Abraham our father came into the world he began to reign over the heaven and the earth (Gen. 24:3)." "If Reason had demanded from our father Abraham the apple of his eye, he would have given it to him, just as if he had demanded his life to save Isaac, his only, his life." This identification of Isaac and Abraham's own life is interesting.

72. Thus the etiological observation has injured H. Gunkel's interpretation. Likewise among modern writers: E. A. Speiser seems to us to have forced the note of the polemic against infant sacrifice, G. von Rad that of a moral orientation centered in obedience.

73. H. W. Wolff's article brings to light the importance of the transitions of the Elohist, the art of placing value on concrete situations where the fear of God is revealed (Gen. 20:1-18; Exod. 1:15-21; Exod. 18:21), seems convincing to us.

74. We think of the summary but valuable observations of P. Beauchamp, *Etudes sur la Genèse: l'Eden, les sept jours, les Patriarches*, Lyon, 1971, pp. 92-94.

SELECT BIBLIOGRAPHY

Some Commentaries

O. Procksch 1924[3]; J. Skinner, *ICC* 1930[2], A. Clamer, coll. Pirot-Clamer, 1953; H. Gunkel 1901, 1964[6]; G. von Rad, *ATD* 1958[5]; E. A. Speiser, *Anchor Bible* 1964; E. H. Maly, *Jerome Bible Commentary*, 1968.

Questions of Introduction

See the Introductions of O. Eissfeldt; G. Fohrer-E. Sellin; lire également H. Cazelles, art. "Pentateuque," *DBS*; M. Noth, *Überlieferungsgeschichte des Pentateuch*, Stuttgart, 1948[2], p. 38, 121 and *passim*; R. De Vaux, *The Early History of Israel*, Philadelphia, 1978, pp. 283-285.

Interpretations of the Whole

E. Auerbach, *Mimesis. La représentation de la réalité dans la littérature occidentale*, Paris, 1968 (ed. allemande, 1946 and 1949).

G. Fohrer, "Theologische Züge des Menschenbildes im Alten Testament," in *Studien zur alttestamentlichen Theologie und Geschichte, 1949-1966*, Berlin, 1969, pp. 176-194.

A. George, "Le sacrifice d'Abraham. Essai sur les diverses intentions de ses narrateurs," in *Mélanges Léon Vaganay. Etudes de critiques et d'histoire religieuses*, Lyon, 1948, pp. 97-110.

J. L. McKenzie, "The Sacrifice of Isaac (Gen. 22)," *Scripture* 9 (1957), pp. 79-84.

R. Kilian, *Die vorpriesterlichen Abrahamsüberlieferungen, literarkritisch und traditionsgeschichtlich untersucht*, Bonn, 1966, pp. 263-278.

R. Kilian, *Isaaks Opferung*, Stuttgart, 1970.

I. Maybaum, "Die Opferung Isaaks," *EvTh* 17 (1957), pp. 249-264.

H. von Reventlow, *Opfere deinen Sohn, Eine Auslegung von Gen. 22*, Neukirchen-Vluyn, 1968.

J. L. Vesco, "Abraham: Actualisation et relectures. Les

traditions vétéro-testamentaires," *RSPhTh* 55 (1971), pp. 33-80.

C. Westermann, "Arten der Erzählung in der Genesis," in *Forschung am alten Testament*, München, 1964, pp. 9-91.

Particular Studies

Etiology

J. Fichtner, "Die etymologische Aetiologie in den Namengebungen der geschichtlichen Bücher des alten Testaments," *VT* 6 (1956), pp. 372-396.

F. Golka, "Zur Erforschung der Aetiologien im alten Testament," *VT* 20 (1970), pp. 90-98.

B. O. Long, *The Problem of Etiological Narrative in the Old Testament*, Berlin, 1968.

L. Sabourin, "L'étiologie biblique," *BThB* 2 (1972), pp. 201-206.

On the Old Testament and Judaism

R. Le Déaut, "Le Targum de Gen. 22, 8 et I Pt. I, 20," *Rech SR* 49 (1961), pp. 103-106.

R. Le Déaut, "La présentation targumique du sacrifice d'Isaac et la sotériologie paulinienne," in *Studiorum paulinorum congressus...*, II, Rome, 1963, pp. 563-574.

R. Le Déaut, *La nuit pascale*, Rome, 1963, pp. 131-212.

M. McNamara, *The New Testament and the Palestinian Targum to the Pentateuch*, Rome, 1966, pp. 164-168.

A. Jaubert, "Symboles et figures christologiques dans le Judaïsme," *RevSR* 47 (1973), pp. 373-390.

R. Rendtorff, *Studien zur Geschichte des Opfers im alten Israel*, Neukirchen-Vluyn, 1968.

L. Sabourin, "Aqeda Isaaci et sacrificium paschale," in "Mysterium paschale et nox messianica," *VD* 44 (1966), pp. 65-73.

L. Sabourin, "The Paschal Lamb and the Binding of Isaac," in *Sin, Redemption and Sacrifice*, Rome, 1970, pp. 261-267.

G. Vermès, *Scripture and Tradition in Judaism*, Leiden, 1961, pp. 193-227.

On the New Testament

J. Daniélou, "La typologie d'Isaac dans le christianisme primitif," *Bib.* 28 (1947), pp. 363-393.

A. Gaboury, "Deux fils uniques: Isaac et Jésus. Connexions vétéro-testamentaires de Mc I:II (parallèles)," in *Studia evangelica* 4, Berlin, 1968, pp. 198-204.

D. Lerch, *Isaaks Opferung christlich gedeutet*, Tübingen, 1950.

I. Lévy, "Le sacrifice d'Isaac et la mort de Jésus," *REJ* 64 (1912), pp. 161-184.

H. J. Schoeps, "The Sacrifice of Isaac in Paul's Theology," *JBL* 65 (1946), pp. 385-392.

J. E. Wood, "Isaac, Typology in the New Testament," *NTS* 14 (1967/68), pp. 583-589.

Some Studies Utilized

R. Le Déaut, "A propos d'une définition du midrash," *Bib.* 50 (1969), pp. 395-413.

R. Le Déaut, "Un phénomène spontané de l'herméneutique juive ancienne: le 'targumisme'," *Bib.* 52 (1971), pp. 505-525.

A. Diez Macho, "Le Targum palestinien," *RevSR* 47 (1973), pp. 169-231.

Ph. Derchain, "Les plus anciens témoignages de sacrifices d'enfants chez les Sémites occidentaux," *VT* 20 (1970), pp. 351-355.

J. Jeremias, "Les paroles des trois jours dans les évangiles," in *Herméneutique et eschatologie*, Paris, 1971, pp. 187-196.

A. Paul, "Littérature intertestamentaire," *RechSR* 60 (1972), pp. 438-442.

P. Zerafa, "The Land of Moriah," *Angelicum* 44 (1967), pp. 84-94.

THE PARABLE OF THE PRODIGAL SON
(Luke 15:11-32)

by François Bovon

FIRST READING

I. INTRODUCTION

The Immediate Context

According to Luke 15:1-2, the situation is tense: Jesus, whose teaching attracts the tax collectors and sinners, provokes murmuring among the Pharisees and the scribes. Three contrasting poles appear, therefore, in the parable of the prodigal son: the blameworthy who take part in the story, the "righteous" who blind themselves, and Jesus who creates the crisis.

Verse 3 poses two exegetical questions:

1. To whom does Jesus address the parable? Who are the αὐτούς? It was probably neither the multitudes--the last interlocutors mentioned (14:25), nor the disciples--the next hearers mentioned (16:1), but the scribes and the Pharisees of verse 2.

2. Why does Luke use the singular παραβολή when he proceeds to relate three parables? The singular does not cover the first parable alone (for the third is a better rejoinder to the criticism of the righteous); nor does it refer only to the last parable (in the light of an eventual traditional link between verses 1-2 and 11-32, Luke would have been able to restore the plural form at the time of the insertion of verses 3-10). The singular παραβολή probably designates the

parabolic form of discourse, as in Luke 12:41, or it defines a collection of small units (Lk. 12:22-39).

The parable which follows this historic introduction, that of the lost sheep (Lk. 15:4-7), is interrogative (τίς ἄνθρωπος). It also contains three poles: the flock, the lost sheep, and the shepherd. It ends with an explicit application.

Equally interrogative, the parable of the lost coin (Lk. 15:8-10) is a replica of the preceding. Luke--as is well known--is fond of putting things in pairs, and he often utilizes a feminine illustration to elaborate a masculine incident.

Here (vs. 10), as there (vs. 7), the application brings into prominence the speaker (in the first person) and the hearers (in the second person): λέγω ὑμῖν.

We admit willingly that Luke handles the connecting links between pericopae and composes with art. Such is not the case with verse 11: the author writes simply εἶπεν δέ. The addressees of the third parable, who are not named, doubtless remain the same: the scribes and the Pharisees of verse 2. In Luke 16:1 (the parable of the Unjust Steward, which immediately follows that of the Prodigal Son), the connecting link, which is also a summary there, is very precise: "He also said *to the disciples*." From Luke 15 to Luke 16, then, the hearers have changed. With Luke, an instruction intended for the disciples alone is sometimes succeeded by a general and public teaching (the same phenomenon appears in Mark, cf. Mk. 10:10-12; and in Matthew, cf. Mt. 13:36-43).

If the connections with what precedes and what follows are few and tenuous, it is otherwise with the inner texture of the narrative. Beginning as other biblical stories or popular tales ("There was a man who had two sons"), the parable logically relates the fate of one, then the reaction of the other. In spite of the first conclusion in verse 24, the second part of the parable is not surprising. Singled out at the beginning, the older son must again appear at the end. As Dan O. Via, Jr., has noted,[1] the younger brother is the first figure who blocks the action (the joyous feast) by his journey and his sin. After having triumphed over this first obstacle, the joy cannot be restored immediately: a second figure, that of the older brother, prevents it from reaching its height.

The Broader Context

The author of the Third Gospel and of the Book of the Acts, Luke proposes a religious vision of the history of God and of his people. The Gospel and the Acts form the last two panels of a triptych inaugurated by the Old Testament. The period of the law and the promise is followed by the period of Jesus, to which in its turn follows the period of the Spirit, of the Word, of the Church, and of mission.

A triple division also marks the rhythm, as is well known, of the Gospel itself: Galilee--Journey--Judea. H. Conzelmann[2] attributes a Christological function to the journey. Other authors[3] have rightly pointed out the ecclesiological perspective of chapters 9:51-19:23. The travel document opens on the theme of "following Jesus" and continues by a series of instructions directed to the disciples.

Luke 15, which is at the center of this second part, hence at the very heart of the Gospel, reminds us, in its structure, of the whole work. If, as we have often been reminded,[4] the three parables of chapter 15 resemble each other because of the divine mercy and the joy which each time mark their recovery, a characteristic difference should not be forgotten: the parables of the Lost Sheep and the Lost Coin insist on the initiative and the activity of the one who comes to save that which was lost. The parable of the Prodigal Son, for its part, underlines rather the voluntary return of the younger son. It follows that, in imitation of the entire Gospel of Luke, the fifteenth chapter reveals the active presence of the Saviour before depicting the decision of the saved. In the Gospel, the mercy of God, which is pointed out repeatedly in Luke 1[5] and made concrete by the sending of the Messiah Jesus (from Chapter 2 on), precedes the conversion of the people narrated in what follows. Luke 15:3-10, then, comments in parabolic fashion, on the beginning of the *logion* of Jesus: "I have not come to call the righteous, but sinners"; Luke 15:11-32 illustrates the end: "that they may be converted (εἰς μέτανοιαν)" (Luke 5:32).

The mercy of God (or of Christ) and Christian commitment appear in an even brighter light in that Luke, as E. Fuchs[6] has noted, follows chapter 15 with various parables which set forth the opposite of salvation, perdition (Luke 16:1ff.).

Luke 15:11-32 allows us, moreover, to analyze at close range the process of human decision. It confirms the peculiarly Lukan features of μετάνοια which one detects in the Book of the Acts: to attain to faith and salvation, men decide first to stop, then actively to commit themselves. Thus, in a first stage, the Prodigal comes to himself in order to assess the meaning of his situation and to prepare his decision. Then he carries out his purpose in a second stage. The halt caused by the inner meditation (εἰς ἑαυτὸν δὲ ἐλθὼν ἔφη, vs. 17) is followed by a movement in a new direction, toward the father (καὶ ἀναστὰς ἦλθεν, vs. 20).

Study of the Text

At the risk of schematizing, we may distinguish four stages in the history of the interpretation of our parable.[7]

The first period, the longest, goes from the earliest days to the end of the nineteenth century: this period on the whole may be grouped in three successive types of interpretation, the allegorical, the dogmatic, and the historical. Each of these methods presupposes that the meaning is beyond the text--in an upper world, a doctrinal truth, or an ecclesiastical past. By discovering the pagan and Jewish, or pagan-Christian and Jewish-Christian, background of the two brothers, F. Ch. Baur and A. Hilgenfeld prolonged an ancient patristic interpretation.[8]

Beyond the symbolic interpretation of the two sons, we must point out the fate which verses 22-23 had during the allegorical period: Christ was seen in the μόσχος (calf) and the priests behind the δοῦλοι (servants); an allusion to the Cross or to the altar was read into the verb θύειν (to kill or to sacrifice), and a mention of the communion in the participle φαγόντες (eating).

A. Jülicher[9] opened a second exegetical period by the attacks he hurled against allegory and dogmatism. He reproached in particular the theologians for dissecting the movements of the repentance of the younger son in order to draw out an *ordo salutis* and for enumerating the gestures of love by the father as the successive expressions of divine grace. They are there only in the "frostige Erörterungen der Theologen".[10]

Marked by romanticism, Jülicher wished to be a partisan of life, of the feelings of nature and of the heart. Under his pen, the parable--if one may be permitted the play on words--left the drawer (*le tiroir*) of the theologians to recover its original soil (*terroir*). In his eyes the parable evoked a concrete story, simple and touching: a story so probable--may we add--that it becomes banal. All reference to the irruption of the Kingdom or of the Saviour is absent, to the degree that we no longer understand how the Jesus of Jülicher could arouse the hatred of his contemporaries.[11]

C. H. Dodd and J. Jeremias, marked by the rediscovery of eschatology, introduce a third period in the study of the parables.[12] Applying the method of literary forms, they uncover the successive roots of the parable in the being of Jesus and in the life of the primitive Church. Starting from there, they distinguish the successive meanings, original, traditional, and redactional.

For Jeremias, our parable is *zweigipfelig*[13] (has two applications): not that one point (the welcome of the prodigal son) is ancient and pre-Easter and that the other (the murmuring of the elder brother) is post-Easter, indeed redactional. No, the duality pertains to a situation in which Jesus had to defend the legitimacy of his message to the Pharisees and the scribes. The historic situation of verses 1-2 of Luke 15 explain the episode of the elder brother (vss. 24b-32). Consequently, the parable is "primär nicht Verkündigung der Frohbotschaft an die Armen, sondern Rechtfertigung der Frohbotschaft gegenüber ihren Kritikern".[14]

It is E. Fuchs who has advanced the furthest in this direction: "Die 'Verständlichkeit' des Gleichnisses liegt freilich eher in Jesu Verhalten."[15] To understand the parables, it is necessary to consider the behavior of Jesus. History serves as the key to the interpretation of the text.[16]

The final stage of the study of the parables is characterized by certain investigations on language. Various exegetes observe that language may have diverse functions. Sometimes it gives evidence; at other times it informs.

It also happens to *persuade*. The parable takes up this persuasive language which constrains the hearer to take a position.[17] Its principle function is not to facilitate the understanding of abstract religious truths, but to challenge those addressed and force them to take a stand for or against Jesus, by disclosing to them a mystery. E. Jungel utilizes the happy expression "Die Gottesherrschaft *als* Gleichnis",[18] the Kingdom of God in so far as it is parable, to point out that Jesus conceived his parabolic teaching as a form of the real presence of the Kingdom.

The structural study of tales in other fields throws a new light on the parables. Dan O. Via, Jr., speaks of figures which block the movement of the story, and by that the denouement, or outcome.[19] Others, following V. Propp,[20] analyze the functions and the actants of parabolic stories. E. Güttgemanns[21] advocates the application of linguistics to exegesis. There is a current movement, then, which favors the analysis of the text, independently of history, even though it should be the history of Jesus himself. This analysis should be done according to aesthetic criteria which find their theological legitimacy in the use of parabolic language by Jesus himself. In loosening itself thus from concrete reality, such language gains in universality.

We conclude this survey by pointing out some divergent interpretations: for the majority of critics, A. Jülicher[22] in particular, the traditional title of the parable is correct, for the prodigal son thoroughly occupies the center of the text, which treats of conversion.

D. Buzy, on the contrary, holds that "the first part plays the role of an introduction only and prepares for the subject matter".[23] In his opinion, the text intends to focus attention principally on the figure of the elder brother.

For E. Fuchs,[24] the parable is interested equally in

both sons. They are both lost sons who owe their salvation solely to the grace of God. Fuchs proposes, therefore, to entitle the parable: The Parable of the Two Lost Sons.

J. Jeremias[25] moves in another direction, for he places the father at the center of the story. For this reason he supports the new title: The Parable of the Love of the Father.

J. D. M. Derrett,[26] finally, is of the opinion that the perspective of our pericope is centered on the community. There is no question of individual salvation. The single concern is for the threatened, then recovered, unity of the family, the cohesion of the social group.

II. EXEGESIS

Textual Criticism

Four variants merit discussion:

1. At verse 16 we prefer γεμίσαι τὴν κοιλίαν ("filled his belly") to χορτασθῆναι ("to be filled"), for this common expression would have shocked the copyists who, taking their cue from Luke 16:21, have substituted a more decorous word.

2. Several important manuscripts have a long text at verse 21 which goes back to the text of verse 19. This is doubtless a secondary development. Certain copyists have determined that the younger son should utter exactly the speech he had promised himself to make.

3. At verse 22 we propose to keep the reading ταχύ ("quickly") whose disappearance is explained thus: the quickness with which the father pardoned likely displeased certain copyists of a church whose penitential discipline took a certain time for reasons of religious pedagogy.

4. Relatively poorly attested, ἀριστήσω (vs. 29) is as valid as εὐφρανθῶ (this last verb has been used twice

before, at vss. 23 and 24b). If one retains this reading, the modest lunch, imagined by the elder brother, contrasts thoroughly with the banquet organized for the younger brother.

Comments on the Text

Vs. 11: According to J. Jeremias,[27] ἄνθρωπός τις is a semitism characteristic of the *Sondergut*, the distinctly Lukan materials. Luke customarily writes ἀνήρτις.

Vs. 12: ὁ νεώτερος: with the definite article, the comparative has the force of the superlative. The difficulty of precisely determining the meaning of νεώτεροι in certain New Testament texts is well known. Does it refer to a group of youth or to the class of new converts (cf. Acts 5:6 and I Peter 5:5)? It is nevertheless improbable that Luke here reflects the "ecclesial" meaning of the term.

J. D. M. Derrett[28] analyzes the psychology and the destiny of younger sons in Scripture. He concludes that the younger is more often weak, rebellious, violent, criminal, filled with wanderlust, and elected. As for the older brother, he sometimes loses his rights or is duped out of them. The parable is scarcely conceivable with a reversal of roles, the departure of the older brother and the acrimony of the younger.

The Oxyrhynchus Papyrus 715 twice contains the expression we read here: τὸ ἐπιβάλλον μέρος ("the share of property that falls to me").[29]

Here, and at verse 13, are the only New Testament uses of the word οὐσία in the sense of property, possessions, a meaning which was widespread in the Hellenistic epoch. As for βίος, life, that which one needs to live, it may also signify property, possessions.

A legal problem is posed here. It appears to be established that if he did not wish to live in the family,[30] a son had the right to demand his share and leave. The Talmud allows a father to give his part of the inheritance to a son. But the son does not lose his right to the succession. Now, here the younger son had lost this right and no longer dares to hope for anything.

Diverse solutions have been proposed. We discard easily any explanation which stems from a Roman legal system.

According to J. Dauvillier,[31] it is a question of the *distribution of the ascendancy*. A father could tender, while he was living, a part of his patrimony to one of his children. Normally the heir paid a lifetime revenue to his father. The distribution of the ascendency effected, the beneficiary could no longer lay claim to that which remained of the paternal inheritance at the time of the death of the father. Although legally permitted, this distribution was nevertheless discouraged: "Whilst thou art yet alive... give not any creature power over thyself. For it is better that thy children ask of thee than that thou shouldst look to the hand of thy sons" (Sirach 33:20-21, cf. vss. 19 and 22-23). One could also deviate from the legacy law laid down in the Torah[32] in achieving the distribution of the ascendancy by means of a deed of gift between the living and carefully avoiding the use of terms which have a succession in view. The difficulty of this solution is that it anticipates that only the younger son has received his part of the inheritance while the father was living.[33]

If we have understood him rightly, D. Daube[34] proposes a solution which is not very different: the father gives his part to the younger son and remains the owner of the rest of his property until his death. The remainder then would go to the older son alone, for the younger son has decided no longer to remain with his father and no longer to participate in the family enterprise. This very simple scheme, which agrees with the text of Luke, appears to be attested by various rabbinic traditions (contrary to the official talmudic solution), by several Jewish legends, and even by certain texts of Genesis.[35] This solution also admits a difficulty. According to verse 12, the father divides his estate between his two sons and is not satisfied merely to give his part to the son who does not wish to live at home.

The problem, then, has not yet received a satisfactory solution. This stems perhaps from the Lukan redaction which has little interest in Jewish legal rules: verse 12 speaks of a division between the brothers (without regard to the traditional proportion of two-thirds to the oldest brother and one-third to the younger), even though verse 31 is indifferent to whether the father keeps possession of the property which he has not given to the younger son, or whether he has retained the usufruct of it.

What meaning should be given to ζῶν ἀσώτως (vs. 13)? Etymologically ἀσώτως signifies "without hope of salvation" (ἀ-σωτ). In its present context, the expression evokes an irretrievable squandering (cf. vs. 14a: "he had spent everything"). But there is perhaps a deeper meaning in these two words, for ἀσωτία has to do with moral language and may include the vices which one indulges by this squandering.[36] However that may be, the text implies that the fault resides less in the demand made to the father or in the departure of the younger son than in the irremediable loss of the inheritance.[37]

A. Jülicher notes with good reason that money plays a large part in the parable and that the economic situation of the interested parties suggests the economic situation of the story.[38]

'Εγένετο λιμός (vs. 14) is a biblical expression (Septuagint, cf. Gen. 47:13). Throughout the text we meet again a vocabulary and a set of expressions which recall the epic of Joseph (Gen. 40-49) and the story of Tobias.[39] J. Cantinat points out that "localized famines are often rife in somewhat desert-like regions, and in a time when commercial enterprise remains very limited...".[40]

The son falls into poverty (ὑστερεῖσθαι): cf. Heb. 11:37, where the ὑστερούμενοι are the poor. The vocabulary of want, which here points to unsatisfied basic needs, will be taken up by Christian theology, beginning with Paul, and by Gnosticism, to define the human condition before God (cf. the falling short of the glory of God, Rom. 3:23).[41] Luke here describes the degradation of the son who, after having lost his goods, falls into poverty because of the famine and feels personally lost (ἐγὼ δὲ λιμῷ ὧδε ἀπόλλυμαι, vs. 17).

The situation forces the prodigal son to attach himself to a foreign landed proprietor (vs. 15): the herd of swine indicates that the πολίτης is not Jewish. The same verb, κολλᾶσθαι, in Acts 10:28 informs us that such an attachment was reprehensible from the Jewish point of view.[42]

The words "sent him into his fields" reveal a semitism: the subject of the phrase changes without the change being marked by a new subject of the verb.[43]

The word κεράτιον, the diminutive of κέρας (horn), in the plural designates the fruit of the carob tree. Lycophron, an Alexandrian poet, indicates also that this was used to nourish pigs (vs. 675-678). "Carobs (*keratia*), the size of large beans, horny (*keras*), crooked, and dark-colored, with a sourish taste when they are dried, have always served as food for the animals of the Near East and are readily nibbled by poor people, the same as chick peas, earthnuts, or watermelon seeds."[44]

Εἰς ἑαυτὸν δὲ ἐλθών (vs. 17). One of the primary meanings of ἔρχομαι is to return, to come back (cf. John 9:7). The expression "came to himself" is found in Epictetus (*Discourses*, III, I, 15) and especially in the *Testament of Joseph* (3:9). In a context of πορνεία and of conversion, the author cites the temptation of Joseph by the Egyptian woman. The patriarch sought to deter the seductress from her evil desire (ἐπιθυμία) by the words of the Most High. "When she had gone out, I came to myself (ἦλθον εἰς ἐμαυτόν) and lamented for her many days." The inner impulse of Joseph, to which, alas, there was no analagous impulse on the part of the Egyptian woman, seems, as in our parable, to be inscribed in accord with the ancient Jewish tradition of conversion, that is to say, of a return to God.

The present loss (ἀπόλλυμαι) will be followed by σωτηρία, salvation, later called life (ἀνέζησεν or ἔζησεν), and being found again (εὑρέθη) (vss. 24 and 32). Such cries of distress (cf. Luke 8:24) were occasioned by everything which threatened life. Mortal dangers, such as the sea, the sword, famine, had taken on a symbolic meaning in the Old Testament. The salvation oracles promise that they will finally be removed by God: "And I will provide for them prosperous plantations so that they shall no more be consumed with hunger in the land, and no longer suffer the reproach of the nations" (Ezek. 34:29).

The condition of μίσθιος (the New Testament also uses μισθωτός, cf. Mk. 1:20), without being necessarily the most miserable, was in any case the most despised. Having himself become μίσθιος, the son thought of the servants of his father, who were treated better.[45]

ἀναστάς (vs. 18), a pleonastic participle having a semitic meaning, often accompanies verbs which mark a movement, a departure (e.g., Gen. 32:23 in the LXX).[46] It would be false, then, to attribute to this word an independent meaning and make it a sign of amendment which could be interpreted in a moral or allegorical manner.

The future (πορεύσομαι) points out the voluntary and energetic purpose of the son who will return to his father's home.

Often the verb ἁμαρτάνω, following the substantive σκοποῦ (in the sense of missing the mark), in the Septuagint has the religious meaning of "to sin". It may be followed by εἰς or by ἐνώπιον. The question has been raised whether, influenced by the language of the Targums, ἐνώπιον after ἁμαρτάνω does not appear when the transcendance of God is threatened: God becomes so inaccessible that one no longer sins against him, but before his face. Curiously, here it is εἰς which precedes heaven, hence God, and ἐνώπιον which is followed by "you", hence the father.

Several exegetes have used verse 18 to deny an identification between the father and God, who are distinguished both here and in verse 21. An equation of an allegorical sort is, indeed, impossible, but a connection between the whole of the story and the relations between God and man forces itself upon the mind. The *Shepherd of Hermas* indicates that to sin against the Lord and against one's parents is a grave offense (*Visions*, I, 3, 1).

In the perfect passive, καλέω ("I am no longer worthy to be called your son", vs. 19) has become almost a synonym of the verb "to be". We may ask, however, if the choice of this verb does not remind the readers that men are not naturally children of God, but become such by call and adoption (cf. Mt. 5:9).

Verses 20-21 are edited in a style which recalls the prose narrative of the Old Testament. The repetition indicates that the plan set forth (vss. 18-19) begins to be realized (vss. 20-21). Nevertheless, the repetition is incomplete, thus avoiding monotony: the father interrupts the discourse of his repenting son and thus expresses his love, more exactly his compassion (rare in Greek, the verb σπλαγχνίζομαι, used especially by the Septuagint, has a Semitic coloration[47]).

This affectionate regard of the father is underlined by various touches: besides the mention of compassion, it is requisite to point out the embrace and the kissing. The fact that the father ran (δραμών) is an additional mark of this, for the haste was beneath the dignity of a head of a family.

Certain exegetes have pointed out that this movement of the father towards the younger son impartially corresponds to a similar gesture toward the older brother (ἐξελθών, vs. 28).

Turning toward the servants, the father ordered the robe to be brought forth (ἐξενέγκατε) from the wardrobe where it was hanging, understood but not expressed (cf. II Kings 10:22: Jehu told the one who was in charge of the wardrobe: "Bring out the vestments, ἐξάγαγε ἐνδύματα, for all the worshippers of Baal"; one variant of the Septuagint reads ἐξένεγκε).

We know that the expression στολή ἡ πρώτη is ambiguous. It could designate the most beautiful robe, which was reserved for guests. In this case, the text suggests that the prodigal was not welcomed as a servant, but as a guest of honor. It could also call to mind the robe of the son which had been carefully put in order and kept ever since his departure. Luke thus evokes the reintegration of the prodigal into the family. (P. E. Haulotte has taught us to respect the symbolism of clothing as a sign of identity.[48]) The ring and the shoes incline us to accept this second interpretation.

The ring, in fact, which often serves as a seal, is an emblem of power and not a present handed over to a visitor.

Compare Genesis 41:42: "Then Pharaoh took his signet ring from his hand and put it on Joseph's hand, and arrayed him in garments of fine linen, and put a gold chain about his neck."

Contrary to guests who remove their shoes, the prodigal has shoes put on his feet. Without saying so, to walk about on the property or in a house signifies a taking possession.

K. H. Rengstorf[49] has carefully studied this triple bestowal of goods. He has rightly underlined the symbolic meaning of it. To infer an investiture, as he has done, however, is perhaps excessive. We believe that Luke wanted to suggest by these acts a complete reintegration of the prodigal into the family.

The bond which verse 23 establishes between the banquet and joy corresponds to the meaning which Semites give to eating together. This bond is seen again in the communal meals mentioned in the Book of the Acts (cf. Acts 2:46).

K. H. Rengstorf would like to give a juridical meaning to verse 24 (and to verse 32), in the sense of an official reinvestiture.[50] For our part, we deem these verses to be characteristic of the Lukan redaction. They are to be placed, then, neither in the juridical nor the moral level, but should be understood in a religious sense springing out of parabolic narrative. Νεκρός has a religious meaning in Acts 3:1, and the theme of salvation as a return to life runs throughout the various New Testament traditions. The theological interpretation of these verses is confirmed by εὑρέθη ("is found") which does not correspond to traditional narrative. The parable is entirely ignorant, indeed, of any attempt of the father to recover his son.

It is necessary to connect the words, "And they began to make merry" (vs. 24c), to the remainder of the story, as the recent *Traduction OEcuménique de la Bible*[51] has clearly seen.

The older son is in the fields, not in a field (vs. 25).[52]

This presence of the proprietor on the land pictures a domain of moderate importance and not that of a large landed estate. It is not necessary to use this verse as a springboard to dogmatize or to moralize, as F. Godet has done: "Here is the image of the Pharisee busied with his rites, while repentant sinners are rejoicing in the serene sunshine of grace."[53]

συμφωνία (vs. 25) may be interpreted in two ways: either the musical tune of the voices or the sounds, or, on the other hand, instruments of music, such as the bagpipe or the tabor.[54]

The χοροί also may be understood in two ways: either the sound of the dancing, or the choral singing. The current interpretation, according to which the elder brother first heard the music, then the sound of the feet of the dancers, is not necessary. We may simply presume that he heard the instruments and the voices (Plato, in his *Republic*, 475d, associates ἀκούω and χοροί).

The παῖδες of verse 26 are undoubtedly to be identified with the δοῦλοι of verse 22. Questioned by the elder son, the servant relates the welcome of the recovered son in an accurate resumé. Note the use of ὑγιαίνω and ἀπολαμβάνω: at the time when Luke was writing, ὑγιής could suggest a Christian quality (attachment to the true faith[55]) as well as bodily health. The *Shepherd of Hermas*, moreover, has recourse to the verb ἀπολαμβάνω in an identical sense and in a similar context: "And then the Son of God will be exceeding glad, and shall rejoice over them, because He has received His people pure" (ἀπειληφὼς τὸν λαὸν ἀυτοῦ καθαρόν)" (*Similitudes*, IX, 18, 4).

As to the anger of the elder brother, we see in the Old Testament a series of parallels: that of Samuel at the time of the rejection of Saul (I Sam. 15:11); that of David at the death of Uzzah (II Sam. 6:8); that of Job before his lot (Job

18:4, it is Bildad who evokes it); that of Jonah against the mercy of God for Nineveh (Jonah 4:1, 4, 9); that which is in danger of arising in the heart of the righteous over the prosperity of the wicked (Ps. 37:1, 7; Prov. 3:31f.). Several Old Testament texts, then, point out the anger of those who believe over what appears to be favorable treatment with regard to the blameworthy. Already censured by the Old Testament, the expression of this jealousy, and more generally of all anger, are condemned by the New Testament (cf. Mt. 5:22 and James 1:20).

The parable seems to characterize each character by a verb chosen with care: the prodigal "came to himself" (vs. 17), the father "had compassion" (vs. 20), and the elder brother "was angry" (vs. 28). Three parts of the story correspond to these three verbs.

Going out to meet the older brother, as he had run to welcome the younger brother, the father, according to the text παρεκάλει αὐτόν: he invited his recalcitrant son to come in (παρακαλεῖν here does not mean to comfort).

If money played a large role in the beginning of the parable, the house, as a communal dwelling, occupies an important place at the end of the story.

Several commentators have thought they had discovered an allusion to Pharisaism in verse 29a: wrongly, it would seem, for δουλεύειν does not necessarily describe a servile attitude. This verb may designate filial piety. It does not hinder the older son from placing himself in a relation to his father determined by duty rather than love.

The father's partiality is deeply resented by the older brother: faithful to his post, he has never been feasted with a kid, while the shrewd youth is tasting the fatted calf and the most delicate wine. To underline his anger, the older son did not say "my brother", but "this son of yours" (vs. 30). The οὗτος which follows could well be pejorative.

The older brother reminds the father that the worthless son has squandered his estate. The same verb κατεσθίω is used, in a figurative sense, in Aesop's fable 248, "The Young Man and the Swallow": Νέος ἄσωτος καταφαγὼν τὰ πατρῷα....[56]

The older son points out that the prodigal has devoured the family patrimony by living in luxury.[57] We have seen that ἀσώτως can imply a squandering which accompanies an immoral life.

One may point out here a final breach in an otherwise impeccable composition of the story: if the older son was acquainted with the licentiousness of his brother, the father should have been also. In this case, why has he done nothing to track his son down? K. H. Rengstorf answers: because he no longer has any desire to save his son. By reason of the rite and the legal process of the *kesasah* (or *kesisah*), the father has solemnly declared the death of his unworthy son: to signify publicly this cutting off of a member of the family, "the assembled clan smashed in the street a jar filled with parched grain and nuts, while they all wailed, to proclaim that such and such was henceforth separated, lost, that is to say, dead to the clan".[58] We have said earlier that this hypothesis appears to us unlikely.

The response of the father manifests an indefectible affection toward the elder son: the vocative τέκνον, even as the σύ, grammatically superfluous, are two indications of this paternal love.

The father, moreover, does not accept the arguments of his son: he opposes the "never" (οὐδέποτε, vs. 29) with an "always" (πάντοτε, vs. 31). "Son, you are always with me." We know the force of the biblical expression "to be with" which adds a communion of love to mere physical proximity.

Two explanations of the words καὶ πάντα τὰ ἐμὰ σά ἐστιν (vs. 31) are possible. Following D. Daube,[59] one may set the phrase in a juridical framework: the father has kept the ownership of the property which he has not bequeathed to the younger son ("mine" would then be juridically correct). The older son will inherit the estate only at the death of his father. But as he lives with his father, for all practical purposes it is already at his disposal. With Madam L. Schottrof,[60] however, one may view it on the simply human plane. Luke is not concerned with the juridical aspect. The only thing that is important for him is that the father and son, by reason of their mutual affection, have everything in common. Perhaps he will agree not to oppose justice and familial love.

Let us note, at verse 32, the tact of the father who does not say "it was fitting", but more generally, "it was fitting to make merry and be glad". Another mark of the finesse of the father is that he speaks of the younger brother as "your brother" and not as "my son" and thus discreetly reminds the older son that the one who has returned is, and remains, also his brother. The final mark of the tenderness of the paternal feelings is the absence of all explicit reproach.

The verbs εὐφραίνω and χαίρω are frequently found in the Septuagint side by side, but in reverse order: Joel 2: 21, 23; Lamentations 4:21, and Esther 9:17 (this last is an instance of the substantives χαρά and εὐφροσύνη).

K. H. Rengstorf,[61] as we have said with regard to verse 24, explains the opposites life-death and lost-found (vs. 32) with reference to the rite and the legal procedure of the *kesasah* (or *kesisah*). By his own choice, the son was dead to the family. Here he recovers life, that is to say, re-enters familial society. It seems to us more consonant with the theology of Luke (we accept the editorial character of verses 24 and 32, against K. H. Rengstorf) to relate the coupling of these two terms to the two preceding parables, the lost sheep and the lost coin, and to the broader context of the ministry of Jesus which Luke understands as an effort to seek and to save that which was lost (cf. Lk. 5:32, and 19:10). Thoroughly integrated into the story, verses 24 and 32 would then have the same hermeneutical function as the conclusions drawn from the two preceding parables (Lk. 15:7 and 10).

Along with the three striking verbs ("came to himself", "had compassion", and "was angry"), these two verses on the passing from death to life and from lostness to salvation would be loaded with meaning, the very epitome of the message of the parable.

NOTES

1. D. O. Via, *The Parables. Their Literary and Existential Dimension*, Philadelphia, 1967, pp. 165ff.

2. H. Conzelmann, *The Theology of St. Luke*, New York, 1960, pp. 60-65.

3. Cf. among recent works P. von der Osten-Sacken, "Zur Christologie des lukanischen Reiseberichts," *EvTh* 33 (1073), pp. 493ff., who points out certain predecessors and inserts this ecclesiological function of the journey into a Christological framework.

4. For example, J. Cantinat, "Les paraboles de la miséricorde (Luc 14:1-32)," *NRTh* 77 (1953), pp. 246ff.

5. Luke 1:50, 54, 58, 72, 78.

6. E(rnst) Fuchs, "Das Fest der Verlorenen. Existentiale Interpretation des Gleichnisses vom verlorenen Sohn," in *Glaube und Erfahrung*, Tübingen, 1965, pp. 402ff.

7. On the history of German interpretation of parables since A. Jülicher, cf. E. Jüngel, *Paulus und Jesus. Eine Untersuchung zur Präzisierung der Frage nach dem Ursprung der Christologie*, Tübingen, 1967^3, pp. 87-139.

8. F. Ch. Baur, *Kritische Untersuchungen über die kanonischen Evangelien...*, Tübingen, 1847, p. 510f.; A. Hilgenfeld, "Das Gleichnis von dem verlorenen Sohne, 15, 11-32," *Zw Th* 45, N. F., 10 (1902), pp. 449-464.

9. A. Jülicher, *Die Gleichnisreden Jesu. Zweiter Teil. Auslegung der Gleichnisreden der drei ersten Evangelien*, Freiburg i. B., Leipzig, Tübingen, 1899, pp. 333-365.

10. A. Jülicher, *op. cit.*, pp. 349-350.

11. The exegesis of A. Jülicher is sharply criticized by A. Hilgenfeld, *art. cit.*, which reproaches him a) for neglecting the Western text of the parable and b) for rejecting the exegesis of the Tübingen school in favor of an interpretation less convincing.

12. C. H. Dodd, *The Parables of the Kingdom*, London, Glasgow, 1961^2 (the first edition dated 1935); J. Jeremias, *The Parables of Jesus*, 3d rev. ed., London, 1972.

13. Jeremias, p. 131.

14. *Ibid.*

15. E(rnst) Fuchs, *art. cit.*, p. 406.

16. It is necessary to recognize also that the German exegete reestablished the inverse movement which goes from the text to the history: by means of the parable the behavior of Jesus finds, in his eyes, its truth: "Zuerst empfängt das Gleichnis von Jesus Mahl seine *Verständlichkeot.* Dann aber empfängt Jesu Mahl durch das Gleichnis seine *Wahrheit*" (*art. cit.*, p. 409).

17. Cf. J. Kopperschmidt, *Rhetorik. Einführung in die Theorie der Persuasiven Kommunikation*, Stuttgart, Berlin, Köln, Mainz, 1973.

18. Such is the subtitle of Paragraph 16 of his book (*op. cit.*, pp. 139ff.).

19. D. O. Via, *op. cit.*, pp. 165ff.

20. V. Propp. *Morphology of the Folktale*, 2nd ed., Austin, 1971.

21. E. Güttmanns, "Die linguistisch-didaktische Methodik der Gleichnisse Jesu" in *Studia Linguistica Neotestamentica. Gesammelte Aufsätze zur linguistischen Grundlage einer Neutestamentlichen Theologie*, München, 1971, pp. 99-183.

22. A. Jülicher, *op. cit.*, p. 335. M. J. Lagrange, *Evangile selon Saint Luc*, Paris, 1927[4], pp. 419ff., estimates first that the traditional title is too narrow. He continues by saying that "the first part, so touching, has its own worth which is, indeed, the principal one" (p. 420).

23. D. Buzy, "Enseignements paraboliques," *RB* 14 (1917), p. 191 (cited by M. J. Lagrance, *op. cit.*, p. 420).

24. E(rnst) Fuchs, "Jesus' Understanding of Time," in *Studies of the Historical Jesus*, Naperville, Ill., 1964, pp. 160-162; and *art. cit.* , n. 3., p. 38. Among the numerous intuitions of Fuchs, let us note these: the parable justifies neither the attitude of the younger son nor that of the older brother, but that of the father; the "fall" of the older brother is apparent in the long discourse which he addresses to his father.

25. J. Jeremias, *op. cit.*, p. 113, particularly note 1.

26. J. D. M. Derrett, "Law in the New Testament: The Parable of the Prodigal Son," *NTS* 14 (1967-1968), pp. 58-59 (reprinted now in *Law in the New Testament*, London, 1970, pp. 100-125. I have cited from the periodical.).

27. J. Jeremias, "Tradition und Redaktion in Lukas 15," *ZNW* 62 (1971), p. 174.

28. J. D. M. Derrett, *art. cit.*, pp. 68-70.

29. B. P. Grenfell and A. S. Hunt, *The Oxyrhynchus Papyri*, Part IV, London, 1904, pp. 184-186. We owe the reference to W. Bauer's *A Greek-English Lexicon of the New Testament and Other Early Christian Literature*, Chicago, 1957, pp. 289-290.

30. ישב יחד, "live together", was the technical term to designate this life of the family; cf. D. Daube, "Inheritance in Two Lukan Pericopes," *Zeitschrift der Savigny-Stiftung für Rechtsgeschichte, Römische Abteilung*, 72 (1955), p. 326.

31. J. Dauvillier, "Le partage d'ascendant et la parabole du fils prodigue," in *Actes du Congrès de Droit Canonique. Cinquantenaire de la Faculté de Droit Canonique, Paris 22-26 avril 1947*, Paris, 1950, pp. 223-228.

32. This law anticipated that two-thirds of the paternal fortune should come to the older brother and one-third to the younger.

33. J. Dauvillier, *art. cit.*, does not observe that, according to verse 12, the older brother also has already received his part of the inheritance.

34. D. Daube, *art. cit.*

35. For example, Gen. 25:5f.

36. Cf. W. Foerster, "ἄσωτος, ἀσωτία," in *Theological Dictionary of the New Testament*, I, Grand Rapids, 1964, pp. 506-507.

37. Only the older son (vs. 30) suggests that his younger brother has spent this money with prostitutes.

38. A. Jülicher, *op. cit.*, p. 341.

39. Tobias, son of Tobit, like the prodigal son, made a journey to a far country, then returned to his father. But unlike the son of the parable, Tobias made this journey through obedience and in a virtuous manner. He brought back from the journey the one who became his legitimate wife, Sarah. He also brought back the money which his father had left in trust with Gabael. These two positive results, owing to the virtue of the traveler, contrast with the squandering of the prodigal son and his dissipation.

40. J. Cantinat, *art. cit.*, p. 262.

41. Cf. the difference between want and plenitude in the unpublished Christian papyrus, undoubtedly from the 2nd century, which J. Rudhardt has just published: J. Rudhardt, "Un papyrus chrétien de la Bibliothèque publique et universitaire de Genève," in *Littérature. Historie. Linguistique. Recueil d'études offert à Bernard Gagnebin.* Lausanne, 1973, pp. 165-188.

42. The author of Luke-Acts perhaps schematizes a little the subtle relations between the Jews and the Gentiles. In the Diaspora, all contacts with Gentiles could not be forbidden. But to work as a keeper of pigs for a Gentile proprietor certainly constituted a transgression of Jewish regulations and occasioned a defilement.

43. A. Jülicher, *op. cit.*, p. 343.

44. J. Cantinat, *art. cit.*, p. 262.

45. A. Jülicher, *op. cit.*, p. 346.

46. F. Blass and A. Debrunner, *A Greek Grammar of the New Testament*, Chicago, 1961, 419, 2 and 5.

47. F. Blass and A. Debrunner, *op. cit.*, 108, 3 and 176, I.

48. E. Haulotte, *Symbolique de vêtement selon la Bible*, Paris, 1966.

49. K. H. Rengstorf, *Die Re-Investitur des verlorenen Sohnes in der Gleichniserzählung Jesu Luk. 15, 11-32*, Köln, Opladen, 1967, pp. 39ff.

50. K. H. Rengstorf, *op. cit.*, pp. 51-62.

51. *Edition intégrale. Nouveau Testament.* Paris, 1972, p. 249.

52. A. Jülicher, *op. cit.*, p. 353.

53. F. Godet, *Commentaire sur l'Evangile de Saint Luc*, II, Neuchâtel, 1871, p. 188.

54. J. Wellhausen, *Das Evangelium Lucae übersetzt und erklärt*, Berlin, 1904, p. 85, leans toward the bagpipe and M. L. Lagrange, *op. cit.*, p. 427, toward the tambourine, preferring however to translate it by "the playing of instruments".

55. Cf. Titus 1:13 and 2:2. The excursus of M. Dibelius will be read with interest, *Die Pastoralbriefe, dritte Auflage neu bearbeitet* by H. Conzelmann, Tübingen, 1955, pp. 20-21.

56. In the critical edition of E. Chambry, *Aesopi Fabulae*, II, Paris, 1926, pp. 405-406, this fable is numbered 249. In the edition and translation by the same author, Esope, *Fables*, Paris, 1967, p. 110, it appears as number 248.

57. It is better to read the feminine μετὰ πορνῶν, "with prostitutes", than the masculine μετὰ πόρνων.

58. K. H. Rengstorf, *op. cit.*, p. 73 (French abridgement of the work).

59. D. Daube, *art. cit.*

60. L(uise) Schottroff, "Das Gleichnis vom verlorenen Sohn," *ZThK* 68 (1971), pp. 39-41.

61. Cf. *supra*, p. 61.

SELECT BIBLIOGRAPHY

Some Commentaries

F. Godet, 2 vol., 1871; A. Plummer, *ICC*, 1901[4]; B. Weiss, *Meyer's Kommentar*, 1901; A. Loisy, 1924; M. J. Lagrange, *Etudes Bibliques*, 1927; E. Klostermann, *Handbuch zum Neuen Testament*, 1929[2]; A. Schlatter, 1931; K. H. Rengstorf, *NTD*, 1937, 1968[13]; A. R. C. Leaney, *Black's NT Commentaries*, 1958; E. E. Ellis, 1966; W. Grundmann, *Theol. Handkommentar zum NT*, 1969[5].

Some Books on the Parables

A. Jülicher, *Die Gleichnisreden Jesu*, I, Freiburg i. B., Leipzig, Tübingen, 1899[2], II, 1899.

C. H. Dodd, *The Parables of the Kingdom*, 1935, revised ed., London, Glasgow, 1961.

J. Jeremias, *The Parables of Jesus*, 3d rev. ed., London, 1972.

E. Linnemann, *Parables of Jesus*, London, 1966.

D. O. Via, *The Parables. Their Literary and Existential Dimension*, Philadelphia, 1967.

Legal Problems

J. Dauvillier, "Le partage d'ascendant et le parabole du fils prodigue," in *Actes du Congres de Droit Canonique (Cinquantenaire, 1947)*, Paris, 1950, pp. 223-228.

D. Daube, "Inheritance in Two Lukan Pericopes," *Zeitschrift der Savigny-Stiftung für Rechtsgeschichte, Römische Abteilung*, 72 (1955), pp. 326-334.

J. D. M. Derrett, "Law in the New Testament: The Parable of the Prodigal Son," *NTS* 14 (1967-1968), pp. 56-74, reprinted in *Law in the New Testament*, London, 1970, pp. 100-125.

K. H. Rengstorf, *Die Re-Investitur des Verlorenen Sohnes in der Gleichniserzählung Jesu Luk. 15, 11-32* (Arbeitsgemeinschaft für Forschung des Landes Nordrhein-Westfalen, Geisteswissenschaften, 137), Köln, Opladen, 1967.

Tradition-Redaction

E. Schweizer, "Zur Frage der Lukasquellen, Analyse von Luk. 15, 11-32," *ThZ* 4 (1948), pp. 469-471.

J. Jeremias, "Zum Gleichnis vom verlorenen Sohn, Luk. 15, 11-32," *ThZ* 5 (1949), pp. 228-231.

E. Schweizer, "Antwort an Joachim Jeremias, S. 228-231," *ThZ* 5 (1949), pp. 231-233.

E. Rasco, "Les paraboles de Luc, XV. Une invitation à la joie de Dieu dans le Christ," in *De Jésus aux Evangiles. Tradition et Rédaction dans les Evangiles synoptiques*, éd. I. de la Potterie, Gembloux, Paris, 1967, pp. 165-183.

J. T. Sanders, "Tradition and Redaction in Luke XV. 11-32," *NTS* 15 (1968-1969), pp. 433-438.

J. Jeremias, "Tradition und Redaktion in Lukas 15," *ZNW* 62 (1971), pp. 172-189.

L(uise) Schottroff, "Das Gleichnis vom verlorenen Sohn," *ZThK* 68 (1971), pp. 27-52.

Parallel Texts

Ch. Schöttgen, *Horae hebraicae et talmudicae*... I, Dresde, Leipzig, 1733, pp. 296-297 (illustration, in Schemoth Rabba 46, fol. 140, 2, on Isaiah 64:7 and Psalm 77:3, by the story of the son of Archiater who, after having attached himself to an evil man as to a father, fell ill and called on his true father for help. This one, who was irritated at the infidelity of his son, in spite of all had compassion.).

Th. Mangey, *Philonis Judaei opera quae reperiri potuerunt omnia*, II, London, 1742, p. 676 (a fragment of a concatenation on Gen. 26:6ff: the father of two sons, one good and one culpable, gives himself by preference to the culpable who has more need of him).

J. J. Wettstein, *Novum Testamentum Graecum*..., I, Amsterdam, 1751-1752, pp. 758-762 (especially valuable for the vocabulary).

Ps-Quintilien, *Declamationes maiores*, ed. G. Lehnert, Leipzig, 1905, pp. 88-110 (the case of the ransoming father who, through lack of means, had to choose between his two sons captured by brigands and finally redeemed the sick one who died on the way back; pointed out by L. Schottroff, *art. cit.*).

Aesopi Fabulae, ed. E. Chambry, II, Paris, 1926, p. 405 (the fable of the young prodigal and the swallow).

A. Deissmann, *Light from the Ancient East*, London, 1927, pp. 187-192 (letter of the "prodigal son" Antonis Longon to his mother Nilus).

H. L. Strack and P. Billerbeck, *Kommentar zum Neuen Testament aus Talmud und Midrasch*, II, München 1924, --. 212-218 (Lev R^132c: If you observe the Torah, you will eat bread; if not the rod is there to strike you.--When the Israelites are humiliated to the point of eating cabors, they will then be penitent; Deut. R^198d: Apropos of Deut. 4:30, parable of the son of a king. Behaving badly, he is invited by an educator sent by his father to return to himself.).

G. Rosenkranz, "Das Gleichnis vom verlorenen Sohn im Lotos-Sutra und im Lukas-evangelium," *ThLZ* 79 (1954), col. 281-282.

J. Alonso Diaz, "Paralelos entre la naración del libro de Jonás y parábola del hijo pródigo," *Bib* 40 (1959), pp. 632-640.

W. G. Braude, *Midrash on Psalms*, I, Yale, 1959, p. 131 (on Psalm 1:1: a king had two sons; he preferred the small one covered with dust to the larger one properly bathed). (This work was inaccessible to us.)

H. Braun, *Qumran und das Neue Testament*, I, Tübingen, 1966, p. 90.

K. H. Rengstorf, *op. cit.*

Other Studies

H. Baumgartner, "Christologie (Soteriologie) und Parabel vom verlorenen Sohn," *Theologische Zeitschrift aus der Schweiz* 4 (1887), pp. 178-199.

A. Hilgenfeld, "Das Gleichnis von dem verlorenen Sohne, Lc 15, 11-32," *ZwTh* 45 (N.F., 10) (1902), pp. 449-464.

J. B. Russel, "The Word of the Cross and the Parable of the Prodigal," *The Expository Times* 24 (1912-1913), col. 358-360.

A. D. Martin, "The Word of the Cross and the Parable of the Prodigal," *ibid.*, col. 526-527.

W. P. Robertson, "The Word of the Cross and the Parable of the Prodigal," *ibid.* 25 (1913-1914), col. 181-182.

D. Buzy, "Enseignements paraboliques," *RB* 14 (1917), pp. 168-207 (on the prodigal son, pp. 188-192).

K. Bornhäuser, *Studien zum Sondergut des Lukas*, Gütersloh, 1934, p. 103-137.

J. Schniewind, *Das Gleichnis vom verlorenen Sohn*, Göttingen, 1940 (this remains inaccessible to us).

L. Cerfaux, "Trois réhabilitations dans l'Evangile," *Bulletin des Facultés catholiques de Lyon* 72, I (1950), pp. 5-13. Reprinted in *Recueil Lucien Cerfaux*, II, Gembloux, 1954, pp. 51-59.

J. Cantinat, "Les Paraboles de la Miséricorde (Luc, XV, 1-32)," *NRTh* 77 (1955), pp. 246-264.

E. Fuchs, "Jesus' Understanding of Time," in *Studies of the Historical Jesus*, Naperville, Ill., 1964, pp. 160-162.

C. H. Giblin, "Structural and Theological Considerations on Luke 15," *CBQ* 24 (1962), pp. 15-31.

E. Jüngel, *Paulus und Jesus. Eine Untersuchung zur Präzisierung der Frage nach dem Ursprung der Christologie*, 1962, Tübingen, 1967[3], pp. 160-164.

E. Fuchs, "Das Fest der Verlorenen. Existentiale Interpretation des Gleichnisses vom verlorenen Sohn," in *Glaube und Erfahrung. Zum christologischen Problem in Neuen Testament*, Tübingen, 1965, pp. 402-415.

G. Crespy, "Psychanalyse et foi," *EThR* 41 (1966), pp. 241-251, reprinted in *Essais sur la situation actuelle de la foi*, Paris, 1970, pp. 41-56.

J. Dupont, "Le fils prodigue, Lc 15, 1-3. 11-32," in *Assemblées du Seigneur* 17 (1969), pp. 64-72.

D. Vasse, *Le temps du désir. Essai sur le corps et la parole*, Paris, 1969, pp. 31-34.

J. D. M. Derrett, "The Parable of the Prodigal Son. Patristic Allegories and Jewish Midrashim," in *Studia Patristica* X, Berlin, 1970, pp. 219-224.

P. Bonnard, "Approche historico-critique de Luc 15," in *Foi et Vie. Cahiers Bibliques* 12 (1973), pp. 25-37.

I. Broer, "Das Gleichnis vom verlorenen Sohn und die Theologie des Lukas," *NTS* 20 (1973-1974), pp. 453-462.

Supplementary Bibliography

B. M. Metzger, ed., *Index to Periodical Literature on Christ and the Gospels,* 1966, pp. 316-318.

E. Rasco, *art. cit.*, p. 166, n. 3.

H. Schürmann, *Das Lukasevangelium, Erster Teil, Kommentar zu Kap. I, I-9, 50,* Herders Theologischer Kommentar zum Neuen Testament, Freiburg i. B., Basel, Wien, 1969, pp. XIff. (one will note in particular the long list of commentaries).

PART TWO

The Origin of Historical Criticism

FERDINAND CHRISTIAN BAUR
METHODOLOGICAL APPROACH AND INTERPRETATION OF LUKE 15:11-32

by Christophe Senft

I. INTRODUCTION

Among the men of learning of the 19th century who have reflected on the presuppositions and the method of the exegesis of the New Testament, the most important is assuredly F. C. Baur. No one has pushed reflections as far nor encompassed the totality of the problem as he. He is a model of methodological research: perspectives have certainly changed, other aspects have appeared; but even in the errors which he committed, he remains a stimulating partner of discussion and a master from whom one never ceases to learn.

Born in 1792 of a pastor father, he took his theological studies at Tübingen, where the spirit of G. Ch. Storr (1746-1805), a supernaturalist with an apologetic tendency, still reigned. In the years which followed his studies, Baur freed himself little by little from this spirit, especially under the influence of Schleiermacher and Schelling. In 1826, in spite of a certain distrust aroused by his new orientation, he was named to the Faculty of Theology at Tübingen, to teach the historic branches--New Testament, the History of Dogma, and Church History. In each of these fields, he had been an innovator and had published some works of the first order. He died in 1860.

Among the precursors of Baur, several were and remain conspicuous: J. S. Semler, with his *Traité de la libre investigation du Canon* (1771-1775), J. D. Michaelis, author of the first *Introduction au Nouveau Testament* (1750), Fr. Schleiermacher with his *Doctrine de la foi chrétienne* (1821-1822), and also a nontheologian, B. G. Niebuhr, whose *Histoire romaine* (1810-1812) oriented him towards the study and the criticism of sources. But that which gave to Baur and his work a particular importance is the manner in which he turned everything to account and gathered everything together into an astonishing synthesis; a synthesis which, far from being a compilatory or harmonizing aggregate, is the type which gives knowledge an immense leap forward, the sort which several subsequent generations find it needful to employ on multiple lines--until a new synthesis appears of similar importance.

The enumeration of the principal works relating directly or indirectly to the New Testament gives an idea of the orientation and the subjects of Baur's research, and their order of succession indicates in what way he made discoveries and progressed, how he expanded the historical and theological knowledge of the New Testament, from a first discovery up to the final blending together of the whole in a coherent interpretation.

The first important work is the article, appearing in 1831 in the *Tübinger Zeitschrift für Theologie*, on "The Party of Christ in the Church at Corinth, the Opposition Between Pauline and Petrine Christianity". On a number of points, even important ones, he has not outlasted criticism (we know, for example, that Baur saw in the Christ party, I Cor. 1:12, a Judeo-Christian breach). Nevertheless, by bringing to light the existence, in the primitive Church, of two strongly different groups, Judeo-Christian and Gentile-Christian, he established a decisive phase of research. Baur discovered a primitive Church with a diversified history, marked by oppositions and tensions between persons and groups; he discovered that which gave direction to his subsequent investigations and made them fruitful, resulting in the impressive syntheses which are to be found partly in his *Geschichte der christlichen Kirche der drei ersten jahrhunderte* (1853), and partly in his *Vorlesungen über die christliche dogmengeschichte* (1864). It is well to point out that at the date when this article appeared, the influence of the Hegelian dialectic of history on Baur, which, from 1835 on, plays an important role in his analyses and his interpretation of New Testament history, is not yet perceptible. But one understands the welcome which Baur is going to give to it, when one knows that at this date he already sees the characteristic movement in this history to be the conflict and the reconciliation of opposites.[1]

The weighty monograph on *Die christliche Gnosis* (1835) does not relate directly to the New Testament. It is nevertheless necessary to mention it here, because the study of the Gnostic phenomenon sensitized Baur to signs of its presence in certain writings of the New Testament. In fact, the same year Baur published a study making evident the anti-Gnostic polemic of the Pastoral Epistles, giving with the same stroke new proof of their inauthenticity.[2] His thesis is interesting: the Pastorals are the work of Paulinists disturbed at seeing Paulinism used and monopolized by the Gnostics, and struggling to reclaim it for the sound tradition of the Church. They belong, then, to a late phase of the history of primitive Christianity, and if it is necessary to give up knowing Paul and his theology through them, we have gained in return a vital document on the Church of the second century.

In 1845 the admirable work *Paulus, der apostel Jesu Christi* appeared. It includes three parts: the life and work of the apostle; the authentic and inauthentic letters--

the criterion of authenticity is the presence of the doctrine of justification which, according to Baur is found only in Romans, I and II Corinthians, and Galatians--analyses and settings in the history of the Church of the apostolic and post-apostolic generations; finally, the theology of the apostle. The influence of Hegel is perceptible here by the interpretation of the history of the early Church as the history of the Christian "consciousness" (*Bewusstsein*), above all in the third part, where the doctrine of justification is presented as the sign of the transition from the "objectivity" of Jewish legalism to the "subjectivity" of the consciousness taking possession of itself.

The results of inquiries undertaken to clarify the problem posed by the *Das Leben Jesu* (1835-36) are collected in the second important work devoted to the writings of the New Testament: *Kritische untersuchungen über die kanonischen evangelien, ihr verhältniss zu einander, ihren charakter und ursprung* (1874).[3] Attempting to define, by a precise analysis of their content, the particular tendency of each of the four Gospels, John, Luke, Mark, and Matthew, Baur sought to understand their relations and their contradictions in order to be able to situate them in the dialectic process of which the Gospel of John, according to him, is the outcome. Although in the Gospel by Matthew the "Christian principle" still expresses itself in the language of the legalistic milieu from which it sprang (The Sermon on the Mount), it severs itself from it by "negation", the Pauline phase represented in the Gospels by Proto-Luke. Then the opposites are brought together in the middle by canonical Luke, which is Proto-Luke amended by Matthean or neuter additions; by Mark, a digest of Luke and Matthew; and finally by John, which marks the final synthesis, the "absolute realization of salvation" by the "immediate communication" of the divine essence to humanity.

Complementary to these studies, the little work on *Das Markusevangelium nach seinem ursprung und charakter* (1851) is a quite peevish polemic against the defenders of the primacy of Mark, all the more aggressive in that this thesis fundamentally calls in question the picture which Baur has drawn of the history of the primitive Church.

The *Ausführlichere Vorlesungen über die christliche dogmengeschichte* was published after Baur's death on the basis of his lecture notes (1864). The work gathers together and synthesizes the results of earlier inquiries. A second elaboration of Pauline theology is found here, on which Baur had worked in view of a second edition of his *Paulus*.

II. HISTORIC PRESUPPOSITION AND THE NECESSITY OF THE HISTORICAL-CRITICAL METHOD

That which makes Baur's work a valuable model is partly his rigor in the application of a perfectly elaborated scientific method; but above all it is the constant presence of *methodological reflection*. Certainly, Baur's adherence, often criticized, to Hegelian theses on the progress of history, is the cause of numerous errors on his part, as much in the field of dogmatics as in the strictly historic field, which particularly interests us here. It is none the less necessary to establish the very important positive role which these theses have played as a tool for penetrating the meaning of history. Supported by them, Baur was able to reflect more usefully and profoundly on the conditions and the rules of historical and exegetical research than many others who were in appearance less compromised.

The introductions to the works of Baur, whether brief or extended, are regularly, either in whole or in part, devoted to questions of method.[4] They impress the reader by the lucidity with which Baur has perceived and gone forward with the analysis of the place of historic research in theology.

How is it that the critical elucidation of New Testament history, an unknown concern for centuries, should impose itself at a given moment as a necessary step to theological knowledge and to faith? Baur was not content with the explanation--often given, but superficial--according to which, by virtue of a more exacting science, we desire today (whatever should be the consequences for faith) to know with complete objectivity that which has really happened. That which makes historical-critical examination possible and necessary, we may say, is the inner state of faith and theology today.

In the Introduction to his monograph on the Apostle Paul, in Hegelian terms Baur accounts for the theological necessity of the critical task as follows: "Thought, reaching autonomy ...after several centuries of laborious effort, very naturally turns its attention towards the past; the spirit, assured of itself, conscious of resting on itself, now simply occupies a position from where it can perceive the ways over which it has traveled under the constraint of circumstances, and it follows them by thought, in order to retrace with the consciousness of the inner necessity of its being what has unconsciously constituted one's self."[5]

The language is Hegelian. But the phenomenon and the posture which he describes are obviously not the doing of Hegel. They proceed from a day long before him, from the Reform of Luther, in the distance which was then set up between the individual consciousness and the inherited norms of history, and in the criticism of the traditional teaching of the Church, which later showed itself forcefully in the Aufklärung. Thought has become "autonomous". That does not signify, either in principle or necessarily in fact, that it intends to exalt itself as a judge of truths heretofore indisputable, or that it lays claim to a rival pattern of historic norms; but it wishes to recognize itself, or better, to know itself in the truths which come to it from a distant past. Without so much rejecting what he is taught, the individual intends to adhere to a truth which will be apparent as such to his consciousness and which will be his truth.

What Baur describes is *a situation of reality.* The critical attitude does not result from a decision taken arbitrarily one day, perhaps in a movement of rebellion, deist or atheist; it does not arise from a strategy invented to escape the truth coming from the groundwork of history. It appears in a given moment, as Baur said, under the pressure of "circumstances". One could say that a *situation of criticism* has preceded the criticism, in the sense that the conditions of the criticism were given by the progress of history before it was methodically developed. From that time, the theologian is not free to approach or not to approach history and his traditions by critical examination; this is imposed on him by the situation and even by the form of his consciousness (*Bewusstsein*). To refuse critical examination would be to refuse a situation of reality, this "autonomy of thought", by virtue of which we are now obliged, in order to grasp the truth, to become aware of the "inner necessity of being" from that which has become, that is to say, to understand the historic becoming of truth, and to understand it from within as the becoming of our own consciousness.

It is clear that we are dealing here with a profound reflection on the fact and the necessity of historical criticism in theology, with a valid explanation, although formulated in Hegelian terms, of the critical pathos which has animated theology since the 18th century. Historical criticism, then, is not only what it has been for numerous scholars both before and after Baur, first and fundamentally a valid technique for analyzing historic facts, for making relations and contradictions evident, with completely scientific objectivity. It is that, assuredly. But it is primarily an activity of the consciousness which exercises *the freedom of knowing* what is its own, whether it should choose it or not, face to face with the truth transmitted by history.

This does not mean, of course, that the methodic and objective elucidation of the facts of the past should be, after all, of secondary interest. Baur meant, on the contrary, that this has now become inevitable necessity. It is a theological necessity, since the consciousness, *to understand itself*, must necessarily retrace the paths of its becoming in the past and know them again *in their objective truth*. This is the other aspect of what we have called the situation of criticism. Indeed, to quote Baur once more, "it is a purely historical question of knowing what Christianity is in its essence, and the answer cannot be found in the past, in that in which Christianity itself had its origins; it is a question which can only be resolved, then, by a critical attitude of the present consciousness face to face with the past."[6]

Removed from its context, this sentence could be nothing other than the statement of the program, for example, of the *Théologie biblique* of J. Ph. Gabler (1789)--critical study of the New Testament (that is to say, study not governed by Dogmatics), in the light of criticism of traditional Dogmatics. But the program of Baur is different. What he wishes is not, as his predecessors of the age of the Enlightenment, a control or a rectification or even a destruction of dogmas, but *a bringing to consciousness of the faith* through the historic expression of its truth.[7]

For faith can no longer be the simple adherence or submission to objective dogma which relieves it, so to speak, of the obligation of its self perceiving the truth. To become an "autonomous" thought, a thought which must know its object in innerly discerning the path of its knowledge, is to turn itself toward the *history* of its origins, which is no longer dogma fixed at the end of its becoming, impenetrable, but rather the expression of the "Christian consciousness" in the movement of its becoming, accessible to knowledge, because it is penetrable and in this sense capable of being interiorized. This knowledge is necessarily *critical*, since it is precisely criticism which transforms the compact block of the canon into an ongoing history open to a consciousness which is itself in movement. The history of origins, heretofore covered by dogma, is uncovered by criticism.

Indeed, in the dogmatizing path, whether of orthodox tradition or of the *Aufklärung*, one looks in the New Testament for timeless truths either of traditional dogma or of enlightened dogma; hence, the obligation of seeing in the "differences" only some variants to harmonize or some diverse accommodations of timeless truths to the mentality of the age. The arrival of "autonomous" thought forced an abandonment of this sort of docetism. To harmonize, by submitting the documents to a norm exterior to them, is to mask history, to cover the mirror in which the "consciousness of the present" discloses itself, and which, in revealing to itself its becoming, reveals what it is. If, for example, governed by the idea of a monolithic unity of the apostolic witnesses, one minimizes, by harmonizing the Pauline and Lucan images of Paul, the conflict which put Paul in opposition to the original apostles, not only is one a shabby historian, but also and especially one is prevented, in masking the conflict, from acceding to the truth of the faith, since the Pauline "antithesis", the No to legalism, is the path of access and a constitutive stage.

To summarize: Baur recognizes in the dialectic process of history, in history concrete and differentiated, the becoming and the expression of the truth. By criticism, he frees history as the object of his knowledge. Guided by the "circumstances" beyond dogmatic objectivism, obliged to know his faith not only in dogma, but in itself, not only is he no longer prevented from perceiving the movement of history, but also *he must* perceive and understand it in order to perceive and understand in himself the movement and the truth of his own consciousness.[8]

III. THE DEVELOPMENT OF THE HISTORICAL-CRITICAL METHOD

The situation of criticism having been produced in the "subjectivity" of the Reformation, *method* was not constituted in one stroke. Considerable time was necessary for critical thought truly to gain knowledge of itself, to discover its laws and to settle on its tools. It developed by searching for itself. In the introduction to his work on the canonical Gospels, where he made a lengthy exposition of the development of method, Baur distinguished four successive phases, yet interpenetrating in a certain measure. We here present a simplified presentation of them.

a) *The dogmatic phase*[9] was the consolidation and the codification of Protestant theology after the agitated years of the Reformation. At this stage, criticism barely existed only as a dogmatic principle, in the form of a distinction theoretically made between the doctrine of the Church and the Scriptures. For the Reformers, it is true, the Scriptures had been in reality the critical norm with regard to dogma, which automatically had the consequence--on the part of Luther alone, it is true--of a critical look at the Scriptures themselves.[10] But for those who followed, and for a long time, critical dialogue between the doctrine of the Church and the Scriptures lost all reality in actual practice. On coming out of this brief period of liberation, the knowledge acquired at that time solidified itself in a rigid dogmatism, which blockaded anew the movement which had primed it: the Scriptures had no other function than to furnish the *dicta probantia* for dogmatics, which became again in fact the norm of exegesis, and which subjugated the texts as well as the faith to its own formalism.

b) *The phase of abstract criticism* is bound to the Aufklärung. This looked for every means one can drag up, in the battle against the dogmatism of the Church, for a criticism squeezed from the biblical texts. It was easily demonstrated that the New Testament is not the homogeneous whole on which they believed they could rest. Apostolicity became an extremely problematic notion, the limits of the Canon--heretofore defined by apostolicity--became uncertain. It was possible henceforth to attack the doctrines of the Church in the name of the Scriptures, whose contradictions and incoherences were made evident. Criticism then registered astonishing progress. Nevertheless, it was still far from possessing all its powers, for two principal reasons otherwise linked. On the one hand, the viewpoint is still largely dogmatic: the traditional dogma is merely exchanged for that of the *Aufklärung*; on the other hand, criticism remains provincial: the relations are not yet discovered between the parties in the New Testament, and the history which conjoins the observed facts among them. The critic still does not situate himself in history; he sees and judges from without--"abstract" criticism. For this reason, even in this phase, there were many relapses into attempts at harmonizing.

c) *The negative or dialectic viewpoint*[12] is represented by D. F. Strauss.[13] In defining the position of his student in these terms, Baur only brought to light one of the aspects of his work, the one which he considered decisive for the advancement of New Testament knowledge: the radicalism of his destructive criticism.[14] The positive deposit, if one may call it that, of the radical criticism of Strauss is, in reality, in Baur's eyes, to have demonstrated the blind alleys into which the principles and methods applied until then lead. Indeed, if, as those holding to the traditional dogmatics desired, the Gospel accounts had the value of revealed truth only on condition of being the faithful reflection of historic facts, then there was no longer any truth, for nonhistoricity was everywhere manifest. If, on the other hand one sought with the rationalizing apologists to save their historicity by so-called natural explanations, then they were deprived of their meaning, which appears precisely in "mythic" expression. In thus striking at the incapacity of both approaches to the New Testament, in extinguishing by his criticism all false lights, Strauss did a useful work: he occasioned a situation which forced criticism to raise itself to a new point of view.

d) *The historic point of view.*[15] We have spoken of the circle which is necessarily set up between the subject and history from the moment when consciousness, in possession of itself, turns toward history to recognize there its own pathways; this is the fundamental circle. What Baur describes now is the other discovery, closely tied to the first, which could be called the *philological circle*, where the knowing spirit, if one may so say, travels from history to history to discover its movements: the knowledge of history gives access to the meaning of history, the knowledge of meaning permits the elucidation of history; the "criticism of history" leads to the "criticism of documents", and inversely. If one makes evident the incompatabilities, the "differences" of all types, for example, between the Gospel by John and the Synoptics, which necessitates staying close to their own character and "tendencies", one will be led to conclude that they are nonhistorical, in the sense that neither one nor the others may any longer be regarded as objective reports of historical facts. But by the same stroke, one will be given the means of establishing a footing in history, of knowing it again and reconstructing it; even their diversity enables one to perceive the unfolding of history, the becoming of truth, which justifies the successive and contradictory clarifications of the Christian consciousness. Writings such as the Gospel by Matthew with its Judaizing legalism, and the Epistle to the Galatians with its radical criticism of the Law, certainly cannot be coordinated at the level of "abstract criticism"; but this is precisely what furnishes the higher criticism, "historical criticism", the bench marks which permit them to be situated in history, and by coordinating them in history, to know their meaning.

This was a capital discovery for science and for faith. The dubious and painful apologetic feats intended to save the honor of the biblical authors and the truth of the texts, no longer have any reason for existence. At the higher level of criticism, a pseudepigraphic text such as I Timothy will no longer be a contemptible and a false writing; its pseudepigraphic nature appears as a positive datum, since it allows it to be placed in the post-apostolic history, and consequently to know through it a portion of the path which the Church traveled and its debates over the Gospel which were heretofore unknown.[16] Or still more, if it affirms that nothing, or almost nothing, in the Christological discourses of the Fourth Gospel reflects the preaching of the historic Jesus, one does not reject it as "myth", nor feel the need to confer on it a counterfeit historicity, by integrating it into a synopsis of the four Gospels,[17] but one will elucidate the meaning of it by setting it in the historic place which is its own expression of the "Christian consciousness" proper to it.[18] The fact that the movement of history, the historic movement of truth, has entered into criticism's field of perception, while giving access for the first time to history, also, for the first time, gives full access to its own freedom. It knows that it does not injure faith when it brings divergences and contradictions to light. On the contrary, it is useful for faith: it frees it from the insincerities of an anticritical apologetic heretofore inevitable, but more and especially, it restores to the texts their authority, by making them free to develop and to exhibit the expression of the truth which is native to them. The fact that the Hegelianism of Baur intervenes constantly, both as a working hypothesis and as a tool of analysis--which was perhaps then the only means of advance--cannot devalue this result.

IV. THE INTERPRETATION OF THE PARABLE OF THE PRODIGAL SON

In his study on the Gospel by Luke, Baur gives a brief but significant interpretation of the parable of the Prodigal Son.[19] Conforming to the method which he brought to its height, it was based on the conclusions of the analysis which he had made of the position of the Gospel in the history of the early Church. A summary glance at this analysis is indispensable. It aims at proving that the Gospel by Luke resulted from the transformation, by an author of the post-apostolic generation, of a Pauline and Gentile-Christian Proto-Luke, still known in the second century, into a Gospel of mediation between Judeao- and Gentile-Christianity.

a) It is known that Irenaeus, Tertullian and others have accused Marcion of having mutilated the canonical Gospel by Luke, to make it conform to his heretical doctrine. Baur refutes these accusations by showing that a number of these so-called passages and pericopae sacrificed by Marcion (especially the parables of the fig tree, 13:1-9; of the prodigal son, 15:11-32; and the wicked husbandmen, 20:9-18) present no quality that could explain their excision. Conclusion: Marcion has not mutilated the canonical Gospel by Luke, but an anonymous commentator has revised and augmented an *original Luke* still unknown by Marcion.

b) The original Luke was Pauline, which exhibited characteristic differences with Matthew, who has served as a model for the author. These attest the universalism of the author: the Samaritan itinerary of Jesus, 9:51ff. (Matt. 10:5: "enter no town of the Samaritan"); the mission of the seventy, 10:1ff.; the absence of the Petrine blessing, in Matt. 16:17ff. The additions of the commentator are of a diverse nature. Alongside passages with any discernible tendency, one finds, on the one hand, some Judaizing notes (the enduring role of the law, 16:17; the reign of the twelve apostles over the tribes of Israel, 22:30), on the other hand, some texts where a tendency toward the *reconciliation* between Judeo- and Gentile-Christians appears, especially the *Vorgeschichte*, chapters 1-4, with its genealogy retouched in a universalistic sense; the entry of Jesus-Messiah into Jerusalem, 19:28-40; the parable of the Prodigal Son, 15:11-32, which neutralizes in a way that of the invited guests, 14:15-24.

The conclusion: the canonical Gospel by Luke bears the marks of its history. A witness at first of the Pauline "antithesis", it has become, by a second redaction, a witness of the "synthesis", not certainly on the high level of the Gospel by John, but on the lower level of a reconciliation by the juxtaposition and balancing of antagonistic elements. It is this which the exegete must know to give to the Lukan texts an objective and specific interpretation.

The meaning of the Parable of the Prodigal Son, then, becomes evident: it reflects the reconciliation, occurring after the conflicts of the apostolic period, between Gentile- and Jewish-Christians.

The Jewish-Christian and Gentile-Christian churches are represented by the older son and the younger son. The jealousy of the older son: the Jewish-Christians look unfavorably on the afflux of numerous pagan converts into the church, because this marks the end of the privileged situation of Israel as the people of God. "Who does not recognize here the behaviour, just as it appears in the letter to the Romans, of Jewish-Christians in the face of Gentile-Christians and Pauline Christianity?" But the younger son is invited and welcomed as the older son: Gentiles and Jews, the one as the other sons, are received with equal rights into the messianic kingdom, since God is also the God of the Gentiles (Rom. 3:29). The difference is solely that the older son possesses his rights from the very beginning, while they become effective for the younger son only after his return. In the good will of the younger son, humble and repentant, and in the joy of the father who welcomes him, is expressed the feeling which the Gentile-Christian Church had of its importance and of the strength of its position. From then on, it belonged to the "Paulinians" to do everything possible to avoid the separation which ran the risk of provoking the jealousy of the Jewish-Christians. Paul himself had previously made use of this in the letter to the Romans. His followers should be likewise preoccupied: to unite the Church in recognizing the same rights for all. It is in this sense that the appeasing words of the father to the older son must be understood: "Son, you are always with me", and the invitation which he addressed to him to take part in his joy. Baur concludes: "All the traits (irenic and conciliatory), relating to a much later epoch (post-apostolic), are of a truth so concrete that it is obviously out of these circumstances that the parable was born, at least in the form in which we know it."

NOTES

1. I Peter, with its Pauline character, still considered then by Baur as authentic, marks the appeasement of the conflict between Peter and Paul.

2. Schleiermacher had already brought forward this evidence for I Timothy, but by showing that the biographical and narrative elements which are taken up there are not reconcilable with those of the other Pauline epistles and the Book of the Acts.

3. In the same year also the *Lehrbuch der christlichen Dogmengeschichte* appeared.

4. The most complete, in the sector with which we are dealing, appear at the beginning of *Kritische Untersuchungen über die kanonischen Evangelien, ihr Verhältniss zu einander, ihren Charakter und Ursprung* (1847) and the *Vorlesungen über neutestamentliche Theologie* (1864).

5. "Die nach...der mühevollen Arbeit vieler Jahrhunderte errungene Selbständigkeit des Denkens wendet von selbst den Blick in die Vergangenheit zurück; der in der Selbstgewissheit seines Bewusstseins in sich ruhende Geist steht nun erst auf dem Standpunkt, auf welchem er auch auf die Wege zurücksehen kann, die er, durch die Macht der Verhältnisse getrieben, gegangen ist, er geht ihnen nach, um das bewusstlos Gewordene mit dem Bewusstsein der inneren Notwendigkeit seines Werdens zu durchlaufen" (*Paulus*..., Leipzig, 1845, p. 1f.).

6. "Auf der anderen Seite ist, was das Christentum seinem Wesen nach ist, eine rein historische Frage, deren Lösung nur in der Vergangenheit liegt, in welcher das Christentum selbst seinen Ursprung genommen hat, eine Frage, die ebendarum auch nur durch die kritische Stellung gelöst werden kann, die sich das Bewusstsein der Gegenwart zu der Vergangenheit gibt" (*Paulus*, p. 2).

7. This purpose is manifested constantly in the works of Baur on the history of dogma.

8. Here, evidently, is a Hegelian interpretation of the relation between faith and history: faith is the "consciousness" which grasps itself by an immanent dialectic process, and history--in the occurrence of New Testment history--the mirror in which it looks at itself to make out its own be-

coming. An essential aspect of the New Testament, its kerygmatic character, is thus eclipsed. Let us observe, nevertheless, 1) that by his reflection on the grounds and the data of criticism in the theological domain, Baur did a pioneering work; 2) that by demonstrating that both the expression of biblical truth and the theology which studies it are set into history, he made a decisive step in theology leading to fruitful developments.

9. *Kritische Untersuchungen über die Kanonischen Evangelien...*, Tübingen, 1847 (= *Kan. Evangel.*), pp. 2-22; cf. *Vorlesungen über Neutestamentliche Theologie*, Leipzig, 1864 (= *Neutest. Theol.*), pp. 1-7.

10. We recall the judgment brought by Luther on the Epistle of James and the Epistle to the Hebrews.

11. *Kan. Evangel.*, pp. 22-40; cf. *Neutest. Theol.*, pp. 7-12.

12. *Kan. Evangel.*, pp. 40-71.

13. D. F. Strauss, *Das Leben Jesu* (1835-36). Strauss himself called it, perhaps more clearly, a "reciprocal refutation" of supernaturalistic and rationalistic points of view (Preface to the first edition).

14. We know that Strauss wished also to rebuild. Baur passed over this undertaking, deprived of any interest for him, in silence: Strauss, beclouded by his total "mythical" interpretation of the New Testament, did not add anything to the knowledge of history.

15. *Kan. Evangel.*, pp. 71-76.

16. *Die sogenannten Pastoralbriefe des Apostels Paulus aufs neue kritisch untersucht*, Stuttgart, Tübingen, 1835, pp. 143-146.

17. *Kan. Evangel.*, p. 62f.

18. *Kan. Evangel.*, p. 75f.

19. *Kan. Evangel.*, pp. 510-512.

SELECT BIBLIOGRAPHY

H. Stephan, *Die Geschichte der evangelischen Theologie seit dem deutschen Idealismus*, Berlin, 1938.

K. Barth, *Protestant Theology in the Nineteenth Century, Its Background and History*, London, 1972.

E. Hirsch, *Geschichte der neueren evangelischen Theologie*, V, Gütersloh, 1949-1954, pp. 518-553.

C. Senft, *Wahrhaftigkeit und Wahrheit*, Tübingen, 1956, pp. 47-86.

M. Tetz, art. "Ferdinand Christian Baur," *RGG*[3], I, Tübingen, 1957, col. 935-938.

W. G. Kümmel, *The New Testament: History of the Investigation of Its Problems*, Nashville, 1972, pp. 126-142.

R. Bultmann, *Theology of the New Testament*, 1955, Vol. 2, pp. 244-245.

JULIUS WELLHAUSEN
HIS HISTORICAL AND CRITICAL METHOD

by Grégoire Rouiller

I. INTRODUCTION

The researches of J. Wellhausen have been widely diffused. Even if many of the results which he believed he had acquired were later contested,[1] they exercise a major and durable influence. This is without doubt the result of his scientific honesty, but especially of the simplicity of his proceeding and his power of rigorous synthesis.

This success was not without serious reserves. From the side of the churches, he was accused of radically destroying the presentation of the Old Testament, of ruining the faith in every form of revelation and ending in a complete naturalism. B. Baentsh echoes such currents of thought:

> One especially reproaches Wellhausen's conception of the history of the people of Israel for not resting on an impartial study of the facts transmitted by Scripture but establishing itself on an arbitrary reconstruction of history, of being in fact wedded to a conception of history whose intention is to eliminate as far as possible every divine factor and to make the history of the people of Israel appear as the necessary product of a natural and human evolution.[2]

In certain quarters, his scientific objectivity is no longer believed. His *Weltanschauung* is considered rationalistic and Darwinian. His philosophy, under the influence of his teacher, W. Vatke, is, they say, a Hegelianism of inferior quality, and his presentation of the history of Israel is an ideological construction. Here again B. Baentsch well summarizes such reproaches:

> He desires, one may say, to subject holy history very simply to a fashionable theory, that of the natural sciences. In philosophy, he is a dilettante, as I have many times heard it said. Through the medium of his teacher, W. Vatke, he has made his own the Hegelian ideas of his time, according to which the history of humanity should unroll itself in conformity to a precise law, established *a priori*. The law to which he has subjected the history of the religion of Israel he has borrowed, according to the fashion of the time, from Darwin's theory of evolution. Cavalierly ignoring the providence of an all-powerful God as well as the freedom of individuals, he has applied this law in a coarse and mechanical fashion to the domain of the spiritual and religious life.[3]

Modern authors have scarcely attenuated the rigor of such judgments, recognizing nevertheless the methodological and critical deposit of Wellhausen. Thus A. Robert says of Wellhausen: "Very rationalistic, profoundly Hegelian, powerful and logical mind, endowed with a strong force of persuasion, he widens the perspective (concerning the Pentateuch) and carries the (documentary) theory to its final consequences, while stating in very simple form what will remain definitive."[4] G. von Rad, for his part, affirms: "Wellhausen was, in the last analysis, strongly influenced by Hegel: he looked on Israel's history as a history of ideas, and presented it above all from the standpoint of a spiritual evolution."[5]

We believe that it is without reason that H. J. Kraus still places Wellhausen in a too direct dependence on Hegel, in spite of the work, in our opinion decisive, of L. Perlitt. In any case, it is the latter which inspires our brief presentation.

II. BIOGRAPHICAL INDICATIONS

Born at Hammeln in 1844, Julius Wellhausen attended the lectures of H. Ewald at Göttingen from 1862 on, and, at 27 years of age, in 1871, published some textual critical notes on the Books of Samuel. From 1872, he taught at Greifswald. It was there that, in 1876, he met the renowned Hellenist, U. von Wilamowitz. The difficulties and the critics to whom we have alluded made him aware of an hiatus between his scholarly purposes and the pastoral mission which had been entrusted to him. This is why, on April 5, 1882, he wrote to the Prussian Minister of Worship: "I became a theologian, because the scientific study of the Bible interests me. Then slowly, it has become apparent to me that the professor of theology equally has the concrete task of preparing students for service in the evangelical Church. I am not equal to such a mission and, despite all my reserve, I make my students more unfit for such a service."[6]

Thus, he became successively professor of Semitic languages at Halle in 1882; he pursued some philological researches at Marburg from 1885 on, before teaching at Göttingen beginning in 1892. His studies, beyond the criticism of materials indispensable for the history of Israel, carried him to almost the whole of the ancient Arab domain on the one hand, and towards the New Testament on the other.[7]

III. AN ANOMALOUS RELATIONSHIP

A long study will be necessary. But at the very beginning it is important to note that Wellhausen chose to be too attentive to the texts and to reality to subject himself to an ideology or even to a single teacher. He knew how to admire, but never without discrimination. When he consented, it was always in rational fashion and on a very precise matter.

Thus, he acknowledged that he owed much to his teacher H. Ewald. It was by him that his interest in research on the history of Israel was awakened. This admiration, however, by no means led him to a servile initiation into the field. He hoped, indeed, to go beyond his teacher, thanks to the more rigorous contribution of W. M. L. de Wette or W. Vatke.[8]

In fact, from 1867 he was seduced, after a visit to Göttingen, by the hypothesis of K. H. Graf (*lex post prophetas*) without yet perceiving the possibility of an exact demonstration. The researches of W. M. L. de Wette aided him here;[9] those of W. Vatke equally helped him, even if he sometimes deplored in the latter an insufficient criticism of the sources.

But what is clear is that he constantly refused to do that for which he has been mostly reproached: to surrender to an *a priori* construction of history, starting from philosophical ideas to end in a sculpting of the facts.[10] What he wrote in 1908 in his studies in the Gospel by John should serve as an earmark in all his work:

> One should not look at the outset for what is valuable or authentic nor for what is without value or inauthentic. Generally, one has no right to establish *a priori* any privileged points of view. One must end there, not begin. One must rather proceed from certain impulses furnished by exegesis itself....
>
> I hold firmly to the principle that it is necessary to begin by being attentive to striking details, if possible exterior and formal; beginning with that, one can pass to the discovery of meanings of a more profound nature.[11]

We are very far, at least in intention, from all ideology.

IV. A HISTORIAN

As O. Eissfeldt has well seen, Wellhausen is a *historian*. But this demands some precision. He is the historian of total suspicion, except with regard to his own instruments of research. In this he is right for his time. A strongly romantic climate in no way undermined confidence in reason and in the possibility of objective research. He is the historian of clarity, of an almost ascetic simplicity, of an honesty which verifies, then subdues. The lively criticism which he made of historic dilettantism and of the position taken by Renan are revealing of his own intellectual integrity: "What pleases is accepted; what does not please is modified to fit his taste, or ignored."[12]

He is a historian who keeps silent when he is not able to verify his knowledge. He wants to see with his own eyes, utilizing intuition, but as a stimulus to verification.[13]

Without doubt, Wellhausen accomplished this rigorous task, which he constantly wished to insure, with his preferences and his allergies, individual or collective, conscious or unconscious.

He has a *passion for origins*. He is allergic to everything which is *artificial*. The connotations of the two terms "origins" and "artificial" are innumerable in his work. He never hides his sympathy for the original, for the natural life, for primitive worship (because it is nearest to nature), for the individual, free of all constraint. Contrarywise, he mistrusts instinctively everything which is *derived*: all political, ecclesiastical or cultural institutions, all collectivism or internationalism, all sacred or transhistoric supernaturalism, every exterior norm or philosophic system, all dogma.

Let us give some examples where his aversions and his attractions appear at the same time. We could cite many a passage of the *Prolegomena*, especially chapter 8. Here are some sentences:

> As with the legend of the beginnings of things, so with the legend of the patriarchs: what is essential and original is the individual element in the several stories; the connection is a secondary matter, and only introduced in the stories being collected and reduced to writing. But in the Priestly Code the individuality of the several stories is simply destroyed: to such an extent is the connection dwelt on.[14]

Further on we read:

> The Jehovist still lives in the spirit of the legend, but the Pristly Code is strange to that spirit.[15]

The same opposition to the cultus is seen in the following statement:

> We may compare the cultus in the olden time to the green tree which grows up out of the soil as it will and can; later it becomes the regularly shapen timber, ever more artificially shaped with square and compass.[16]

Also, as a historian, he wanted to avoid "dissolving everything which is individual and concrete into the general and the schematic".[17]

To appreciate the work of Wellhausen as a historian, we must remember that with him there is a double purpose. He wished to submit himself rigorously to the testimony of the texts. And, as we shall see, it is in view of this that he never turned aside from a rigorous method. But, from another point of view, he did not lack the occasion to manifest his versatile and warm attachment to the authentic, to the germinal charm of life. The two purposes are united when he affirmed: "This is not putting logic in the place of investigation",[18] when he fought against the construction of history, yet totally recognizing that the historian must construct and order.[19]

V. HIS METHOD OF WORK

His method of work, in essentials, has become a boon to all biblical scholars. Wellhausen understands that there are two stages to honor in the scientific study of the Bible: a slow preparation which it is necessary never to slight, followed by synthetic accounts where history properly so called is written.

1. *The Preparatory Investigation*

According to Wellhausen, it is necessary to devote particular attention to *textual criticism*. If in the history of his own research it was there that he began with his notes on the Books of Samuel, he never ceased in his historic investigation to establish the best possible textual foundation. The notes of his translation of the Minor Prophets, those which he published on the Psalms, many a remark in his Introduction to the three Synoptic Gospels, all testify to this. From 1871, his keen discernment appeared. Several rules utilized for revealing a corrupt text or copyist's errors, and his suggestions for using the Septuagint to improve the text, were innovations in that period. He said this of himself: "What I said in 1871 about the text of the Books of Samuel, holds more surely yet for the text of the Gospels."[20] Also, the reading of some pages of his Introduction to the three Gospels reveals how methodically and minutely he examined the text of the Gospels.[21]

Once the text was determined, Wellhausen excelled in the *translation*. His profound knowledge of Hebrew, of Aramaic, of Arabic and of Syriac, and his philological lucidity helped him much in this. A dictionary such as Gesenius-Buhl indicates how much Hebrew lexicography owes to him. Several publications of Wellhausen illustrate what many scholars forget: an exact and intelligent translation permits a considerable reduction of the commentary and the notes. It renders them superfluous. Gunkel paid homage to the competence of Wellhausen in this domain when he affirmed that after Luther it would be necessary to be Wellhausen to attain to such warmth and fullness in the translation of the Psalms.

But the largest part of this preparatory work lies certainly in *literary criticism*. His studies on the composition of the Hexateuch teach us in precise fashion the manner in which Wellhausen understood this. Setting out from hypotheses more or less assured in his time concerning the date of the four documents of the Pentateuch, he proceeds to an analysis of each layer, being preoccupied less with the structure or the construction of the whole of a passage (*Gattungsgeschichte* had not yet arisen) than with the localization of each element established on philological foundations and with the help of literary sources.

If we read what he says of our text of reference, Genesis 22, the principal tendencies of this literary criticism are perceptible.[22] First, his *extreme sobriety*. Having established with evidence that verses 15-18 were an addition of the Jahwist abounding in reminiscences, he refuses to take up again the demonstration of it. At the most he will remark, because it is a new element, that this is perceptible from verse 15 where שנית recalls Joshua 5:2 and is not far from I Samuel 11:14.

Then there is *a simultaneous attention to form and content*. Verses 11-14 are Elohist as to their content[23] in spite of formal modifications due to the Jahwist. Finally, *that which is principal, the examination of sources*. Taking account of philology, of parallel passages carefully examined, of historical indications previously checked, he moved forward with prudence and discretion. We have here a beautiful example of this versatile and rigorous process: to elucidate the enigma of the place where the sacrifice of Isaac should have taken place, he will appeal to a comparison of the other patriarchal traditions, to the Jewish tradition and even to the Samaritan tradition concerning the site of the temple, to geographical data, to parallel places, and finally to the requirements of the story itself which postulates a region rather than a precise spot.

This literary criticism is never dissociated on his part from a *historical criticism*. If we distinguish them here, it is to underline how much his double comparative process remains methodologically valuable.[24] In his *Prolegomena*, it is applied successively to places of worship, to the distinction between priests and levites, to sacred ground rents and to feasts. Wellhausen starts from the hypothesis which places the documents of the Pentateuch in the following historic order: J, E, D, P. In a first approach, he compares some passages situated on a diachronic axis, he studies their natural coherence, he interests himself less in their evolution than in their probable genesis. Thus, one passes easily, according to him, from the ancient testimonies of J and E, in Exodus 20:24-26, affirming the multiplicity of altars and of places of worship, to the peace around one place and a single altar attested by the priestly text of Leviticus 17, while passing over the tensions still perceptible in D (cf. Deut. 12, for example). Wellhausen can then proceed to a second comparative work which has the tone of verification. The question which he poses is this: having provisionally admitted a plausible date for each document, do the assured synchronical data confirm this date or not? In the example indicated above (that of the places of worship), he will examine the data of Genesis and of Judges to compare them with the stories of J and of E, those of the reform of Josiah which he will confront with D, those of the birth of Judaism and of the exile in relation to P. He could, after that, affirm that the chronological order J E D P is confirmed and can henceforth be utilized in drawing up the history of Israel.

Slowly he became aware that this long work constituted the indispensable approach to all serious historical synthesis. It was a preparation. One understands then why he modified the title of one of his works: in 1871, he had published *Geschichte Israels*. The edition of 1883 carried the title *Prolegomena zur Geschichte Israels*.

2. *The Historical Synthesis*

On the part of Wellhausen, this comes methodologically into its own, even if it is excessive or weak on a number of points. It is, indeed, here that the preferences of Wellhausen manifest themselves, sometimes unfortunately. Let us pause before some of his principal positions.

Wellhausen distributed his historical materials in all directions from the deep chasm of the exile. Contrary to what one might imagine if he were the defender of a facile Hegelianism, his favors go to the period which precedes the exile, not to that which follows. The exile, he said, "has shattered the natural bond between the present and the previous epochs to such a degree that an artificial reconstruction of these epochs, on the basis of ideas, no longer finds any obstacle".[25]

The priestly document as a witness to nascent Judaism serves him as a negative reference, as a universal repudiation.[26] Based on some ideas (those of theocracy, of covenant, of internationalism), P is constructed according to a scheme (that of three covenants); it unfolds itself according to a monotonous, rigid, abstract mathematics. All sacerdotalism is hardness of heart.

Faithful to his methodological principles, he believed it possible to exhibit strong skepticism about the nomadic period of ancient Israel. The sources in our possession do not, in his opinion, permit us to affirm what that period was. In reading the stories concerning the patriarchs in J or E, "It is true, we attain to no historical knowledge of the patriarchs, but only of the time when the stories about them arose in the Israelite people; this later age is here unconsciously projected, in its inner and its outward features, into hoar antiquity, and is reflected there like a glorified mirage."[27]

On the contrary, the documents assembled in the way he preferred allow him to extol the period of the initial occupation of the land of Canaan. That period was somewhat like the life of a happy savage, flexible and multiformed, abounding and natural, without institutional hardening. According to him, there existed a sort of harmony between God, the nation, life, religion and revelation. It is not without jubilation nor approval that he writes: "Of administration and of police, as exercises of authority, there was no discussion."[28]

As to the prophets, his position is ambivalent. He extols them as individuals, bearers of revelation on the margin of the institution which hardened itself.[29] He read them as continuators of the work of Moses,[30] as the restorers of the course of moral life, flexible and pluralistic. But he sees no cleft between them and Deuteronomy. Deuteronomy seemed to him to be the crowning of the prophetic work.[31]

Let us simply note again that he approached the New Testament with the same rigor and the same sympathies. Jesus appeared to him as the herald of the natural life, of religious individualism which he did not hesitate to call the salt of the gospel (in opposition to the Church).[32]

It is necessary to read, as highly significant of the spirit of his historical synthesis, the concluding chapter of his *Israelitische und jüdische Geschichte*. Let us cite from the closing lines of it:

> Faith in liberty and faith in God, are one and the same thing; one does not exist without the other.
>
> Jesus did not establish the Church, he condemned the Jewish theocracy. The gospel is only the salt of the earth. Where it wishes to be more, it is less. It proclaims the most noble individualism, the liberty of the children of God.[33]

VI. OBSERVATIONS AND QUESTIONS

The general effect of our study reveals how much the historical-critical method pursued by Wellhausen inspires us still, even if its limits are perceptible to us. We conclude our reflections then with a certain number of statements and questions.

1. We cannot reproach Wellhausen for the deficient character of his extra-biblical information. In his time, he could only cover the Arab domain which he cleared up magisterially. He foresaw what one could take from other cultures. Nevertheless, we may not affirm that he had the time to practice what he caught a glimpse of when he affirmed:

> Although in earlier times the Old Testament was obliged to illuminate the rest of the ancient Orient, henceforth it itself receives the light of the Egyptian and Babylonian-Assyrian monuments recently discovered and deciphered. Israelite antiquity can no longer be isolated....Beyond the demonstrable historical contact, it should be studied by anal-

> ogy with the general cultural evolution. The Israelite nation should be compared with the other nations, and we know that religion should not be separated from the nation. Nevertheless, neither the historic attention open to the rest of the world, nor the work of comparison have the mission of a complete leveling. We ought not to try to prove that there was nothing specific in the Israelite and Jewish religion. Because of the resemblance of the beginnings and the analogy of evolution, the difference in the results ought not to be denied.[34]

2. One may easily recognize the deficiency of his instruments of analysis. In his time there was a myth about writing. This prevented him from doing justice to oral tradition, sometimes as trustworthy as the written document. Even more, his literary criticism is often atomist. It is not sensitive to wholes, to literary form, to the simultaneous presence of the elements of a language. It grievously misunderstands the power of poetry.[35]

3. A fixed resolve against all forms of the sacred, against all ecclesiastical institutions and against all dogmatism has narrowed the possibilities of his instruction. Hence, he cannot thrill to the wholly liturgical majesty of Genesis 1. He reads there only schematics, ideas, and abstractions. Likewise, instead of seeing in the Deuteronomic theology of the covenant a legitimate development very rich with ancient historical traditions, he sees disclosed there only an impoverishment respecting the religious practices of the period of the Judges.

4. His individualism (deeply rooted in the mentality of his time) seems to us to be extremely fertile when it has as a connotation liberty, simplicity, flexibility, life, creation, and authenticity. On the other side, however, I ask myself if he is not sometimes prevented from reading even the his-

tory of Israel as the history of a people. The depth of the notion of the Torah, for example, contains the dawn of Judaism.

5. Many other questions could be posed. Is his notion of revelation sufficient? Is his interpretation of the preaching and the person of Jesus acceptable? etc.[36]

These observations are not at all designed to tarnish the greatness of Wellhausen. We have yet to receive from his rigorousness much humility, from the example of his never satisfied research. Let us simply conclude our remarks with an example of his integrity. In the seventh edition of his *Israelitische und jüdische Geschichte*, he adds a note before the last chapter (Das Evangelium) to caution: "I have let this chapter appear, although I only partially acknowledge it today." It is our turn not to harden.

NOTES

1. Cf. article by J. J. Roberts, "The Decline of the Wellhausen Reconstruction of Israelite Religion," *Restoration Quarterly* 9 (1966), pp. 229-240.

2. "Man macht der Wellhausenschen Auffassung von der Geschichte des Volkes Israel in der Hauptsache den Vorwurf, dass sie nicht der unbefangenen Betrachtung der in der Schrift überlieferten Tatsachen entspreche, sondern auf einer willkürlichen Geschichtsconstruction beruhe, und zwar näher auf einer Geschichtsconstruction, die in ganz bewusster Weise darauf ausgehe, den göttlichen Faktor möglichst zu eliminieren und die Geschichte des Volkes Israel als das Produkt einer naturnotwendigen, rein menschlich-natürlichen Entwicklung erscheinen zu lassen." B. Baentsch, *Geschichtsconstruction oder Wissenschaft?* Halle, 1896, p. 1.

3. "Er wollte, sagt man, ganz einfach die heilige Geschichte der modischen, naturwissenschaftlichen Entwicklungstheorie, die in allen Köpfen spukt, unterwerfen. Er ist eben ein philosophischer Dilettant, so habe ich mehrmals sagen hören. Durch Vermittlung seines Meisters Vatke hat er seiner Zeit hegelsche Ideen in sich aufgenommen, nach denen die Geschichte der Menschheit nach einem ganz bestimmten a priori feststehenden Gesetze verlaufen muss. Das Gesetz nun, dem er die Geschichte der israelitischen Religion unterstellte, hat er...dem Zuge der Zeit folgend und ganz à la fin du siècle der Darwinschen Entwicklungstheorie entnommen. Die Vorsehung eines allmächtigen Gottes und die Freiheit der menschlichen Individuen stolz ignorirend habe er dieses Gesetz in ganz roher, mechanischer Weise auf das Gebiet des geistigen und religiösen Lebens übertragen." B. Baentsch, *op. cit.*, p. 21 (cited by L. Perlitt, *op. cit.*, p. 155).

4. A. Robert, *Notes sur le Pentateuque*, Paris, n.d., p. 5.

5. G. von Rad, *Old Testament Theology*, I, New York, 1962, p. 113.

6. "Ich bin Theologe geworden, weil mich die wissenschaftliche Behandlung der Bibel interessierte, es ist mir erst allmählich aufgegangen, dass ein Professor der Theologie zugleich die praktische Aufgabe hat, die Studenten für den Dienst in der evangelischen Kirche vorzubereiten, und dass ich dieser praktischen Aufgabe nicht genüge, vielmehr trotz

aller Zurückhaltung meinerseits, meine Zuhörer für ihr Amt eher untüchtig mache. Seitdem liegt mir meine theologische Professur schwer auf dem Gewissen." Letter to the Prussian Ministry of Worship of May 4, 1882, as a sequel to the violent criticisms occasioned by his first publications (cited by L. Perlitt, *op. cit.*, p. 153).

7. A list of the principal works of Wellhausen is found at the end of this article.

8. Of de Wette, he affirmed: "Was ich im alten Testament gemacht habe, steht ja schon alles bei ihm" (cited by L. Perlitt, *op. cit.*, p. 167).

9. Notably his publications on Deuteronomy.

10. He did not hesitate to take a position against Baur and Strauss on this point. Cf. Perlitt, *op. cit.*, pp. 205f.

11. "Man darf nicht fragen, was wertvoll und echt sei, oder wertlos und unecht. Man darf überhaupt nicht von vornherein grosse Gesichtspunkte aufstellen; damit muss man aufhören, nicht anfangen. Ausgehen muss man vielmehr von einzelnen Anstössen, die sich bei der Exegese ergeben..."
"An dem Grundsatze halte ich fest, dass man bei auffallenden, wo möglich äusserlichen oder formellen Einzelheiten einsetzen muss und erst von da zur Aufdeckung durchgehender Unterschiede von tieferer Art fortschreiten darf." *Das Evangelium Johannis*, Berlin, 1908, p. 4f. (cited by L. Perlitt, *op. cit.*, p. 205.

12. "Was gefällt, wird aufgenommen; was nicht gefällt, wird gefällig gemacht oder ignoriert." Review of E. Renan's *Histoire du peuple d'Israël* (cited by L. Perlitt, *op. cit.*, p. 170).

13. We can apply to him that which he said about C. G. Wilke, in his *Einleitung in die drei ersten Evangelien*, Berlin, 1911^{2}, p. 34: "Der Pfarrer von Rothenburg ist (...) ein merkwürdig selbständiger Forscher, der immer mit eigenen Augen sieht und Alles seiner eigenen zähen Arbeitkraft verdankt."

14. J. Wellhausen, *Prolegomena to the History of Ancient Israel*, New York, 1957, pp. 335-336.

15. *Prolegomena...*, p. 336.

16. "We may compare the cultus in the olden time to the

green tree which grows up out of the soil as it will and can; later it becomes the regularly shapen timber, ever more artificially shaped with square and compass. Obviously there is a close connection between the qualitative antithesis we have just been expounding and the formal one of law and custom from which we set out. Between 'naturaliter ea quae legis sunt facere' and 'secundum legem agere' there is indeed a more than external difference. If at the end of our first section we found improbable precisely in this region the independent co-existence of ancient praxis and Mosaic law, the improbability becomes still greater from the fact that the latter is filled with a quite different spirit, which can be apprehended only as Spirit of the age (*Zeitgeist*). It is not from the atmosphere of the old kingdom, but from that of the church of the second temple, that the Priestly Code draws its breath. It is in accordance with this that the sacrificial ordinances as regards their positive contents are no less completely ignored by antiquity than they are scrupulously followed by the post-exilian time." *Prolegomena*, pp. 81-82.

17. "...dass alles Individuelle und Concrete sich ins Allgemeine und Schematische auflöst." Review of E. Renan (cited by L. Perlitt, *op. cit.*, p. 213).

18. *Prolegomena*, p. 367.

19. *Prolegomena*, p. 367. The entire page is enlightening.

20. *Einleitung in die drei ersten Evangelien*, Berlin, 1905 (= Einleitung), p. 2.

21. Especially *Einleitung*, pp. 2-6 and his nuanced judgment on the text called Western.

22. *Die Composition des Hexateuchs und der historischen Bücher des alten Testaments*, Berlin, 1899[3], pp. 18-19.

23. Which he proves very skillfully: "vgl. v. 11 mit 21, 17 und dagegen 16, 7; 18, 1 ss; 19, 1 ss aus J, ferner v. 14 mit v. 8, wo der Name durch אלהים יראה vorbereitet wird." It can be with difficulty more concise.

24. Utilized in exemplary fashion in *Prolegomena*, pp. 17-167.

25. *Geschichte Israels*, Berlin, 1878, p. 40.

26. The whole of chapter 8 of the *Prolegomena* witnesses to this, pp. 295-362.

27. *Prolegomena*, pp. 318-319.

28. "Von Verwaltung und Polizei, als Aufgaben der Obrigkeit, war nicht die Rede." *Israelitische und jüdische Geschichte*, Berlin, 1894 (= *Israelitische*), p. 85. The entire fine chapter: "Gott, Welt und Leben im alten Israel," pp. 78-103, illustrated what we are saying.

29. Cf. *Prolegomena*, p. 398f.

30. *Prolegomena*, p. 399.

31. *Israelitische*, p. 129: "Das Deuteronomium krönt die Arbeit der Propheten."

32. *Skizzen und Vorarbeiten*, I, Berlin, 1884, p. 102.

33. "Der Glaube an die Freiheit und der Glaube an Gott ist das selbe, eins nicht ohne das andere. Beide sind nur dem Glauben vorhanden" (...) "Jesus hat die Kirche nicht gestiftet, der jüdischen Theokratie hat er das Urteil gesprochen. Das Evangelium ist nur das Salz der Erde; wo es mehr sein will, ist es weniger. Es predigt den edelsten Individualismus, die Freiheit der Kinder Gottes." *Israelitische*, p. 371.

34. "Während ehedem das Alte Testament den übrigen alten Orient beleuchten musste, empfängt es nunmehr auch selber Licht von den neu entdeckten und entzifferten ägyptischen und babylonisch-assyrischen Denkmälern. Das israelitische Altertum kann nicht mehr isoliert werden....Auch über die historisch nachweisbare Berührung hinaus muss es unter die Analogie der allgemeinen Kulturentwicklung gestellt werden. Das israelitische Volkstum muss den anderen Nationen verglichen werden, und von dem Volkstum lässt sich die Religion nicht trennen. Nur hat die weltgeschichtliche und die vergleichende Betrachtung nicht die Aufgabe, alles zu nivellieren. Sie darf nicht darauf ausgehen, nachzuweisen, dass an der israelitisch-jüdischen Religion nichts Besonderes sei. Sie darf über der Ähnlichkeit der Anfänge und der Analogie der Entwicklung die Differenz des Endergebnisses nicht übersehen." *Kultur der Gegenwart*, Berlin, Leipzig, 1906, p. 1f. (cited by L. Perlitt, *op. cit.*, p. 224).

35. The poem of Job 3, for example, is disparaged in comparison with Jeremiah 20.

36. His judgments are often categorical. "Jesus war kein Christ, sondern Jude." *Einleitung*, p. 102.

SELECT BIBLIOGRAPHY

a) Principal Works of J. Wellhausen

Der Text der Bücher Samuelis untersucht, Göttingen, 1871.

Die Pharisäer und die Sadducäer, Greifswald, 1874.

Geschichte Israels, Berlin, 1878.

Prolegomena zur Geschichte Israels, Berlin, 1883, 1927[6] (resumption of *Geschichte Israels*) (= *Prolegomena...*). [*Prolegomena to the History of Israel*, Edinburgh, 1885.]

Reste arabischen Heidentums, Skizzen und Vorarbeiten, drittes Heft, Berlin, 1887.

Israelitische und jüdische Geschichte, Berlin, 1894 (first drafts in 1878; 1880; 1885) (= *Israelitische*).

Die Composition des Hexateuchs und der historischen Bücher des alten Testaments, Berlin, 1899[3] (articles of 1876, 1877, 1878).

Das arabische Reich und sein Sturz, Berlin, 1902.

Einleitung in die drei ersten Evangelien, Berlin, 1905 (= *Einleitung*).

Das Evangelium Johannis, Berlin, 1908.

For a complete list of Wellhausen's writings until 1914, cf.:

K. Marti, *Studien zur semitischen Philologie und Religionsgeschichte, Festschrift J. Wellhausen*, Giessen, 1914, pp. 353-368.

b) Some Studies on Wellhausen and His Work

W. Baumgartner, "Wellhausen und der heutige Stand der alttestamentlichen Wissenschaft," *ThR* 2 (1930), pp. 287-307.

O. Eissfeldt, "Julius Wellhausen," in *Kleine Schriften*, I, Tübingen, 1962, pp. 56-71.(text of 1920).

P. Humbert, "Wellhausen," *RThPh* n.s. 6 (1918), pp. 58-64.

H. J. Kraus, *Geschichte der historisch-kritischen Erforschung des Alten Testaments von der Reformation bis zur Gegenwart*, Neukirchen, 1956, 1969[2], pp. 255-274.

L. Perlitt, *Vatke und Wellhausen*, Berlin, 1965.

J. J. Roberts, "The Decline of the Wellhausen Reconstruction of Israelite Religion," *Restoration Quarterly* 9 (1966), pp. 229-240.

H. Weidmann, *Die Patriarchen und ihre Religion im Licht der Forschung seit J. Wellhausen*, Göttingen, 1968 (especially pp. 11-35).

JULIUS WELLHAUSEN'S EXEGESIS OF LUKE 15:11-32

by François Bovon

The five pages which Julius Wellhausen devoted to the Parable of the Prodigal Son in his 1904 commentary disappoints the reader at first.[1] The exegesis seems scanty, cold and insignificant. A second reading proves to be more stimulating, for the intention of the author becomes more evident, the method more bold and the results more original.

Wellhausen's progress is achieved in six stages. In a first stage, the author offers an original translation which presupposes an analysis of the state of the text. The criticism does not retain the variants of the Western text, but the more rugged forms of the Egyptian and Byzantine texts. Thus Wellhausen reads at verse 16 "filled his belly" rather than "satisfy himself".

To give the meaning of the first part of the parable (vss. 11-24a) is the aim of the second stage, singularly brief. The story of the younger son is transparent: it signifies that the divine pardon and a joyous welcome are assured to the "true sinner" (p. 82) who returns to God. In specifying that the real sinner is not the man who is a sinner by nature (pp. 82-83), Wellhausen doubtless bares his fangs against the dogmaticians who speculate on original sin.

He affirms further on that what counts is only the religious meaning of the parable (p. 83) and adds that the perspective is individualistic (p. 84). As we shall see, these two observations probably are aimed at the interpretation of F. C. Baur.

The third stage permits Wellhausen to demonstrate the secondary, adventitious nature of the second part of the parable, which recounts the offended reaction of the older son (vss. 24b-32).

Wellhausen advanced three indices favoring his thesis:

1. The words "and they began to make merry" (vs. 24b), which serve as a transition between the two parts, clearly project the moral drawn at verse 24a as the conclusion of the story ("for this my son was dead, and is alive again; he was lost, and is found").

2. The second part concludes with the same words as the first (vs. 32 takes up vs. 24a). But, Wellhausen notes with subtle discrimination, the tone has changed. In verse 24a the pure joy of the father bursts forth. In verse 32 the same words appear to be the expression of the embarrassment of the head of the family who explains to his older son that he could not do other than rejoice. For the German exegete, this change of tone is suspect ("*Das ist verdächtig*", p. 83). This is to say that the original nature of the second part is uncertain, indeed unlikely.

3. A contradiction between the two parts finally confirms the inauthentic character of verses 24b-32. According to the first story, the father has really divided his goods between his two sons (vs. 12), while the second part implies that only the younger son has received his part of the inheritance (hence, the recriminations of the older son).

Wellhausen then pursues a criticism of the sources and reveals himself as a partisan of *Literarkritik*, but to our surprise the arguments which he advances in favor of the inauthenticity of verses 24b-32 take up a thematic content. He is aware of the contradictions of meaning and perceives that the second part deranges the coherence of the first. But he does not note the literary difference of style and of vocabulary which nurture, for example, the criticisms which E. Schweizer addresses to the partisans of the integrity of the parable.[2]

In a fourth stage, Wellhausen raises the question of the origin and the *raison d'être* of the addition of verses 24b-32. Two principal reasons have occasioned this excrescence, the one literary, the other theological.

The second part of the parable has seen the light of day in response to a *narrative* preoccupation of the reader. Aware of the existence of the older brother, the reader asks himself what has become of him. Verses 24b-32 were created to satisfy his curiosity.

More important is the theological reason. The reader of the first part compulsively asks himself the question: Is it fair that the guilty convert should finally be treated better than the virtuous son who has no need of repentance? "Der zweite Teil des Gleichnisses stellt das Problem der Theodicee, das dem ersten fern liegt" (p. 84).

Resorting then to *Sachkritik*, Wellhausen condemns the response which the second part of the parable gives to this agonizing question. The reply of the father (vs. 31) does not satisfy him for two reasons: 1) The father has nobly said "all that is mine is yours", but the older son in fact does not have the right freely to receive the paternal goods. This indicates why the older son remains totally disappointed. 2) Then, the younger son not only is feted upon his return, but also positively reinstated into the family domain. This amounts to saying that he will not cease to be in a superior position.

We may suppose that Wellhausen arrived at this judgment by reason of the normative and durable value which he conferred on the original parable (vss. 11-24a). As we have had occasion to point out, this importance is in his eyes religious and individual. Religious, for it places the believer in his real existence (Wellhausen here takes up a *doctrinal* scheme of conversion). Individual, for it does not comprise a collectivity, such as the Gentile-Christian Church (Wellhausen attacks the schematism of F. C. Baur without naming it). Inadequate rather than bad, the theological reflection of verses 24b-32 cannot then be, for him, the fruit of the preaching of Jesus.

In no way does Wellhausen attempt to situate in the history of primitive Christianity the concern for distributive justice which he discloses in verses 24b-32. Surpassing Baur in an analysis of sources, although still very rudimentary, he remains on this side of the master of *Tendenzkritik* by inserting the texts into history.

The contemporary reader is also astonished at the little interest Wellhausen grants to the comparative history of religions. At the moment when his *Evangelium Lucae* appeared (1904), the work of A. Jülicher which signaled several parallel texts--certainly to reject them--had left the press several years before.[3]

In a fifth stage, Wellhausen compares the parable of Luke 15:11ff. to that of the two sons conveyed by the first Gospel (Matt. 21:2kff.). For this last text, he permits an interpretation similar to Baur's,[4] in seeing there a "historical allegory" (p. 84). The attitude of the two sons of Matthew 21 for him reflects without doubt a situation of the time of the Church (to hold that view of the text is to give what he calls a historical explanation). The two sons of Luke 15 do not yield themselves to such an interpretation: "...man darf das Verhältnis des verloren Sohnes zu dem anderen so wenig *historisch ausdeuten*, wie das Verhältnis des verloren Schafes zu den anderen (14:4ff.). Die dem Lc eigentümlichen Parabeln sind meistens *auf das Individuum gerichtet*" (p. 84; the italics is ours).

The exegesis of Wellhausen concludes with some explanations of philological and historic details. Drawing upon his Orientalist erudition, the learned scholar uncovers some Semitisms and explains various expressions with the aid of Syriac or Aramaic.[5]

In conclusion, let us state that Wellhausen reveals himself here as a philologist, historian and *Literarkritiker.* Sensitive to the coherence of the original parable, he prunes the canonical text without reflecting on the ecclesiastical milieu which has brought the primitive text to completion nor concerning himself with the author who has imparted such beauty to the parable of the Prodigal Son in the composition of his Gospel.

NOTES

1. J. Wellhausen, *Das Evangelium Lucae übersetzt und erklärt*, Berlin, 1904.

2. E. Schweizer, "Zur Frage der Lukasquellen, Analyse von Luk. 15, 11-32," *ThZ* 4 (1948), pp. 469-471.

3. Volume II of the *Gleichnisreden Jesu* of A. Jülicher, entitled *Auslegung der Gleichnisreden der drei ersten Evangelien*, appeared in Freiburg im Breisgau, Leipzig and Tübingen, in 1899.

4. In fact, curiously enough, F. Ch. Baur arrived at an opposite result. He deems that in distinction from the parable of the prodigal son, the parable of the two sons (Matt. 21:28ff.) does not reflect the situation of the primitive church. Does it not, then, in his opinion, yield a "historical" interpretation? "Die Parabel bei Matthäus (21, 28-31) von den beiden Söhnen eines Vaters, von welchen der Eine im Wort ungehorsam, in der That gehorsam, der Andere im Wort gehorsam, in der That aber ungehorsam ist, lässt sich mit der unsrigen [that of the prodigal son] nicht vergleichen, da sie gerade den die Judenchristen betreffenden charakteristischen Zug nicht enthält, und der den Zöllnern und Huren vor den gesetzeseifrigen Pharisäern gegebene Vorzug, auf das Verhältniss der Heiden und Juden bezogen, nur dieselbe Verstossung der Letztern aussagt, von welcher auch sonst die Rede ist." F. Ch. Baur, *Kritische Untersuchungen über die kanonischen Evangelien, ihr Verhältniss zu einander, ihren Charakter und Ursprung*, Tübingen, 1847, pp. 511-512.

5. These remarks bear successively on the carob pods (vs. 16), the variants "fill his belly" and "fed" (vs. 16), the condition of the servants (vs. 17), the verb "came to himself" (vs. 17), "heaven" (in the sense of God) (vs. 18), εἰς and ἐνώπιον (vs. 18), the adjective "best" (vs. 22), διδόναι (vs. 22) and συμφωνία (vs. 25).

HERMANN GUNKEL, HISTORIAN OF RELIGION AND EXEGETE OF LITERARY FORMS

by François Bovon

Gunkel was too ardent a partisan of the historic method for us to avoid noting from the very outset two historic contingencies which marked the life of this scholar and, through him, the lot of biblical science.

In reality, Gunkel wished to become a specialist in the New Testament, as is shown by his doctoral thesis, defended at Göttingen in 1888: it was devoted to the work of the Holy Spirit according to St. Paul.[1] Nevertheless, through the insistence of a secretary of State in the ministry of worship of Prussia, Friedrich Althoff, according to some,[2] or of the faculty of theology at Halle, according to others,[3] he turned to the field of Old Testament studies. From *Privat-Dozent* of New Testament at Göttingen, he became *Privat-Dozent* of Old Testament at Halle in 1889.

Now, at this point, Gunkel did not possess a philological preparation sufficient to thrust himself into the domain of semitic studies. This weakness, which he recognized,[4] induced him to interest himself in the literature and the literary forms[5] rather than in textual criticism and philology.

I. THE THEOLOGICAL SITUATION AT THE BEGINNING OF GUNKEL'S CAREER

When Gunkel wrote his thesis at Göttingen, A. Ritschl and his partisans dominated the Faculty of Theology. In spite of his attachment to historical science, and in spite therefore of the influence of F. Ch. Baur, Ritschl believed that he could go beyond his teacher in reconstructing a theological system of a dogmatic nature. In fact, he understood Christianity as an ellipse with two foci, one of which was the forgiveness of sins and the other the Kingdom of God.

Under the intellectual direction of a man who had written relatively little, A. Eichhorn, a group of young scholars was formed at that time. Besides Eichhorn, the leader, some young theologians from Northern Germany participated: H. Gunkel, W. Wrede, and W. Bousset.[6] These young Turks also claimed to be theologians. But, in their eyes, theology should be exclusively historical. History is the only access to truth and to revelation. In the interest even of the Church, it is expedient to disengage theology from all ecclesiastical tutelage and from all systematizing of a dogmatic type. For what is of value is not dogmas, but piety and its history. The issue for them, then, was to oppose Ritschl in the name of theology, but of a theology understood as history, more precisely as the history of religion and of piety.

Gunkel and his friends did not wish to attack the Bible. On the contrary, the most rigorous possible study from the philological and historical point of view could, in their opinion, only reveal the *specificity* and the *superiority* of the Israelite and Christian revelation, according to a necessity which determined the history of the human spirit (Hegel influenced directly or indirectly all theologians of that epoch). The prophets, for Gunkel, are at the summit of the spiritual history of Israel, as Jesus is the zenith of the New Testament. The law and the cult are far below these heights!

In comparing the Old Testament literature to the Babylonian, or even the Egyptian literature, and in describing Israel as a people young, very small and open to outside influences, the Göttingen group did not seek either to minimize Israel nor her literary treasures.[7]

The *religionsgeschichtliche* method,[8] extolled by A. Eichhorn and his friends, concerned itself with the history of *the* Religion and not of *religions*. Gunkel reminds us of this expressly in the preface to his collection of articles of 1913.[9] Against Friedrich Delitzsch and Pan-Babylonism, Gunkel notes the important transformations to which Israel had submitted the materials borrowed from other people of the East: Israel had assimilated nothing which she had not at the same time, if one may say so, *monotheized and ethicized*.

II. THE SITUATION OF OLD TESTAMENT STUDIES

If from the theological point of view Eichhorn, Gunkel and their associates were opposed to Ritschl, from the exegetical and historical point of view they confronted the giant Julius Wellhausen, the most classical of Old Testament exegetes.[10] Wellhausen's ideas dominated German Old Testament scholarship: the young scholars of Göttingen followed him in the greater part of his views. They admired his construction of the history of Israel and lived in genial fashion with his criticism of sources (*Literarkritik*) and his historic perspective (Gunkel, for his part, preferred his ingenuity in synthesis to his analysis of documents). They accepted the chronological inversion effected by the master: the *law*--which Gunkel never liked--is secondary; the prophets precede and tower above it.

On two points, nevertheless, Gunkel vigorously opposed Wellhausen. Wellhausen's system of explanation functioned in a closed vessel: the history of Israel is to be explained by internal reasons. The *religionsgeschichtlich* effort of

Eichhorn and Gunkel was precisely--Gunkel was very conscious of it--to insert the history of Israel and its literature into the history of the ancient Near East. The archaeological and literary discoveries of the 19th century permitted this intention to be realized with success. But in spite of the opinion of R. Kittel, Gunkel always refused to overvalue the impact of archaeological discoveries on the birth of the school. It was a question, according to him, in the *religionsgeschichtliche* school, of an intrinsically theological (*innertheologisch*) movement.[11]

The first conspicuous work of Gunkel (*Schöpfung und Chaos*, 1895)[12] revealed the originality and the fecundity of the new method. It also permitted Gunkel to address to Wellhausen a second criticism: the *Literarkritik*, that is to say, the criticism of sources, the dating of documents, was not a sufficient step in his eyes. The written texts are never a point of departure: the religious ideas which they contain and the literary forms which they utilize are the fruit of a slow gestation, of a prehistory. Behind the written lies the oral; before the writer, the popular tradition; before the whole compositions, the small units.

Wellhausen shut himself off from this perspective and saw in the work of his young rival--he told it to several colleagues--"more chaos than creation".[13] The historic and the literary was not the only stake in the debate. The problem was also theological: Wellhausen became the defender of the text (he thus anticipated *Redaktionsgeschichte*). He refused to accord a *theological* importance to the early traditions (the meaning is in the text and not before it). The traditional elements are in his eyes only archaeological elements.[14] Gunkel does not deny the importance of the texts (to the extent that, according to the dogma going back to Schleiermacher, the text reflects the thought, and the thought the soul of the writer). He even gives his preference to the prophetic texts and, through them, to the great figures of the Old Testament who were the prophets. Prophetism was in his eyes the *zenith* (*Höhepunkt*). But the popular oral traditions (we find here the legacy of Herder) were nonetheless an indispensable *link* of the Hebrew history and literature.

III. THE *RELIGIONSGESCHICHTLICH* METHOD

Let us characterize the *religionsgeschichtlich* method utilized by Gunkel. It is not a question of a simple search for parallels, since for a long time men have gone on quest for religious themes analogous to those read in the Bible. The originality of Eichhorn, Gunkel, Bousset, Wrede, Gressmann, and later Reitzenstein, was *to substitute genealogy for analogy*. Thus, according to *Schöpfung und Chaos*, the resemblance between the myth of Marduk who fights against Tiamat, the chaotic monster, and the story of Genesis 1 where Elohim creates the universe, becomes a real relationship when Gunkel can set down the history of this mythic tradition, analyze the evolution of the themes (for example, the passing from polytheism to monotheism), and discover above all the famous *Zwischenglieder*, the missing links between the original Babylonian and the Israelite version of this myth. And if the text of Genesis has its roots in Babylon, it spreads its roots as far as the Apocalypse. From the mythic prehistory follows, indeed, the apocalyptic posthistory: the myth pursues its existence. Following a transfer known elsewhere, the themes tied to creation have, in reality, been projected into the end of time: it was not henceforth surprising to meet again the primordial combat in the Apocalypse of John, in a version which could be called terminal.

In many respects, *Schöpfung und Chaos* is the prime example of the *religionsgeschichtlich* method. It should not be forgotten that if Gunkel calls to our minds the *Literaturgeschichte*, he saw his professorial ministry and his theological task to be the diffusion of *religionsgeschichtlich* ideas among the people and their implantation in the scholarly world. Even if the strictly personal deposit of Gunkel was greater in the study of *Gattungen*, he himself preferred to center his existence on *Religionsgeschichte*, plainly a very burning issue: hence his effort at popularization by numerous conferences to the four corners of Germany and his scholarly work of extending the *religionsgeschichtlich* method to all domains of theology by the publication of *Religion in Geschichte und Gegenwart*, of which he was one of the pioneers and pillars (especially for the second edition).

IV. THE *GATTUNGSGESCHICHTLICH* METHOD

Schöpfung und Chaos led Gunkel to introduce *the question of literary forms* into the orbit of his thought. For to apply the *religionsgeschichtliche* method was above all to classify, to compare and to understand the texts. Now Gunkel, influenced by J. G. Herder and E. Reuss, had a mind sharpened by aesthetic requirements (he spoke of "die Kraft der Anschauung, die edle Phantasie").[15] He was aware that a content required a corresponding formal expression. To utilize his own terms, to understand the history of religion properly is to understand the history of literatures, oral then written, and to understand this history is to grasp the life of the various literary forms.[16] The establishment of this truth permitted him to surpass Wellhausen on this point.

The search for the *Sitz im Leben* itself was already inscribed in *Schöpfung und Chaos*: for Gunkel, the text is, in reality, the access to the *life*. To understand the text is to determine the sociological rootage of its literary form. In the case of the myth of creation, the feast of the god Marduk is the *sociological* cause of the mythic narrative.

It appears erroneous, then, to *distinguish* two Gunkels, the one of the first period, *religionsgeschichtlich*, and the other of the second period, *literaturgeschichtlich*. The one does not exist without the other. There is no hiatus in the life of the German scholar. At the very most, we may speak of a change of accent:[17] in the commentary on Genesis (1901),[18] in the Introduction, especially paragraph 3, devoted to *Kunstform der Sagen*, the interest in literary forms is emphasized. Gunkel distinguishes myths from tales (in the first two editions, the myth is primary; in the third, the tale is original), then the *Sagen* and their various categories. Without yet using the term *Sitz im Leben*, he imagines what he still calls the *Situation*, the situation in which the *Sage* was narrated.

At the time when he was interested in Genesis (around 1900), his attention undoubtedly was focused on the origins of the literature, a literature still oral. Influenced by Romanticism, he cherished the primitive, naive, pure soul of the people: he thought that the simplest forms, the briefest forms, the purest forms, were the oldest. Certainly, he knew--contrary to what has been sometimes said since then--that popular literature did not mean literature written by the people: the people did not compose it. It is the work of an *individual*, but of an individual *mouthpiece* of the community.

In the *Mêlanges* which were presented to him in 1923[19] (with a year's delay caused by the economic situation) the disciples of Gunkel[20] placed these words on the exergue: "To Hermann Gunkel, teacher and friend, the scholar who, among the first, has placed the religion of the Bible in the framework of the religious history of the Near-East, who has thrown a new light on the narratives of the Old Testament proceeding from the tales and popular *Sagen*, who, in plunging with love into the spirit of Hebrew poetry, has recognized the history of its literary forms, who has felt and described the power of the religious experience of the inspired men and the prophets of the Old Testament and the New Testament...."

This dedication, each word of which is important, places the history of religion in the first rank. We have already spoken of this. Then comes the commentary on Genesis: the accent is rightly placed on the literature compared and on literary forms. In this field, he had no true predecessors: he found too late (between the second and third edition) support among the specialists of German and Greek oral literature. The dedication evokes, in the third place, the work on the Psalms. It was there that Gunkel truly brought to significance his theory of literary forms.

He had worked on the Psalms throughout his life. In 1904, he published a popular work (*Ausgewählte Psalmen*) and innumerable articles thereafter. At the end of his life he published his large commentary without introduction. Death surprised him in the editing of the sixth chapter of the Introduction which he prepared as a complement to his commentary. His disciple J. Begrich completed the work.

Gunkel described there the various literary forms and classified the one hundred and fifty Psalms according to their *Gattungen*: the hymn, the individual complaint, etc. He showed how the form evolved, how, with time, some *Mischformen* were formed, how the *Sitz im Leben* changed, and how from the cultic it became private.

Here the question of Gunkel's originality in this domain is raised: Gunkel pointed to Karl Budde as a pioneer, "the first", he wrote, "to have described a Hebrew *Gattung*",[21] the lamentation, the song of mourning. A silence is astonishing: he nowhere makes mention of de Wette. Now de Wette had written a commentary on the Psalms and among the ten portraits of theologians who adorned the walls of Gunkel's study was one of de Wette. In the light of this, how can the fact that Gunkel does not make note of de Wette's commentary and never discusses the classification of the Psalms which he had there proposed be explained? Nobly, W. Klatt in his thesis[22] deems that Gunkel was not acquainted with this commentary. That is possible. Gunkel had never been exhaustive in his bibliography. He preferred to read the texts of antiquity rather than examine the commentaries of which he often complained. However that may be, de Wette, in spite of his merits, had not arrived at a classification which rested on formal criteria. Moreover, he explained the origin of these literary forms by historic and individual contingencies. The unquestionable originality of Gunkel resides in the discovery of the sociological and collective *Sitze im Leben* and in the utilization of formal criteria in determining literary forms.

Too late Gunkel discovered a precursor, an outsider, named E. Meier, author of a history of Hebrew poetry which dated from 1856.[23] In our time, an author named K. F. Stäudlin (1761-1826) has been rescued from oblivion, a precursor in the subject of prophetic literary forms of whom Gunkel was certainly ignorant.[24]

Gunkel, therefore, was not content to bring to realization the ideas of others. If for *Religionsgeschichte*, the best part comes from Eichhorn, for *Literaturgeschichte* Gunkel was truly the pioneer, even if he leaned on Herder and Reuss. This must be said to contradict H. J. Kraus.[25]

V. CONCLUSION

Among the exegetes of his time, Gunkel has, in our opinion, three principal merits:

a) He *brought to realization* the *religionsgeschichtlich* program worked out with others under the direction of Eichhorn.

b) He integrated into this program a sorting mechanism devoted to *the history of literature.* He not only fancied this, but brought it to realization as a history of literary forms.

c) Finally, he never ceased to reflect on the problems of method. How should one be a theologian? He replied: by being a historian. How does one train himself for the study of history? By philology; but he added that philology is only one stage--by aesthetic sensitivity (he stated expressly[26] that for him exegesis is more an art than a science, and he complained bitterly of those commentaries which amassed philological and historical notes on details to the detriment of the *text* taken in its coherence and its totality). Psychology is also necessary, for it is a case of communing with the great souls of Israel. Finally, the exegete must be a religious man: one understands nothing in the Bible, if he does not share the faith of the sacred authors.[27]

Obviously, the limitations of Gunkel are obvious to an exegete of the end of the twentieth century.

a) As E. Güttgemanns has indicated,[28] Gunkel did not sufficiently reflect on the passage from the oral to the written. He neither surmised nor analyzed the repercussions and the perturbations to which an oral tradition is submitted in being put into writing.

b) As W. Klatt remarks,[29] Gunkel did not have sufficient theological strength to think through the relations which are set up between history and revelation. He could say sometimes that revelation is disseminated in the varied religions (especially at the beginning of his life), sometimes that revelation is centered in Israel. To this uncertainty is added an absence of the knowledge of the *meaning* of history. According to Gunkel, history has only highs and lows, the summits of prophetism or the Gospel, the depths of the law and the cult. Thus he did not succeed in resolving the problem of the relationships between the two Testaments. He left them in juxtaposition.

c) Finally, Gunkel certainly succeeded in justifying a formal analysis of the texts; he also practiced it. But, here again, the power of thought, of theological thought, made him deficient in analyzing the bonds which unite the literary form of a text with its religious content. He contented himself with saying that there was a correspondence between the two, but he did not know how to say what the nature and the theological importance of this correspondence were.

Let us not end, however, on a negative note. One sentence strikes the reader of his article devoted to exegetical method: he declares that the intuition of the exegete should cause him to read between the lines. It is often, he tells us, between the lines that the most profound meaning of a text is hidden: the spirit of the man does not say everything, "so dass oft die Hauptaufgabe der Exegese ist, das Unausgesprochene, Vorausgesetzte, Mitschwingende zwischen den Zeilen herauszuhören".[30] He thus discovered the importance of the *non-spoken*. What the text does not say, but is there as the background of what is said, is important to the vividness and the meaning of the text. By this intuition, Gunkel reveals what he is: a great exegete.

NOTES

1. Cf. the Bio-Bibliography *infra*, p. 139, where the reference will be found.

2. Cf. W. Klatt, *Hermann Gunkel. Zu seiner Theologie der Religionsgeschichte und zur Entstehung der formgeschichtlichen Methode*, Göttingen, 1969, p. 40f. Our pages owe much to this work.

3. Cf. W. Baumgartner, "Zum 100. Geburtstag von Hermann Gunkel," in *Congress Volume, Bonn 1962*, Leiden, 1963, p. 5. W. Baumgartner notes that the Minister of Worship strongly supported the candidacy of H. Gunkel.

4. W. Baumgartner, *art. cit.*, p. 6.

5. He compares their functioning to the rules of grammar: "Jenen Antiken waren die Gesetze der literarischen Formensprachen von Kindesbeinen an ebenso vertraut wie etwa die Regeln der hebräischen Grammatik." H. Gunkel, "Die Grundprobleme der israelitischen Literaturgeschichte," *Deutsche Literaturzeitung* 27 (1906), col. 1797-1800 and 1861-1866, reprinted in *Reden und Aufsätze*, Göttingen, 1913, p. 32, to which we refer.

6. The group was later joined by E. Troeltsch, who became the dogmatician among them, W. Heitmüller and H. Gressmann. Without directly becoming a part of the team, R. Reitzenstein, the philologist, in reality employed the same method. Cf. W. Klatt, *op. cit.*, pp. 20ff.

7. The breadth of view of Gunkel appears in that throughout the *Babel-Bibel* conflict he recalled the existence of Egypt and disclosed in the Egyptian literature various parallels to the Wisdom literature of Israel.

8. On the appearance of the term, cf. the Bio-Bibliography, *infra*, p. 139.

9. H. Gunkel, *Reden und Aufsätze*, Gttingen, 1913, p. v.

10. "Der Klassiker unter den alttestamentlichen Theologen," following the words of Gunkel, cited by W. Baumgartner, *art. cit.*, pp. 8-9.

11. H. Gunkel, "Was will die 'religionsgeschichtliche'

Bewegung?" *Deutsch-Evangelisch* 5 (1914), p. 356f. (cited by W. Klatt, *op. cit.*, p. 26).

12. Cf. the Bio-Bibliography, *infra*, pp. 140-141, where the reference will be found.

13. On this oral tradition, cf. W. Klatt, *op. cit.*, p. 70.

14. Cf. W. Klatt, *op. cit.*, p. 71.

15. H. Gunkel, "Ziele und Methoden der Erklärung des Alten Testaments," *Monatschrift für die kirchliche Praxis* 4 (*Zeitschrift für die praktische Theologie* 26) 1904, pp. 521-540, reprinted in *Reden und Aufsätze*, Göttingen, 1913, p. 14. "Denn Exegese im höchsten Sinne ist mehr eine Kunst als eine Wissenschaft," p. 14. Certainly not an unbridled impressionism, "sondern vielmehr um eine methodisch geschulte, bewusst und kraftvoll auf das eine Ziel gerichtete Strenge," p. 15.

16. H. Gunkel, art. "Literaturgeschichte, 2," *Die Religion in Geschichte und Gegenwart*, 2d ed., Tübingen, 1929, III, col. 1677-1680.

17. With W. Klatt, *op. cit.*, p. 104.

18. Cf. the reference in the Bio-Bibliography, *infra*, p. 141.

19. The reference to this work is found in the bibliography, cf. *infra*, pp. 140-141.

20. These disciples were counted more among the specialists of the New than of the Old Testament. Throughout his lifetime, Gunkel never succeeded in thrusting himself truly into his own discipline, the Old Testament.

21. H. Gunkel, "Die Grundprobleme der israelitischen Literaturgeschichte," *Deutsche Literaturzeitung* 27 (1906), col. 1797-1800 and 1861-1866. Reprinted in *Reden und Aufsätze*, Göttingen, 1913, p. 32.

22. W. Klatt, *op. cit.*, p. 234.

23. E. Meier, *Geschichte der poetischen National-Literatur der Hebräer*, Leipzig, 1856, mentioned by W. Klatt, *op. cit.*, p. 112.

24. Cf. J. M. Schmidt, "Karl Friedrich Stäudlin--Ein Wegbereiter der formgeschichtlichen Erforschung des Alten Testaments," *EvTh* 27 (1967), pp. 200-218.

25. H. J. Kraus, *Geschichte der historisch-kritischen Erforschung des Alten Testaments von der Reformation bis zur Gegenwart*, Neukirchen, 1956, p. 309.

26. Cf. note 15, p. 137.

27. We refer the reader to the article on method, "Ziele und Methoden der alttestamentlichen Exegese," reprinted, under a slightly different title, in *Reden und Aufsätze*, Göttingen, 1913, pp. 11-29.

28. E. Güttgemanns, *Offene Fragen zur Formgeschichte des Evangeliums. Eine methodologische Skizze der Grundlagenproblematik der Form- und Redaktionsgeschichte*, München, 1970, pp. 158-159. [Eng. tr., *Candid Questions Concerning Gospel Form Criticism; a methodological sketch of fundamental problematics of form and redaction criticism*, Pittsburgh, 1979.]

29. W. Klatt, *op. cit.*, p. 77.

30. H. Gunkel, "Ziele und Methoden der Erklärung des Alten Testaments," reprinted in *Reden und Aufsätze*, Göttingen, 1913, p. 13.

BIO-BIBLIOGRAPHY OF HERMANN GUNKEL
(May 23, 1862 - March 11, 1932)

1862: born at Springe (Hannover).

1881: studied at Göttingen from 1881-1885. Intellectual formation: the total life of the spirit, in literature and in religion, must be understood historically.

Became part of a group of young theologians of Northern Germany, of whom Albert Eichhorn was the leader, who wished to detach themselves from Ritschl (H. Gressmann, *A Eichhorn und die religionsgeschichtliche Schule*, Göttingen, 1914, p. 5). Birth of the *Religionsgeschichtliche Schule* (Gunkel used this term for the first time in 1889, it seems, in an article appearing in *ThLZ* 20, 1889, col. 369).

From 1882-1883, at Giessen, where he came under the influence of A. Harnack; from 1885-1888 various sojourns at Lüneburg, Göttingen and Leipzig.

1888: *Die Wirkungen des heiligen Geistes nach der popularen Anschauung der apostolischen Zeit und nach der Lehre des Apostels Paulus*, Göttingen. A thesis which permitted him to become *Privat-Dozent* of New Testament at Göttingen.

1889: *Privat-Dozent* of Old Testament at Halle.

1895: *Schöpfung und Chaos in Urzeit und Endzeit. Eine religionsgeschichtliche Untersuchung über Gen. 1 und Ap. Joh. 12. Mit Beiträgen von H. Zimmern*, Göttingen. The work is dedicated to A. Eichhorn. Gunkel sent an author's copy of it to Wellhausen. The latter judged the work severely: cf. J. Wellhausen, "Zur apokalyptischen Literatur," in *Skizzen und Vorarbeiten VI*, Berlin, 1899, pp. 215-249.

From the period at Halle, we may remember:

1) some scholarly works which apply the *religionsgeschichtlich* method: *Zum religionsgeschichtlichen Verständnis des Neuen Testaments*, Göttingen, 1903 (the first work in the collection "Forschungen zur Religion und Literatur des Alten und Neuen Testaments" set up by Gunkel and his friend Gressmann); the co-management of the first edition of *Die Religion in Geschichte und Gegenwart* (= *RGG*) ("The scientific method of *Religionsge-*

schichte shall, as a methodical principal, govern the entire work in the Dictionary," declared a circular in 1906 signed by F. M. Schiele and H. Gunkel);

2) some methodological articles: "Ziele und Methoden der alttestamentlichen Exegese" (1904), reprinted in *Reden und Aufsätze*, Göttingen, 1913, pp. 11-29, under the title "Ziele und Methoden der Erklärung des Alten Testamentes"; "Das Alte Testament im Lichte der modernen Forschung," in *Beiträge zur Weiterentwicklung der christlichen Religion,* Göttingen, 1905, pp. 40-76.

3) some conferences and some popular works; for example, the *Ausgewählte Psalmen*, Göttingen, 1904. Less radical than certain liberals, he refused to trace everything back to Jesus (differing from A. Harnack). Against the Pan-Babylonism of Friedrich Delitzsch, he defended the particularity of the religion of Israel and of the Christian religion: "We have understood from the very beginning under 'Religionsgeschichte' not the history of religions, but the *history of religion*" (Foreword to *Reden und Aufsätze*, Göttingen, 1913, p. v).

1894: Professor-extraordinary at Berlin.

1901: *Genesis übersetzt und erklärt*, Göttinger Handkommentar zum Alten Testament, I, 1, Göttingen. The third edition is dated 1910. Read the introduction and, in the introduction, section 3 ("Kunstform der Sagen der Genesis"). Note the difference between the first and the third edition: in the first edition, myth is the primitive literary form; in the third, it is the tale.

1906: *Die israelitsche Literatur*, in *Die orientalischen Literaturen, Kultur der Gegenwart*, I, 7, Stuttgart, pp. 51ff. Reprint in a fascicle, Darmstadt, 1963. The first history of Israelite literature.

1907: Professor-ordinary at Giessen.

The principle works of this period are devoted to the prophets: the *Einleitung* to the prophets in *Schriften des Alten Testaments* (*SAT*), II, 2, Göttingen, 1915; and *Die Propheten*, Göttingen, 1917.

It was during this period that *Reden und Aufsätze* appeared, Göttingen, 1913.

1920: Professor-ordinary at Halle.

1926: *Die Psalmen übersetzt und erklärt*, Göttinger Handkommentar zum Alten Testament, II, 2, Göttingen.

1927: *Einleitung in die Psalmen*, I. Hälfte, Göttingen.

The work of introduction to the Psalms remains unfinished. It was completed by the disciple of Gunkel, J. Begrich, under the title: *Einleitung in die Psalmen. Die Gattungen der religiösen Lyrik Israels* of Hermann Gunkel, brought to completion by Joachim Begrich, Göttinger Handkommentar zum Alten Testament, Ergänzungsband zur II. Abteilung, Göttingen, 1933.

This last period is devoted to the Psalms. In fact, Gunkel was interested in the Psalter throughout his life, as earlier articles and the popular work *Ausgewählte Psalmen*, Göttingen, 1904, testify.

Gunkel shared with L. Zscharnack the scholarly responsibility for the second edition of the *RGG*. He wrote a number of articles, of which one of the most important is: "Literaturgeschichte, biblische, 2," in *RGG*², Tübingen, 1929, III, col. 1677-1680.

1932: death of H. Gunkel.

BIBLIOGRAPHY OF WORKS DEVOTED TO THE WORK OF GUNKEL

W. Baumgartner, "Hermann Gunkel," *Neue Zürcher Zeitung*, 1932, nos. 489/499, reprinted in *Zum Alten Testament und siener Umwelt, Ausgewählte Aufsätze*, Leiden, 1959, pp. 371-378.

K. Galling, "Hermann Gunkel," *Zeitschrift für Mission und Religionswissenschaft*, 1932, pp. 257-274. (This work is still inaccessible to us.)

P. Humbert, "Hermann Gunkel, un maître des études hébraïques, 1862-1932," *RThPh*, n.s., 20, 1932, pp. 5-19.

H. Schmidt, "In memoriam Hermann Gunkel," *Theologische Blätter* II, 1932, pp. 97-103. (This work is still inaccessible to us.)

L. Hennequin, art. "Gunkel, Hermann, " *DBS*, III, Paris, 1938, col. 1374.

H. J. Kraus, *Geschichte der historisch-kritischen Erforschung des Alten Testaments,* Neukirchen, 1956, pp. 309-334.

W. Baumgartner, "Zum 100. Geburtstag von Hermann Gunkel," in *Congress Volume, Bonn, 1962*, Leiden, 1963, pp. 1-18.

K. v. Rabenau, "Hermann Gunkel," in *Tendenzen der Theologie im 20. Jahrhundert Eine Geschichte in Porträts*, ed. by H. J. Schutz, Stuttgart, Olten, 1966, pp. 80-87. (This work is still inaccessible to us.)

W. Klatt, *Hermann Gunkel. Zu seiner Theologie der Religionsgeschichte und zur Entstehung der formgeschichtlichen Methode*, Göttingen, 1969.

E. Güttgemanns, *Offene Fragen zur Formgeschichte des Evangeliums. Eine methodologische Skizze der Grundlagenproblematik der Form- und Redaktionsgeschichte,* München, 1970, pp. 154-166.

EXHAUSTIVE BIBLIOGRAPHY OF THE WORKS OF HERMANN GUNKEL

One will find this bibliography for the period which extends up to 1922 in the Essays offered to Gunkel on the occasion of his sixtieth anniversary (the economic difficulties of the period delayed the appearance of the double volume): *Eucharisterion. Studien zur Religion und Literatur des Alten und Neuen Testaments*, II, Göttingen, 1923, pp. 214-225 (bibliography assembled by J. Hempel).

For subsequent bibliography and for complementary works, cf. W. Klatt, *op. cit.*, pp. 272-274.

THE INTERPRETATION OF GENESIS 22:1-19 BY HERMANN GUNKEL

by Grégoire Rouiller

H. Gunkel devoted scarcely seven pages to the narrative of Genesis 22. But they are of such a compactness as to furnish an excellent illustration of his method of reading. He published his large commentary on Genesis in 1901, that is to say between the publication of *Schöpfung und Chaos* (1895) and his studies on the Psalms (1926/1927). This is to say that, if we follow the ascent of his general evolution, we find ourselves in the presence of a commentary more attentive to the history of religion than to that of literary forms, more "*religionsgeschichtlich*" than "*gattungsgeschichtlich*". This edition of 1901 will see some serious improvements in the third edition of 1910. From that date the numerous reprintings leave it practically unchanged. (In these notes, we follow the pagination of the sixth edition of 1964.)

Gunkel proceeds in a transparent fashion. On the basis of a very temperate documentary criticism (admitting the preponderant part of E in verses 1-14 and recognizing that verses 15-18 are added), he first follows the text step by step with rigor and sensitiveness. (1) Then, taking leave from that which the reading has revealed to him, he attempts to trace the genealogy of it: from the Elohist *Saga* to a Phoenician *Saga*. (2) Let us underline some points of these two stages.

1. Hardly devoting any attention to the final redaction as such, Gunkel is very sensitive to the beauty of the Elohist text. Several times he underlines this: in verse 3 "the emotion of the narrator is not perceptible in the words, but

the hearers discover it in the sound of his voice" (p. 237); on verses 7-8: "it is a magisterial page of psychological painting" (p. 237); on verses 9-10, he underlines how well the father-son dialogue adequately expresses the tension of this journey toward the mountain of sacrifice.

He is conscious of the high degree of spiritualization attained by the Elohist redactor. He notes this particularly in commenting on verse 12: "The consummation of sacrifice is not necessary; for it is not the act itself that God wishes, but the resolute intention to grant such an act: that is a highly spiritual idea" (p. 238).

His reading confirms, by a series of remarks on detail, the documentary division which prevailed before him: the name Elohim, the recoil from too concrete anthropomorphisms, the orientation toward a greater psychological and theological finesse, the stylistic stamp of the introductions, all of which, according to him, confirm the dependence of verses 1-12 on the Elohist stratum.

But, already in the first part, Gunkel is very attentive to the traces left in the Elohist story by earlier ideas. From encountering the term Moriah (vs. 2), he discovers "a late modification of a text of Jerusalemite origin" (p. 237). But it is especially verse 14 which claims his attention. There a careful examination permits him to affirm that the primitive *Saga* which still shows through rests on a place name. That this appellation has been modified, indicates a displacement of tradition. The responsibility for this displacement could rest with J.

The rite of sacrificing the ram is likewise considered as an ancient, pre-Elohist, element. A comparison with the Iliad, he thinks, is clarifying.

His analysis of verses 15-18 reveals the aim of his interpretation. One recognizes in it, at the same time, both his perspicacity and his tendency to devalue final redactions. Everything, he affirms, reveals the secondary character of these verses: the affirmation of a new recompense accorded to Abraham (as if the preservation of a beloved son were not sufficient!); the stylistic redundancies; the anthropological character of the elements enumerated.

2. Gunkel's interpretation is very attentive to the intricacies of the story. Is it sufficiently attentive to the joining of the parts? In any case, so his interpretation assures us in one place, Gunkel is able to move on to the chief stage of his research. He wishes to go beyond the plane of analogies in order to arrive at a plausible genealogical explanation.

We divine that for him the redactor who has modified certain verses (introducing the term Moriah, for example) and added verses 15-18, has hardly established a new and significant stage in the tradition. Also, when he speaks of the "present narrative", it is already a question of the Elohist narrative disencumbered of all late additions. The Elohist story itself should be interpreted in an exclusively moral fashion. "The author wishes to present in Abraham a religious ideal: his narrative offers 'a character portrait', the temptation of the righteous" (p. 240). Further, he even introduces a characteristic restriction: "The narrative, in its present state, is 'only a character painting'" (p. 240). It is also this highly moral character of the Elohist narrative underlined by comparing it with a more unpolished story, that of Judges 11, which allows Gunkel to affirm that Genesis 22 is relatively recent.

Then Gunkel asks: beyond this Elohist exaltation of the faith of Abraham and of the mercy of God, did the primitive *Saga* (written or not; on this point the commentary is very cautious) not have a concrete meaning in relation to a *sacred place*? Here the search for the name of the sanctuary takes on its full meaning. Gunkel underlines the play on words, the assonances, the allusions:

יראה אל vs. 8

ירא איל vs. 13; ירא אל vs. 12

He was led with strong probability to two possible names:

יריאל; ירואל

which are of known formation (cf. Gen. 32:31, 32) and which in reality coincide, the first as the name of a family (I Chron. 7:2), the second as the designation of a desert in Judah (II Chron. 20:16). That is why Gunkel concludes in a categorical manner: "Genesis 22 is 'die Kultussage von J^{e}ru'el'" (p. 241).

But moreover, a *rite* is mentioned. The story which contains it must be an etiological myth which explains a rite which is lost (as in Judges 11). A careful examination allows us to infer that the sacrifice of infants was not rare among the peoples surrounding Israel, that it was sporadically practiced in Israel and that the prophetic polemic condemning such practices is raised against that which was at first widely accepted.

These ideas allowed him a new preciseness: Genesis 22 was in the beginning "die Sage von Kinderopfer zu J^{e}ru'el" (p. 247). The substitution of a ram for the infant--an etiological trait justifying a later practice--does not conceal the primitive practice. At the beginning, then, we uncover a custom (heroic?), that of the immolation of infants.

With extra-biblical documents, Gunkel believed that he could go one step further. We find a similar *Saga* in Phoenicia where El has established an analogous cult immolating a son by his father Ouranos. Gunkel adds, in the third edition of his commentary, that we perhaps have there the *proto-*

type of our *Saga*. This discloses his concern to survey the phases of a complete genealogy.

SOME REFLECTIONS

1. This commentary on Genesis 22 illustrates both the method of exegetical approach used by Gunkel (well summarized in the articles collected in 1913 under the title *Reden und Aufsätze*), and his conception of biblical theology which is intertwined with a reading of history.

2. The fashion in which he studies the inconsistencies of the text and his recourse to extra-biblical parallel customs, clearly demonstrates at what point Gunkel separated himself from the school of J. Wellhausen. He began his true work where the others believed it to be terminated.

3. We feel, meanwhile, in him a painful conflict between an astonishingly acute aesthetic perception and a desire to strip off the layers of the text so as to lead him to the native home of the tradition. Obeying the first, he exalts the perfection and the feeling of the Elohist story. But when he surrenders to the imperatives of the second, the Elohist story loses its worth, it is "nur ein Charaktergemälde". Sometimes the conflict between the two aims is patent. Thus, at verse 2, the name of Isaac is necessary to the literary creation of the child to be sacrificed. On the other hand, one who, following the etiological traces of the story, is in quest of the original can achieve such exactness. The commentary on verse 2 oscillates between these two necessities.

4. The limitations of this commentary arise precisely, in our view, from this too exclusively "archaeological" and diachronic aim. More than in the present text of Genesis 22, there is a divorce between the residue of aeteological inter-

pretation still perceptible and the aims of the written redaction (whether Elohist, or whether finally including verses 15-18). Gunkel can scarcely take account, on a synchronic plane, of all the elements of the text, without leaving a residue; he hardly understands the liturgical character of the whole and he does not grasp the significance of the considerable echo encountered by such an episode in the consciousness and the practice of the Jewish people as well as the writers of the New Testament. Thus it is not without some disdain that he concludes his commentary on Genesis 22 by this sentence: "An earlier theology saw in the sacrifice of Isaac a prefiguring of the sacrificial death of Jesus." It is true that this sentence was removed from the third edition on.

PART THREE

Dialogue with Human Sciences

Literary Criticism

GÉRALD ANTOINE

A Glance at Critical Methodology

The Sacrifice of Isaac.
Exposition of Genesis 22:1-19

The Three Parables of Mercy.
Exposition of Luke 15:11-32

Psychoanalysis

LOUIS BEIRNAERT

The Parable of the Prodigal Son
(Luke 15:11-32) Read by an Analyst

Sociology of Literature

JACQUES LEENHARDT

Methodological Preliminaries and an Interpretation
of a Sermon of Massilon on Luke 15:11-32

Hermeneutics

PHILIBERT SECRETAN

Hermeneutics and Truth

PAUL RICOEUR

The Task of Hermeneutics

The Hermeneutical Function of Distanciation

Philosophical Hermeneutics
and Biblical Hermeneutics

Literary Criticism

A GLANCE AT CRITICAL METHODOLOGY

by Gérald Antoine

You have desired, in the guise of a preamble to a double interpretation of biblical texts, a statement on the present tendencies of criticism and the paths which it could take tomorrow.

It so happens that the editor of *Français Moderne* has asked me, on his part, for an article on what is currently called "the new criticism". Allow me, then, to take it up again here, in presenting some reflections proper to a more direct response to your inquiry.

After all, if I trust what M. Bovon and Canon Rouiller have told me, it is not deplorable that I submit a discourse from which all concern for the application of the exegesis of the sacred texts is excluded. You will be thus more at ease in judging, yes or no, whether the most recent methods of the criticism of literary texts can be of some service to you and what problems the existence of these methods pose for you.

The number of books, small treatises and articles written on the New Criticism is impressive, even disquieting, and one feels a little uneasiness in enlarging the volume of these critical works on the work of criticism. My objective is above all to free the subject from a certain "contemporary rubbish", to quote Peguy, indeed passionately, and to attempt to recover its true meaning.

Whoever wishes to deal with this proposes to himself right from the start two sorts of criteria: the first, from a distance, the most elementary and the most external, simply makes an appeal to chronology. "Linguistic" research in its broad meaning evolves very quickly--in particular that which is devoted to the methods of analysis of literary texts. As Serge Doubrovsky once said, I believe, it is necessary for us to distinguish between an old and a new New Criticism. The second perspective will assuredly be that of doctrinal orientations, from whose bias we very naturally first approach the great problems which they raise, before delineating a classification of methods. By way of conclusion, why not play on the "futurible" and not pose the question: what new criticism should we foresee for tomorrow?

I. CHRONOLOGICAL BENCH MARKS

1. It is certainly difficult to assign a beginning to the premises of the New Criticism. But it appears more and more legitimate to consider as its great ancestor Gaston Bachelard and his bouquet of cosmogonic thematics, the principal five blossomings of which appeared at intervals from 1937 to 1948.

2. Around the same time Georges Poulet, who remains very much alive and continues to produce, already invented the image which brought forth from him numerous relevant studies, of an expansive and *a priori* thematic, or if one prefers, voluntarist thematic, bound as it is to the two universal categories of space and time.

3. From about 1955 to 1967, all the major works on literary criticism could be grouped, in spite of their extreme diversity of inclination, under the banner of "the old new criticism": new in that it broke with literary history, with the criticism of taste, with a certain literary stylistics of the former period devoted invariably to studying

"the language and the style of..."; but old in that it did not make up its mind to detach the work from one or several elements of its external conditioning--from the social order, or the psychological (more and more frequently: psychoanalytic), or the ideological.

4. From about 1967, in concurrence with some works which continued to reflect the preceding tradition, two fresh or resurgent currents appeared: on the one hand, that for which the name "New Criticism" is too exclusively reserved and which forms a group of brilliant essays utilizing the work studied as a springboard toward an effort at recreation or invention at a second remove; on the other hand, that where sharp investigations of a neostylistic fashion converge, but which reject the term "stylistic" and prefer to be known as an autonomous discipline baptized, in a fashion moreover very ambiguous, "poetic". With these we are truly engaged with the methods of a "new New Criticism", in the more precise meaning of the term.

For the use of those among you who are the least in contact with this sector of linguistic research, here are some studies which, in my judgment, are to be placed on the top shelf.[1]

It is not a case of setting up a complete prize list, but of pointing to a limited number of works whose thought is sometimes, even often, put to debate if not to trial, but of which, nevertheless, neither the importance nor the quality are denied by any of those who know them. Whoever says "method" signifies by virtue of etymology "to put on the way". Regard these, then, very simply, as some trainers among whom each one can keep his colleagues on the preferred way.

1. *Books and Articles on Doctrine*

I go no further back than 1964, for the flowers fade and the thorns grow very quickly in the garden of criticism.

J. Mourot, "Stylistique des intentions et stylistique des effets," in *Cahiers de l'Association internationale des études françaises*, 1964.
R. Picard, *Nouvelle critique ou nouvelle imposture*, Pauvert, 1965.
R. Barthes, *Critique et vérité*, Seuil, 1966.
G. Poulet, 4 conferences on the "new criticism", supplement of No. 34 of *Studi Francesi*, 1968.
G. Poulet, editor, *Les chemins actuels de la critique, Entretiens de Cerisy*, Plon, 1967.
S. Doubrovsky, *Pourquoi la nouvelle critique*, Mercure, 1966.
J. Starobinski, *La Relation critique*, Gallimard, 1970.
J. Starobinski, "Considérations sur l'état présent de la critique littéraire," *Diogène*, No. 74, April-June, 1971.
A. Henry, "La stylistique littéraire, Essai de redéfinition," *Français Moderne*, January, 1972.
P. Guiraud and P. Kuentz, *La Stylistique. Lectures,* Klincksieck, 1970.
H. Meschonnic, *Pour la Poétique* I, Gallimard, 1970; II and III, Gallimard, 1973.

2. *Books and Articles on Method and Experimentation Together*

a) *The Bachelard series of five, from 1937 to 1948:*

La Psychanalyse du Feu, Gallimard, 1937.
L'Eau et les Rêves, Corti, 1940.
L'Air et les Songes, Corti, 1942.
La Terre et les Rêveries du Repos, Corti, 1948.
La Terre et les Rêveries de la Volonté, Corti, 1948.

b) *A series of theses:*

L. Goldman, *The Hidden God; A Study of Tragic Vision in the* Pensées *of Pascal and the Tragedies of Racine*, London, 1964.
M. Riffaterre, *Le style des Pléiades de Gobineau*, Droz-Minard, 1957.
J. Starobinski, *J.-J. Rousseau, La Transparence et l'obstacle*, Plon, 1957.
J. Mourot, *Chateaubriand. Rythme et sonorité dans les Mémoires d'Outre-Tombe*, Colin, 1960.
J.-P. Richard, *L'Univers imaginaire de Mallarmé*, Seuil, 1962.
Ch. Mauron, *Des Métaphysiques obsédantes au mythe personnel*, Corti, 1963 (Corneille, Molière, Baudelaire, Nerval, Mallarmé, Valéry).
M. Arrivé, *Les Langages de Jarry*, Klincksieck, 1972.

c) *Some "classics":*

G. Poulet, *Etudes sur le temps humain,* Plon, 1950.
R. Barthes, *Le degré zéro de l'écriture,* Seuil, 1953.
M. Blanchot, *L'Espace littéraire,* Gallimard, 1955.
R. Jakobson, *Essais de linguistique générale,* IVe Partie: Poétique. Trans. by N. Ruwet, Minuit, 1963.

II. PROBLEMATICS OF CURRENT CRITICISM

A good means of knowing where one is in the increase of doctrinal orientations is without doubt to group by couples a certain number of questions and tendencies. Here are four which seem major to us:

1) critical method (or stance) and objectivity;
2) criticism, the knowledge of literature or the literature on literature, with the variant: criticism of the work in itself, which from that time is no longer a "work" but an "object", or criticism of the work regarded as inseparable from the one who has made it or the one (or those) who receive it;
3) thematic criticism or stylistic criticism;
4) stylistic criticism or poetic criticism.

1. *Criticism and Objectivity*

This is probably the Gordian knot of the matter, even if it is seldom mentioned.

One fact, however, cannot be neglected: numerous universities compete in the ranks of criticism. They classify this, only in the sense of professional (or professorial!) classification, among the human sciences. And this single word *science* is seen by them as carrying the obligation of objectivity. Or it places this concern for objectivity in the first rank and cuts off from the critical process everything which could draw the reproach of lacking it. In this hypothesis, it is the integrity of the "object" which is threatened.

In this regard, it is very curious to compare three passages of the study, in other respects so rigorously conducted, of J. Starobinski (*Considerations on the Present State of Literary Criticism*):[2]

Page 62: "All objectivity presupposes an aim."

Page 80: "Stylistic criticism, on the other hand, try though it may to get to grips with language, is nonetheless only neutral attention with no bias towards any particular theory of history or of man...."

Pages 87-88: "It is obvious...that we study only what interests us, things the meaning and value of which have aroused our attention."

Would we not have a fine time understanding and choosing between a "neutral attention" and an "interested attention"?

Add to that, at the end of a humorous, but nonetheless serious, confrontation, a rejoinder of Zenobia in *Les bâtisseurs d'Empire* of Boris Vian:

"If he observes, he is not impartial, he already has a desire, the desire to observe. In that case he observes inattentively. And he is no longer a good observer."

Who will suggest the means of getting out of that? In any case, we repeat, it is not in the power of a person to do away with the heavy constraint of a double subjectivity; and to put it beyond a game as is done by certain ones at present, is to get relief too cheaply. P. Claudel once[3] analyzed the matter in a most clear manner: "...Between each human being and ourselves there are always two partitions to breach, his and then ours. We reach inmost reality only dubiously, by way of sign, conjecture and inference." That at least one of the two beings in the action should be a writer does not eliminate the difficulty, but increases it by concentrating on the datum of the work, a partition oh how resistant!

2. *Critical Science of Literature or "Literature on Literature"?*

This is always only another way of formulating the preceding problem, whose advantage, nevertheless, is twofold: on the one hand its transparency, on the other its contemporaneity.

a) *Critical science of literature*

This project has never ceased to haunt certain people. Cf. Doubrovsky, in the conversations at Cerisy:[4]

"In the vicinity of the humanities, the critic dreams, in his tower, of becoming a scholar; and since all science, according to Bachelard's formula, 'designates itself as a principle of harmony without supports and without reporter', there is necessary to this new criticism *its object* (here, language) *less consciousness* (that of the writer or the reader). The literary object, without origin or destination, cut off from all return to reality, functions then as a pure linguistic object freed from the ballast of all contingency and dragged out of the mire of all existence."

Starobinski expresses himself in very similar but, happily, complementary terms (*loc. cit.*, pp. 83-84):

"'Scientific' analysis must also intervene, but at the right moment, i.e. after the text has been allowed to develop all its powers, produce all its effect. To study a text cut off from its effects would in itself be a truncated study. The objective structure of the work is the finished form in which an unfinishable relationship[5] is established; the tension which gives rise to this form in its own dimension, and its own time, is a historical vector whose presence should never be neglected by the critic."

A little further on, he does not hesitate to divulge the first trap, for which he should be thanked; for it is not so often, in this domain more and more encumbered by abstruse meditations, that we see someone go back to the clarity of the sources:

"It is a reproach which all good philosophy will address to 'scientific' criticism: this science, so zealous to relativize literature in the sphere of its causal references, forgets to bring itself into question and to examine itself on the meaning of its design to be a science."

One would not know how to say it better. It is in any case the question Jakobson and Lévi-Strauss should have posed to themselves before risking their 'scientific' reputation in the famous double analysis of Baudelaire's sonnet "The Cats" reduced to its objective substance--an attempt which sought to be structuralist in the strictest obedience.

As B. de Schloezer put it, "this reduction...clearly destroyed the poem: since it systematically eliminated its meaning, the work was no longer more than a laughingstock of 'sonorous inanity'."[6] The result was foreseeable: never was a more beautiful "fiasco" seen on the soil of experiment in criticism.

b) *Criticism as "literature on literature"*

The formula is from G. Poulet (*loc. cit.*, p. 32). The only reproach one may address to him is the play on words--which belongs not only to him but to the whole family of the New Criticism: G. Poulet himself, then R. Barthes, J.-P. Richard, etc.

Truly it is not necessary--it is even dangerous for the critic--to think that he must make an art on the art. Rigor, clarity and above all fidelity to the work studied run the risk of suffering too much from this; for the moment the critic changes himself into an author, he opens himself to the unceasing temptation, whether conscious of it or not, to prefer the inclination of his creative fertility to that of holding himself to listen with humble attentiveness to the work produced by others.

I have already had occasion, on this subject, to denounce the ambiguity, so revealing, contained on the last page of the little book of R. Barthes (*Critique et Vérité*, Paris, 1966, p. 79):

"To pass from reading to criticism is to change the desire; it is no longer to care for the work, but for his own language. But by the same token, it is to dismiss the work in the desire for writing from which it had sprung."

Delightful game of mirrors, but how deceiving to the eye! For "his own language" is not related to the work but to the critic, and to forget the work in the desire for writing which animates or consumes the commentator is no longer criticism: it is in reality literature in the common meaning of the term. That is why there will be little question here of this form of exercise: however engaging it may be, it lies outside our subject.

3. *Thematic or Stylistic?*

What remains, then, of ways to borrow from a criticism which admittedly is neither science nor literature?

Let us be reassured: the possibilities of itineraries across this median are not lacking. They seem, however, to group themselves in large measure around two main axes: "*thematic*" on the one hand, "*stylistic*" evolving toward the "*poetic*" on the other. At any rate, it is thus that the field of criticism is usually divided, while perhaps assigning one or several false meanings to the detriment of the thematic.

It is on this point that I should like to pause for an instant, before proposing, in concluding with current tendencies in criticism, an acceptable means of classifying them.

a) I recall the amazement--errors happily excepted--which G. Poulet displayed at Cerisy, when, truly without wishing to seduce nor annex anyone, I regarded his own efforts, as well as those of many of his friends, entered with full right into the scheme of "stylistic" studies as I conceived them.

In fact, if one could define stylistic criticism as a systematic analysis of the means of expression which make up a work of art in producing its style, it is still necessary to ask what orientation this analysis is going to take.

Does it go from the signifiers to what is signified, that is to say, from the means of the expression and the orchestration of the themes, or does it start, conversely, from the things signified, from the themes and the network of ideas and feelings which they command, in order to go to the signifiers, that is to say, the universe of forms where the imaginary universe of the artist is incarnated?

In both cases there happens to be implicated, but according to a different order, a stylistics and a thematics, to use the vocabulary of certain ones. But it appears to me more clear and exact, in the one, to speak of a formal stylistic (taking as a basis the study of signifiers), and in the other a thematic stylistic (taking as a basis the themes or the things signified).

Is a concrete application desired from this? Happily, an opportunity is offered to us in two analyses of the *Maximes* of F. de La Rochefoucauld, one of R. Barthes in his preface to the edition of the French Book Club (Paris, 1961), the other by J. Starobinski in the *Nouvelle Revue Française* of July-August, 1966. R. Barthes begins with the entirety of forms seen as structure and goes toward the meaning of the message; J. Starobinski starts from the *cosa mentale* (according to the expression dear to Leonardo de Vinci), that is to say, from the meanings and values in a perspective at the same time psychological, psychoanalytic and sociological, then goes toward the formal structures.

The first makes a stylistics of forms, in a structuralist direction, while the second experiments with the ways of a stylictic of themes, in a psycho-sociological direction.

b) Since on the whole we have evoked Poulet and Starobinski, let us elucidate one point more: it so happens that the first has spoken of the other (*loc. cit.*, pp. 83-84) by refusing to define his criticism "as a thematic criticism". Why? Because the privileged analysis of the space-time (or time-space) dimensions of knowledge expressed by the work effects that "subjectivity is here filtered out, stripped of its emotional determinations, dissociated from the aesthetic form in which it appears". Perhaps there is some contempt here for the ambition of G. Poulet's critical effort; but surely there is a misinterpretation with respect to thematic analysis which consists precisely in separating the themes, or certain chosen themes, at first, in order afterwards better to discern the manner in which they are expressed. The truth is--but curiously Starobinski has not whispered a word of it--that a thematic study can be, or is content to be, in the extreme and not without peril, a profound investigation of the "imaginary universe" little concerned to get down to details by setting it in a formal work, or on the contrary it hastens to go towards the forms to assure itself against extrapolations and phantasms.

On the whole, just as we have distinguished between a

stylistics of forms and a stylistics of themes, so, and by way of symmetry, it will be allowable to the one who desires to be a thematician to distinguish between a psychological thematics with a literary tendency and a formal thematic--or a stylistics with a more grammarian tendency. But that is, after all, to say the same thing as was said a moment ago, while simply inverting the perspective.

4. *Stylistic or Poetic Criticism*

"Poetics" is one of the latest born of criticism, descended from some Russian formalists and from some theories of linguistic structuralists or functionalists: in particular those of Benveniste.[7]

The point of departure for the proceeding is a demand to be "scientific" which none of the stylistic attempts has fulfilled--which sees itself challenged, not without contempt and sometimes vehemence, when, all things considered, the poetic is only a variety of the stylistic armed with a particular rigorousness, at least at the level of language, willingly esoteric when it is not attached to a certain courtship--which can wed it, but in appearance only, to the literary side of the New Criticism.

Historically, the vogue of poetic criticism stands in the line of revolt of the sons against the fathers--a revolt situated more on the level of signs, of "costume", than of essence.

In principle, poetics is occupied with discarding the concepts of "language" and of "literature", leaving these to semiotics (semiology), the science of signs, in order better to isolate and to particularize those of "discourse" and of "writing" relevant to semantics, the science of expression. This explains definitions such as this: "Writing produces a system of significance, not a system of signs. From whence, a particular 'semantics', which is poetics" (H. Meschonnic, *Pour la poétique*, t. II, p. 180).

Again: "The text is composed of formants which are form-meanings." This last expression clearly indicates one of the fundamental preconceptions of poetics: its *antidualism*--but one which does not exclude the recognition of the two sides of the poetic object.

Likewise, the poetician readily insists on unity, the identity of knowing how to write and of knowing how to be or to live. Flaubert (letter to Louise Colet of December 18, 1853) is cited in this regard:

"Continuity creates style."

Also Proust is cited (letter to Antoine Bibesco, p. 177):

"Style is not only an ornament, as certain people believe; it is not even a question of technique; it is as color to painters, a quality of vision, a revelation of the singular universe which each one of us sees and which is not seen by the others."

This produces, under the delineation of "poetician", some axioms for this genre:

"The aim of poetics is the work, in what its language has of uniqueness. It is the work, a syntagmatic *unity of vision* and the work, a unity of rhythmic and prosodiacal diction--plan and creativity, object and subject, form-meaning, form-history" (Meschonnic, *ibid.*, I, 62).

Or once more:

"Poetics is the study (and the study of the conditions of this study, inseparably) of a work as object and subject, *closed as a system*, open to its own inwardness as creativity, and outwardly as reading--the study of an imaginary rhetoric, which gives a form its uniqueness" (*ibid.*, p. 138).

These excellent axioms only repeat, in a form perhaps more precise but surely less accessible, what stylistics has taught for a long time, in resting itself, when opportunity offers, on the testimony, among others, of Flaubert and Proust.[8]

Two ideas, however, appear to be put forward with a particular insistence: the not very clear idea of "form-meaning" and the idea of a work, on the one hand "closed as a system" but, on the other hand, as discourse, given over to its own creativity.

H. Meschonnic likewise calls up a sponsorship, that of Max Jacob and the preface to his *Cornet à dés* whose true importance, moreover, he is not certain is yet wholly perceived.

To have style, declares Max Jacob, a work must satisfy two conditions: first it must be situated, then it must give the sensation of exclusiveness. It is especially this second precept which has held the attention of current criticism and of which it recognizes itself the heir. But it is probably no less indebted to the first. In fact, that which serves to situate a work, according to Max Jacob, is the capacity which it must have to call forth a proper atmosphere, a genre,[9] an index of values, in brief, to possess a style of content even before revealing a style of expression.

That is clear and beyond dispute. Why, starting from here, should paraphrases be launched such as those cited from H. Meschonnic or those from G. Genette:

"That which constitutes language as a system of signs (in a "narrative" idea), is the way in which the content and the expression show themselves and structure themselves in their relation of reciprocal articulation, determining the conjoint appearance of a *form of content* and a *form of expression*" (*Les Chemins actuels*, p. 243).

What is most troublesome is that by the grace of this play on ambiguous formulas, Genette has come to invert the common meaning of *form* and of *theme*--for our poeticians find themselves, in their turn, the prey of a double postulate by which the stylistics were already found to be captive:

"The theme is an opening on the plane of the signifier, proportionate to that which is given to the notion of form on the plane of the signified" (*ibid.*, p. 244).

To us this is a full perversion of meaning, and one can scarcely doubt that the *rimbaldisme* of Genette is here for something. But this is the danger of this label of "Poetics", which is too easily interchangeable, from writer to critic.

Let us, by way of compensation, retain the following as profitable acquisitions:

--a reassuring coherence as to the basis of stylistics, and at the same time as to the forms and themes of poetics;

--the putting into relief of the idea of a style of content without which there is no true style of forms;

--the notion of a work as a "closed system" concealing its own creativity--and that which springs from it which is without doubt the most fruitful: that of a rhetorical or poetical "model", of a "pattern" proceeding from which a work or a specific aspect of a work can be begotten. The risk here is of generalizing and systematizing too much. The truth is that it is necessary to know how to choose its fields of application: *work* or privileged *procedure*: how, decisively, one may ask himself if the distance between one school and the other is not above all a mere difference in language.

III. ATTEMPT AT CLASSIFICATION

Our last reflections suffice to show how delicate any attempt is to classify current methods of criticism: each, (or almost each) exegete, seeks to carve out a kingdom for himself and to give to it the status of an independent state;

but in reality the observer is led to reveal a host of interpenetrations among them.

It is probably this which will permit a subjoining of two attempts at making an inventory which have extant value--one that of Dominique Noguez at the end of the collection of addresses at Cerisy on *Les chemins actuels de la Critique*, the other that of J. Starobinski whose "Considerations on the Present State of Literary Criticism" is organized around the principle of arranging the schools and tendencies in logical order.

a) I do not reconsider the possibility, always open, of a balance sheet resting on simple chronology which, as is natural, makes a sort of law of evolution by opposition or at least by differentiation appear. Hence, the feeling, perfectly founded, that criticism proceeds by fashions, not to say infatuations, followed by disaffections.

b) It is well to forget a division springing from philosophical or ideological "options". To cite some examples:

--Marxist criticism opposed to a criticism that is bourgeois or reputed to be as such;

--Existential criticism to which the personality of J. P. Sartre, at once a philosopher, writer, creator and essayist, has given a particular prominence in France: cf. his *Questions de méthode* and his work of criticism properly speaking, from *Baudelaire* to *L'Idiot de la Famille*.

c) It remains to establish the most desirable classification, but also the most difficult, in pursuing the varieties of disciplines from which criticism solicits cooperation. It is a classification of the sort which has led Starobinski to the following outline:

1) necessity of history
2) sign and causality (precursor in fact of 3 and 4)
3) literary sociology

4) problem of philological analysis

5) study of forms

One may hold himself here, in specifying this, to the course of the rubrics.

Point 1: Starobinski seems to think only of literary history. But how can he not make place at least:
--for the internal history of works: studies of "genesis";
--for the history of language;
--for that of groups and of literary forms.

To illustrate the importance of taking into account the history of language, let us remind ourselves of the title of a chapter of M. Riffaterre: "Effets de style sur fond de langue", taken up under a more precise form by S. Doubrovsky (in *Les Chemins actuels...*, p. 270):

"Such is the insurpassable ambiguity of subjective existence, which is encountered again in its linguistic manifestation, where the individual word is carved out on the basis of a pre-personal language, but where the language only exists uttered by the individual word; a tongue dies, we sometimes seem to forget, with the men who speak it."

Points 2-3-4: It will be permitted to indicate, more explicitly than Starobinski has done, the possible combinations of signs and of causalities, of an order which is at the same time historical, psychological and social. Nothing can overcome the elementary, but fundamental, statement of Sartre in *Situation*, IV, 33: "A work of art is at the same time an individual production and a social event."

It is not amiss either to remind ourselves that psychological analysis leads naturally enough toward a type of *thematic* criticism, and on the other hand that, more and more frequently, psychoanalysis is importuned to furnish its contribution to criticism.

Finally, whatever be the human sciences called in for

reinforcement, one would prefer not to cite a reflection owed to the frank malice of the one whom we have taken as a guide in this labyrinth:

"It is easier for linguists, sociologists and philologists, already wholly formed, to turn towards literature than for literary experts to make themselves linguists, sociologists or philologists" (*loc. cit.*, p. 70).

Unfortunately, almost all of our current critics are literary experts in origin, in formation and in taste, who are more or less hastily coming into contact with one or the other of these three disciplines. This is a setting in which to plead for a vast effort of early interdisciplinary formation, to which I permit myself to urge not only the literary experts, but also the theologians!

Point 5: Just as psychological analysis inclines toward the thematic, so textual study moves toward the stylistic of forms--or let us say toward one or the other of the formal stylistics in fashion--whether it be the stylistic of effects, or transformational, or structural; or again whether it be rebaptized as literary semantics; or finally, let us remember, whether it appears in the rejuvenated term of *poetics*.

So much for the old New Criticism and for the less old--up to their most recent embodiments. The champions of these are, surely, within their rights in saying to me: what do you have better to propose?

It remains, then, to ask ourselves what kind of New Criticism to wish for today.

IV. SOME PROPOSALS FOR A FUTURE NEW CRITICISM

S. Doubrovsky (*loc. cit.*, p. 78) helps me to formulate a first wish: "The difficulty is not: what is true in each one, then what is not true; it is rather: how to combine the truths among them, genuine or inconsistent, of each one?

That is why it is important to establish a classification and an arrangement within the methods. Some have as their objective to situate the works in their historical, social, psychological, or linguistic context. Their aim is to secure the criticism of object-works by all preliminary precautions without which they will be in danger of error--and the more the talent, the greater will be the peril!

Only let us be careful: these preliminaries should have as their end not to explain the work, but only, once more, to determine it by situating it.

The "clearing of the situation"[10] which is at one and the same time historic, social, psychological and verbal, having been accomplished, this is criticism--this is fundamental. And it is here that the difficulty is increased.

It is well to encounter the echo on the part of experienced observers who have not taken the plunge themselves, but have more or less strayed into the profession. One man, fortunately instructed in the history of literature and of scientific ideas, coming one day to listen to some critics,[11] concluded by telling them the essential thing in a most simple manner:

"A work of art is not to be read as an instrument of a notary public; there is a difference of nature about which I have implored and still implore some information."

Hence, the importance of works which give themselves and will give themselves more to the task of fathoming the nature of a work of art, as much as possible through examples, for it seems to me that we should tolerate less and less those books in which a reasoned affectation is poured out, all the more at its ease when it never meets the resistance of the concrete nor the living.

There are at present two very hopeful responses; the very general one of Riffaterre (reproduced by A. Henry in the article mentioned below): "the whole text which engages the attention of the reader by its form is literary, independent or not of its content"; the other of Starobinski, much more precise: "(in a literary work) the word, added to desire, forms a complex body, whose unity lives in its double origin: *appropriation* of a social tool (vocabulary, syntax, rules of fixed forms) by *desire*, then interpretation of the desire by the act of elocution or of writing (*loc. cit.*, p. 92).

This task of definition again makes certain some concerns stemming from the "clearing of the situation", but it places us very directly before our duty which G. Poulet, an exact follower in this of Péguy, has so well named "the internal seizure of the work" (*loc. cit.*, p. 461).

With regard to Péguy, why not start from one of his most striking pages on critical methodology to suggest--*a fortiori* let us say--how the remarks which are made on the subject of literary texts are applicable to the sacred texts?

What, in fact, in the eyes of a secular critic, is a sacred text; how does he regard it?--As a literary text, belonging to a very strongly "marked" genre which is the biblical genre. If he undertakes to explain it, he should first analyze with care the "style of genre", then that of the particular text offered to his investigation in that which, in his turn, he has of specificity.

But will not a nonsecular critic, after all, be more able, if he wishes, to give an exact account of the sacred text which he studies, to conform rigorously to this method? --This is without doubt the true question which fundamentally you wish to ask me. It so happens that the author of *Clio* replies to it--listen well how.[12] The sacred text to which he refers is, it is true, among all texts impressive, since it involves the prayer of Jesus on the Mount of Olives:

"...And we, if we had not been stupified, my child, by years and centuries and generations of catechism (...) more or less ecclesiastical, generally of the university, generally academic, if we should take up the sacred texts *as it is necessary to take all texts, all great texts*,[13] and as we take them up, if we should take up the sacred texts as it is necessary to take up (also) (all) the classic texts, in their fullness, in their breadth, in all their crudity..., if we should not permit to come between them and us the obstruction of habit and the blunting of custom, we would be, my friend, we would be terrified by this text...."

All that follows should be read. What I deduce from it for the moment is that the best new criticism does not speak otherwise, nor with more austere severity.

At this point it is very suitable and gratifying to take up the series of A. Henry whose recent evaluative article, "Literary Stylistics--An Attempt at Redefinition",[14] has the same importance, with regard to the methods of inner analysis of literary works, as that of J. Starobinski in relation to literary criticism taken in its entirety. The present attempt alleges that it knows an approach of its own. Let us be content to note its point of approach: A. Henry insistently demands that there be conducted a "study of organic relationships between thematic development and *forms* (at all levels) of expression, both on the *local* plane and that of the *whole*."

The solidarity which joins this demand to what precedes, as well as what R. Barthes has taught for some time under the title of "intertextual criticism", should be emphasized. This encourages us to move toward this by two series of propositions:

a) There is no theme beyond the forms of its expression; conversely, no longer a form which expresses nothing.

On this subject--how can one not recall L. Spitzer and his method of the intuitive-deductive circle--one is no longer able to be faithful to the proper process of the experimental sciences. Let us lay out a scheme: an honest reading of the texts puts the observer on the trail of one or several themes (intuition). He goes from there to encounter them through the methodical analysis of signifiers (verification). Finally, he arrives at the nature and the reciprocal characterization of the themes and their forms of expression. This criticism of the day before yesterday merits being rediscovered in the criticism of tomorrow.

b) Critical work should be conducted on the scale of works regarded as systems and structures, and at the same time considered in their elements which take their meaning and value only from the function of their unity. There is no possibility of attaining a true stylistic characterization without recourse to this double movement.

And here I should like to call attention to the existence of an old book which has perhaps not received adequate publicity: the thesis of J. Mourot, *Rythme et sonorité dans les Mémoires d'Outre-Tombe* (Colin, 1960). I do not know where "the internal seizure" of the work should at this point be realized, thanks to the methodical observation of convergences between some privileged themes and certain forms of expression which recompose themselves each time the themes recur--such as that of vast space, that of silence, etc.

Is it a question of science, or of observation?--It is a question in truth of an excellent model for this science of observation which should be a well conducted stylistics. It would not henceforth disavow its bonds with linguistics itself, of which J. Vendryes wrote not long ago with a simplicity too much forgotten today, but which should be restored for use tomorrow:

"Linguistics is a science of observation which should be kept in contact with the reality of facts."

The most weighty champions of "Poetics" will, moreover, not contradict this. Let us recognize simply that when they aspire to place in equation the components of "discourse"--though it be literary!--they clearly submit to the influence of science and of mathematical technique, powerful and fascinating at the time when the empire of "modern mathematics" and those who ordained it were born.

At present, it seems to me, it is the turn of the physical sciences, especially the biological, to occupy the forefront of the scene. No doubt the inventors of the future New Criticism will be induced by that, as by the working of the law of alternation mentioned earlier, to reintegrate into their total schemes all the empiricism underlying discourse.[15]

The subject is by no means exhausted, far from it. It is in particular a question of importance that one evades in general, about which one becomes dizzy by the fatality of the subject: criticism being a discourse on the modes of improving discourse, it does not know how to escape the problem of the choice of a language for itself.

I confine myself here to citing S. Doubrovsky (*Pourquoi la nouvelle critique*, p. 253) to sharpen the appetite. The meal properly so called will be left for another time:

"Critical language can be neither ordinary language, nor literary language, nor philosophical language, nor scientific language; irreducible in principle to these various languages. It must, therefore, invent a synthesis of them. Critical language, because of this, is a mongrel language, an odd language, a strange language, which has not only its usefulness, but can and should have its own beauty."

I would add only to these qualifiers, however numerous already, those which are perhaps the hardest but the most useful to understand: the critic being the servant and the interpreter of a work of art, his language should be, in addition to these, modest; and it should be transparent.

NOTES

1. I will restrict myself to writings in the French language.

2. In *Diogenes*, No. 74 (April-June, 1971).

3. In *Présence et Prophétie*, Fribourg, 1942, pp. 239-240.

4. Collected under the title, *Les Chemins actuels de la critique*, Paris, 1967, p. 271.

5. Listen very clearly: the relationship of the work to the reader which, if it is truly great, never ceases to renew itself.

6. B. de Schloezer, "L'oeuvre, l'auteur et l'homme," in *Les chemins actuels de la critique*, Paris, 1967, p. 165.

7. Convenient references: H. Meschonnic, *Pour la Poétique*, I, II and III, Paris, 1970-1973. See in particular, in Volume II, the chapter, "Sémiotique et poétique, partant de Benveniste," pp. 173-187. And T. Todorov, *The Poetics of Prose*, Ithaca, N.Y., 1977.

8. We know, from the publication of *Contre Sainte-Beuve*, how far Proust felt himself alienated from the critical method of the illustrious guest of Lausanne. And yet...let us reread the dedication of the first edition of his *Port-Royal*, engraved on an imposing table a couple of steps from here:

> "To my hearers of Lausanne.
> Thought and formed under their eyes,
> this book belongs to them."

Is not this very audacious alliance, "thought and formed", a prelude to "forms-meaning", and in any case, to the antidualism of our current critics?--I take this opportunity to point out also a very interesting question posed to me by M. Secretan: does not the word "form" have the same meaning when I speak of the "stylistic of forms" as it does when the poeticians discuss "forms-meaning"?--Are they not very near to using it as Kant did in his *Esthetique transcendantale*?

9. Some observations of this sort would, nevertheless, have some very classic guarantees. Do we not read from the pen, I believe, of Père Rapin, this remarkable sentence: "The style is the genre"?

10. The expression is from Paul Valéry, in *Variété*, "Poésie et Pensée abstraite" (*OEuvres*, Vol. I, p. 1316).

11. J. Roger, in *Les chemins actuels de la critique*, p. 472.

12. *Deuxième Elégie* XXX, p. 381ff. (*Clio*).

13. The italics is mine.

14. In the *Français Moderne* of January, 1972.

15. You will indeed wish to believe me if I affirm that at the moment I said this, I did not have in mind certain pages of the paper of Péguy (he again!) devoted to *Zangwill*, where he sought to show how the famous historical criticism so cherished at the beginning of this century was born of a seduction exercised over the "literati" by the progress of the *science* then in great vogue--history: "It is essentially, and eminently, the modern historical method, acquired by the exportation, by direct transfer, as a whole, of modern scientific methods into the domain of history" (*OEuvres en prose*, Vol. I, p. 696). But to come across that statement, which to us is truly correct, proves that the newest criticism ever made which reopens routes formerly traced goes a little further (*ibid.*, p. 720): "...it is exactly through the progress of the natural sciences that we are today led back to conceptions more human, and, as the word says it, more natural." These lines were written in October 1904!

THE SACRIFICE OF ISAAC
Exposition of Genesis 22:1-19

by Gérald Antoine

How above all not to "explain" myself, first on the difficulty of a critical exercise applied to a translation (*a*), then on the method adopted for commenting on it (*b*)!

a) Indeed, the exposition of a text--as we have seen clearly enough this morning--is always a delicate enterprise. What does one say, on this score, of the exposition not of a text, but of a translation of this text?

I do not broach here the problems implied by the translation of poetry in general, or biblical poetry in particular. See on this:

E. Nida, *Toward a Science of Translating*, Leiden, 1964.
E. Nida and Ch. Taber, *The Theory and Practice of Translation*, Leiden, 1969.
H. Meschonnic, "Pour une poétique de la traduction," in the preface of his translation of *Cinq Rouleaux*, Paris, 1970.
H. Meschonnic, "Poétique de la traduction," in *Pour la poétique* II, Paris, 1973, pp. 305ff.

That said, and for us to restrict ourselves to the passage chosen, the comparison of the translation made from the Hebrew text by the French Rabbinic team and reviewed by Rabbi Elie Munk (a publication of the Odette S. Levy Foundation, 1964) with the translation made by the École Biblique de Jerusalem (éd. du Cerf, 1956), is suitable to reassure us: the differences are inconsequential. The only one which would be of any importance relates to verse 14, which, in the opinion of all, is not clear in the Hebrew text.

Munk's translation reads: "Abraham called this place: the Lord will see; from whence it is said today: 'On the mount of Adonoi-Jirah'."

The translation of the Jerusalem Bible reads: "Abraham called this place 'Yahweh provides', and hence the saying today: On the mountain Yahweh provides."

In fact, the Hebrew yields: "On the mountain of Yahweh, he will be seen." And I must confess that, looking at the text as a layman (to speak as in the lecture this morning), I do not find it at all so obscure. It is, indeed, the mountain of the salvific presence--of the ram sent by whom, if not by Yahweh himself!

b) As to the method, it will suggest, if you wish, some reflections which I have confided to you on current tendencies in criticism and on the advantages of a stylistics which can speak of forms, but is constantly careful to identify their meaning, still more their worth, and is anxious to get at, if it can, the reciprocal characterization of the themes and their modes of expression.

In order to show you that all this is not incompatible with certain structures which the New Criticism gives itself, I adopt the order of presentation which Roland Barthes has chosen when he wished to give an example of the "L'Analyse structurale du récit", apropos of Acts 10:1-11, 18 (*Recherches de Science religieuse*, 58 [1970], pp. 17-37). Of all these questions of placing a thing in its setting and in the work I will speak to you a little more at length in another connection by approaching the study of the second text.

I. STRUCTURE OF THE NARRATIVE

It is a narrative in episodes, presented in their succession in a most simple linear manner:

1. Message from God.
2. Departure and journey of Abraham with Isaac and the two servants.
3. Dialogue of father and son.
4. Preparation of the sacrifice.
5. Sudden turn of fortune (twofold): *a*) the intervention of the angel of God; *b*) the appearance of the ram and the substitutionary sacrifice.
6. Second intervention of the angel, in the form of an announcement, that is to say, of prophecy.
7. Return of Abraham with Isaac (not named) and his two servants.

II. THEMATIC ASPECTS

The topographical, onomastic, chronological code is of a remarkable neatness--not very full nor detailed, but sufficiently precise. I limit myself to pointing out two traits which merit special attention:

a) The place of chronological notations, and more particularly of *successivity*. The initial utterance governs everything: "After these events (acts)..." The story is put in perspective from that time.

b) The very calculated effect of suspense, in the order of the topography. The precise place destined for the sacrifice remains and should remain the secret of God: at first for Abraham as for us; but afterwards it remains so for us and the text does not tell us how Abraham was able to know it. Hence the commentary of Rashi, who feels obliged to explain--but such an "explanation" goes against the explanation of the text!--: "He saw a cloud fixed on the mountain."

In fact, it is when the action is achieved, and the miracle accomplished, that the place finds itself named--baptized--and by that takes its place in the geography of men.

As to the code of "action" [*actionnel*], it is no less clear. The unity of action is perfect, and the action perfectly plotted--like a truly dramatic play:[1] exposition; main problem of the action; sudden turn of fortune; denouement.

If we look at things from the standpoint of the characters and their arrangement, we find the following sequence:

God → Abraham; Abraham--Isaac; Abraham--Isaac--the angel; Abraham--the angel (very curiously Isaac disappears); Abraham (→ God).

The arch is very well constructed, and all is organized in such fashion that the scene of the sacrifice appears as the apex--from every standpoint!

III. THE THEMES AS MEANS OF EXPRESSION

The analysis of the "symbolic" code makes us pass very naturally from the themes to the figures, that is to say, to the realm of the means of expression, the image (metaphor, metonymy, symbol, etc.) being the principal one, especially when one is dealing with a poetic text.

The theme itself--that is to say the sacrifice of Isaac--is a symbol, and a double symbol. No doubt a scholar of poetry would find there (let us note it in the passage) a magnificent specimen of form-meaning, or of meaning-form, if one prefers.

Whatever it may be, on the one hand *hic et nunc* as well as *ad aeternum*, it is the most testing and consequently the most moving symbol of obedience to the commandment of God. And, on the other hand, in relation to the realm of hope, it is the announcement, the prefiguration of the sacrifice of Christ--the Lamb of God.

The first of these two symbols (*a*) is expressed through the first five paragraphs; the second (*b*) is expressed through the prophecy of the angel.

The stylistic mark proper to *b* is lyric effusion, signified by a cascade of three images--two comparisons and a metaphor. Then this ensemble of images serves, let us not forget, to elucidate a declaration which is itself a symbol. It is necessary also to acknowledge that--stylistically speaking--the passage is out of tune with the rest of the story.

As to symbol *a*, I would call attention to but one aspect of its modes of expression: it is a question, materially speaking, of the sacrifice of *Isaac*. He is the symbol-object; but he is only the signifier, the instrument of the thing signified, which, once more, is the obedience of the creature to his Creator.

Now this fact becomes transparent through at least four features of the story:

1. At the beginning: "Take your son, your only son, whom you love, Isaac."

How can we fail to notice the triple projection pointing forward to the extraordinary price of the sacrifice demanded? The name also comes only afterwards.

2. At the third unit: Isaac poses to his father a question which could not be more pertinent. But the equivocation of the response is such that it poorly explains how it could satisfy Isaac: strange silence!

3. In the fourth unit, even more strange yet are the silence and the total passivity of Isaac, when his father binds him and places him on the altar. We are in complete *unreality*. Isaac no longer exists as a subject: he has become pure symbol.

Finally, in the last verse: "Abraham returned to his young men...." There is no longer even a question about Isaac, who has completely disappeared--as if he had been sacrificed for good!--The truth is that he has accomplished his office and has returned to his ordinary anonymity. The symbolic actor disappears with his function.

I conclude here, for all the rest is only detail with regard to this convergence of expressive motifs, all contributing to the suggestion of what is nothing other than the theme of the absolute of sacrifice employed through the relation of the father and the son.

NOTE

1. We know, moreover, that the episode furnished the material for several medieval *Mysteries* before inspiring Theodore Beza's tragedy of *The Sacrifice of Abraham* (1550).

THE THREE PARABLES OF MERCY
Exposition of Luke 15:1-32

by Gérald Antoine

This time, we do not begin with empty hands. From the side of methodology, the articles by Roland Barthes and Louis Marin are offered to us, in the *Recherches de Science religieuse*, 58 (1970), pp. 17-37 and 39-61--with a practical application devoted to Acts 10:1-11, 18.

Also, for commenting on our passage, the aid of two scholars likewise presents itself: E. Rasco, S.J. whose article is contained in I. de La Potterie, *De Jésus aux Evangiles* (Gembloux, 1967), pp. 165-180, and W. Trilling, who devotes a chapter of his book, *L'annonce du Christ dans les Evangiles synoptiques* (Paris, 1971), pp. 105-120 to the first two of our parables, while introducing some elements of comparison with Matthew 18:12-14.

This is not the place to examine in detail the bases and the content of the method called "the structural analysis of the narrative". Let us mention only the "operative principles" recommended by R. Barthes:

1. Division of the text into reading units;
2. Inventory of codes (to discern the themes well);
3. Coordination, that is to say, the establishment of correlations, at once intra- and intertextual.

It is necessary to state precisely that a good stylistic method demands this as an ensemble of preliminaries, but it is not at all fulfilling, for the goal--I recall once more--is to seize that which makes the specificity of a text, form and content reunited in this mystery of incarnation which is a wholly genuine work of art.

Having said that, it is difficult to avoid the problem of the orientation of the analysis: should it begin with forms or with themes? With the sacrifice of Isaac, the second formula may be tested in a wholly empirical manner. But when it comes to the Gospel, hesitation appears hardly permissible, since: "In principio erat Verbum, et Verbum erat apud Deum, et Deus erat Verbum...." A change of dance partners could be the justification for one or the other methodological directions, if *Verbum*--the signifier--were not at the departure as at the arrival!

The gospel, you tell me, is the Good News. Yes, but to get at it, to captivate it, it offers us precisely a collection of *texts*--today, for example, that of Luke 15. Let us start then from this "woven fabric" of forms, of modes of expression, to ascend once again to its meaning and its worth. And since the recommendations of R. Barthes do not go counter to this, let us follow them, at least to begin.

I. DIVISION INTO SUB-UNITS OF READING

I refer you here to P. Rasco whose scheme of reading appears to me to "stick" rigorously to the text:

a) an introduction: verses 1-3;

b) the first two parables, twins: that of the shepherd and that of the diligent woman;

c) the third, much longer, bound to the preceding "by a feeble εἶπεν δέ", and itself divided into two parts:

  1) the departure and return of the younger son: vss. 11-24;

  2) the resistance of the older son: vss. 25-32.

The figure and the attitude of the father affirm the unity of 1) and of 2).

However, even if this proposal for reading is correct, it appears to call for a certain number of complementary observations: first, it must be seen that the parallelism of the first two parables is at this point displayed in such fashion that they could be sufficient unto themselves and truly form a whole.

That poses the question, how is the third united to the other two?--By two *themes*: on the one hand, that of the object, or the animal, or the cherished person, lost and found; on the other hand, that of joy, of the rejoicing which marked the rediscoveries.

Thus, let us be more precise: there is a thematic unity, but a formal duality--so much so that (as P. Rasco has well seen) the first two parables not only correspond term for term, but present themselves in one unit as two *interrogations*--while the third stands off by itself.

II. INVENTORY OF CODES

If one goes back to the inventory drawn up by R. Barthes in relation to Acts 10, he is obligated to state that he finds here only one very partial application of it. It is important to stress this fact from the methodological point of view, for it reveals that in the matter of the analysis of literary texts, structuralism is very unequally rewarding. A very simple observation, but one that it is necessary to have the courage to make.

Let us look rather at the pieces: the topographical, onomastic, historical code is here found to be reduced to nothing. It is interesting to note, however, that we thus register a *zero degree* of references to these codes. And here I agree entirely with a very useful reflection of R. Barthes:

"Confronted with a statement...it is necessary always to think of what happens if the feature were not noted or if it were different. The good analyst of a narrative ought to have a sort of imagination of a *counter-text*."

The author would naturally have been able to add to his first phrase: ...or if, contrarywise, such an absent feature of the story appeared there.

It is, for example, very remarkable that--in the ensemble of our three parables--no exact notation of place, of time, or of names of persons obtrudes:

"Now the tax collectors and sinners were all drawing near to hear him."

As Trilling notes, the "all" is incredible. I would add: this is a generalization, or an indefiniteness, the same as the two articles so badly named "definite" which precede. In fact, these are generic tools, as in the titles of the fables by La Fontaine.

The part played by anonymity is still more manifest in the third parable:

"*A* man had two sons. *The younger*...departed for *a* far country and there squandered his property in *a* life of prodigality."

Afterwards there comes, it is true, a picturesque passage all the more gripping as it contrasts so strongly with the neutral background of the story. But let us examine very closely here: this picturesqueness in no way personalizes the protagonists of the action; it does not adhere to them--or rather, they do not adhere to it. Thus, the younger son who, keeping the swine for the benefit of an owner, receives nothing from him and does not even touch the carob pods which he envies: traits as "incredible" as the "all" pointed out earlier, or--let us not hesitate before this intertextual parallel--as the misconduct of Isaac toward his father which we discussed before.

The same is true of the summing up of the circumstantial indications in the second occasion--that of the return:

"His older son was in the fields. When...he came near to the house..."

Here it is easy to decipher the zero degree of the code: we are in the presence of a complete symbolic; the parable prescribes its own law.

If we pass to the phatic and metalinguistic code, we find ourselves in turn, at least in a certain manner, before a profusion. Curiously, this trait does not seem to have struck either Rasco nor Trilling. It nevertheless appears very fundamental.

If the narrative is not enlivened by looking for details which serve to *situate* it, in repayment it lives continually by the influence of the word of those personnages of whom, as for other matters, we are totally ignorant. Especially remarkable is the part played by direct discourse:

Introduction: "This man, *they said*...
He *spoke* to them, then, this parable:"

First parable: "Who among you...": the entire parable is then already, in itself, a direct discourse of Jesus, at the heart of which there is a series of quotations, then other bits of direct discourse:
"When he has found it..., he calls together his friends and his neighbors, *saying* to them.... Even so, I tell you..."

Second parable: a design identical to the preceding.

Third parable: it contains an outstanding masterpiece of this genre. I wish to point out the occurrence, in the

second paragraph [in the paragraphing of some French translations], of the inner monologue, explicitly announced as such:
"But when he came to himself he said..."

But that is not all: at the heart of this soliloquy, the prodigal son finds the means of putting his thoughts into words, always in direct style:

"I will arise and go to my father, and *I will say to him*, Father, I have sinned against heaven and before you; I am no longer worthy to be called your son; treat me..."

In short, he recites to himself what he is going to say to his father, who does not, moreover, give him time to finish the sentence. We are here in the presence of a discourse by anticipation--by reflection in the inner mirror.

This is a remarkable variety of what R. Barthes learnedly calls "the diagrammatic structure", with regard to Acts 10--a text very astonishing to him by its sequence: vision--story of the vision--story of the story of the vision. From one text to the other, the pace of the diagram is inverted.

There would be, certainly, a complete study to be done on this process of important style--and its gamut of varieties --in the Gospels. From there we could make the transition toward some explorations which are no longer intra- but intertextual.

III. INTERTEXTUAL CORRELATIONS

We meet here, in truth, not one correlation, but a collection, which shows in a very clear fashion the legitimacy of a recourse to this method.

I would add that--if one may discuss it, at least in theory, at a loss for arguments when it is a question of secular authors--in the case of the Gospels and *in a Chris-*

tian perspective hesitation does not seem permissible to me: the Word of God is *one*!

In this regard, let me share with you a matter of surprise: how is it that neither Rasco nor Trilling have called attention to an intertextual relation clearly uniting the Gospel parable of the lost sheep to at least one passage of the Old Testament--that of the Book of Ezekiel traditionally titled "the shepherds of Israel"?--Yahweh speaks in these terms to the evil shepherds:

"The weak you have not strengthened, the sick you have not healed, the crippled you have not bound up, the strayed you have not brought back, the lost you have not sought....

"For thus says the Lord God: Behold, I, I myself will search for my sheep, and will seek them out...so will I seek out my sheep; and I will rescue them from all places where they have been scattered on a day of clouds and thick darkness....I will seek the lost, and I will bring back the strayed, and I will bind up the crippled, I will heal those who are sick."

Thus the theme of the lost sheep is at the hinge of two movements which constitute a symmetrical whole.[1]

But while remaining humbly on the plane of literary criticism alone, we may say this: each time we are confronted by a text bearing in a certain degree the marks of a form--that is to say, referring itself, implicitly or not, to a model (*pattern*)--to deny the concurrence of an intertextuality becomes a willful mutilation of criticism.

Here--or never--it is the case. I will limit myself to three examples, of which the last two have significance as counterproof:

a) The first trait is pointed out both by Rasco and Trilling. It touches on the composition of a passage such as we have analyzed above: two twin parables, in interrogative form, followed by a third, more ample.

Now this *type* of composition appears again in Luke several times, and we need not concern ourselves to look very far, since it appears in chapter 13 with the parables of the grain of mustard seed, then the leaven, then finally the householder whose door is shut. The texts in Matthew to which Trilling refers testify likewise, namely:

13:31-33: which likewise give the parables of the mustard seed and the leaven;

13:44-46: the parables of the pearl and the treasure in the field;

5:13-14: the parables of the salt and the light, etc.

The comparison of these texts alone proves that we are in the presence not of a stylistic trait characteristic of the passage studied today, but a trait which participates in the typology of the gospel narratives.

b) The first counterproof.--The same W. Trilling, explaining Luke 15:1-19, cites with approval Kahlefeld: "The discourse is bold but, at the same time, is of great discretion"--a discretion marked by the fact that Jesus avoids a direct reference to the name of God ("there will be more joy in heaven...there is joy before the angels of God...") and that he "veils the declarations relative to his love".

A single misfortune: if he had only extended his reading to the parable of the prodigal son, he would have encountered the episode where we see that the father "embraced him and kissed him", before giving him everything, which is a lively and spectacular demonstration of tenderness!

c) Another counterproof, even more clear.--Trilling notes the fact that "the conversion is realized at first *by God*: it is the shepherd who goes to look for the lost sheep; he does not wait until he comes to himself..." Hence, the consequences which we may infer on the nature of grace and the ways of salvation.

Unfortunately, that is not at all true of the parable of the prodigal son, which roundly rejects this by itself!

It consequently is apparent in the clearest way that the explanation is not valid in the example chosen, which breaks a correlation which one hesitates, moreover, to say whether it is intra- or intertextual--which reveals with the same stroke both the correspondences and the differences between the first two parables on the one hand and the third on the other.

But the observation could be further enriched by a broadened intertextual search. I think, among others, of the episode of the Samaritan woman: there also, it is true, Jesus took the first step, to the great scandal of the Pharisees. Nevertheless, he did not wait to ask--and in what tone!--the sinful woman to carry out the second: "Woman, give me a drink."

It is, consequently, the sight of three possible approaches to salvation which we comprehend: 1) God alone takes the step; 2) the sinner alone; 3) the act is shared.

You will observe here how the intertextual method incites, or at least invites, interpretation. Just a word in this regard, to conclude, on the problem of hermeneutics.

IV. WHAT TO THINK OF EXPLANATIONS OF A HERMENEUTICAL CHARACTER?

It happens that P. Rasco, explaining Luke 15, presents it to us as a twofold and excellent example: what, he asks first, is the essence of the sin incarnated in the prodigal son?--"He does not wish to be a son, nor to receive the love of the father; but like Adam in paradise earlier, he wishes to be independent."

Without doubt through modesty and scrupulousness of method, P. Rasco does not speculate upon his comment; but it is sufficiently clear to all that he suggests a contemporaneity to the Gospel which we can no longer make perceptible and burning: it is totally the problem of the strife among youth, of the revolt of sons against fathers, which is stressed.

The second question posed by the analyst is: did the older son finally accept the invitation of the father?--we do not know: the latter parable remains "mysteriously open". And he adds: "This is, without doubt, to pose the question *for ourselves*: are we willing to rejoice with God at the entrance of our sinful brother into the Kingdom?"

The expression "without doubt" sufficiently denotes the character of relative gratuitousness of this interpretation which is only one possible interpretation--among others. What should we think, from the point of view of literary criticism, of this sort of interpretation?

Chance orders things well. Indeed, it likewise so happens that R. Barthes, theoretician of the structural analysis of the narrative cited in the study of Rasco, has written elsewhere a well known work entitled *On Racine* (Octagen, 1977). It serves us as a star witness.

Now, in this book, there is no question of codes or of structures, but of observations as personal as possible, rich with excitements, I dare to say, at once specious and effective. Barthes' methodological position does not settle any uncertainty. Or rather, it is ostensibly open in the sense that, even when it makes use of structuralism, it is careful to dissociate this method which touches the means of expression, the forms, from all preoccupation directed towards ends, that is to say *meaning*. On the question of meaning, it poses on the contrary the "principle of plurality":

"The structural analysis of the narrative...aims to trace what I would call the geometrical basis, the basis of meanings, the basis of the possibles of the text....For me, the meaning...is not one possible, it is *the very being of the possible*. It is the being of the plural."

"Under these conditions, structural analysis of the narrative can be only one method of interpretation..., it does not search for the secret of the text: for it, all the roots of the text are up in the air...."

It is true that R. Barthes, not at all malignantly, and hardly maliciously, introduces an important reservation when it is a question of biblical texts. But this is no longer structuralist criticism which speaks on its own account; it seeks to put itself in the place of the theologian:

"...does a text possess in some fashion a final signifier ...Theologically, it is certain that a final signified is postulated; the metaphysical or semantic definition of theology assumes a final signified" (*loc. cit.*, p. 34).

Well, I am no more a doctor in theology than R. Barthes; but I am not sure that he is entirely right. My point of departure will be, as is his--but not in the same sense--that of a grammarian habitually devoting attention to the analysis of literary texts.

He observes that the writer of genius distinguishes himself from the talented writer in that he writes not to seduce the public of his own epoch--on the contrary he rather baffles it--but in such fashion that his work offers to coming generations strong and ceaselessly renewed nourishment.

Now, if God exists, he exists for Eternity, and his message is a word given to teach the generations of men to infinity. Truly, it is a case of taking up the beautiful image of R. Barthes: all its roots are up in the air and mount as high as the tree of Jesse!

Note in the passage that Barthes has passed, wittingly or not, from the expression "final signifier" to "final signified". Let us not play with words or not let them play with us: there is certainly an initial signifier: "In principio erat Verbum." But he would know how to have a final signified: "...et Verbum erat apud Deum....Hoc erat *in principio* apud Deum!'" That is to say: the signifier was from the beginning incorporated in the infinite signified, in the infinity of meaning--in the semantic infinity if you prefer.

On this, let us return, for a moment, to the simple point of view of stylistic explanation engaged in a purely positivist perspective, and say: it is a fact that a number of elements of the typology of Gospel discourse lend themselves, by nature, to the infinity of interpretation: the definite character of so many forms; their simplicity, their openness, their brevity; the blanks in the story. All these call for explanation; all these blanks demand to be completed, furnished, peopled.

But to conclude, the grammarian must give way to the poet--and why not to Péguy of Orleans, who lived to be a centenarian and who, better than anyone, has, on the one hand, explained and commented on our three parables--and with what abundance, and on the other hand, has defined our duty with regard to the entire Gospel text, the Book which contains the Word.

This explanation and this definition both appear in *Le Porche de la deuxième Vertu*. I am only able to send you back there, not knowing too well what fragments to highlight on this flood of inexhaustible verses. For Péguy, our three parables, which he named the parables of hope, are the most admirable of all:

"All the parables are beautiful, my child,
all the parables are grand, all the parables
are dear.
(...)
But among all the three parables of hope
Stand out
(...)
This is perhaps because they have in them
a youthfulness, an unknown childlikeness."
(ed. Pléiade, p. 620)

Nevertheless, among the three, it is still the last which he prefers:

"...
A man had two sons. It is beautiful in Luke.
It is beautiful everywhere.
It is only in Luke, it is everywhere.
It is beautiful on the earth and in the heavens.
It is beautiful everywhere.
Merely to think about it, a sob arises
in your throat."
(*ibid.*, pp. 622-23)

As to the manner of receiving not only this parable but all the others, let us listen a little (too little, alas!) to what he says. It is our souls which speak:

"We are summoned to nourish the word of the
Son of God.
O misery, O misfortune, it is to us it returns,
It is to us it belongs, it is on us it depends
To make it understood from century to century,
To make it sound forth.
O misery, O happiness, it is on us that
it depends,
Trembling with happiness,
We who are nothing, we who pass on earth
Some years of nothingness,
What poor, miserable years,
(Our souls immortal)
We who are nothing, who do not endure,
Who do not endure so much as to say anything
(On earth),
This is senseless, it is yet we who
are charged

To conserve and to nourish eternal things
On earth
The word spoken, the word of God."
(*ibid.*, pp. 588-89)

What may be said after that which you do not already know: the text of the Gospel addresses itself to us, youthful as on the first day, "ageless". As such, it offers itself for the taking to the professional critic, who applies his best methods to it. These make progress gropingly in the directions which I have tried to indicate to you. But at the same time--why not keep the word of Péguy?--the Gospel, as much and more than every great book, has that which "nourishes" humanity, generation after generation. When it no longer has anything to give, then the end of time will be near!

NOTE

1. M. Bovon has pointed out to me that the opposition of the older son to the younger is a frequent theme in the Old Testament: the younger son is always an undisciplined figure, clever in getting himself out of evil scrapes, while the older brother takes the most thankless part.

Psychoanalysis

THE PARABLE OF THE PRODIGAL SON (Luke 15:11-32) READ BY AN ANALYST

by Louis Beirnaert

Faced with a text as widely commented on as this one, the analyst, as such, begins by freeing himself of all that tradition has brought to him. For the theologian, Luke's narrative elucidates the revelation of the divine mercy with regard to the sinner. For the analyst the parable is a narrative which is to be interpreted as a function of his experience as an analyst. Like a dream, it betrays and does not betray a certain position in relation to desire. It is a road toward an unconscious truth.

Does it follow that he has for an aim to substitute one exegesis for another, to make what is sometimes called "a psychoanalytic exegesis" which will result in manifesting a hidden meaning, a disguised text called "psychological" under the apparent text? But the psychoanalyst does not seek to discover the truth behind falsehood. He does not suspect the text. He takes it as an enigma to be deciphered. Now the enigma is not a facade. It speaks the truth, but in such fashion that the task of decoding a cryptogram is required to grasp it. The psychoanalytic reading, then, is not a sort of a counter-reading which is set in opposition to the theological reading, but *another* reading which causes another thing to emerge on another scenery, to which it will be necessary hereafter to accommodate oneself, for it cannot remain without effect on all reading.

At the beginning, there emerge certain phrases, certain words, which detach themselves in the fabric of the text. Thus I can witness to the confusion in which I was left before the parable, before having noticed the repetition of the sequence "lost and found" and the insistence on the joy of the finders. Up till then one could say that the text remained pure enigma for me. It is by the marking of certain signifiers that the reading begins. They indicate that this story concerns desire, its object and the satisfaction which is bound to the possession of this object. Now this last one is presented in the parable of the prodigal son, and in the two preceding parables--that of the lost sheep (Luke 15:4-7) and that of the lost coin (Luke 15:8-10)--as a *lost* object. This loss which affects it makes part of the law of the object which creates the desire. What is it that this wishes to say? Besides, and this is a second remark, this object is found again. His return to the place which he had left empty awakens joy. This is clearly bound to the *re*-finding. It is to it that the satisfaction in the text which occupies us is due. But can the lost object always be refound? Finally, I note the enigma which what is told of the older son constitutes in the parable. He has lost nothing nor refound anything. What is there of his desire and of his object?

I am, then, going to resume the reading proceeding from these remarks, while applying myself successively to each of the three characters placed on stage, the father and his two sons.

The Younger Son

The younger son demands from his father the goods which should come to him. These are immediately given by the father. Let us pass rapidly over the story of what happens to him. He dissipates what he has received; he engages himself as a hired labourer to people who let him perish with hunger; he recalls then what goes on at the home of his father; and he returns repentant, asking only for a place as a servant. Briefly, his first demand has been granted and this was a defeat.

For G. Crespy, who attempted a "psychoanalytic exegesis" of the parable,[1] "we are in the presence of an Oedipean situation....It is clear that in claiming the part of the property which should come to him after the death of his father, he symbolically *killed* the father, he deprived him of his prerogatives in so far as the father (the "legal" father Lacan would say) was defined by *possessions*. He asked him, in short, to disappear so that he himself could become the father."[2] It does not seem that this interpretation answers to that which is in the text.

Everything indicates that not only has the younger son not killed the father--even symbolically--since this one accedes immediately to his demand, but he keeps the reassuring memory of his existence: "How many of my father's hired servants have bread enough and to spare..." (Luke 15:17). If he returns, it is to escape his own death, while making himself dependent on his father.

If it is true, according to psychoanalysis, that the Oedipus myth indicates the path of access to desire, it is clear that here the Oedipean situation is denied. Among the goods which he possesses, there is one which the father cannot distribute, that is his wife. Now, the figure of the father's spouse, the mother, is completely absent from the text. Where in the Oedipean myth she represents the object forbidden to desire, her effacement in the parable signifies that the possibility of acceding to castration in recognizing the rule of the father, after the phase of imaginary rivalry with him, remains closed. To have immediately received the goods which are not forbidden to him, which is here concealed, the younger son stands on the record of his demand to the Other, not recognizing his desire and the object of this one. That is why he remains dependent on his father. Is that to say that all possibility of one day finding access to his desire is henceforth removed?

The text does not say that the subject finds joy in this dependence. From the moment when he returns to the house and makes confession of his fault, the younger son remains silent and the parable speaks only of the rejoicing of which he is the *object for the others*. Nothing is said about what he feels. This blank in the text leaves open the possibility of another text which takes up again the question of the desire of the younger son, at the point where it remains in suspense, whether it be a repetition of the same flight from the paternal house, as A. Gide has done with it by unfolding the figure of the prodigal son,[3] or whether it be the recognition of the Oedipean situation which continues to work in the unconscious. The fate of desire remains suspended on the part of the younger son.

The Father

With the figure of the father, something new occurs. The son who occupied the place of the lost object is refound and joy is born of this rediscovery. Thus the wide chasm in the family caused by the departure is filled in by the return. It should be noted that in this parable, as in those which precede it, the reconstitution of a totality, of a collection of numerous elements, is at the forefront. One sheep is lacking in the hundred. And then the number is again complete. The lost drachma is returned and the collection of the ten drachmas is constituted anew. Of the two sons, there remains only one. And behold, they are two again.

In short, the shattered totality forms itself again. The empty place is reoccupied. "Rejoice."

The text of the story indicates that that which was lost and therefore was wanting, arousing desire by that, can return to its place. The defective breach in the familial domain of the father is only provisory. Completeness is not only possible, it exists. This is at least what is shown in the entire first part of the parable (Luke 15:11-25).

And the feast to which the servants are urged is the manifestation of a joy which is born of the satisfaction of desire in refinding the lost object. Thus there is no longer any want for the father. At least at the moment of the story. For the text proceeds and something new is going to be introduced.

The Older Son

The other of the two sons returns from the fields and sees the feast. Far from rejoicing, he becomes angry with his father. It is the first time that the text speaks of agression. It is connected to what? Listen: "Lo, these many years I have served you, and I never disobeyed your command; yet you never gave me a kid, that I might make merry with my friends. But when this son of yours came, who has devoured your living with harlots, you killed the fatted calf for him!" (Luke 15:39-40). Thus what interests the older son is that which has been given to *another*, that which has not been given to him. There is awakened the desire of an object which he will never have, since it is the very same thing which is for another.

It is necessary to see clearly that the desire of the older son does not rest on the real gift of a kid or a calf, as if it would suffice him for the father to reestablish an equilibrium by procuring for him the same goods as those which he had given to the younger son. The fact that the object had been given to the other is the integrating part of the envy felt. To speak the truth, the question of a kid or a calf has no importance. It is the gift made to the other which is here the object of desire. And it is before "the image of a completeness which is enclosed",[4] a rejoicing from which he is separated, that he is irritated.

When the desire of his father is satisfied, his own is not and cannot be. The lost object of which it is a question for him can never be refound. He was well established in his submission: "I never transgressed a single one of your orders" (Luke 15:29), he had all the property of the father: "all that is mine is yours" (Luke 15:31), but a crevice has opened in this tranquil life, and with it a totally new moment of desire: his suspension has lost something structural, in so far as it is a question of another's object.

Would the older son have acquiesced in this lost object which in the Oedipean myth is marked out by the mother? No again, for in the irremediably lost object, he only sees again the gift which the father has not given to him, but which *would have been made to him*, since another had benefited from it. That of which he has been deprived would be in the place of the object radically impossible, he knows nothing of it again. Hence his anger against the one who deprived him who, according to him, could have been the donor. As if the object was not that which in any case and to whomever could not be given. At the point where he is, the object on which his desire remained suspended is still imaginary. Totally irrecoverable though it may be in fact, he still comes undone on the basis of a possession which had been possible.

There is in the anger of the older son a desire for

the death of the father, in response to the privation of which he imagines him to be the cause. The object is certainly irremediably lost, but it is the fault of the Other: that is why the older son constitutes a lost object for the father. The text says nothing of it for reasons which we will see later, but the logic of desire leads us to suppose it.

The Challenging of the Father

In refinding one son, the father of the parable at the same time lost the other son by a loss different from the first, for the loss of the younger son was reparable. The place which he had left empty in the house could be reoccupied. The shattered wholeness could be restored. But the older son had never left his place; he is then not lost with a loss which permits a return. Besides, did he not always enjoy the father's goods? He never went away, so he cannot be looked for. Plainly at the heart of this possession, he is roused to the desire of that which he cannot possess, deprived as he is of it by the other. From then on, he does not leave the father by going away, he leaves him from the inside, if I may so put it. He is lost in so far as the estate governed by his father and his tenderness crumbles in its sufficiency. It is by this that the dimension of desire to which he accedes necessarily puts in question the father himself as he is presented in the first part of the parable, for the entire operation of his mercy is passive. The older son is the remainder who does not reenter the framework posed at an earlier time. In so far as he is lost with the sort of loss which we have indicated, he shatters the figure of the father in the tranquillity of his benevolence, in the sufficiency of his possession. The desire of the father finds its satisfaction in the refinding of his object. And here arises a lost object in this older son to whom he cannot give either the goods which he already has, nor with still more reason those goods which he has given to the younger son. That is to say that his desire finds itself before an object which this time cannot be refound. Thus an image of the object is sketched for the father which puts his whole universe in question, because he even attacks his benevolence. We have evoked earlier the death wish registered in the anger of the older son. It is before this death that the father of the parable finds himself, and by that he faces this irreparable deficiency which is at the very heart of his desire.

An inversion of the parable proposes itself here then. It is the figure of the older son who introduces into the dialectic, as we read it in the text, this essential deficiency of the desire. But if the object lost, with this loss of which we have been speaking, is at the end, it is because it was already at the beginning. It is there from the opening word: "A man had two sons" (Lk. 15:11). The one who is lost is not the one who left, since he is refound, but rather the one who remains.

Such a reading is psychoanalytic, that is to say, that it effects an unveiling of that which the text does not manifestly speak. It allows a share of reconstruction legitimate in psychoanalysis,[5] in particular for everything which concerns the effect of the loss of the older son on the figure of the father. But this effect the father rejects in an interpolation, since he effects a closing of the story by substituting a lesson for it: "It was fitting to make merry and be glad, for this your brother was dead, and is alive; he was lost, and is found" (Lk. 15:32). Thus he escaped the opening up of the question of his desire, by taking the position of a teacher. To speak truly, he has never ceased taking this position. From the beginning it is a question for him of illustrating a lesson: to know that the refinding of the lost object gives joy. It is this position of mastery of knowledge which closes off from the father of the parable access to a new dimension of loss, and by that to where he truly stands in desire.

Certainly our text thus closed is not very separable from the entire text of Scripture where the question of desire and of the death *of* and *to* the recoverable object is reopened.[6] But for an analyst, it is the story itself which can be read as a function of that which it does not say explicitly. As a dream, it must be deciphered so that the articulations, the omissions, the substitutions, in brief the mechanisms which play in its production, may be revealed in order to have some access to the unconscious discourses which support it. For neither the father nor the two sons have any conscious knowledge of all this.

It should be remarked that the current reading of the parable practically engages only the first part. Everything takes place as if the episode of the older son did not constitute an essential part of the narrative. Some exegetes have even seen an interpolation in it, although from the opening of the play it should be granted that there are two sons. They keep only the story which illustrates the "mercy", while omitting any analysis of the effect on the other of that which is accorded to one. There is in this a significant blotting out, a sort of rejection of the revolting son, in the shadows where those dwell whose "egoism" prevents them from understanding the lesson.

For manifestly, the older son does not understand. He is all caught up in his anger against the one whom he thinks deprives him unjustly. And by that, paradoxically, he is nearer to his desire than the younger son. That one had received immediately what he had demanded. He had not yet arrived at the point where it appeared that desire is produced by that of which one is deprived by another, by a deprivation which cannot cease. The time of aggression has been frittered away. That is why he remains in the perspective of a good which can be given, even though the older son has gone beyond this stage.

In this story of the three, it is the record of the onset of desire which is called forth. But it is not ended. We end with something suspended, in the measure that the father in his function of teaching does not place himself in the perspective of renouncing the sufficiency of having everything and of every gift of property, which alone will make him arrive at the final truth of desire. He has, in fact, for good reasons an object from whom the subject is radically separated. This is what the Oedipus myth expresses in the figure of the forbidden mother.

At the end of this reading, which has only the character of an outline, I want to return to my endeavor, in order to clarify it further.

SOME REFLECTIONS ON METHOD

We have dissected a text in order to submit it to a psychoanalytic reading. We have compared it to the telling of a dream which puts on stage the desire and its object, but who is the subject of the narrative? The one who produced it? It is represented in the context by the personal pronoun in the third person: "*He* said again" (Lk. 15:11) which designates Jesus who speaks. And he speaks at a datable moment, in precise circumstances, for hearers who are designated: "Now the tax collectors and sinners were all drawing near to *hear* him. And the Pharisees and the scribes murmured, saying, 'This man receives sinners and eats with them.' So he told them..." (Lk. 15:1-3). Of what is it an issue, then, if not of calling into question Jesus' bearing toward sinners? To this calling into question of which he is the object, Jesus responds by three parables, and notably by the parable which has held our attention. But, as it happens when a subject in analysis responds by a dream to a conflict situation, the response does not place itself on the same level as the question. It reveals what it contains of the position of the subject in relation to the desire which has been importuned by the event. It manifests the position from which the subject responds.

The same is true here. The demeanor of the Pharisees reaches the attention of the Jesus of Luke and results in the production of a parable in which we have seen what it conveys of desire and its object.

Was this the desire of Jesus as a "real person"? If so, credence could be given to the reference we have made to the event which has given rise to the parable. But we have only the account of this event. It concerns Jesus whose presence there is represented only by a pronoun, "him", and by the indication "this man". Our analysis of the parable in no way concerns itself with the "real subject", which is not in the text. If the producing of the parable supposes a context, it only supposes a representative of Jesus who Himself could not be there. Therefore, the reply of the parable-riddle bears only on the position and the object of desire implied in *the account* which immediately precedes it.

That the whole text and the pre-text fall beyond itself and all the other texts and the subject called real, would not prevent our analysis from being valid precisely to the extent that it does not pretend to give an analysis of the desire of Jesus implied in the *whole of Scripture.*

With regard to the analytical character of the method used here, several remarks are to be made. We have not taken the Oedipean myth as a discourse by which we would fit together the different elements of the narrative in order to make them consonant with it. It is not our concern to rediscover in the text what the myth says. The myth does not function as a plain discourse, it functions in the unconscious, and it does so there precisely as a mask and a repression. We have disclosed this clearly with regard to the figure of the mother. The reference which we have made has its function only to point out, in harmony with a constellation which is normative for desire, what is, for each of the three persons in the scene, his desire and his object, and then what he does not recognize and the fashion in which he ignores this.[7] That our endeavor calls for a good deal of construction, as we have observed, is not injurious to its pertinence, for these constructions, which take the place of the speaking of the analyst himself in the direct experience of psychoanalysis, are articulated on the basis of analytic experience and theory. As for the fact that we have never introduced into our work any reference whatever to the theological interpretation of the narrative (save once in a note), this indicates clearly that our reading cannot be taxed with reductionism, in the sense that it substitutes another text called psychological for a theological text. No more have we made evident in the text its agreements with a text which would tell what the conduct of God toward us is.[8] They will perhaps say of us that we have omitted the explicitly religious confession of the prodigal son: "Father, I have sinned against heaven and before you" (Lk. 15:21). If we have not taken up this text, it is because it constitutes a theological interpretation which leaves entirely open the question of knowing where the younger son is in relation to his desire and its object.

Thus the psychoanalytic reading of a text neither does away with this nor other possible interpretations. But it brings to light in the text something of the unconscious discourse which supports it; discourse which is discourse of this desire, indeed, which is always more or less unrecognized, but whose modes of disavowal can be traced. In the parable, the father and the two sons are, let us say, embarked in the same galley, but they do not occupy the same place.

NOTES

1. "Psychanalyse et foi," in *Essais sur la situation actuelle de la foi*, Paris, 1970, pp. 41-56.

2. *Op. cit.*, p. 43.

3. *Le retour de l'enfant prodigue*, Paris, 1945[18], pp. 195-235.

4. J. Lacan, *Les quatre concepts fondamentaux de la psychanalyse*, Paris, 1973, p. 106.

5. Cf. S. Freud, "Konstruktionen in der Analyse," in *Gesammelte Werke*, 16, London, 1950.

6. This is one way of reading the narratives of the Passion and the Resurrection.

7. The work of G. Crespy which we have already cited (cf. *supra*, p. 199, note 1) appears to us to be an illustration of what it is not necessary to do from the analytic point of view. The Oedipean myth there functions as a model, under the form of an obvious discourse.

8. Cf. L. Beirnaert, "Psychanalyse et vie de foi," in *Problèmes de psychanalyse*, Paris, Bruges, 1973, pp. 193-204.

Sociology of Literature

SOCIOLOGICAL APPROACH TO A SERMON OF MASSILLON ON LUKE 15:11-32

by Jacques Leenhardt

I. METHODOLOGICAL PRELIMINARIES[1]

People have the habit of speaking of the sociology of literature as if, whatever its object, it were always and everywhere a question of the same process. Now is it likely that faced with a novel, a systematic philosophy, or a sermon, the sociologist would conduct his investigation on identical bases? That would be to suppose the homogeneity of these different forms, while in any case erasing the specifecity. Since, then, today we find ourselves confronted with a sermon by Massillon, preached at Court at the end of the reign of Louis XIV, it is necessary to inquire about the type of discourse which it is legitimate to have, from the sociological point of view, on such a text.

The first remark which is permissible to make consists in placing this sermon in the oratorical genre, within the interior, then, of the flourishing rhetoric of the 17th century. This recollection is not without importance for, as we see it, it permits us to make a double movement. Habitually, the Court sermons present a quality of singularity, reinforced by the fact that the authors of the sermons moved about at the express demand of the king; consequently, they adorned themselves to the maximum with all the resources of rhetoric, an *inventio* which surprises, a *dispositio* which best supports the subject, and finally an *elocutio* whose effects are never too vehement. But, instead of following, as we would expect, the rules of oratorical discourse, Massillon offers a simple homily, an explanation and paraphrase of the Gospel, in which the main point of his rhetorical effects will consist in a remarkable *dispositio*.

This particularity implies, then, that we set the homily of Massillon exactly in opposition to a *sermon* properly so called, the revealer of the mysteries of religion and of morality, and in a general manner relate it to the evolution of the rhetoric at the turning point of the 17th and 18th centuries.

Rhetoric presents assuredly a significant history;[2] it does not, however, offer us a single guiding thread for a sociological analysis of a precise literary text. Still it is suitable to examine this notion of a "literary text". Preaching is situated somewhere near the encounter between dogmatic theology, oratorical styles and philosophical systems. To approach a text such as that of Massillon's it will then be permissible, ideally, to give it a triple analysis. The fullness of such a project obliges us to choose, without exempting us from some explanation about this choice.

Everyone will admit that rhetoric alone will not offer a satisfactory explanation, even for a genre as typed as the sermon; it is in return difficult to choose, without appearing arbitrary, between an explanation which is founded on a theological conceptualization, thus giving its full meaning to the fact that our text is that of a minister of religion, and a philosophical conceptualization which will more easily open our way toward the description of a vision of the world. In truth, it will be difficult to say which of these two possibilities we have chosen, by taking Malebranche's work as a philosophico-theological indicator of Massillon, since the system of this Cartesian Oratorian holds the two parts of his heritage so intimately bound together. Our subsequent development will indicate the choice with evidence from the work of Malebranche.

What is a sociological interpretation if not the attempt to situate a text or a work not only within its appropriate paramaters, but in relation to other works and other producers of works? Thus, to pass from Massillon to Malebranche, from Melebranche to the occasionalists, and from the occasionalists to a certain part of the class of nobles to whom one may suppose that the texts were implicitly addressed, is not to run away from the difficulties of the text itself, but to insert them as problem, as moment in the interior of structures more vast where they take their meaning; it is to affirm that the form of the antithesis which, on the rhetorical level, totally structures the arrangement of the sermon of Massillon has no significance in itself, but that related to the occasionalist system and to the power structure in French society of the second half of the 17th century, it takes its meaning, it becomes concrete, that is to say, it is an interpretation set in the world according to the laws of men with the same eyes as those who hereafter have some sorrow to find themselves there.

The sociology of literature reads the text, but always as a dialogue, as a question-response between sociological entities, groups, or social classes of whom the evolution of society renders the position problematic and consequently necessitates an ideological filling in, an explanation, and the restoration of meaning.

Rather than effecting a sliding back and forth from the theological to the philosophical, one would prefer a confrontation, even within the dogmatic field, where would be set over against each other, for example, the preaching of Bourdaloue and that of Massillon on the Return of the Prodigal Son, the first insisting on repentance and the resolution of the one who confesses his guilt, the second radically eliminating this intermediate dimension only for the sake of antithetically opposing the excess of mercy to the excess of passion. For comprehensible though it may be, this method would have had the inconvenience of sending us back constantly to the interpretation of the biblical text itself, to justify one or the other reading in founding itself on the pericopes which each one of them put forward, at the risk of making us miss what is essential here: the casting into form of a system of representation of man faced with God and with the world.

Such, then, is the work of sociology, to designate the manner in which a text enters into an ideological whole, establishes it and works for its transformation. But it will not know how to understand correctly the text on which it leans without making the objective meaning of the text spring forth, a meaning which, to be sure, goes beyond the consciousness of the one who produced it, and which, properly speaking, can only be pointed out by the insertion of the text as a significant structure within a much vaster structure, itself of an ideological character and before, in its turn, receiving the explanation of its meaning by its insertion into the social structures. The understanding of a text, then, is built on the explanation of its position within the ideological field, that is to say, in conceiving it as part of a vaster totality. Whether it fashions the ideological structure, and consequently modifies it, or whether it reflects it, the text is always founded on mental categories produced within the social practice by the groups and classes who constitute a given society. The text of a discourse from one of the class in power reproduces its ideology, without a rupture, without the slightest crack. If, on the other hand, he speaks in the name of those whom power oppresses, he shakes off the heavy cloak of the dominating ideology not from the outside, a utopian place, but from the borders of his interiority. The text, then, "labors", grates, and by dissonance produces a novelty, a design for a different order, founded on a new power.

II. THE READING OF MASSILLON

The text: Sermon of Friday of the second week of Lent delivered in 1704 by Jean-Baptiste Massillon, on the parable of the Prodigal Son. Luke 15:11-32.

Here is the beginning of the sermon:

> The parable of the penitent prodigal is one of the most consoling features of the entire Scripture for sinners; and as I propose today to expound to you all its circumstances, it appears necessary to speak to you first of its setting.
>
> A large number of publicans, and of people of bad life, touched by the words of grace and of salvation which came from the mouth of the Savior, had renounced their dissoluteness, and appeared in his following among his disciples. This heavenly physician, who had come only for those who needed to be healed, honored their houses by his visits (...) (pp. 196-197).[3]

From the beginning, very briefly, and what is often absent in sermons, the speaker establishes the two elements of his sermon: to expound in circumstantial fashion the magnificent consolation which Scripture contains on which the homily is to be supported; to relate moreover, because that is necessary, the *occasion* of this marvel of grace. Massillon feels the need of holding together the efficacy of grace and the occasion by which it is produced. We shall see how these two elements mutually condition themselves in his "system".

Let us see, then, how he places himself before the text. From the second paragraph, the central figure of the Savior is interposed, and qualified here as the "heavenly physician". The expression reappears twice in the sermon (p. 228) and is supported by the use of the word "remedy" (p. 229). It is with the person of this heavenly physician that we are going to begin our investigation. The image is indeed striking, since it sends us back at the same time to a theology of sin and to a conception of the universe as order, to a cosmology in the etymological sense of the term. In his *Entretiens sur la métaphysique et la religion*, Malebranche also posits the world as a creation of an *order*, marred by sin but not definitively since a "restorer"[4] is foreseen from the beginning, destined to restore the order. From Massillon to Malebranche we have, then, the paradigm Physician-Restorer-Redeemer. Here is how Malebranche introduces this restorer:

> Nevertheless, God has foreseen and permitted sin. That suffices; for it is a certain proof that the Universe *restored* by Jesus Christ is of more value than the same Universe in its first construction....[5]

The function of the physician is then included in the system of order itself. He has come, as Massillon says, for the single reason that there were (or there will be) *disorders* (p. 197). This brings us back to the second paragraph of our sermon, where disorders and renunciation take their full meaning, the first expressing the rupture of the regular, fixed activity of the world as order; the second, the result of the action of grace by the physician, permitting the re-establishment of this order.

Thus from the outset the great theme of the theology of Massillon is presented to us, which the development of the peroration will only resume and illustrate. Unhappily, it will not be a process of following the text of the sermon step by step. We will content ourselves with a certain number of significant halting-places, which explain the progress of the preacher.

Let us read the first two paragraphs of the first part:

> The vice of which I attempt today to explain the mortal consequences; this vice so universally spread over the earth, and which wastes with so much fury the heritage of Jesus Christ; this vice of which the Christian religion had purged the universe, and which today has gotten the better over religion, is characterized by certain marks all of which I rediscover in the story of the wanderings of the prodigal son.
>
> First, it is not the vice which further alienates the sinner from God; secondly, it is not the vice which after alienating him from God, allows him less resources to return to him; thirdly, it is not the vice which renders the sinner more insufferable to himself; finally, it is not that which renders him more despicable in the eyes of other men. Observe, I pray you, all these qualities in the story of the sinner of our gospel (pp. 199-200).

If we relate this to the diversity of the behavior to which Massillon makes reference throughout his sermon, one can only be astonished by the unicity of *this vice* to which he refers his hearers. Now Massillon is entirely clear; there is *one* vice which begets mortal consequences. What are commonly called the Court vices are, in fact, in his perspective only multiple consequences of one unique vice. And, although he devotes half of his sermon to detailing this vice in the form of the vices encountered at Versailles, we see clearly that Massillon's interest rests on this origin and not on its diverse manifestations.

You know that this Lenten sermon was preached in 1704 at the Court of Louis XIV, an aging monarch surrounded by young and less young debauched or devout nobles. The debauchery there was no less absolute than the monarch. Without that constituting a sociology of the text in the sense that I intend, one could pick up in Massillon's homily all the traces of this immediate connection with a select public of noble heads. We note, then, that the speaker refers preferentially to the kings, to the sons or wives of kings, that he makes constant allusion to the ancestors and the lineage of his hearers, to their name, to their rank, to the eminence of their lot and their fortune, to their dignity, to their glory, to the service of the state and the fatherland, to the embellishment of history, etc. One will find in the volume by B. Groethuysen, *Les origines de l'esprit bourgeois en France*,[6] all the profit that one can draw from this type of analysis of the texts. We know that Massillon addressed himself to a small elite group of the Court, we know, but in that which concerns the interpretation of the text, the establishment of this fact leaves us pretty much deprived of ammunition.

In order that the diverse picture painted by Massillon may recover a little coherence, it is helpful to lean on this vice of which he speaks all the time without naming it. If he names it only in images, in examples and through its manifestations, it is definitely so as not to use the language of the pulpit, of the homily, but of metaphysics. In the pulpit, Massillon could not undertake the explanations which I will try now to develop. They are implicit in his text, they alone permit us to understand the reduction of a multiplicity of actions to the metaphysical unicity of this vice. This unnameable, this unspoken, vice is *concupiscence*, desire badly directed.

In making this nomination, we pass *ipso facto* from the homily of Massillon to the metaphysics of Malebranche. What follows in no wise pretends to be a complete picture of the philosophy of the great Cartesian. At best, we may recall some essential points for our demonstration.

For Malebranche, the world created by God is a totally mechanized system, ordered, immutable and directed toward the greatest glory of the creator. There derives from this, among other things:

1. Order says that a spirit is superior to a body; it wills that in the creature the spirit should have dominion over the body.

2. Adam, master of his body, was master of his *senses*; his imagination and his passions dwelt in a respectful silence and did not trouble his *thoughts*. All was according to order.

3. *The sin of Adam.* It is natural to love pleasure, that was not forbidden. But, since Adam did not have an infinite capacity of spirit, his pleasure diminished the clear vision of his reason and made him *momentarily* forget that God was his good:

> The first man, having little by little ceased to take part in or to refill the capacity of his spirit by the lively feeling of a presumptuous joy or perhaps by some love or some sensible pleasure, the presence of God and the thought of his duty were effaced from his spirit.[7]

Sin was then a "voluntary distraction" which brought concupiscence into the world:

> Men were at first dissolute only by weakness; they grew dissolute by reflection and by principle; the pleasures which are purchased by remorse cost too much; one would like to enjoy his offenses peacefully (p. 207).

Since the sovereignty of Adam over his body was not founded on *natural law* but on the *immutable order of justice*, it was bound to *reverence for order*. Now, as it has been said, order wills that the body be submitted to the spirit. The disorder which ensues otherwise is not so much a disorder of the senses as of the will:

> ...our senses then are not as corrupt as we imagine; but it is the very core of our being, it is our liberty which is corrupted. It is not our senses which deceive us, but it is our will which deceives us by its hasty judgments.[8]

By this brief detour into the metaphysics of Malebranche, we know what the vice is, and why it is the one at the center of all the reasoning of Massillon. The soul-body relationship is the key to the theory of grace, this is what Malebranche is content to make the structural efficacy of a system perfectly conceived for the glory of its author.

Let us now return to Massillon's text, page 200:

> In the first place, it is not vice which alienates the sinner from God; secondly, it is not vice which, after having alienated him from God, leaves him less resources to return to him; thirdly, it is not vice which renders the sinner more insufferable to himself (p. 200).

Let us rapidly examine these statements in the form of theorems:

I. It has already been seen how the false appeal of the senses can make men forget God.

II. If this vice does not permit any recourse, it is because it is written into the very matter of the brain. This carries hereditarily the traces of the sin of Adam:

> Concupiscence resides principally in the traces of the brain, which incline the soul to the love of sensible things.[9]

III. The forgetting of God, that is to say of order (let us recall that the Fall is defined by Malebranche as the disregard of order), can only be induced by *disorders*, themselves contrary to the nature of the creature and consequently unsupportable by definition.

IV. The corollary: "Finally, it is not that which renders him more despicable in the eyes of other men", is drawn from the preceding proposition.

The first part of the sermon thus develops the implications of these theorems. I only want to insist, in this regard, on some scattered points. We read, p. 206:

> Recall the first feelings of modesty and of virtue with which you were born [unbelieving person]...

Massillon presupposes in each of his hearers an earlier state of innocence, in the light of which alone the stigmatization of concupiscence and its ravages can take any meaning. Further on, he insists in these terms:

> Not alone the benefits of grace are dissipated, but more the benefits of nature. You have received in birth a soul so chaste, a taste so tender and so discreet about modesty, a delicacy so noble concerning glory: heaven had taken pleasure, it seems, in forming you for virtue, and in placing in you a thousand resources and a thousand bonds to attach you to duty: and these happy barriers which nature herself had opposed to your dissoluteness, an unjust passion has surmounted them (p. 208).

The accent put by Massillon on original goodness permits him not only all sorts of oratorical effects but, on a more interesting level, serves him as a canvas for a large fresco articulated entirely on the binary opposition of rest-unrest:

> *The blessings of nature.* You were born gentle, equable, and accessible: you have had for your share a simple and sincere heart; a *candor of soul*, a *serenity* of temper which opened a thousand favorable dispositions to Christian *sincerity*, and to the *peace* of a pure conscience: and since this fatal passion has corrupted your heart, since this impure *fire* has entered into your soul,

> one no longer recognizes you: you are similar, says Saint Jude, to a sea *always tossed* by the most *violent* waves; one finds you *gloomy, odd, restless, dissembling*; this *serenity* which comes from *innocence*, is extinguished; this *equanimity*, which had its source in the *calm of passions*, is now only an inexhaustible fund of *moods* and *caprices*; this *candor*, which showed your soul fully whole, now lets you see only *black* and *secret thoughts* (pp. 208-209).[10]

The classic arsenal of antitheses functions here fully, from the simple register where "candor" and "black thoughts" are set opposite, to the subtle cross-fire of *impure fire* which enters into the soul and extinguishes its innocence whilst the sea tossed by violent waves is set opposite the equanimity of soul which slakes its thirst at the calm source of the absence of passions! Here is a double play of the antithesis of water and fire where the thematic symbolism is rejected in order finally to come out at the single significant opposition, that of calm and of agitation.

Thus far, these remarks have led us to the end of the first part of Massillon's sermon. The demonstration of the catastrophic effects of vice is ended; it remains for the preacher to show how this terrifying picture can constitute a consoling word.

Now the second part, which will be the last, offers us a very extraordinary demonstration, compared to the usual art of the pulpit. What first strikes us is the bipartition of the sermon. The sermon of Bourdaloue on the same subject, entitled *Le Retour de l'enfant prodigue*, gives us a model of tripartite structure: 1. Distress; 2. Plan; 3. Trust. Sin, through conversion and victory over itself, leads to salvation.

The effacing of the intermediate phase, of the mediation of penitence, sends us back once more to Malebranche's anthropology. When Massillon writes "his repentance makes reparation for all the consequences of his disorders" (p. 221), we rediscover in reality the two central ideas: disorder as a temporary disease of order, and the repair of the ordinary mechanism by the intervention of the repentance borne by Jesus Christ, the Restorer. Thus the life of mankind is understood as equilibrium (or eventually disequilibrium), a quantative notion par excellence, thoroughly in accord with the physiological cosmology of Malebranche which is affirmed by Massillon from the introduction of this sermon:

> ...the same disorders which have angered God against us, excite his clemency and his pity... (p. 198).

or elsewhere:

> The excess of passion in the wanderings of the prodigal son. The excess of the mercy of God in the bearing of the father of the family (p. 199).

and in another fashion:

> Grace abounds where sin had abounded (p. 228).

All of these formulas by Massillon manifest the primordial concern for equilibrium which leads the preacher to repeat "excess/excess", "abounds/abounded". In order for the system to regain its equilibrium, it is necessary that the scales of the balance be identically weighted. It is not until the "irritated" and the "excite" of the first citation that we are sent back to such notions as stimulus/reflex, although in the genre of the physiologism that we noted above.

Fitting the economy of the mediating term, of the moral conversion which separates the "physiological" from the "mental", Malebranche comes back to a binary stance, the same as Massillon has put in practice in so extraordinary a manner in his sermon, a stance where order can, but above all, must triumph, for it cannot escape from the natural law of order which it itself has established. This leads Massillon to this natural philosophy of equilibrium which he expresses (p. 228):

> The greatest sinners are the most worth of his pity and his mercy (...).

Thus the binary structure of the whole of the preaching reflects a necessity and a fundamental theology and metaphysics. One will not be astonished, then, to see it reappear at every moment in the development of the sermon. Everything plays on the category of yes/no, of here/yonder:

> The first mark of his deplorable passion had been to put an abyss between him and grace (...) (p. 222).

This abyss is the null point of the binary stance, that on which one does not know how to say anything, the no bill. At the two extremes of this missing continuum appear, then, the only strong tenses of the demonstration: *peregre*, he had departed into a foreign country; *profectus est*, he is lost towards himself, he is alienated, and from the other side, radically other, he is *in himself, reversus est*,[11] he has recovered his proper place, he has returned to himself, he is himself. But between these two abysses there is no place for a middle term which would be the ascesis of a repentance. In a philosophy of equilibrium there is, or there is not, equilibrium, order.

This logical exigency, which imposed itself on Malebranche when he constructed his system, imposes itself no less strongly on Massillon when he presented the efficacy of grace in the sinner. Also the preacher dwelt with insistence on the *instantaneousness* of grace:

> Now, the first *act*...alienated...(p. 222),

and further on:

> The charm which fascinates fell *all at once* (*ibid.*).

In a like movement, it is the whole lexicon which becomes in its turn the interpreter of the inversion:

> it is then that all that *change of name* in his eyes...(*ibid.*), passion becomes steadfastness, depravity of heart becomes goodness of heart, debasement becomes nobleness.

Then the basic image of returning appears, that of the Adamic priority, of the state of innocence which represents the natural equilibrium of the powers of the spirit and of the body.

After the spatial duality, which serves simply to lead into the metaphor of returning (*in se autem reversus*), appears the temporal duality, the before/after which engenders the same lexical effect and induces the same idea of immediacy:

> ...touch and already enlighten...(p. 223).

Massillon insists strongly on simultaneity. As soon as it is touched, it is enlightened. This trait takes on all the more importance when one emphasizes that it forms the economy of the *bearing* of the father. To reenter into his rights, the son of the parable must pass through a sort of ceremony of reestablishment. This turn of events, this mediation is impossible in the perspective of Massillon on account of the physiological law of error, sin, and vice. This last is a physical trace and, consequently, is or is not. Before sin there are no traces of it; after grace there are none either. Where the doctor has moved through the physiological functions according to order, there is nothing to add.

If one reflects on the climate of preaching in this second half of the 17th century, one could not insist too much on the rupture which is here marked by this total absence of concern on the part of Massillon to engage the faithful in a process of pious imitation. The instantaneousness of the change repudiates every mediating act:

> Thus, my brothers, our happy penitent chooses *instantly* to enter into the society of the just... (p. 225).
> He does not cling to simple desires of imitation...(*ibid.*).
> Our changed prodigal does not henceforth delay...(*ibid.*).

Massillon leaves to his hearer no empty hope of one day following the holy rules of virtue. It is not a question of reaching heaven by sublime virtues. From this instant we are not very far away, with Massillon, from Fenelon's quietist attitude. Conversion is not a path, but an instant,[12] a voluntary decision which does not have to be disturbed about knowing what the response of God will be:

> The certainty of pardon? ah! I have a tender and merciful father; he only *asks* the return of his child (...) (p. 226).

God only *asks* the return of the sinner, all the more certainly as he has let sin into the world partly to cause Christ to appear for his greatest glory:

> Man, Ariste, is a sinner; he is not at all what God has made him. God has permitted his work to be corrupted. Reconcile that with his wisdom and his power; deliver yourself alone from this evil action without the help of the God-Man, without permitting a Mediator, without imagining that God has had the Incarnation of his son principally in view. I challenge

> you to do it with all the principles of the best philosophy.[13]

In a certain manner, Malebranche hints, God loves sin as an occasion for manifesting his greatness. He makes himself greater by his opposite, and the greater the evil which he combats, or reclaims, or puts in order is great, the greater is the glory which he takes from it.

Massillon, moreover, is very clear on this point:

> ...without doubt He [God] has only permitted you to fall into this whirlpool, and to lack nothing of misfortune, in order the more to show forth in you the riches and the power of his grace (p. 228).

This hydraulic borders on the ridiculous, if one does not know what to relate it to when Massillon adds:

> Indeed it is not greater when he withdraws Jonah from the bottom of the deep then when he only holds Peter up who alone began to sink on the waters (pp. 228-229).

The principle of equilibrium, guaranteed by the natural laws of cosmic and divine order, demand *proportionality*, and as the greater glory of God is always the final cause of creation, the greatest evil is necessarily the best occasional cause. Thus:

> If your sins have mounted to the highest point, ah! that is perhaps the moment of [the releasing] of his grace (...) (p. 229).[14]

We find here again the function of "the occasion" mentioned by Massillon in the first paragraph; the parable is consoling because it describes the fullness of the decadence of the prodigal, and, *ipso facto*, this being the occasion of the intervention of grace, it describes the grandeur and the plenitude of the latter. This kindness of God in effecting his own glory through the adventure of the world, so striking in the thought of Malebranche, so evidently illustrated in this text, does not, nevertheless, omit posing a problem, which is felt by Massillon. The problem is not expressed, just suggested. The preacher, astonished and intrigued at the same time, cries:

> O paternal clemency! O inexhaustible source of goodness! O mercy of my God! how do you then regain the salvation of the creature? (p. 232).

Less a metaphysician than Malebranche, Massillon raises the question with himself: what, then, is this hidden interest of God? For Malebranche, the interest is systematic. It is necessary that the ultimate goal of God be his own glory for the system to hold together. As soon as one forgets this logical necessity, there is a question, the beginning of a scandal.

We may here pass directly to the last sentence of the sermon:

> ...in order to return from their strayed ways, they find you near to receive them into the bosom of your glory and your immortality (p. 237).

Glory and immortality indeed form the center of the divinity of God, in opposition, for example, to love, or mercy: it is from this core that the fact that God is *ready* to receive the sinner is to be understood.

Here we are at the end of this second and last part of Massillon's sermon, who we have seen, working from the structure of the homily and the principal themes on which it is articulated, is a great connoisseur and a profound adept of Malebranche. I would add, for the sake of probability, that it is well established that the two men regularly spent long days together in discussion, at the home of the Marquis de l'Hopital at the chateau of Saint-Mesmes.[15]

It is fitting now to inquire about Malebranche himself, dean, although rather willingly unawares, of Cartesianism.

An Oratorian, Malebranche appeared to sum up the currents which agitated that congregation. Now accused of Jansenism, then of Molinism, he had to defend himself on all the important ideological fronts of the epoch. What is problematic, then, is the specific coherence which Malebranche gave to ideological elements which we are accustomed to see represented in diverse philosophical syntheses. The question to pose is the following: to what unexpressed, implicit question does this specific coherence bring forward a response?

When Descartes died in 1650, his system, which revolutionized philosophy as much as the sciences, left obviously a certain number of difficulties or contradictions. There is one, notably, to which the philosophers do not cease to return: that of the relationships between the absolute substance and the finite world, a point particularly acute for every theory of knowledge, both physical and moral. No less important is the other problem, which was going to call forth some notable developments, that of the relationships of the soul and the body, considered as substances which are mutually exclusive and yet must be in reciprocal action. Such is the philosophical field in which Malebranche did his work. He likewise would take up again the problems linked to the "solution" brought to these questions by Descartes. To say it in one word, the coherent response which Malebranche brought to these two questions was occasionalism, a philosophy strongly oriented towards a mysticism having a tendency to condense all reality and all causality in absolute substance.

To define quickly the doctrine of occasional causes, or the occasionalism of Malebranche, I will content myself to restate the exposition given in the Lalande dictionary:

> Malebranche designated by this word the relation which exists, according to him, between the events of the world (especially between the modifications of the soul and those of the body, which are ordinarily considered as directly dependent on one another). By reason of the independence of the moments of time, and of the principle of continuing creation..., there is no change which has the will of God as its direct and effective cause.[16]

Here a remark arises which is no longer systematic but historic. Occasionalism appears as a "solution" in numerous philosophers, and not only to Malebranche. One could in this connection mention Louis de la Forge, a French physician, with his *Tractatus de mente humana* (*Traité de l'esprit de l'homme, de ses facultés et de ses fonctions et de son union avec le corps, composé par M. de la Forge selon les sentiments de M. Descartes*) (1666), which proposes that since the single driving force is God, all contact and all movement of bodies and of souls is done, taking into account the necessary laws, by his unique causality.[17] The case of Géraud de Cordemoy is even more interesting. Councillor to the king and reader to the Grand Dauphin, he published, likewise in 1666, *Dix discours sur la distinction et l'union du corps et de l'âme*. In this work he reveals to us that his ideas have been discussed for some years and that they had been the occasion of friendly debates among his acquaintances. As E. Bréhier remarks in his *Histoire de la philosophie*:

> One sees at what point that which was later called occasionalism was in the air and attracted most of the Cartesians.[18]

Finally, it is necessary to cite *l'Ethique* (1665) of Arnold Geulinx--and the posthumous appearance of his *Metaphysica vera* and *Metaphysica ad mentem peripateticam* (1691-1698)--in which the thesis developed later by Malebranche is already present in full clarity.

The omnipresence of the occasionalist "solution" makes us attentive not only to the fact that numerous philosophers have had recourse to it, but that this recourse only appeared as pertinent between 1660 and 1700.

However, before studying this brief historical period, it is fitting again to approach an idea intimately linked to occasionalism and omnipresent in the preaching of Massillon: *rest*. This notion is brought together with that of *renunciation* (p. 197), which expresses the resolution of the misfortunes engendered by disorders and irregularities. Renunciation is the rule of the spirit over the passions.

The "reversal" of the attitude of the sinner characterized by *in se autem reversus*, by this reentry into himself in the natural perfection of the creature, is bound to the silence of the passions. We did not complete citing the words which Massillon found to describe the agitation of the life of the sinner:

> troubles and inquietude, his life, always agitated and restless (p. 223),

etc. Now, as Malebranche put it in a text which illuminates our subject very well:

> What means of reentering into oneself when they [the senses] call us and hold us outwardly, and can one understand the responses of inner truth during the noise and tumult which they excite.[19]

The discovery of this "inner truth" is, then, bound to the repose of the passions. Now this repose of the *senses*, which should permit a just equilibrium in the relations of the soul and the body, cannot be practiced in the "world".

We know that the theme of rest is deeply anchored in the literature of the end of the 17th century, and notably in the masterpiece of Madame de La Fayette, *La Princesse de Clèves*, which concludes precisely with a retreat from the world. This does not have the marks of a Jansenist retreat,[20] although Madame de La Fayette had frequented the circles of the *Amis de Port-Royal*, but rather draws near to a well tempered *ataraxia*, where the world is not absolutely evil--Malebranche is very clear on this--but an impediment to the happiness which springs from rest, because it assures the harmony of the soul and the body.

I read from *La Princesse de Clèves*. She is speaking to her husband:

> The tumult of the heart is so great, and there are always so many great people with you that it is impossible for the body and the spirit not to get tired, and one cannot find rest.

And Massillon, in a sermon during the same Lenten period which occupies us:

> Yes, it is to the upright man that the worldly-minded go to be consoled every day from the treachery of the world and the caprices of fortune; it is there that they go to refresh themselves from the ennui of pleasures, from the constraint of thraldom and of manners, from the unrest of expectations and of schemes; it is there that they go to breathe the air of candor, of good faith, of truth which they cannot find in the world: it is in their bosom that they go to pour out the most secret emotions of their heart, the interests of their fortune, the hidden measures of their schemes, the mysteries of their hopes; and they confess after that that men are very senseless to be so restless, and that the world is a very small thing; it is there that they do not fear at all, as one always fears elsewhere, to confide in an enemy, a rival, a traitor; it is there that their heart is poured out, that it *rests*, that it spares itself the fatigue of wariness and mistrust, and has the pleasure of laying itself bare without fear.[21]

Rest appears, then, as the *concrete solution* to the problems of the relationships of the soul and the body.

But it is necessary to go further. The end of the 17th century had been agitated, if I dare say so, by the quarrel over *quietism*. I will not repeat its content, which is well known. I simply point out that quietistic mysticism is in germ completely integral to the system of Malebranche, and that Massillon, for his part, readily allowed it to stand there:

> Love only him who can give all that one desires and whose love alone creates the true happiness of those who love him.[22]

In his *Considérations sur la Doctrine d'un Esprit universel unique* (1702), Leibniz notes in addition the kinship of Spinozism and quietism:

> Spinoza, who admitted only a single substance, did not remove himself much from the doctrine of the unique universal Spirit, and even from the new Cartesians [i.e. Malebranche] who pretend that God alone operates the establishment almost without thinking about it.[23]

We are not far from the "holy rest" of Miguel Molinos, condemned by Rome in 1687:

> It is necessary that man annihilate his powers. To wish to do an action, even good, is to offend God who wills to be the sole agent.

The condemnation was directed toward the latent "immoralism" which was echoed in this refusal of the practice of virtues which we have seen on the part of Malebranche and Massillon. Nearer to the doctrine of *pure love* of Fenelon than to the excesses of Madame Guyon, Massillon could subscribe to this affirmation of the Bishop of Cambrai, according to which God

> is himself his unique and essential end in everything,[24]

which is pure Malebranche.

These too rapid reflections on rest have a double object: on the one hand they throw a bridge between occasionalism as a doctrine necessary to the systematic quality of the philosophy of Malebranche, and quietism where, more prosaically, rest, as the concrete demeanor of individuals and as an essential category, places the absolute ascendency of politics and of theology in relationship to private ethics.[25] In addition to this, the fact that the philosophical problem had been felt with sufficient strength to produce specific attitudes on the level of living only underlines the importance which this unuttered question should have; which will permit us, once it is expressed, to understand the place of occasionalism at the end of the 17th century.

Consequently: why did occasionalism as a theory of the relationship of finite substances to the absolute substance, and rest as a practice of this relationship, appear in France between 1660 and 1700? To reply to this question, it is well to invert it: to what question posed between 1660 and 1700 are occasionalism and rest a response? Whence the inquiry: what happened between these dates which posed a new problem?

Here again, unhappily, I am obliged to procede in an extremely schematic manner. We have seen that occasionalism aimed to bring forward a new response to the problem of the relationships between finite substance (the individual) and the absolute substance, God, universal or sovereign. Thus the theological question and the metaphysical question are closely bound to the political question. The state, insomuch as it was absolute substance, maintained relations with parties, and individuals, and under what mode? If, under philosophical and theological aspects, the question had been very largely expounded by Malebranche, by contrast the political aspect remained in the shadows; or, from the sociological, philosophical, or theological point of view debate had no reason for being in itself, but presented itself as the echo of a political preoccupation which I now wish to develop a little.

It is well-known that the 17th century saw taking place, through a spasmodic but constant process, the concentration and consolidation of the power of the State in the person of the king of France. We may very schematically summarize this evolution in three stages:

Henry IV, who died in 1610, and whose heritage was discussed by the States General in 1614, when the nobles demanded the abolition of the annual tax paid to the king by the holders of office, assured the right of taxes and raised up some lawyers;

Louis XIII. From 1624, Richelieu was chief of the Council. He crushed the great and the attempts to return to feudalism (The Day of Fools--Saint-Mars--Special Commissions). He succeeded in dispossessing Parliament of the right of looking into the affairs of the State. When Richelieu died in 1642, he bequeathed a strong government;

Louis XIV. Born in 1638, the Regency of Ann of Austria --Mazarin. The feudal danger had not disappeared: in the Cabal of Importants, Parliament redemanded power in the affairs of the State; the arrest of Broussell, a member of Parliament of the Fronde party--the siege of Paris, the Peace of Rueil in 1649; Fronde of Princes (Conde), defeat. These jolts precede the great period of the personal reign of Louis XIV (1654) and of his economico-politics: Colbertism.

Colbertism

I must here again make a brief informative digression on mercantilism as an economic and social theory. I borrow from the great lines of the classic book of Elie F. Heckscher, *Mercantilism*.[26] For him, mercantilism is at one and the same time:

a) a system of unification, in particular of a territory, which involves freedom of commerce;

b) a system of power, in particular of the State in its relations with the Princes (abolition of the privileges of remonstrance by Parliaments) and with regard to Rome (Gallican politics);

c) a political system, which operated notably on demography to supply the needs of a large army.

Without entering into detail about the extremely numerous measures which spring from these principles, let us remember:

1. The State, the legal representation of the nation, knows no master and, as we are dealing with royalty (which is not a necessary condition of Colbertism), State and sovereign are one: "I am the State."

2. Royal absolutism, which built the omnipotence of the State, profited in addition to this from the ideological concurrence of circumstances. Thus the king would be king by the grace of God, a prerogative which nourished a Gallicanism always in battle with the Pope and Jesuit ultramontanism. The worship which Louis XIV organized around his own person is well known, and it is enough to recall that at the chapel in Versailles the assembly turned their back to the altar during the Mass, in order to look at the king. We may thus recall that the Grande Mademoiselle, addressing herself to Bussy-Rabutin, wrote of the king: "He is as God; it is

necessary to await his will with submission and wholly to hope in his justice and his kindness...."

3. The sovereign is superior to the laws since he is the law; I am the law, he had said, giving himself the authority of the practice which he propagated with his privy-seal. Thus, through the person of the king, the State itself became an end in itself, even as it is with God in the system of Malebranche:

> God acts only for his own glory, only for the love which he bears for himself....[27]

4. Finally, mercantilism and Colbertism, in their specific application in the century of Louis XIV, desired to be rational. The economic order is a natural order, to know whose laws suffices to act in the best interests of the State and of individuals. This rationalization of power Massillon held as one of the essential exigencies of a good government when, in the *Mémoires de la minorité de Louis XV*, he showed how the monarch ought to be supported by the knowledge of his ministers without, however, letting himself be governed by them. And in order not to place on trial the high hand which the monarch should keep over the affairs of the country, Massillon underlines at what point Louis XIV had, with reason, always expressly chosen as ministers individuals without any illustriousness, who offered the double advantage of having no other concern than to please[28] their sovereign, and having in return no appeal to public opinion if the bad services which they rendered directed that they be replaced.

It is not questionable that Massillon, favorable later to the experiment of Jack Law, with whom he was not far from sharing the idea that a transaction which ruined a large number of individuals was not prejudicial to the State, saw with an approving eye the disappearance of the Princes from the political scene, to the advantage of capable ministers, permitting the formation of what he called "an economical government established in finances".[29]

The period which began under Louis XIV after the defeat of the Fronde party seemed to take its essential characteristics from a recently ended contest for power between the king of France and the feudal Princes on the one hand--a contest which was certainly not completed in the minds of these princes--and on the other hand, from the very marked trend toward the establishment of a social and political policy centered in the State, through the person of the king.

There are, then, two elements to be considered here, although the second alone, under the name of absolutism, appears to define this period. In that which concerns our purpose, the first--which represents the quasi-definitive rupture of the feudal system of social and political relationships--created a void which the second--the specific solution brought forward by the tandem of Louis XIV-Colbert--attempted to fill. The crushing of the Fronde party, the always greater humiliation of the Parliament, the massive entry of the bourgeois into the administration of the State, was all a very brutal transformation of the image of the world, in so far as it rested on the relationship of finite substances (the citizens) to absolute substance (the sovereign, the State).

While the feudal epoch preserved a series of mediations, both political and religious, between the two, absolutism, like mysticism, occasionalism and in a general manner all the currents in which individualism was fermenting, abolished intermediaries and hierarchical mediations, leaving only abstract relationships, the ancestors of universal suffrage. On the mediations assumed by the feudal system, I refer you to the analysis of the vassalage bond by Marc Bloch.[30] But what concerns us here is the effect on the consciences, the minds, etc., of the downfall of the mediating system. We may here borrow the terms of Foucault's analysis, with the restriction that the level to which he limits himself, that of *epistemology*, disregards its proper relation to the transformation of society which I wish to point out. Michel Foucault writes:

> First, the substitution of analysis for the *analogical hierarchy*: in the 16th century, they granted from the start the universal system of correspondences..., henceforth all resemblance will be submitted to the test of comparison, that is to say that it will be admitted only, when once found, by the measure, the *common unity*, or more radically by the *order*, the identity and the series of differences.[31]

In the orbit of religion, one can find this analogical hierarchization already surpassed in the ultramontane struggle. The *Hexaples* or the *Six colonnes sur la Constitution Unigenitus* (1721) speak thus of the simple and good Catholic, opposed to "strong" and wicked believers:

> He is united to his pastor, his pastor to the bishop, and by his pastor and his bishop, he is united to all Catholics dispersed throughout the provinces and kingdoms, to the ends of the earth.[32]

Such was the traditional image of this joining of the finite substance (the Christian) to the infinite substance ("to the ends of the earth"). As has been repeated a hundred times, the structure of it is homologous to that of feudalism.

True to life, the hierarchical arrangement by stages like stair landings, then, permitted the construction of a system of representation and an analogical theory of the sign ever since the Middle Ages. In return, and I refer here again to Foucault's book, beginning with the 17th century, and particularly with capitalism:

> ...the activity of the mind no longer consisted in *comparing* things among themselves, by going in quest of everything which could reveal a kinship, an attraction, or a nature secretly shared among them, but on the contrary in *perceiving*: that is to say, in establishing identities [and differences].[33]

It is a question, then, of understanding the transition from "comparing" to "discerning" at the same time as the addition to this "discerning" of a totalizing factor assuring the vicariousness of the hierarchical homogeneity. Do not forget, the true socio-political finality of the movement we are observing will be the Republic of 1789, with universal suffrage as mediation, assuming the individual-State relation.

But between 1660 and 1700 we are not yet there. Certainly the Colbertian centralism, which found its logical achievement in the Jacobinism of 1789, provoked a radical rupture in the systems of power. It will again be necessary, meanwhile, that the royalty, in ruining the feudal society, itself prepare the ways of democracy, and singularly by opening the doors of power to the *bourgeoisie*. In this interregnum, while the knowledge of it is still undecided, the occasionalist theories present all the necessary elements to assume philosophically the order of the world, during the time of transition. The passing character of the social structure with which they are in accord, absolutism, explains their own rapid obsolescence.

Royal absolutism is a transient solution to the problem of the State. But the incision which it made in the system of representation wrought a crisis which called forth a theory, a new metaphysics, not yet that of liberalism, but one which could no longer belong to the orthodoxy of the world of Catholicism. Occasionalism restored reason to this rupture by organizing a new rationality, that of order, a system of general dependence where the absolute position of God and/or the monarch are homologous.

Whether one examines the practical politics of Louis XIV, the historical reflection which Massillon made to support him, or again the "physiologist" theory of the universe of Malebranche, one perceives in all these domains that Cartesianism has here, in a certain manner, regressed to Aristotle,[34] retaking from him his notion of the whole, where the parts are rationally conceived as the medium of the finality of the whole, in so far as the whole is, then, as a static structure, the product of the composition of these parts.[35] In a physiology constructed on the technological mode, as in the politics and the theology which we have examined, the finite substance--organ, citizen, or believer--is nothing in regard to the absolute substance--body, monarch, God--from whom everything emanates for His own greater glory. It will be necessary to wait for 1789 and Claude Bernard in the domain of biology, passing from the technological model to an economic and political model, for the conception which was formed of the relations of the part to the whole to be radically changed, to the point that this same Claude Bernard, in his *Leçons sur les phénomènes de la vie communs aux animaux et aux végétaux*, could write: "The organism, as society, is constructed in such fashion that the conditions of elementary or individual life should be respected."[36] The economic and political model, based on the notion of the individual, radically reversed the relation of the part to the whole, making this a relation of integration whose end is the part, this last henceforth no longer considered as a piece of the interior of a technological montage, but as an *individual* endowed with full autonomy.

To reach this result, the mediation of the philosophy of Leibniz will be necessary, as well as all the romantic developments to which it has given place; but it will be especially necessary that both the social and economic development themselves give a new credibility to this notion of the individual propounded for a long time, a credibility still very far from being acquired at the end of the 17th century. At that time, the rupture of the hierarchical universe wrought by monarchic absolutism did not lead to the affirmation of the autonomy of the parts, henceforth released from their bonds with the hierarchy, but on the contrary, was interpreted as the mark of the abasement of finite substance in relation to absolute substance, an abasement which gave place, historically, to two variant philosophies.[37] The one, Jansenism, declared a world evil where the lawyers had lost all power;[38] the other, a mystical tendency, decreeing that it was necessary, if not to flee the world, at least to turn aside from it in order to enjoy *rest*, a compensatory ideological theme which appeared at the moment when the nobles were replaced in the offices by the *bourgeoisie*. There is henceforth vested in this nobility only a role of maintaining the dignity of their station, a figurative role which opens the way for it to a new idea of life which places rest at its center, as a replacement for the commotion of offices. This re-evaluation, an ideological justification which responds to the political demands of the peculiar structure of absolute monarchy, induced Massillon frequently to draw his inspiration from the work of Horace. Thus, in one of his celebrated passages on "The vanity of human enterprises", he has this development:

> but all that is a secret worm which devours you without ceasing, and poisons all this empty bliss which deceives the spectators, while it cannot make you happy....[39]

It is necessary to follow here all the unfolding of the reasoning. The point of departure is the fact that the activity of the nobles is now only a spectacle for the spectators, henceforth irremediably removed from any effect on the real world. Having on his part welcomed with satisfaction this transformation of the political function of the nobility, Massillon can only invite them to play their decorative role in the calm. And this is certainly not an accident, if the borrowings from the poet of the reign of Augustus furnishes any clues; thus this aphorism: "The superb palace hides cruel cares", which reflects the line of Horace: *Curas laqueata circum terta volantes* (the cares which hover around the gilded paneling).

To depoliticize the princes, to make them understand that there is for them only unhappiness by fancying that they can recover a lost power which the evolution of the State forbids returning to them, in brief, to furnish them with an ideology of replacement by showing them that, as for the prodigal son, there is for them abundance of goods in the house of the father on condition of submission to him, for henceforth thus the Order wills it, that is to say the State--such seem to be the grand axes of a preaching which leans permanently on a metaphysic of order, of profound accord with the universe and of submission to a quasi-transcendent sovereign.

ADVENTITIOUS REMARKS

Every totalizing demonstration, seen from the sociological reading, exposes itself, when it is reduced as here to some rapid sketches, to the criticism of superficiality. We counter this, not by the affirmation that we have exhausted the field which we proposed to examine--that would be laughable--but in arguing from the thesis according to which abstraction, and consequently another and more insidious form of superficiality, undermines every enterprise which, in order to be able to conform to the practices of demonstrative erudition, tries to be thrifty with the multiple landings and levels which we have only very imperfectly touched upon.

NOTES

1. I have decided against prefacing this lecture by a theoretical and methodological exposition on method. A few remarks will suffice, I think, to place this work in relation to what can be consulted elsewhere, calling to mind here for memory and preliminary bibliographical guidance: Lucien Goldmann, *Pour une sociologie du roman*, Paris, 1964; *Marxisme et sciences humaines*, Paris, 1970; Jacques Leenhardt, *Lecture politique du roman:* La Jalousie *d'alain Robbe-Grillet*, Paris, 1973; Georg Lukacs, *Theory of the Novel*, Cambridge, 1971.

2. See the article by Pierre Kuentz, "Le 'rhétorique' ou la mise à l'écart," *Communications*, No. 16, 1970, pp. 143-157.

3. The page references correspond to the J. B. Massillon edition, *OEuvres complètes*, III, Paris, 1822, pp. 196-237.

4. Malebranche, *Entretiens sur la métaphysique et la religion*, Paris, 1922, XII, p. 292.

5. *Ibid.*, IX, pp. 200-201. The italics is mine.

6. B. Groethuysen, *Les origines de l'esprit bourgeois en France, I, L'Eglise et la bourgeoisie*, Paris, 1927.

7. Cited from H. Gouhier, *La philosophie de Malebranche et son expérience religieuse*, Paris, 1946, p. 106. Cf. *Entretiens, op. cit.*, I, V, p. 38.

8. Malebranche, *op. cit.*, I, V, p. 40.

9. *Ibid.*, II, I, ch. VII, §5.

10. The italics is mine.

11. Massillon frequently takes up this type of reasoning. See, for example, the sermon on the Day of Pentecost, *Sur les caractères de l'Esprit de Jésus-Christ et de l'esprit du monds*, on I Cor. 2:12.

12. It is difficult to see what place purgatory would have in such a conception.

13. Malebranche, *Entretiens, op. cit.*, IX, p. 203.

14. I add "the unlatching" to underline the mechanical aspect of this theory.

15. Cf. Abbé L. Pauthe, *Massillon*, Les maîtres de la chaire en France, Paris, 1908, p. 239.

16. A. Lalande, art. "Occasionnelle (cause)," in *Vocabulaire technique et critique de la philosophie*, Paris, 1947[5], p. 694.

17. We know that Melbranche was familiar with the *Traité de l'Homme* of Descartes in a copy annotated by La Forge (cf. H.-J. Martin, *Livre, pouvoirs et société à Paris au XVIIe siecle (1598-1701)*, Geneva, 1969, p. 891.

18. E. Bréhier, *Histoire de la philosophie*, Paris, 1950, tome II, vol. I, p. 122.

19. Malebranche, *Entretiens, op. cit.*, IV, p. 93.

20. It is necessary here to insist strongly on the fact that Massillon and Malebranche here turned their backs resolutely on the Jansenist ideology in that this distinguishes mundane nonperformance from spiritual nonperformance, the fruit of the always infinite distance of the creature from his Creator, a distinction on which the tragic character of the Jansenist vision of the world is built. As Michel Clouscard remarks (*L'être et le code*, Paris, The Hague, 1972, p. 494), only the Jansenist position as a radical criticism denying order opens the way to the constitution, properly called, of subjectivity. With Malebranche, on the contrary, the synthesis was achieved always to the advantage of order.

21. Massillon, *Morceaux choisis*, a selection by H. Hignard, Paris, 1852, pp. 224-225.

22. *Paraphrase du Psaume IV,* in *op. cit.* in the preceding note, p. 230.

23. Leibniz, *Considérations sur la Doctrine d'un Esprit universel unique*, 1702, cited by L. Brunschvig, *Spinoza et ses contemporains*, Paris, 1923, p. 361.

24. Fénelon, *OEuvres spirituelles*, Paris, 1954, p. 238; cited by G. Gusdorf, *Dieu, la nature et l'homme au siècle des lumières*, Paris, 1972, p. 72.

25. Cf. M. Clouscard, *op. cit.*, p. 424ff.

26. E. F. Heckscher, *Mercantilism*, London, 1935, 2 volumes.

27. Malebranche, *Entretiens, op. cit.*, Paris, Lyon, 1792, IX, §7, p. 64.

28. Compliance, as a mode of behavior, effects precisely the synthesis of private and public life called for by the structure of power, when the ascendancy of the sovereign over the individual is acknowledged and all eventuality of rebellion removed.

29. Massillon, *Mémoires de la minorité de Louis XV*, Paris, Lyon, 1792, p. 64.

30. M. Bloch, *La société féodale*, Paris, 1968.

31. M. Foucault, *Les mots et les choses*, Paris, 1966, p. 69. The italics is mine.

32. *Les Hexaples*, an anonym by Boursier, Le Fevre, Fouillon, Quesnel d'Ettemare and Nivelle, from Barbier, IV, Amsterdam, 1721, p. 259.

33. M. Foucault, *op. cit.*, p. 69. The italics is mine.

34. We could equally, rather than pleading a regression (however it may be stripped of all value judgment), speak of a progressive opening toward the Voltairian philosophy and its great Architect.

35. Cf. G. Canguilhem, "Le tout et la partie dans la pensée biologique," in *Etudes d'histoire et de philosophie des sciences*, Paris, 1968, p. 323.

36. Cf. Bernard, *Leçons sur les phénomènes de la vie communs aux animaux et aux végétaux*, I, Paris, 1878, pp. 356-357; cited by G. Canguilhem in *op. cit.*, p. 330.

37. It is interesting to know that the work of Malebranche, *La Recherche de la Vérité*, had a very complicated and flashing entrance into the book market. On the one hand, the religious authorities, in the person of the censor Pirot, refused their approval for a license. The manuscript was then sent on to the Abbey of Aligre, the son of

the Keeper of the Seals. He forwarded it for information to the great historian Mezeray in order to assure himself that the work contained nothing contrary to the doctrine of the State (cf. H.-J. Martin, *op. cit.*, p. 879). After a favorable opinion from him, the book received its license for publication from the Keeper of the Seals.

Thus the opposition which was manifest in ecclesiastical opinion, always very haughty since it was a question of Descartes and his followers, is ultimately negligible, and had regard for the merits of the work and the conformity of its views on the State.

38. See with regard to this the study of Lucien Goldmann, *Hidden God*, London, 1964.

39. Massillon, *Paraphrase du Psaume IV*, in *op. cit.*, p. 230.

HERMENEUTICS AND TRUTH

by Philibert Secretan

Presented to Paul Ricoeur,
on the occasion of his 60th birthday

Every hermeneutics ought, at a given moment, to raise the question of truth. H.-G. Gadamer has given his philosophical law of hermeneutics by imposing on it the double task of examining itself on its method and its truth. Paul Ricoeur has echoed this double demand in writing: "In this way...we will resist the temptation to separate *truth*, characteristic of understanding, from the *method* put into operation by disciplines which have sprung from exegesis."[1] Expressions such as: *reappropriation of meaning, the hermeneutics of "I am"*, the themes of: *hermeneutics and existence, progressive hermeneutics and the effort to exist*, return definitively to the relation set forth by Jaspers between reason and existence. Hermeneutics is entered in the task of the illumination of existence [*Existenzer-hellung*], and from this fact likewise in a Treatise on Truth.

Understand in truth in order to exist in truth: such is the horizon and the embodiment of all interpretation which does not limit itself to taking account of the validity of its procedures. Methodical, analytical interpretation moves in a horizon of an "ideal" understanding which motivates and inspires the scientific work of interpretation. The hermeneutic maxim professes to be: interpret in order to understand. But is the truth proper to comprehension assured, or attested by the validity of the procedures of interpretation? Or is it the truth understood which, *a posteriori*, validates the methods of interpretation? Is this not the question in the signification relation--meaning: is it the truth which gives meaning to the methodical research of signification, or is this the regular, critical effort agreeable to the task of setting free the signification which will render the truth "perceptible"? What relation is established between the spirit of geometry: disengagement from signifying structures, and the spirit of understanding: sensibility to meaning?

The hermeneutic sphere, to be vital, postulates a transcendence of meaning to signification, and likewise the long way of passage through interpretation, opposed to the short way of a comprehensive ecstasy of meaning (Heidegger). Thus the transcendence of meaning does not separate itself from the signification: it requires on the contrary the work of the interpreter and of fact to validate it. In its method, interpretation is the "servant" of comprehension.[2]

But again, this transcendence in some way comes to dwell even in that which it interprets. The "text" is not the mediator between a transcendent meaning and a structured signification; it is the bearer of meaning even in its signification. This immanent transcendence takes account of the tension which confers on a "text" its value as symbol, or on an image its value as metaphor. The play of the metaphor, analyzable certainly in its linguistic structure, is in the last analysis the impact of the event of meaning on the signifying structure. The metaphorical image does not permit itself to be reduced to two univocal statements joined by an *as*; the force of the image is irreducible to the simple comparison; at best, comparison is the lowest degree of the metaphor.

The truth is the horizon, and the meaning is the center of the text.

Starting with that, it is the text which creates a problem: what text, what works, is it necessary to interpret? I call enigmatic a text, a story, which makes a sign to the interpreter, which alerts him. This enigmatic character is the sign by which I recognize that the message is ciphered. This mark of strangeness puts me on the alert; and my wonder puts me on the path of work and inquiry. And that will be to arrive at the center of the text, understanding the meaning of the "world" of which the text is the tissue--the texture--which will disclose the horizon, the "sky" of truth.

From enigma to unveiling, that is the hermeneutical path; it is the one already traveled by Oedipus, that the enigma of his birth led him to Colonus. This road is method --the rigorous approach of interpretation (*hodos*) and the way to meaning (*meta-hodos*). It proceeds by the discipline of reasons. It is this, I believe, that Paul Ricoeur calls the long way and makes necessary the traversing of this discipline of reasons which make up the "disciplines issuing from exegesis".

This relationship between enigma and unveiling requires to be made precise. Is it summed up in the relationship of the hidden to the revealed, of the initially hidden to the finally revealed? Why is the meaning, finally understood in truth, hidden under the features of the enigma? And is the enigma already the promise of a "manifestation" ["*phanie*"]?[3] In what is the manifestation ["*phanie*"] already implied in the enigma? With what dialectic have we here to do?

This relationship appears to me dialectic in that the enigma contains, as a lost dimension, the strength of the "manifestation" ["*phanie*"], and that the manifestation ["*phanie*"] surpasses, but conserves something of the enigma. Or again: the truth understood is still enigmatic, when the enigma is already revelatory. The enigma, we see, is not abolished by the "manifestation" ["*phanie*"], it finds itself on the contrary reinforced, justified. And it is this which the old term *mystery* expressed.

To express the mysterious truth is in another way to militate against the tradition of the *Aufklärung*, from which the Hegelian dialectic is tributary, which sees in Knowledge, in Reason, the victory of truth over mystery. The way from the unknown to the known is that of science, and as such it is incontestable. That which, in return, is contestable is the meta-epistemology which has engendered, in the name of science, the rationalism prescribing as the only truth that which knowledge extracts from mystery.

The enigma is not to be conquered; it is not a void to fill up, but a presence of meaning not unveiled. The "manifestation" ["*phanie*"] does not abolish, but on the contrary confirms and reinforces this presence yet veiled by absence; the moment of the enigma finds itself promoted to the rank of time as a symbol. Promotion and not abolition; but dialectic promotion in that which imposes the negative work of reduction.

This promotion, in fact, is inseparable from reduction, for all interpretation participates in the reduction of the unknown to the known, in the explanation of the unknown by the known, or resorts to assured methods where the enigmatic is assumed in an operative field already well explored. The conflict of interpretations can from that time be defined as the conflict between the explanatory reductions of the enigma and the production of the symbol.[4] Such is the work of hermeneutics. Every method of interpretation stakes its validity on the double work of removing what the enigma has of the hidden, and the penetration of what the symbol manifests.

The path is properly philosophical. It is described in a text which is neither symbol, nor allegory, but story--*mythos*--an appeal to the imagination by that which should prepare the way for the intelligence, and the discussion of the intelligible in the image. And this story is par excellence the *myth* of the truth. I wish to speak of the myth of the cave. The philosophical path is indeed the one which ascends from the cave toward the sun. In the cave, the enigma resides in the duplicity of a world of shadows which are at the same time the source of illusion, fatal charm, phantasmic obscurity, *and* the ultimate reflection of the light projected to the lower limits of the world. To reascend this path of light, is to go on to the light itself, to undergo the test of the manifestation ["*phanie*"]. But the sun is unbearable in human eyes; it is only enlightening in so far as it is a symbol, in so far as it is fire, at the same time a pattern of the enigmatic fire of the cave and the image of the light itself. Between these two extremes of the illusory and the unbearable, progress is possible. It destroys the shadows and sends back to the real. It is the moment of disillusionment, of painful passing from desire to the real, to the objectal and the objective; it is the way of science, of sobriety (*Ernüchterung*) and of mourning. But each reality won from illusion is *at the same time* a higher call, a progression toward this light in which the sober and naked real is also an intelligible and desirable form. Each time the real, in its truth and its blessing, is an image (*eidos*), and an image analogous to another infinite reality. The Idea, participating in this infinite, is however a finite form. Its law is not that of intermixture, but rather that of the center of a "sphere of meaning" of which the empirical world is an enigmatic reflection and of which the truth is the ultimate horizon.

This Platonic symbolism has been suffocated by an exhaustive understanding of the Idea as rational form, whether by an exclusively epistemological reading of Plato, or deformed by a gnosis which has not feared to substantify the Ideas. The deep meaning of *eidos* has been lost. A hermeneutical reflection can restore to us a Plato in whom the philosophical method cohere profoundly with the dialectic of the enigma and of the "manifestation" ["*phanie*"]. The Platonic *eidos*, intelligible form *and* sign of the infinite, is properly the enigma sublimated and the truth held within the limits of the intelligible or adjusted to the finite intelligence of man. In the symbol, the infinite neither affirms itself nor denies itself, but makes a sign.

The symbolic law of the Platonic idea is a solid anchorage point for a philosophical hermeneutic.

It is philosophical in its structure, but also philosophical in its situation and its struggle. Plato contended in reality against two adversaries: sophistic phenomenalism and Parmenidian dogmatism. Now, the history of philosophy, or philosophy in its historicity, continually goes back to this same battle. As an adventure in the truth, hermeneutics must retake this into its consideration, for this battle is also the one which continually reestablishes philosophy in its truth. Hermeneutics does this in the simultaneous refusal to permit Parmenidian ecstasy--and that is the short way of Heidegger--to obliterate comprehension, and to permit analysis--and this is the power of structuralism--to destroy interpretation. It does it in knowing well that the ultimate object is dogmatic, but that it is necessary to consent to the critical effort. This is the reply of Ricoeur to Heidegger, as it was of Kant to Wolf.[5] It does it in knowing well that the phenomenon of the text demands a rigorous analysis. But it must be repeated that there is no comprehension without interpretation, and that there is no interpretation without comprehension. To isolate one from the other is to condemn oneself to ecstatic silence or to the pattern of a methodical, though insignificant game, of the elements of language. What is at stake is the power of the word.

This statute of philosophy is human. Or more exactly, man has attempted to clarify by reference to two limits. Neither beast nor angel, body *and* spirit are the ontological formulas which correspond to this intermediate position. Kant gave it the critical formula: it is in posing the question of the validity of his knowledge, of his action, of his hope, that man recognizes his limits. Religion within the limits of simple reason desires to be a human religion.

But it is in posing the question of meaning that man is led *to* the limits, running there the risk of an evil infinite or a false infinite, or nurturing his wager on the infinite with intelligibility.[6] If a "dialectic" hermeneutic finds itself caught, according to this truth of the human dimension, *within* the limits of reason, it is also *to* the limits, dispossessed and challenged by the exploration of language in which man expresses the experience of fascination by evil, and the experience of the approach of the sacred or of listening in faith. It is to the limits that it will have to understand itself as a philosophy of the true imagination.

Hermeneutics, similar to Jaspers, attempts to name these limits, or the mysterious field whose limit marks the "symbolic partition". Perhaps it is indeed of the "cipher" that it is necessary to speak with Jaspers: to cipher from the enigma to the limit of non-meaning, to cipher from the manifestation ["*phanie*"] to the limit of the indescribable. To cipher from the horrible or from the splendid, but to cipher from a text, or from a work.

In this world, only the work can guarantee objectivity and legibility "to the limits". Also hermeneutics draws from the ethics of Aristotle, of Kant, of Hegel, the categories necessary to the elaboration of a theory of the work. Aesthetics, in fact, is the royal way by which we have access to the work so far as the texture of meaning is concerned on which the work of hermeneutics may be worthily carried on. But it is on condition of having a concept of the art which should bind it to the truth--and in this sense the *splendor veri* of Thomas Aquinas anticipates the Kantian expression: "the symbol presents to thought"--that we know that the work invokes a comprehension in truth; that it is the work which mediatizes the truth of the ideal horizon and the truth of comprehension.

If it is to the tenor and the bearing of a work, as a readable work, that interpretation should certify to itself its capacity for truth, it is a question of insuring that the abstract truth, the formal truth of the just measurement, of the balance of forms, engage itself in the concrete truth of the work--aesthetic or philosophical.[7] It is necessary that it undergo the test of the particular before pretending to be universal; it is necessary that the formal dimension become "virtue" in action, the deed of meaning in the work. This quasi-Hegelian movement should take cognizance of two critical moments: the moment of the falling of thought into speech, its reification in language which at once speaks and masks the truth *thought*; and the critical moment of restoration, of the resuscitation of the literal object as a work open to a reappropriation of meaning. Leaving the hands of the author, the thing written, subjected to the critics, enters into the world of the interpretable.

But to what universality can this interpretation pretend?

On the response to this question of the universal depends the response to the question of knowing what type of truth hermeneutics deals with.

Or, indeed, the "ideal" image of the critic will be that of the interpreter who, in his congeniality to the work, translates it into a universal language, whether integrating it into the total and universal discourse of Reason or the Spirit: he will then speak the truth in his conception. Or, indeed, universality resides in the network of communications which the work establishes, and in which it is communicated to an interpreting community.

To the speculative response of a philosophy of the Spirit laying a wager on the congeniality of a mind to the Spirit, a speculation which, finally, identifies Discourse and Truth, Universal and Absolute, we should prefer a conception of the universal compatible with the place assigned to the work in the limits of the speakerly ["*discible*"]: then a conception of the universal issuing in a reflection on communication and reciprocity; on that language which is the work, and on the work which is the speech [*parole*]; on the word which *communicates* what is incommensurable. Truth is not a substance but a relation; and a relation maintained or reaccomplishable in the temporal distance which can separate the world of the text and the world of the interpreters.

Also, it is necessary to say of a work that it is never isolable from the system of communications which give it its context, and that it is no longer only a moment of all that gives its meaning to it. It is *between* the two infinities of the atom and of the all that the work is a reality; and it is to the limits that it is a *sign*: its cleansing function renders it jointly answerable both to the tragedy of possible non-meaning and to the splendor of the meaning revealed.

A pretense of essential solitude is deficient in the truth of the communication of works in the system of their correspondences. This system of *relations*, conquerors of the single *difference*, can be understood as the extension of other works of inner correspondences which bind into a whole that which analysis can cut up into parts: scenes, chapters, sequences, figures, images, motifs, colors, and sonorities. This macrocosm of which each work is the microcosm is called style. But to arrive at the truth of a style, we suggest calling this structured and living whole a poem [*poïème*], and the hermeneutical correlative of the poem *poesy* [*poïèse*]. And just as it is necessary to describe the macrocosm of the work as a system of correspondences, it is necessary to see in poesy [*poïèse*] a community of interpretation in which the meaning of the poem [*poïème*] circulates. A constant interchange can then be made between an appropriation of meaning, a living rereading, and a structuration of the interpreting community. This phenomenon characterizes the social cohesion of peoples who live by the interpretation of their myths; it continues in civilizations of the Book or of the Idea. The work of Marx, considered from this point of view, "verifies" itself in so far as it continues to nurture, even in the plurality of its interpretations, the societies which proclaim themselves its interpreters.

This recourse to correlation is bound to the definition of the truth of a work; and of a truth to which it is necessary to discharge the obligation of being apodictic by primary evidence. At this price alone can truth be carried forward from the pole of *cogito* to that of the gift of meaning: it is in the reciprocal movement of a gift of meaning and a structuration by the taking back of meaning that a work is true, concretely true; and it is by starting from this concreteness of the living relation of a work and to a work, that a new apodictic must be recovered. The purely vital comprehension of a work still lacks the universality of truth. Without being apodictic--it should be reconsidered--the work could not yet be *understood*.

Do the truth of the situation of philosophy, and this truth of correlation of and to a work, respond to the expectation of the one who accepts as true only that which can be deduced from evidence, or the one who refers truth to a reality which it would be folly to deny? To put it otherwise, are these the truths of *reason*?

On this, I propose the following reflection:

The idea of truth, as deposited in a proposition deductible from an ontological or logical evidence, is in the last analysis bound to the Parmenidian formula: being is, nonbeing is not. And this formula is properly dogmatic. In it is enunciated a fundamental rule of reason. Reason discovers there its norm, but does not discover there on what it may stand. Reason finds there its rigorousness, but not the knowledge of its fecundity. The return to the real as the mark of truth is no longer adequate. Science there discovers its object, but not the anchorage of its method. Truth is only in the relation between this law and this richness. The medievals called this relation adequation. Now, if truth resides in adequation, one is correct in asking if the logical requirement and the ontological requirement which it unites are not transposable on the specific plane of the *poet-poem* [*poïêtico-poïêmatique*] correlation, where a community structures itself to the meaning which it appropriates. To speak of the reality of a community is to affirm that in it and by it living relationships are established in a real and lasting way. And to speak of an evidence which will give its truth to a work, to an interpeted *poem* [*poïème*], is to require of it that it obtain a sort of immediate and astonishing adhesion. Are these two demands for adhesion and for interpretive comprehension finally compatible?

Adequate means at the same time *ordained to* and *sufficient, ausgerichtet* and *ausreichend*. This sufficiency is opposed to the exhaustive, or more exactly marks the boundary between the plenary abundance which man does not know how to receive, and that which he is capable of receiving. To be *ordained to*...signifies an intention, a direction, but also the boundary between distance and identity. Also one could say that, ordained in an immediate adhesion to the meaning of that which it interprets, the real community will never exhaust the vivifying strength. Thus, in the strong analogy between the truth of knowing and the truth of comprehending, we see the essential of a structure of truth conserved. And thus one sees beyond a conception of truth which could only satisfy the seizure of everything. The truth of the discourse should here yield to the truth of the sign.

Or again: interpretation bears being burdened by the requirements of truth in so far as the work, the sign, has for its function the bringing to the encounter of an interpreting community the unity or the universality anticipated by multiple interpretations which run the risk of dividing it.

The idea of reason is inseparable from that of unity; its unifying function is called synthesis. Its own unity is therefore never the idea which it has of itself. Also it is necessary to call it pure reason, transcendental reason. And since the advent of rationalism, it is indeed this idea of Reason, or this ideal reason, which has been burdened with the task of unifying the human species, and of assuring the universality of the doings of man. The unity of truth is seen suspended in the unique Reason, but this unity was never only a formal unity.

The hermeneutical approach with its philosophical law radically reversed this position. A work of reason, hermeneutics must yet remain as a scheme of systematic unity: How to tie up again, asks Paul Ricoeur, a hermeneutics of desire (Freud), a hermeneutics of the spirit (Husserl) and a hermeneutics of the hope of faith in a single discourse? But is it indeed the discourse of universal Reason which, here, can rejoin these interpretations?

How does one proceed from regional hermeneutics to a general hermeneutics? To pose this question is to postulate the unity of Meaning and the analogy of multiple meanings. And if hermeneutics is inseparable from a reflective philosophy (the hermeneutics of *who am I?*), itself taken again into the scheme of a philosophy of *existence* and of an ethical vision of the world, is not hermeneutics also an occasion of a philosophy of *being*? A philosophy of being, the only alternative to a philosophy of reason when the question is raised: what is truth? For the two things are one: either truth is the operation of the reason, or truth signifies being offered to the inventiveness of the human intelligence.

But it is also a philosophy of being alone capable of supporting a convincing theory of analogy. Now how can one think on the multiple interpretations referring to a single Meaning, if not in the discipline of analogy? How can one hold the real unity of an understanding against the disaggregation of multiple exegeses?

When the gaze is set on the limits, the truth of understanding is no longer suspended in the Reason, the ideal form of all truths, the source of all apodictic, but in Meaning whose synthesizing power is recognizable in the creative power of the imagination: the detour around the true work is also a detour around the capacity of the imagination for truth, falling back to the occasion of the abuse of power which has carried reason to the summit of thought.

It is in the work that the concrete truth finds itself carried to the border of the imaginary; and it is the truth of the concrete imaginary which requires thought in its universality, that is to say *according to* the unity of Meaning.

What is "the reason for the analogies of structure and process" between an economics of desire, a phenomenology of spirit, hermeneutics of religious figures?, asks Paul Ricoeur at the end of *Conflict of Interpretations*.[8] It is an admirable question. But can it be a question only of the isomorphs of structure and of process? The ground, the *logos*, of these analogies is perhaps in the Meaning which gives itself up in multiple fashions. And when I continue to read the questioning of Paul Ricoeur, I am tempted to hazard an analectic version:[9]

> What that question demands of the philosopher is nothing else but this: to undertake again, with renewed energy, the task assumed in the last century by Hegel, of a dialectic philosophy which would take up the diversity of the schemes of experience and reality into a systematic unity.[10]

To restore this systematic unity coherent with the logos of the analogies of structures, is it not of a systematic analectic--and no longer a dialectic--of which it is necessary to dream? And is it not a *politics* of desire which it is necessary to disengage from a Freudian economics? Is it not the *inventions* of the spirit which it is necessary to disengage from a phenomenology of the intentions of the spirit? Is it not the *image* which "I am" which is restored to me in the "religious symbols"? Then, in an analectic hermeneutics, the great regions of the imagination-institution, of the imagination-invention and of the imagination anticipating itself on the same foundation on which it was founded could be brought into agreement: the image of God already restored to man and still dismissed by him.

Neither apodictic truth, nor dialectic truth, the truth of *hermeneia* should reintegrate the grand systematic of the *analogos*. The analysis of the symbol, of the metaphor, has already put us back on this way. And how can its philosophical law be given back to the analogy if not in binding the ancient object of a philosophy of being to a new object of a philosophy of the imagination. "That is the task. But who today could assume it?"[11]

NOTES

1. P. Ricoeur, *The Conflict of Interpretations*, Evanston, 1974, p. 11.

2. This pattern seems to me to assure a better comprehension of the relation between theology and philosophy.

3. We have recourse to this term to avoid the misinterpretations which are occasioned by the use of revelation and appearing, which are words charged with ambiguous connotations oscillating between appearance (*Schein*) and a miraculous phenomenon (*Erscheinung*).

4. At the moment when Oedipus had conquered the Sphinx by resolving the enigma, his destiny, from the enigmatic, becomes symbolic: a parricide and an incestuous person, he ends by *understanding*.

5. Cf. E. Kant, *Critique of Pure Reason*, preface to the 2nd edition, translated by Norman Kemp Smith, New York, 1965, p. 33.

6. Cf. B. Pascal, *Pensées*, text of H. F. Stewart edition, New York, 1950, no. 86, p. 49, *fantastic appraisal* and *rank insolence* of a disordered imagination, are strictly a false infinite and a bad infinite. One asks himself if the wager is not also an affair of the imagination in this positive aspect which renders it similar to the "sentiment" and to the "heart". B. Pascal, *op. cit.*, nos. 274-275, p. 159.

7. Here is the occasion of inquiring about the interpretation and the comprehension of philosophic work: how to read the philosophers?

8. Ricoeur, p. 497.

9. Analectic is the system of analogical thought.

10. Ricoeur, p. 497.

11. Ricoeur, p. 497.

THE TASK OF HERMENEUTICS*

by Paul Ricoeur

This lecture is intended to describe the state of the problem of hermeneutical philosophy as I perceive it and as I receive it before adding my own contribution to its solution in the second lecture. In this first discussion I would like to bring out into the open the terms of an unresolved problem. In effect, I want to bring hermeneutical reflection to the point where, due to its internal aporia, it calls for an important reorientation if it is to enter into serious discussion with the "science of a text", such as semiology and exegesis. My second lecture will be devoted entirely to this revision of the hermeneutical problematic.

I will adopt the following working definition of hermeneutics: hermeneutics is the theory of the operation of understanding in its relations to the interpretation of texts. My guiding idea will be that of the actualization of discourse as a text, and all of the second lecture will be devoted to elaborating the categories of the text. Thus the way should be prepared for an attempt to resolve the central aporia presented in this first lecture--the disjunction, destructive in my eyes, between explanation and understanding. The search for a complementarity between these two attitudes, which hermeneutics with a semantic origin has tended to dissociate,

---

* The two lectures presented here were the first two lectures of a series of six given at Princeton Theological Seminary in May 1973 as the Warfield Lectures.

will epistemologically express the reorientation required of hermeneutics by the notion of text.

The historical survey of hermeneutics which I propose here converges on the formulation of an aporia which is the same one which has prompted my own research. Therefore the presentation which follows is not neutral in the sense that it is meant to be free of presuppositions. Even hermeneutics itself puts us on guard against the illusion of such a claim to neutrality.

I see the recent history of hermeneutics as dominated by two preoccupations. The first is to progressively enlarge the goal of hermeneutics in such a way that all the *regional* hermeneutics are included in a *general* hermeneutics. But this movement from regional to general heremeneutics cannot be brought to its fulfilment unless at the same time the properly epistemological preoccupations of hermeneutics--I mean its effort to constitute itself as scientific--are subordinated to the ontological preoccupations where "understanding" ceases to appear as a simple mode of "knowing" in order to become a "way of being" and of relating itself to beings and to being. So the movement of generalization is accompanied by a movement of radicalization by which hermeneutics becomes not just general but also fundamental hermeneutics.

FROM REGIONAL HERMENEUTICS TO GENERAL HERMENEUTICS

The First "Place" of Interpretation

The first "locality" which hermeneutics undertakes to present is surely that of language and more particularly written language. It is important to recognize the contours of this first place, since my own enterprise in the second lecture could appear as an attempt to "re-regionalize" hermeneutics by means of the notion of text. There is question therefore of specifying why hermeneutics has a privileged relation to questions about language. We can begin, it seems to me, with a noteworthy characteristic of natural languages which calls for a work of interpretation at the most elementary and banal level of conversation. This characteristic is polysemy, the trait that our words have more than one signification when they are considered outside of their use in a determinate context. I will not be concerned here with the economic reasons which justify recourse to a lexical code which presents such a unique characteristic. What counts for the present discussion is that the polysemy of words calls forth as its counterpart the selective role of contexts in determining the current value of words in a given message, addressed by a specific speaker to a hearer in a particular situation. Sensitivity to context is the necessary complement and the unavoidable counterpart of polysemy.

But the use of contexts in turn brings into play an activity of discernment which takes place in a concrete exchange of messages between interlocuters and whose model is the language game of question and answer. This activity of discernment is properly called interpretation. It consists in recognizing which relatively univocal message the speaker has constructed upon the polysemic base of the common lexicon. To produce a relatively univocal discourse with polysemic words and to identify this intention of univocity in the reception of messages is the first and the most elementary work of interpretation. It is within this very large circle of exchanged messages that writing carves out a limited domain which Dilthey, to whom I shall return in more detail shortly, calls "expressions of life fixed by writing". These call for a specific work of interpretation for reasons which we will discuss in the second lecture, which belong precisely to the actualization of discourse as text. Let us provisionally say that in writing the conditions of direct interpretation through the question and answer game, therefore through dialogue, are no longer fulfilled. Specific techniques are required to raise to discourse the series of written signs and to discern the message across the superimposed codifications proper to the actualization of discourse as text.

Schleiermacher

The true movement from regional to general hermeneutics begins with the effort to disengage a general problem from the activity of interpretation which is undertaken in each instance although the texts may differ. The recognition of this central and unifying problematic was the work of Schleiermacher. Before him there was a philology of classical texts, principally those of Greco-Latin antiquity, and an exegesis of sacred texts, the Old and New Testaments. And in each of these two domains the work of interpretation varied according to the diversity of the texts. A general hermeneutics requires therefore that we transcend particular applications and discern the operations common to the two great branches of hermeneutics. But in order to do this, we must not just rise above the particularity of rules and recipes among which the art of understanding was scattered. Hermeneutics as born from this effort to raise exegesis and philology to the rank of a *Kunstlehre*, that is, to a "technology" or "technique" which would not be limited to a simple collection of unrelated operations.

Now this subordination of the particular rules of exegesis and philology to the general problematic of understanding constituted a revolution like the one that Kantian philosophy had achieved elsewhere, principally in relation to the natural sciences. In this respect, we can say that the philosophical horizon closest to hermeneutics is Kantian. The general spirit of critical philosophy, as we know, is to invert the relation between a theory of knowledge and a theory of being. We must measure the capacity for knowledge before raising the question of the nature of being. And it is understandable that it was in a Kantian climate that the project to relate the rules of interpretation, not to the diversity of texts and things in these texts, but to the central operation which unifies the diversity of interpretation could be formed. If Schleiermacher himself was not conscious of carrying out in exegesis and philology the sort of Copernican revolution that Kant carried out in the order of the philosophy of nature, Dilthey was perfectly aware of it in the neo-kantian climate at the end of the 19th century. But this required an insight of which Schleiermacher had no idea--the inclusion of the exegetical and philological sciences within the historical sciences. It is only within this insight that hermeneutics can appear as a global response to the great lacuna of Kantianism, seen for the first time by Herder and also recognized clearly by Cassirer: that in a critical philosophy there is an unbridgeable gap between physics and ethics.

But there was not only question of filling a lacuna in Kantianism, there was also question of profoundly revolutionizing the Kantian concept of the subject. Because it limited itself to investigating the universal conditions for objectivity in physics and ethics, Kantianism could only bring to light an impersonal mind, bearer of the conditions of the possibility of universal judgments. Hermeneutics could not add to Kantianism without taking from Romantic philosophy its most fundamental conviction, that the spirit is the unconscious creator at work in individual genuises. Schleirermacher's hermeneutical program carried the double mark of both Romanticism and critical philosophy. It was Romantic in its appeal to a living relation to the process of creation, critical in its wish to elaborate the universally applicable rules of understanding. Perhaps all hermeneutics is forever marked by this double filiation to Romanticism and critical philosophy. The proposal to battle against misunderstanding in the name of the famous adage, "There is hermeneutics wherever there is misunderstanding", is critical; and the proposal to "understand an author as well as and even better than he understood himself", is Romantic.

We must understand that it is an aporia as well as a first sketch which Schleiermacher gave to his descendents in the notes on hermeneutics which he never succeeded in turning into a complete work. Schleiermacher struggled with the problem of the relation between two forms of interpretation: "grammatical" interpretation and "technical" interpretation. This is a constant distinction in his work, but its meaning changed over the years. Before Kimmerle's edition of Schleiermacher's *Hermeneutics* in 1959, we did not know of the notes from 1804 and the following years. This is why everyone credited Schleiermacher with advocating a psychological interpretation, which in the beginning was actually on an equal footing with grammatical interpretation.

Grammatical interpretation was concerned with the characteristics of discourse which were common to a culture. Psychological interpretation was concerned with the singularity, the genius, of the author's message. Now, even if these two forms of interpretation are equally valid, we cannot practice them at the same time. As Schleiermacher says: to consider the common language is to forget the writer; to understand an individual author is to forget his language, which is just passed over. Either we perceive the common or we perceive the particular. The first type of interpretation is called "objective" since it deals with the distinctive linguistic characteristics of the author, but it is also called "negative", since it simply indicates the limits of understanding. Its critical value bears only on errors concerning the meaning of words. The second type of interpretation is called "technical", doubtless because of the very project of a *Kunstlehre*, a technology. The real project of hermeneutics is accomplished in this second type of interpretation. It is a question of reaching the subjectivity of him who speaks, language being forgotten. Language here becomes an instrument at the service of individuality. This type of interpretation is also called "positive" because it reaches the act of thinking which produces the discourse.

Not only does one type of interpretation exclude the other, each requires distinct talents, as the respective excesses of each reveal. An excess of the first gives pedantry; an excess of the second, nebulousness. It is only in the later texts that the second type of interpretation prevails over the first, and that the divinatory character of interpretation emphasizes its psychological character. But even then psychological interpretation--this term replaces that of technical interpretation--is never limited to an affinity with the author. It implies critical motives in the activity of comparison; an individuality can only be grasped through comparison and contrast. Thus the second type of hermeneutics also includes technical and discursive elements. We never directly grasp an individuality, but only its differences from another and from ourselves. The difficulty in arbitrating between the two hermeneutics is thus complicated by the superimposing on the first pair of oppositions ("grammatical" and the "technical") a second pair of oppositions ("divination" and "comparison"). Schleiermacher's famous *Discourses* witness to this extreme perplexity on the part of the founder of modern hermeneutics. I propose to show in the second lecture that this perplexity can be overcome only if we make clear the relation of a work to the subjectivity of the author and if we shift the emphasis in interpretation from pathetic investigation of submerged subjectivities to the meaning and the reference of the work itself. But first we must push the central aporia of hermeneutics further by considering the decisive enlargement which Dilthey accomplished in subordinating the philological and exegetical problematic to the historical problematic. This enlargement, in the sense of a greater universality, prepares for the displacement of epistemology toward ontology in the sense of a greater radicality.

Dilthey

Dilthey is at the critical turning point in hermeneutics where the scope of the problem is magnified but is still presented in terms of the epistemological debate characteristic of the whole neo-kantian epoch.

The necessity to incorporate the regional problem of interpretation into the larger field of historical knowledge imposed itself on a mind anxious to account for that great success of German culture in the 19th century, the discovery of history as a science of the first rank. Between Schleiermacher and Dilthey were the German historians of the 19th century, Ranke, Droysen, etc. The text to be interpreted from then on was historical reality itself and its inner-connections (*Zusammunhang*). But before we ask how to understand a text from the past, a prior question comes up--how to conceive historical continuity. Before the coherence of the text comes that of history, considered as the great document of man, as the most fundamental expression of life. Dilthey is above all the interpreter of this pact between hermeneutics and history. What we today call "historicism" in a pejorative sense expresses a cultural fact, the transfer of our interest from humanity's main works to the historical interconnections which carry them. The discrediting of historicism was not just a result of the puzzles it raised, but of another cultural change which took place more recently and which makes us give preference to the system over change, to synchrony over diachrony. We will see in the remaining lectures how much the structural tendencies of contemporary literary criticism expresses both the failure of historicism and the deeper subversion of its problematic.

But, even though Dilthey brought to light for philosophical reflection the great problem of the intelligibility of the historical as such, he was inclined by a second major cultural fact to seek the key to a solution not in the domain of ontology but in the reformation of epistemology. The second cultural fact to which we allude is represented by the growth of positivism as philosophy, if we thereby understand, in general terms, the demand that the mind take as its model for all intelligibility the sort of empirical explanation current in the natural sciences. Dilthey's times were those of the complete refusal of Hegelianism and an apologetic for experimental knowledge. Thus the only way of doing justice to historical knowledge seemed to be to give it a scientific dimension, comparable to the dimension which natural sciences had conquered. So it was in order to reply to positivism that Dilthey undertook to endow the cultural sciences with an epistemology and a methodology just as respectable as those belonging to the natural sciences.

On the basis of these two great cultural facts, Dilthey posed his fundamental question: how is historical knowledge possible, or more generally, how are the sciences of the spirit possible? This question brings us to the threshold of that great opposition which runs through all of Dilthey's work, the opposition between the explanation of nature and the understanding of history. This opposition is pregnant with consequences for hermeneutics, thus cut off from naturalistic explanation and forced into the realm of psychological intuition.

Dilthey sought the distinctive trait of understanding in psychology. Every science of the spirit--and by this Dilthey meant every knowledge of man implying some historical relation--presupposes a primordial capacity to place oneself into the psychical life of others. In natural knowledge, in effect, man only reaches those distinct phenomena whose fundamental thingness escapes him. In the human order, on the contrary, man knows man; no matter how foreign the other man may be to us, he is not alien in the sense of the unknowable physical thing. The difference of status between the natural thing and the spirit therefore requires the difference of status between explanation and understanding. Man is not radically foreign to man because he gives signs of his existence. To understand these signs is to understand man. The positivistic school completely ignores the difference in principle between the physical and psychic worlds.

Someone might object that the spirit, the spiritual world, is not necessarily individual. Did not Hegel witness to a sphere of the spirit, the "objective" spirit, the spirit of institutions and cultures, which can in no way be reduced to a psychological phenomenon? But Dilthey still belonged to that generation of neo-Kantians for whom the pivot point of every human science was the individual, considered, it is true, in his social relations, but fundamentally singular. This is why the sciences of the spirit as fundamental sciences need psychology, the science of the individual acting in society and in history. Reciprocal relations, cultural systems, philosophy, art, and religion are all constructed on this basis. More precisely, and more epoch-making, it is as activity, as free will, as initiative and enterprise that man seeks to understand himself. Here we recognize the firm purpose to turn away from Hegel, to leave the Hegelian concept of the *Volksgeist* and thus to stand again with Kant, but, as we said earlier, to stand at the place where Kant had stopped.

The key to this critique of historical knowledge which defaulted to Kantianism is found in the fundamental phenomenon of an "internal connection" or "inner connection" by which the life of another person lets itself be discerned and identified in its manifestations. Because life produces forms and exteriorizes itself in stable configurations, the knowledge of others is possible. Feeling evaluation, rules for willing, etc., tend to be deposted in an acquired structure offered for others to decipher. The organized systems that culture produces in the form of literature constitute a second order stratum built upon the primary phenomenon of the teleological structure of the productions of life. We know how Max Weber in his turn undertook to resolve the same problem with his concept of ideal-types. Both men struggled with the same problem, how to conceptualize the fluctuating experiences of life that are in opposition, or so it seemed, to the regularity of nature. An answer is possible because spiritual life fixes itself within structured wholes capable of being understood by another person. From 1900 on Dilthey depended upon Husserl to give consistency to this notion of "interconnection". Husserl, at that time, was establishing that psychic life was characterized by intentionality, the property of intending a meaning capable of being identified. Psychic life itself could not be reached, but one could grasp what it intended, the objective and identical correlate in which psychic life transcended itself. This concept of intentionality and of the identical character of the intentional object allowed Dilthey to reinforce his concept of psychic structures through the Husserlian notion of meaning.

What happens in this new context to the hermeneutical problem we got from Schleiermacher? The passage from understanding, defined largely as the capacity to transpose oneself into someone else, to interpretation, in the precise sense of understanding the expressions of life fixed by writing, bring up a twofold problem. On the one hand, hermeneutics completed empathetic psychology by adding a supplementary stage to it. On the other hand, empathetic psychology gave a psychological inflection to hermeneutics. This explains why Dilthey retained from Schleiermacher the psychological side of his hermeneutic in which he recognized his own problem, understanding through transference into another person. Considered from the first point of view, hermeneutics consists of something specific; it intends to reproduce an interconnection, a structured whole, by taking hold of a category of signs, signs which have been fixed by writing or by any other process of inscription equivalent to writing. It is then no longer possible to grasp the psychic life of others in its immediate expressions. We must reproduce or reconstruct it by interpreting the objectified signs. Distinct rules are required for this *Nachbilden* because of the investing of expression in objects. As with Schleiermacher, philology, that is, the explication of texts, furnishes the scientific step for understanding. For both thinkers, the essential role of hermeneutics consists in "theoretically grounding, against the constant intrusion of Romantic arbitrariness and sceptical subjectivity, the universal validity of interpretation, the basis of all certitude within history". Thus hermeneutics constitutes the objectified layer of understanding, thanks to the essential structures of the text.

But the counterpart of a hermeneutical theory founded upon psychology is that psychology remains its final justification. The autonomy of the text, which will be at the center of our reflections in subsequent lectures, can only be a provisional and superficial phenomenon. This is precisely why the question of objectivity for Dilthey remains both an unavoidable and an insolvable problem. It is unavoidable because of the claim to respond to positivism by an authentically scientific conception of understanding. This is why Dilthey never ceased to refine and perfect his concept of "reproduction" making it more suitable for the needs of objectification. But the subordination of the hermeneutical problem to the psychological problem of understanding others condemned it to look for the source of all objectification beyond the field of interpretation. For Dilthey, objectification begins very early, beginning with interpretation of oneself. What I am for myself can only be grasped through the objectifications of my life. Self-knowledge is already an interpretation which is not easier than any other interpretation, and probably more difficult, for I only understand myself through the signs I give of my life and which are not returned to me by others. All self-knowledge is mediated through signs and works. This is how Dilthey responded to the *Lebensphilosophie* so influential in his day. He shared this philosophy's conviction that life is essentially creative dynamism. But, against the "philosophy of life", he held that this creative dynamism cannot know itself but can only interpret itself through the detour of signs and works. There was thus in Dilthey's thought a fusion between the concept of dynamism and that of structure--life appears as a dynamism which structures itself. This is how the later Dilthey attempted to generalize the concept of hermeneutics, tying it evermore firmly to the teleology of life. Acquired meanings present values, and distant ends constantly structure the dynamic of life according to the three temporal dimensions of past, present and future. "Man instructs himself only by his actions, by the exteriorization of his life and by the effects these produce on others." He only learns to know himself through the detour of understanding, which is always an interpretation. The only truly significant difference between psychological interpretation and exegetical interpretation lies in the fact that life's objectifications tend to be deposited and sedimented in a stable acquisition which takes on all the appearances of Hegel's objective spirit. If I can understand worlds which have disappeared, it is because each society has created its own instruments for understanding in creating the social and cultural worlds in which it understands itself. Universal history thus becomes the hermeneutical field. To understand myself is to make the greatest detour, that of the great memory which retains what has become significant for men as a group. Hermeneutics is the merging of the individual with the knowledge of universal history, it is the universalization of the individual.

Dilthey's work, more than Schleiermacher's brings to light the central aporia of a hermeneutics which places understanding the text under the law of understanding another person who expresses himself there. If this enterprise remains fundamentally psychological, it is because it takes as the final interpretation not *what* a text says, but *who* expresses himself there. At the same time, the object of hermeneutics is continuously removed from the text, from its meaning and its reference, toward the life that is expressed there. Gadamer has presented well this latent conflict in Dilthey's work (*Wahrheit und Methode*, pp. 205-208). The conflict is finally between a philosophy of life with its deep irrationalism and a philosophy of meaning which makes the same claims as the Hegelian philosophy of the objective spirit. Dilthey transformed this difficulty into an axiom: "Life contains the power to transcend itself in significations." Or as Gadamer says, "Life exegetes itself, it has a hermeneutical structure." But this hermeneutics of life is a history and this is incomprehensible. The passage from psychological understanding to historical understanding presupposes in effect that the interconnection of life's works is no longer lived or experienced by anyone. This is its objectivity. And this is why we can ask if, in order to think about the objectifications of life and to treat them as given, it is not necessary to put the whole of speculative idealism at the root of life, finally to think of life as spirit (*Geist*). If not, how are we to understand that in art, religion and philosophy life expresses itself most completely by most objectifying itself? Is it not because here the spirit is most at home? And is this not to admit that hermeneutics is only possible as sensible philosophy through what it has borrowed from Hegelian concepts? It is then possible to say of life what Hegel said of the spirit: "Here life grasps life."

It is still true, however, that Dilthcy perfectly caught sight of the kernel of the problem, that life only grasps life through the mediation of unities of meaning that are raised beyond the historical flux. Dilthey caught sight of a mode of transcending finitude without complete transcendence, without absolute knowledge--of interpretation. In this way he indicated the direction in which historicism could be conquered by itself, without invoking any triumphant coincidence with some absolute knowledge. But, to continue this work it is necessary to renounce linking hermeneutics to the purely psychological notion of transference into an alien psychic life. It is necessary to unfold the text, no longer backwards toward its author, but forward toward its immanent meaning and toward the sort of world which it discovers and opens up.

FROM EPISTEMOLOGY TO ONTOLOGY

Since Dilthey the decisive step was not to improve the epistemology of the sciences of the spirit, but to question its fundamental postulate, that these sciences can be rivals of the natural sciences by means of an appropriate methodology. This presupposition, which dominates Dilthey's work, implies that hermeneutics is one kind of "theory of knowledge", and that the debate between explanation and understanding can go on within the limits of the *Methodenstreit* so dear to neo-Kantians. It is this presupposition of hermeneutics understood as epistemology that is essentially called into question by Heidegger and later by Gadamer. Their contributions cannot therefore be taken as the simple prolongation of Dilthey's enterprise. Rather they must be seen as an attempt to dig beneath the epistemological enterprise in order to disclose its ontological conditions. If we can place the first movement, from regional hermeneutics to general hermeneutics under the aegis of a Copernican revolution, we must place the second which we are now undertaking under the aegis of a second Copernican reversal which will relocate the questions of method within fundamental ontology. We must not expect therefore from either Heidegger or Gadamer a perfecting of the methodological problematic coming out of the exegesis of sacred or profane texts, by philology, psychology, the theory of history or the theory of culture. On the contrary, there is a new question. Instead of asking "how do we know?", the question will be "what is the mode of being of that being who only exists through understanding"?

Heidegger

With Heidegger, the question of *Auslegung*, exposition or interpretation, coincides so little with that of exegesis that it is joined from the introduction of *Being and Time* to the "forgotten question of being". What we are interrogating is the *meaning* of being. But, in this question we are guided by that which is sought. The theory of knowledge is inverted from the beginning by a questioning which precedes it and which depends upon the manner in which a being encounters being, even before it opposes itself to it as an object in face of a subject. Even if *Being and Time* puts the accent on *Dasein* (that being-there which we ourselves are) more than the later works of Heidegger, this *Dasein* is not a subject for whom there is an object, but a being within being. *Dasein* denotes the "place" where the question of being arises, the place of manifestation. The centrality of *Dasein* is just that of a being which understands being. It is part of its structure as a being to have an ontological pre-understanding of being. Hence to show the constitution of *Dasein* is not at all "to ground by derivation" as in the methodology of the human sciences, but to disengage "the fundamental structure by exhibition" (par. 3). An opposition is thus created between the ontological foundation, as we just said, and epistemological question if the problem was that of basic concepts which regulate regions of particular objects, the nature-region, life-region, language-region, history-region. Certainly science itself moves toward such an explication of its fundamental concepts, particularly where there is a crisis of foundations. But the philosophical task of grounding is something else. It aims at disengaging the fundamental concepts which "determine the preliminary understanding of a region, furnishing the base for all the thematic objects of a science and which thereby orient all positive research". What is at stake in hermeneutical philosophy will thus be "the exposition of that being relative to its constitution of being". This exposition will add nothing to the methodology of the sciences of the spirit. Rather it will dig below that methodology to reveal its foundations: "thus in history what is philosophically prior is not the theory of the formation of concepts about historical matters, not the theory of historical knowledge or even the theory of history as the object of historical science, but the interpretation of historical being relative to its historicity." Hermeneutics is not a reflection on the sciences of the spirit, but an explication of the ontological ground on which these sciences may be built. From this comes what appears to me to be the key sentence: "It is within hermeneutics thus understood that is contained what we must name 'hermeneutics' in a derivative sense: the methodology of the historical sciences of the spirit."

This first inversion found in *Being and Time* calls for a second. For Dilthey the question of understanding was tied to the problem of other minds. The possibility of reaching a foreign psyche through transference dominated all the sciences of the spirit, from psychology to history. It is noteworthy, that in *Being and Time* the question of understanding is freed entirely from the problem of communication with another person. There is a chapter which is called *Mitsein*, being-with, but it is not within this chapter that we find the question of understanding, as one might expect from a Diltheyan approach. The foundations of the ontological problem are to be sought in the domain of the relation with the world and not in the domain of relation with another person. It is in relation to my situation, in the fundamental understanding of my position within being, that understanding in its principle sense is implied. It is not without interest to recall the reason why Dilthey proceeded as he did. It was beginning from a Kantian argument that he posed the problematic of the human sciences. The knowledge of things, he said, leads to something unknown, the thing itself. But in the case of psychic life, there is no thing-in-itself. What another is, we are ourselves. Knowledge of a psychic life therefore has an undeniable advantage over knowledge of nature. Heidegger, who had read Nietzsche, was no longer so innocent. He knew that the other, just as much as myself, is more unknown to me than any phenomenon of nature can be. Here dissimulation is undoubtedly thicker than anywhere else. If there is a region of being where inauthenticity reigns, it is within the relation of each person to every other possible person. This is why the great chapter on being-with is a debate with the "they", as the home and privileged location for all dissimulation. It is thus not surprising that it is not by a reflection on being-with, but on being-in that the ontology of understanding begins. Not being-with another--which would duplicate our subjectivity--but being-in-the-world. This placement of the philosophical locus is just as important as the transfer from the problem of method to the problem of being. The question about the "world" replaces the question about "others". In making understanding "wordly", Heidegger "depsychologizes" it.

This displacement has been completely misunderstood by those so-called existentialist interpretations of Heidegger that have especially flourished in the Anglo-Saxon world. They have taken the analyses of care, anxiety, being-toward-death in the sense of a refined existential psychology. They do not notice that these analyses belong to a meditation on the "worldhood of the world" and that they essentially are aimed at destroying the claim of a knowing subject to be the measure of objectivity. What we must take over from this claim about the subject is the conditions for dwelling in the world in terms of which there is a situation, understanding and interpretation. This is why the theory of understanding must be preceded by the recognition of a grounding relation which assures the anchorage of every linguistic system, and therefore of books and texts, in something which is not in primordial terms a phenomenon of articulation or of discourse. We must first find ourselves (for better or worse), find ourselves "there" and feel ourselves (in a certain manner), before orientating ourselves. If *Being and Time* exploits the depths of certain feelings such as fear and anxiety, it is not to "do existentialism", but in order to disengage by these revelatory experiences a tie to reality more fundamental than the subject-object relation. Through knowledge we already and always have objects before us. The mood of the situation precedes this being in face of, by situating us.

And so arises understanding. But it is not yet a fact of language, writing or text. Understanding itself must first be described, not in terms of regarding or of discourse, but as a power of being. The first function of understanding is to orient us in a situation. Understanding is not addressed therefore to grasping a fact but to the apprehension of a possibility and our utmost potentialities. We must not lose sight of this point when we draw the methodological consequences of this analysis: to understand a text, we shall say, is not to find an inert meaning which is contained therein, rather it is to unfold the possibility of being which is indicated by the text. Thus we will be faithful to the Heideggerian understanding which is essentially a "project" or, in a more paradoxical fashion, a "project" of a prior "being-thrown". Here again the "existentialist" tone is deceiving. "Projecting has nothing to do with comporting oneself toward a plan that has been thought out, and in accordance with which *Dasein* arranges its being; on the contrary, any *Dasein* has, as *Dasein*, already projected itself and as long as it is, it is projecting" (p. 185). What is important here is not the existential moment of responsibility or of free choice, but the structure of being which makes choice problematic. The "either-or" is not first, but derived from the structure of "being-thrown".

It is thus only in the third position in the triad, situation-understanding-interpretation, that the ontological moment enters which interests the exegete. But before the exegesis of texts comes the exegesis of life and world. Interpretation is first an explication, a "development" of understanding, a development which "does not transform understanding into something else but makes it become itself" (185). All return to the theory of knowledge is thus forbidden. What is explicated is the hermeneutical "as" (*als*) which is attached to the articulations of experience. "Explication does not make the *as* appear; it only gives it an expression" (186).

But if the analytic of *Dasein* does not expressly aim at the problems of exegesis, it does provide a meaning for what could appear to be a failure on the epistemological level, in that it relates this apparent failure to a more primitive ontological structure. This failure is what has often been spoken of in terms of a *hermeneutical circle*. In the human sciences, as has often been noticed, subject and object are mutually implied. The subject contributes to the knowledge of the object and in return is determined in its own subjectivity by the hold which the object has on it even before the subject has come to know the object. Stated in the terminology of subject and object, the hermeneutical circle can only appear as a vicious circle. It is the function of a fundamental ontology to disclose the underlying structure which accounts for what in methodological analysis appears as a vicious circle. It is this structure which Heidegger calls "pre-understanding". But we would be entirely mistaken if we tried to describe pre-understanding in terms of a theory of knowledge, that is once again, in the categories of subject and object. The relations of familiarity which we can have, for example, with a world of tools, can give us a first glimpse of what the preliminary having (fore-having) from which we derive a new usage of things might mean. This anticipatory character belongs to the manner of being of every being which has historical understanding. Thus it is in terms of the analytic of *Dasein* that we must understand the proposition that "the interpretation of something, as this or that is grounded essentially on a fore-having, fore-sight, and fore-conception" (191). The role of presuppositions in textual exegesis is thus nothing more than a particular case of this general law of interpretation. Transposed into the theory of knowledge and measured by the claim of objectivity, pre-understanding received the pejorative connotation of being a pre-judgment. But on the contrary, for fundamental ontology, pre-judgment is only understood on the basis of the anticipatory structure of understanding. The famous hermeneutical circle is henceforth no more than a shadow of this anticipatory structure seen from a methodological point of view. Whoever has understood this knows that "what is decisive is not to get out of the circle but to get into it in the right way" (190).

As you will have noticed, the principal weight of this meditation does not bear on discourse nor on writing. Heidegger's philosophy--or at least that of *Being and Time*--is so little a philosophy of language that the question of language is only introduced after the questions of situation, understanding and interpretation. Language, in the period of *Being and Time*, remains a second level of articulation, the articulation of interpretation in "statements" (*Aussage*, par. 33). But the connection of the statement to understanding and interpretation makes us see that its first function is not communication with another person, nor attribution of predicates to logical subjects, but "pointing-out", "showing", "manifestation" (192). This supreme function of language reminds us of its connection to the ontological structures which precede it: "That language only now becomes a theme of our examination," says Heidegger in paragraph 34, "indicates that this phenomenon has its roots in the existential constitution of *Dasein's* disclosedness" (203). And later: "Discourse is the articulation of intelligibility" (*ibid.*). Thus we must replace discourse within the structures of being, and not the latter within discourse: "Discourse is the way we articulate significantly the intelligibility of being-in-the-world" (204).

In this last remark we find the passage to the later philosophy of Heidegger which will ignore *Dasein* and begin immediately with language's power of manifestation. But it follows from *Being and Time* that "saying" (*reden*) appears as superior to "speaking" (*sprechen*). "*Saying*" designates the existential constitution and "speaking" its worldly aspect which falls into the empirical. This is why the first determination of "saying" is not to say something, but the pair, "hearing"-"keeping silent". Here again Heidegger inverts our ordinary, and even our linguistic, tendency to make the operation of speaking primary (locution, interlocution). To understand is to hear. In other words, my first relation to speech is not that I produce it but that I receive it: "Hearing is constitutive of discourse" (206). This priority of hearing marks the fundamental relation of speech to the opening to the world and to the other. Its methodological consequences are considerable: linguistics, semiology and philosophy of language, are all tied firmly to the level of speaking and do not reach the level of saying. In this sense fundamental philosophy no more ameliorates linguistics than it adds to exegesis. While speaking forces us back to the speaking man, discourse forces us back to things said.

At this point one will no doubt ask: Why do we not stop here and simply proclaim ourselves Heideggerian? Where is the famous aporia previously announced? Have we not eliminated the Diltheyan aporia of the theory of understanding, condemned by turns to being opposed to naturalist explanation and to struggling with it as to which is more objective or more scientific? Have we not transcended this aporia by subordinating epistemology to ontology? In my opinion the aporia is not resolved, it is only transferred elsewhere and thereby even aggravated. It is no longer *in* epistemology--between two modes of knowing--but *between* ontology and epistemology taken as wholes. With Heidegger we can move backwards to the ground but any return from ontology to the epistemological question about the status of the human sciences is impossible. This situation is the most unhappy that one can think of, for a philosophy which breaks the dialogue with these sciences is left with only itself. Moreover, it is only on the way back that we can prove the claim that questions of exegesis and of historical criticism in general are "derivative" questions. As long as we have not proceeded to this derivation, the very surpassing of these questions in favor of the questions of grounding remains questionable. Have we not learned from Plato that the ascending dialectic is the easiest one and that it is on the way back of the descending dialectic that the true philosopher declares himself? To me the unanswered question in Heidegger is, "how are we to account for any *critical* question within the framework of a fundamental hermeneutics?" However it is in the movement of return that the affirmation that the hermeneutical circle (in the sense of the exegetes) is "grounded" in the structure of anticipation of understanding at the fundamental ontological level can appear and attest to itself. But ontological hermeneutics seems incapable, for structural reasons, of unfolding this problematic of return. Even in Heidegger this question is abandoned as soon as it is asked. We read in *Being and Time*: "In the circle is hidden a positive possibility of the most primordial kind of knowing. To be sure, we genuinely take hold of this possibility only when, in our interpretation, we have understood that our first, last, and constant task is never to allow our fore-having, fore-sight, and fore-conception to be presented to us by fancies and popular conceptions, but rather to make the scientific theme secure by working out these fore-structures in terms of the things themselves" (153).

Here therefore is posed in principle the distinction between anticipation according to the things themselves and an anticipation which only comes from fancies (*Einfalle*) and popular conceptions (*Volksbegriffe*). But how can Heidegger go any further when he immediately declares that "the ontological presuppositions of historiological knowledge transcend in principle the idea of rigor held in the most exact sciences", and he then avoids the question of the rigor proper to the historical sciences themselves? The concern to ground the circle more deeply than any epistemology can prevent Heidegger from repeating the epistemological question after the ontology.

Gadamer

This aporia becomes the central problem of the hermeneutical philosophy of Hans Georg Gadamer in *Wahrheit und Methode* (1960). This Heidelberg philosopher proposes to take up again the question of the human sciences by means of the Heideggerian ontology and more precisely by means of its inflection in the latest works on philosophical poetics. The basic experience around which his whole work is organized, is that of the scandal for the modern consciousness of the "alienating distanciation" (*Verfremdung*) which seems to him to be the presupposition of these sciences. Alienation is in effect much more than a sentiment or a mood, it is the ontological presupposition which supports the objectivity of the human sciences. The methodology of these sciences inevitably implies, in Gadamer's eyes, the taking of a distance--which in its turn expresses the destruction of the primordial relation of participation (*Zugehörigkeit*) without which there exists no relation to the historical as such. This debate between alienating distanciation and the experience of participation is carried on by Gadamer within the three spheres of hermeneutical experience: the aesthetic sphere, the historical sphere and the sphere of language. In the aesthetic sphere, the experience of being grasped always precedes and makes possible the critical exercises of judgment for which Kant wrote the theory under the title of the judgment of taste. In the historical sphere, the consciousness of being carried by traditions which antedate me is what makes possible all exercise of a historical methodology at the level of the human and social sciences. Finally, in the sphere of language, which in a certain way overlaps the other two spheres, the co-belonging to things articulated by the great voices of the creators of discourse, precedes and makes possible every scientific treatment of language as an available instrument and every claim to dominate the structure of the text of our culture by objective techniques. Thus a single thesis runs through the three parts of *Wahrheit und Methode*.

Gadamer's philosophy expresses the synthesis of the two movements we have described from regional hermeneutics to general hermeneutics and from the epistemology of the human sciences to ontology. The expression of the hermeneutical experience expresses well this synthetic character. But furthermore, Gadamer notes with regard to Heidegger, the attraction of a return from ontology back to epistemological problems. It is in this light that I will speak of Gadamer here. The title of his work also confronts the Heideggerian concept of truth with the Diltheyan concept of method. The question is to what extent the work earns the right to be called "truth *and* method", or whether it should not be called "truth *or* method". If Heidegger escapes any debate with the human sciences by a supreme movement of transcendence, Gadamer achieves a better debate just because he takes Dilthey's question seriously. The section of his work devoted to the historical consciousness in this respect is very significant. The long historical review which Gadamer imposes on himself before presenting his own ideas attests that hermeneutical philosophy ought first to recapitulate the struggle of Romantic hermeneutics against the *Aufklärung*, that of Dilthey against positivism, and that of Heidegger against neo-Kantianism. Without a doubt the declared intention of Gadamer is not to fall back into the same old rut of Romanticism. Romanticism, he declares, only inverted the theses of the *Aufklärung*, without succeeding in displacing the problematic itself or changing the terrain of the debate. This is why the romantic philosophy attempted to rehabilitate pre-judgment, which is a category of the *Aufklärung*, and which continues to reinstate critical philosophy, that is, a philosophy of judgment. Romanticism conducted its struggle on a terrain defined by its adversary on the role of tradition and authority in interpretation. But it is a question of knowing whether the hermeneutics of Gadamer has truly gone beyond the Romantic point of departure of hermeneutics, and if his affirmation that "the being man finds his finitude in the fact that he first of all finds himself in the middle of traditions" (260) can escape the interplay of the reversals in which he sees philosophical Romanticism enclosed in the face of the claims of every critical philosophy. Dilthey is reproached for having remained a prisoner of a conflict between two methodologies and for "not having known how to break away from the traditional theory of knowledge" (260). His point of departure remains the consciousness of self as master of itself. With Dilthey subjectivity remains the last reference. A certain rehabilitation of pre-judgment, authority, and tradition is thus directed against the reign of subjectivity and interiority, that is, against the criteria of reflexive philosophy. This anti-reflexive polemic contributes to giving this plea the appearance of a return to a pre-critical position. However provoking--not to say provocative--this plea might be, it holds to the reconquest of the historical dimension over the reflexive moment. History precedes me and my reflection, I belong to history before belonging to myself. Now Dilthey could not understand this because his revolution remained an epistemological one and because his reflexive criterion prevailed over his historical consciousness. At this point Gadamer is heir to Heidegger. It is from him that Gadamer receives the conviction that what we call pre-judgment expresses the structure of anticipation of human experience. At the same time philological interpretation must be made a derivative mode of fundamental understanding.

This theory of historical consciousness marks the summit of Gadamer's reflection on the foundation of the sciences of the spirit. This reflection is placed under the title of the *Wirkungsgeschichtliches Bewusstein*: word by word, the consciousness of the history of effects. This category no longer comes from the methodology of historical inquiry but from the reflexive consciousness of his methodology. It is the consciousness of being exposed to history and its action in such a way that one cannot objectify this action on us because it is a part of the historical phenomenon itself. We read in the *Kleine Schriften*, p. 158: "By that I mean that we cannot extricate ourselves from historical becoming, or place ourselves at a distance from it, in order that the past might become an object for us....We are always situated in history----I mean that our consciousness is determined by a real historical becoming such that consciousness is not free to situate itself over against the past. On the other hand,

I mean that it is always a question of newly becoming conscious of the action which is thus exercised on us, such that everything past which we have just experienced constrains us to take it totally in hand, to assume its truth in some way...."

I wish to pose my own problem beginning from this concept of historical agency: How is it possible to introduce a particular critical moment into a consciousness of belonging, expressly defined by the refusal of distanciation? This can only occur, I think, to the degree that this historical consciousness does not limit itself to repudiating distanciation, but also sets out to assume it. Gadamer's hermeneutics contains a series of decisive suggestions which will become the point of departure for my own reflections in my second lecture. First, in spite of the great opposition between participation and alienating distanciation, the efficient consciousness of history contains within itself an element of distance. The history of effects is precisely the history which takes place under the condition of historical distance. It is the proximity of the distant, or to say the same thing differently, efficacity at a distance. There is therefore a paradox of otherness, a tension between the near and the distant essential to any historical consciousness.

Another index of the dialectic of participation and distanciation is furnished by the concept of a "fusion of horizons". In effect, according to Gadamer, if the condition of the finitude of historical knowledge excludes every transcendent point of view, every final synthesis in a Hegelian manner, that finitude is not such that I am enclosed in a point of view. Where there is a situation, there is a horizon capable of being narrowed or enlarged. We owe to Gadamer this very fruitful idea that communication at a distance between two consciousnesses differently situated takes place through a fusion of their horizons, that is, from the blending of their intentions about the distant and the open. Once again a factor of distanciation among the near, the far, and the open is presupposed. This concept means that we do not live within closed horizons nor within a unique horizon. To the extent that the fusion of horizons excludes the idea of a total and unique knowledge, the concept implies the tension between the self and the alien, between the near and the far, and therefore the play of difference is included in the coming together.

Finally, the most precise indication in favor of a less negative interpretation of alienating distanciation is contained in the philosophy of language achieved by Gadamer's work. The universal "linguisticality"--this word more or less translates Gadamer's *Sprachlichkeit*--means that my participation in a tradition or traditions passes through the interpretation of signs, works and texts, in which cultural heritages are inscribed and offered for our deciphering. Certainly the whole of Gadamer's meditation on language is turned against the reduction of the world of signs to instruments which we can manipulate at will. All of the third part of *Wahrheit und Methode* is a passionate apology for the "dialogue which we are" and for the preliminary understanding which support us. But linguistic experience only exercises its mediating function because the partners in a dialogue both efface themselves before the things said, which, in a way, guide the dialogue. Now, where is this reign of the thing said over the partners more apparent than when *Sprachlichkeit* becomes *Schriftlichkeit*, or in other words, when mediation through language becomes mediation through a text? Then that which makes us communicate at a distance is the "issue" of the text, which no longer belongs to either its author or its reader.

This last expression, the "issue" of the text brings me to the threshold of my own reflections and it is this threshold which I will cross in the second lecture.*

---

* This essay first appeared in *Philosophy Today*, 7 (1973), 112-128, translated by David Pellauer, St. Olaf's College, Northfield, Minnesota 55057. It is reprinted by kind permission of the publisher.

THE HERMENEUTICAL FUNCTION OF DISTANCIATION

by Paul Ricoeur

In my first lecture I described the background against which I am attempting to elaborate the hermeneutical problem in a way that will be meaningful for a dialogue with semiological and exegetical disciplines. The description brought us to the antinomy which seems to me to be the essential outcome of Gadamer's work, the opposition between alienating distanciation and participation. This opposition is an antinomy because it gives rise to an untenable alternative: on the one hand, alienating distanciation is the attitude that makes the objectification which reigns in the human sciences possible; on the other hand, this distanciation that is the very condition which accounts for the scientific status of the sciences is at the same time a break that destroys the fundamental and primordial relation by which we belong to and participate in the historical reality which we claim to construct as an object. Thus we reached the alternative suggested by the very title of Gadamer's work, *Truth and Method*: either we have the methodological attitude and lose the ontological density of the reality under study or we have the attitude of truth and must give up the objectivity of the human sciences.

My own reflections stem from a refusal of this dilemma and an attempt to transcend it. They find their first expression in the choice of a dominating problematic which seems to me by its very nature to escape the alternative of either alienating distanciation or participation by belonging. This dominating problematic is that of the text. Here, in effect, a positive, and if I may say so, a fruitful notion of distanciation is re-introduced. For me the text is much more than a particular case of interhuman communication, it is the paradigm of the distanciation in all communication. As such it reveals a fundamental character of the historicity of human experience, communication within and by means of distance.

In what follows I shall elaborate the notion of text in light of that to which it testifies, i.e., the positive and productive function of distanciation at the heart of the historicity of human experience.

I propose to organize this problematic around four themes: (1) the text as a relation of speech to writing; (2) the text as a structured work; (3) the text as the projection of a world; and (4) the text as mediating self-understanding.[1]

WRITING AND SPEAKING

Writing is evidently the first problem posed by the notion of a text. But if we must not underestimate this problem, neither must we overestimate it by purely and simply identifying text and writing. We enumerated three other problems which go beyond that of writing and which do not always presuppose it. Moreover, we have not called our first problem that of the "text as writing", but that of the relation of speech to writing. Actually, writing only makes explicit some traits that are already present in oral discourse which we call speech, and all the other traits--work, the world of a text, and self-understanding through a text--presuppose the realization of discourse as discourse. It is a question therefore of first making clear which traits of discourse are significantly altered by the passage from speech to writing.

Now discourse, even in oral form, presents an elementary characteristic of distanciation which is the condition for all those traits which we will consider later. I propose to consider this primordial instance of distanciation in terms of the dialectic of event and meaning.

What do we mean when we say that discourse is an event? This question is especially appropriate since the category "speech event" occupies a central position in theological hermeneutics which I will consider in my fourth lecture.

From what point of view, for what sort of investigation is the notion of the discourse event justified? Modern linguistics gives us the answer to this question. The notion of discourse as event is not only legitimate but even necessary once we consider the passage from a linguistics of language or of code to a linguistics of discourse or of message. This distinction, as we know, comes from Ferdinand de Saussure and Louis Hjelmslev. The first speaks of language (*langue*) and speech (*parole*), the second of schema and usage. We might also add Chomsky's terminology of competence and performance. It is necessary to draw all the epistemological consequences of such a duality, namely, that the linguistics of discourse has different rules than the linguistics of language. It is the French linguist Emile Benveniste who has gone the farthest in distinguishing these two linguistics. For him, these two linguistics are not constructed upon the same units. If the sign (phonological or lexical) is the basic unit of language, the sentence is the basic unit of discourse. Therefore it is the linguistics of the sentence which supports the theory of speech as an event. I will take four traits from this linguistics of the sentence which should help us elaborate the hermeneutics of the event and of discourse.

To say that discourse is an event is to say several things at the same time. First, discourse is realized temporally and in the present, whereas the system of language is virtual and outside of time. In this sense we can, with Benveniste, speak of the "instant of discourse" to designate the occurrence of discourse as an event. Secondly, whereas language has no subject in the sense that the question "Who speaks?" does not apply at this level, discourse refers back to its speaker by means of a complex of indicators such as the personal pronouns. In this sense we can say that the instance of discourse is self-referential. The character of event is now attached to the person of the speaker and the event consists in this, that someone is speaking, that someone expresses himself in taking up speech.

In yet a third sense discourse is event: whereas the signs of a language refer only to other signs within the same system with the result that language no more has a world than it has a time or a subjectivity, discourse is always about something. It refers to a world which it is supposed to describe, express or represent. In this third sense, the event is the advent of the world in language by means of discourse. Finally, whereas language is no more than a preliminary condition of that communication to which it furnishes its codes, it is in discourse that all messages are exchanged. In this sense, discourse alone not only has a world, but an other, another person, a hearer to whom it is addressed. The event, in this last sense, is the temporal phenomenon of exchange, the establishing of a dialogue which can be entered into, prolonged or interrupted.

Together these characteristics constitute discourse as an event. It is noteworthy that they only appear in the movement of actualization of language into discourse, in the actualization of our linguistic competence in performance.

But in thus emphasizing the character of discourse as event, we have only considered one of the two poles that constitute discourse. We must now shed some light on the second pole, that of meaning, because the distanciation which makes writing possible, and the production of discourse as a work, and all the other factors that enrich the notion of distanciation, come from the tension between these two poles.

To introduce this dialectic of event and meaning, I propose to say that if all discourse is actualized as event, all discourse is understood as meaning. It is not the event in so far as it is transient that we want to understand, but its meaning in so far as it endures. Let us be clear about this point. In saying this we are not taking a step backwards from the linguistics of speech to the linguistics of language. It is in the linguistics of speech that event and meaning articulate themselves. This articulation is the kernel of every hermeneutical problem. Just as language in actualizing itself in discourse goes beyond itself in the speech event, so speech in entering into the process of understanding goes beyond itself in the meaning. This surpassing of the event in the meaning is a characteristic of speech itself. It attests to the intentionality of language, the relation of the noesis and the noema in it. If language is a *meinen*, an intending, a meaning, it is so precisely because of this *Aufhebung*--this suppression--by which the event is surpassed and retained in the intending of a meaning. The very first distanciation therefore is the distanciation of the saying in the said.

But what is said? In order to more completely illumine this problem, hermeneutics must appeal not only to linguistics--even understood as the linguistics of discourse as opposed to the linguistics of language as we have distinguished them here--it must also appeal to the theory of the speech-act, as found in the work of Austin and Searle. The act of speaking, according to these authors, is constituted by a hierarchy of subordinate acts which are distributed on three levels: (1) the level of the locutionary or propositional act, the act *of* saying; (2) the level of the illocutionary act or force, that which we do *in* saying; and (3) the level of the perlocutionary act, that which we say *by* saying. If I tell you to close the door, for example, "Close the door!" is the act of speaking. But if I tell you this with the force of an order and not of a request, this is the illocutionary act. Finally, I can stir up certain effects like fear by the fact that I give you an order. These effects make my discourse act like a stimulus producing certain results. This is the perlocutionary act.

What is the implication of these distinctions for our problem of the intentional exteriorization by which the event surpasses itself in the meaning and lends itself to material fixation? The locutionary act exteriorizes itself in the sentence. The sentence can in effect be identified and reidentified as being the same sentence. A sentence becomes an e-nunciation (*Aus-sage*) and is thus transferred to others as being such and such a sentence with such and such a meaning. But the illocutionary act can also be exteriorized thanks to grammatical paradigms (indicative modes, imperatives, subjunctives and other procedures expressive of the illocutionary force) which permit its identification and reidentification. Certainly, in spoken discourse, the illocutionary force leans upon mimicry and gestural elements and upon the non-articulated aspects of discourse, what we call prosody. In this sense, the illocutionary force is less completely inscribed in grammar than is the propositional meaning. In every case, its inscription in a syntactic articulation is itself gathered up in specific paradigms which in principle make possible fixation by writing. Without a doubt we must concede that the perlocutionary act is the least inscribable aspect of discourse and that by preference it characterizes spoken language. But the perlocutionary action is precisely what is the least discourse in discourse. It is the discourse as stimulus. It acts, not by my interlocutor's recognition of my intention, but sort of energetically, by direct influence upon the emotions and the affective dispositions. Thus the propositional act, the illocutionary force, and the perlocutionary action are apt, in a decreasing order, for intentional exteriorization which makes inscription in writing possible.

Therefore it is necessary to understand by meaning the speech-act, or by the noema of the saying, not only the sentence, in the narrow sense of the propositional act, but also the illocutionary force and even the perlocutionary action to the extent that these three aspects of the speech-act are codified and gathered into paradigms, and to the extent that consequently they can be identified and reidentified as having the same meaning. Therefore I am here giving the word *meaning* a very large acceptation that covers all the aspects and levels of the intentional exteriorization which makes the inscription of discourse possible.

But fixation is only the external appearance of a more important phenomenon which affects all the characteristics of discourse which we have enumerated.

First, writing makes the text autonomous in relation to the intention of the author. What the text signifies no longer coincides with what the author wanted to say, verbal significance and mental significance have distinct destinies. This first modality of autonomy invites us to give a positive signification to distanciation which does not at all have the pejorative nuance of Gadamer's *Verfremdung*. In this autonomy of the text there is already the possibility of what Gadamer calls the issue of the text escaping the intentional horizon which limits its author, of what we will later call the world of the text breaking away from the world of the author. But what is true for the psychological conditions is also true for the sociological conditions for the production of a text. The essence of a work of art, a literary work, or a work in general, is to transcend its psycho-sociological conditions of production and to be open to an unlimited series of readings, themselves situated within different socio-cultural contexts. In short, it belongs to a text to decontextualize itself as much from a sociological point of view as from a psychological one and to be able to recontextualize itself in new contexts. The act of reading accomplishes the latter.

The same situation holds as regards the addressee of a text: whereas the vis-à-vis is given in advance by the colloquy itself in the dialogical situation, written discourse is open to an audience virtually understood as made up of whoever knows how to read. Thus to depsychologization and desociologization through writing, we must add the emancipation of the written material in regard to the dialogical condition of oral discourse, by which I mean that the relation between writing and reading is no longer a particular case of the relation between speaking and hearing.

This autonomy of the text has a hermeneutically important consequence. Distanciation is not the product of our methodology and therefore is not something added and parasitic, rather it is constitutive of the phenomenon of the text as written. At the same time, it is also the condition of interpretation. "Distanciation" is not only what understanding must conquer, but also its condition. We are thus ready to find between objectification and interpretation a relation much less dichotomizing and consequently much more complementary than that instituted by the Romantic tradition. The passage from speech to writing affects discourse in several other ways. In particular, the functioning of the reference is profoundly altered when it is no longer possible to show the thing about which we are speaking as belonging to the common situation of the partners in the dialogue. But we will save this problem for another time, for it is not so much writing as the new traits which it introduces and which we are now going to consider that affect the destiny of the reference, especially in the works that we call literary works. This is why I will reserve the analysis of this phenomenon for our discussion of the world of the text.

Such is the triple distanciation introduced by writing: (1) distanciation from the author; (2) from the situation of discourse; (3) from the original audience. But once again this does not mean that the problematic of the text is reduced to that of writing. First, because writing only realizes a trait that is virtual in all discourse--the distanciation of meaning and event. And furthermore, because the problematic of the text passes through other modalities of distanciation that can affect discourse outside of writing, even at the level of oral discourse. This is what I have called the realization of discourse as a work.

DISCOURSE AS A WORK

I propose to consider three distinctive traits of the notion of a work. First, a work is a sequence longer than the sentence, which gives rise to a new problem of understanding relative to the final and closed totality which constitutes the work as such. Secondly, the work is submitted to a form of codification that is applied to the composition itself and which makes discourse into a poem, an essay, a story, etc. The codification is known as literary genre. In other words, part of a work's being a work requires that it belong to a literary type. Finally, a work receives a unique configuration that assimilates it to an individual and which we call its style.

Before elaborating more in detail these three traits considered separately, I want to emphasize their common nature. Composition, belonging to a genre, and individual style characterize discourse as a work. Even the term "work" reveals the nature of these new categories, which are those of production and of labor. To impose a form upon material, to subject a production to genres, and to produce an individual style are ways of considering language as a material to be worked and formed. They are ways in which discourse becomes the object of a praxis and a technique. In this respect there is no radical opposition between the work of the spirit and the work of the hands. On this subject we might recall what Aristotle says about praxis, practice, or production: "All practices and all production relate to the individual. It is not man who is healed by the doctor, unless accidently, but it is Kelias or Socrates or some other individual so designated who is at the same time a man" (Metaphysics A, 981a, a15). In the same sense the French philosopher Granger writes in his *Philosophie du Style*: "Praxis is activity considered with its complex context and in particular the social conditions which give its signification in an effectively lived world." Labor is thus one of the structures of the practical, if not *the* structure. It is "practical activity objectified in its works". In the same way the literary work is the result of labor which organizes language.

We may now consider each of the three distinctive features of discourse as a work, in terms of these practical categories.

First, discourse as a work is a sequence of discourse longer than the sentence presenting a second-order kind of organization, as compared to the sentence taken as the minimal unit of discourse. This is what Aristotle in his *Rhetoric* called *taxis*, i.e., "composition", and which he considered as one of the three main divisions of rhetoric along with the "discovery of arguments" (*heuresis*) and "diction" or style (*lexis*). This kind of complexity and organization is more or less implied in the word *dis-course*, which preserves something of the Greek *dianoïa*. There is *taxis*, because there is *dianoïa*. Discourse is both a course of thoughts arranged in a certain manner, from a beginning through a middle to an end, and a course of utterances constituting a concatenation of minimal units of discourse.

In this sense, a text is not merely a sequence of sentences on equal footing and separatedly understandable. A text works as the first con-text for each partial meaning. As such it delineates a relatively closed space for each individual sentence's interpretation.

We are hitting here on a problem which Kant raised within the framework of the third critique, *The Critique of Judgment*, the teleological structure of a work of art as a system of wholes and parts. This structure is similar, to an extent, to the constitution of a living organism. Like the latter, it requires a specific kind of judgment, the "reflective judgment", to which I shall return in my next lecture when I shall draw the hermeneutical consequences of this constitution. Let us say, for the moment, that to understand a text is not to add partial meanings to one another. The text as a whole has to be "construed" as a hierarchy of topics, of primary and subsidiary topics. This very word "topics" suggests that the production of discourse as a whole implies more than a semantics of the sentence, it implies, say, a "topology" of discourse, which would be the proper semantics of discourse, with the notion of one or more "isotopics" interwoven in a text. (On the concept of "isotopy", see A. J. Greimas, *Sémantique Structurale*, pp. 69-102.)

Secondly, discourse as work admits to being subordinated to the rules of specific kinds of *codification*, which are traditionally called "literary genres". In the same way as grammatical and lexical rules are the required "codes" for producing "messages" in the form of a sentence, the codes which we are now considering are the appropriate conditions for producing those second-order units of discourse which we call a poem, an essay, a narrative, etc.

But the expression "genres" is an important kind of mistake. The word seems to imply that literary genres are *genera*, i.e. classificatory devices invented by literary criticism to master the chaos of individual works. Even in the magistral work of René Wellek and Austin Warren, *Theory of Literature*, the consideration of literary genres comes rather late and does not fit very well within the general framework of the book, which is more or less ruled by the categories of Imgarden's theory of literary work. And the slight discrepancy between this chapter and the rest of the book results from the treatment of genres as classes for individual works, therefore as taxonomic devices.

The consideration of discourse as work suggests that we look at literary genres less as means of classification than as means of production. Literary genres contribute to produce discourse as a work. To master a genre is to master a "competence" which offers practical guidelines for "performing" an individual work. We should have to add that the same competence in the reader helps him to perform the corresponding operations of interpretation according to the rules prescribed by the "genre" for both *sending* and *receiving* a certain type of message.[2]

In other words, a literary genre has a *genetic* function, rather than a *taxonomic* function. Just as "grammaticality", according to Noam Chomsky, expresses the "generative" function of grammar, i.e., it provides the speaker and the hearer with common rules for encoding and decoding individual messages, that is, for uttering and understanding isolated sentences, so the function of literary genres is to mediate between speaker and hearer by establishing a common *dynamics* capable of ruling both the production of discourse as a work of a certain kind and its interpretation according to the rules provided by the "genre".[3]

This "generative" function of the literary genres has two hermeneutical consequences which will be elaborated in Lecture IV. It will be shown that the dynamics of form is at the same time a dynamics of thought. In other words, it is not at all indifferent that a certain "confession of faith" is expressed in the form of a narrative, or of a prophecy, or a hymn, etc. Content and form--to use inadequate categories--are "generated" together. The theological content itself is produced in harmony with the rule of the corresponding literary genre.

The third dimension of discourse as work has been called its *style*. This word designates the aspect of the work that makes it a unique configuration. The style of a work lets the hearer or reader *identify* it as an individual, in the sense of Strawson in *Individuals*. This third category is the decisive one, if Aristotle is correct when he says that man contemplates universals, but produces individuals. "Art" is this field of human experience where the individuality of artifacts is emphasized at the expense of the *anonymity* of technological products, for which individuality is accidental, merely stochastic, and finally irrelevant. The individuality of works of art and of discourse is so characteristic of what is a work that the best examples that come to our minds to illustrate what we call an individual are offered by works of discourse (*this* poem, *this* play) and by works of art (*this* painting, *this* sculpture).

At first sight, this trait seems to contradict the preceding one: how is it possible to treat discourse as a work, first under the concept of genre, then under that of style? But this twofold description would constitute a discrepancy only if by a genre we should have to understand a class. If a genre is a competence, i.e., a set of generating rules, in the way that grammatical rules generate individual sentences, then it belongs to the function of "genres" to be directed toward the production of those individuals which we call works. Genre is generative process ending in the performance of a singular discourse. From this we define the task of *stylistics* as the theory devoted to the general conditions ruling the insertion of structure into an individual practice.[4]

In light of these principles what happens to the traits of discourse outlined at the beginning of this presentation? Let us recall the initial paradox of event and meaning. Discourse, we said, is actualized as event, but understood as meaning. How do we situate the notion of a work in relation to this paradox? In introducing categories proper to the order of production and labor into the dimension of discourse, the notion of a work appears, first, as a new kind of distanciation, then as a practical mediation between the irrationality of the event and the rationality of its meaning. Let me explain this new concept of distanciation, since it is a part of the mediating function ascribed to discourse as work.

The "genre" may be common to both speaker and hearer because it is an instrument of distanciation for both of them. The message encoded according to the generative rules of a genre escapes the vicissitudes of a simple utterance condemned to vanish with the speech-act of the actual speaker. Thanks to the genre, discourse appears as a public object readily memorizable and eventually capable of being written down. In this way its function is not only to establish communication at the time of the first utterance of the message, rather it allows it to survive the initial situation of discourse, it preserves it from all kinds of distortion, thanks to its own relative historical stability, and finally it keeps it available for fresh interpretations in quite new situations. This last function points to a paradox which can play a central role in hermeneutics. The form ascribed to the work by the genre makes it both "closed" and "open": "closed" in the sense that the kind of circumscription imposed on it preserves it from distortion, "open" in the sense that the same process that keeps it from distortion reserves it for new interpretations. This paradox is only apparent. The genre establishes the first contextualization, but, being at the same time a virtual decontextualization of discourse, it makes the subsequent recontextualization of the message possible.

We can now return to the dialectics of event and meaning in discourse. The same traits which rule the distanciation through the "genre" provided mediation through the "style". These two functions are linked in the same way as the "genre" generates the "style" of the individual work.

In fact, it is only within the framework of what we have called with Granger a stylistics that the concept of discourse as "event" becomes fully understandable. Event is the temporal aspect of an individual existence. But isolated sentences are not the only, not even the best, examples of what Emile Benveniste calls an *"instance de discours"*. Individual works are *"instances de discours" par excellence*. The event is the stylization of discourse.

This kinship between event, individual and style in the domain of discourse helps us to eliminate the residual of the expression *"instance de discours"*. We are always tempted to understand an event as a break in temporal continuity, as a leap in existence. The notion of style avoids these irrational connotations because it is a category of production. What appears as a "choice"--the choice of a style, given other available strategies--is not a "leap". Stylization appears as a transaction between a complex concrete situation which presents contradictions, indeterminacies and residues of previous unsatisfactory solutions, *and* an individual project. This transaction between a project and a situation is nothing else than a restructuration within an already structured experience which includes openings as well as obstacles. To grasp a work as an event is to reconstruct the process of this transaction, of this restructuration which *is* the work of stylization.

Such is the way in which the paradox of the fleeting event and the identifiable meaning, which is at the beginning of our mediation on distanciation in discourse, finds a noteworthy mediation in the notion of a work. The notion of style is an accumulation of the two characteristics of event and meaning. Style, we said, occurs temporally as a unique individuality and in this way concerns the irrational moment of decision, but its inscription in the material of language gives it the appearance of a tangible idea, of a "concrete universal", as Wimmsat has said in *The Verbal Icon*. Style is the outcome of a decision which can be read in a work and which by its singularity illustrates and exalts the event character of discourse. But this event is not to be found anywhere else than in the very form of the work. If the individual is theoretically beyond reach, it can nevertheless be recognized as the singular result of a process, a construction, in response to a determinate situation.

As for the notion of the subject of a discourse, it receives a new status from this concept of work as individual style. The notion of style permits a new approach to the question of the subject of a literary work. Once more the key is to be found in the categories of production and labor. In this regard the model of the artisan is particularly instructive (the trademark on eighteenth century furniture, the signature of the artist, etc.). Actually, the notion of the author which here qualifies the notion of the speaking subject appears as the correlate of the individuality of the work. The most arresting example is the least literary one possible, the style of the construction of a mathematical object such as Granger describes in the first part of his *Philosophie du Style*. Even the construction of an abstract model of phenomena, from the moment it is a practical activity immanent in a process of structuration, bears a proper name. And such a mode of structuration necessarily appears as chosen instead of some other mode. Because style is a work which individualizes, that is, which produces something individual, it retroactively points to its author. Thus the word "author" belongs to the stylistic. "Author" says more than "speaker". The author is the artisan of a work of language. But at the same time the category of author is a category of interpretation in the sense that the author is contemporary with the signification of the work as a whole. The singular configuration of the work and the singular configuration of the author are strictly correlative. Man individualizes himself by producing individual works. A signature is the mark of this relation.

But the most important consequence of introducing the category of a work involves the notion of composition. The work of discourse presents in effect characteristics of organization and of structure which permit us to extend to discourse itself the structural methods which were first applied successfully to entities of language shorter than the sentence in phonology and in semantics. The objectification of discourse in a work and the structural characteristics of composition joined to distanciation by means of writing force us to question the opposition between understanding and explanation stemming from Dilthey. This will be the goal of our third lecture. We will limit ourselves here to saying that a new epoch in hermeneutics is opened up by the successes of structural analysis. Explanation is henceforth the required path to understanding. This does not mean, I hasten to add, that explanation eliminates understanding. The objectification of discourse in a structured work does not suppress the fundamental and first trait of discourse, namely, that discourse is constituted by an ensemble of sentences where someone says something to someone about something. Hermeneutics, I would say, remains the art of discerning the discourse in a work. But this discourse is only given within and through the structure of the work. The result is that interpretation is the reply to the fundamental distanciation which constitutes the objectification of man in works of discourse, comparable to his objectification in the products of his work and art.

THE WORLD OF THE TEXT

A third modality of distanciation seems to me to be connected with the trait I called in my introduction "the world of the text". It is no longer a distanciation which affects the relation of the discourse to its speaker, of the writing to the writer, of the work to its author; it is a distanciation which crosses the very world of the work. What do we mean by this?

This notion prolongs what we called earlier the reference or denotation of the discourse. You will recall how we defined it. In every proposition we can distinguish with Frege the sense and the reference. The sense or the meaning is the ideal object that is intended. This meaning is purely immanent to discourse. The reference is the truth value of the proposition, its claim to reach reality. Through this character discourse is opposed to language which has no relationship with reality. Words refer to other words in the round without end of the dictionary. Only discourse, we say, intends things, is applied to reality, expresses the world.

The new question that arises is the following. What happens to the reference when discourse becomes a text? It is here that the structure of the work alters the reference to the point of making it entirely problematic. In oral discourse the problem is ultimately resolved by the ostensive function of discourse. In other words, the reference is resolved by the power of showing a reality common to the interlocutors. Or if we cannot show the thing being talked about, at least we can situate it in relation to a unique spatio-temporal network to which the partners in discourse also belong. It is this network, here and now determined by the discourse-situation, which furnishes the ultimate reference for all discourse. With writing things begin to change. There is no longer a common situation between the writer and the reader. And at the same time, the concrete conditions for the act of pointing something out no longer exist. Without a doubt it is this abolition of the demonstrative or denotative characteristics of reference that makes possible the phenomenon which we call literature where every reference to the given reality may be abolished. But it is essentially with the appearance of certain literary genres, generally tied to writing but not necessarily so, that this abolition of reference to the given world is led to its most extreme conditions. It is the role of most of our literature, it would seem, to destroy this world. This is true of fictional literature--fairy tales, myths, novels, drama--but also of all literature which we can call poetic literature where the language seems to glorify itself without depending on the referential function of ordinary discourse.

And yet if such fictional discourse does not rejoin ordinary reality, it refers to another more fundamental level than that reached by that descriptive, assertive, didactic discourse which we call ordinary language. My thesis here is that the abolition of first order reference, an abolition accomplished by fiction and poetry, is the condition of possibility for the liberation of a second order of reference which reaches the world not only at the level of manipulable objects, but at the level Husserl designated by the expression *Lebenswelt* and Heidegger by "being-in-the-world".

It is this referential dimension that is absolutely original with fictional and poetic works which, for me, poses the most fundamental hermeneutical problem. If we can no longer define hermeneutics as the search for another person and his psychological intentions that hide behind the text, and if we do not want to reduce interpretation to the identification of structures, what is left to be interpreted? My response is that to interpret is to explicate a sort of being-in-the-world unfolded in front of the text.

Here we rejoin Heidegger's suggestion about the meaning of *Verstehen*. In *Being and Time*, the theory of understanding is not tied to the understanding of others, but becomes a structure of being-in-the-world. More precisely, it is a structure that is examined after the structure of *Befindlichkeit*, state-of-mind. The moment of understanding responds dialectically to being-in-a-situation, as the projection of our own-most possibilities in those situations where we find ourselves. I want to take this idea of the "projection of our own-most possibilities" from his analysis and apply it to the theory of the text. Actually, what is to be interpreted in a text is a proposed world, a world that I might inhabit and wherein I might project my own-most possibilities. This is what I call the world of the text, the world properly belonging to this unique text.

The world of the text of which we are speaking is not therefore the world of everyday language. In this sense it constitutes a new kind of distanciation which we can call a distanciation of the real from itself. It is this distanciation that fiction introduces into our apprehension of reality. A story, a fairy tale, a poem, do not lack a referent. Through fiction and poetry new possibilities of being-in-the-world are opened up within everyday reality. Fiction and poetry intend being, but not through the modality of givenness, rather through the modality of possibility. And in this way everyday reality is metamorphized by means of what we could call the imaginative variations that literature works on the real.

Among other poetic expressions fiction is the privileged path to the re-description of reality and poetic language is the language which above all effects what Aristotle, in his consideration of tragedy, calls the *mimesis* of reality. Tragedy in effect only imitates reality because it recreates it by means of a *mythos*, a fable which reaches its deepest essence.

SELF-UNDERSTANDING

But we have not yet spoken of the last and the most fundamental distanciation, that which adheres to the act of writing as well as to the act of reading--the distanciation of the subject from himself. But we are not yet in a position to see just how much the premature reintroduction of the subject into the hermeneutical problem risks leading us back into the illusions of romantic hermeneutics. This latter emphasized the expression of genius. The task of hermeneutics was to be equal to this genius, to become contemporary with it. Dilthey, still close to this sense of hermeneutics, founded his concept of interpretation on the notion of understanding, on the grasping of an alien life expressing itself through the objectifications of writing. The psychologizing and historicizing characteristics of Romantic and Diltheyan hermeneutics come from this. This path is no longer open to us once we take seriously the distanciation by writing and the objectification by the structure of the work.

Is this to say that the problem posed by Romantic hermeneutics is worthless? I continue to think that in the last analysis *the text is the mediation by which we understand ourselves*. But today we cannot begin our hermeneutical work with this theme, at the very most we may end with it. If the last act of understanding is the *appropriation* of the meaning of the text, this appropriation here can only be tied dialectically to the distanciation proper to discourse, writing and a work. Beyond this by joining the existential interpretation of works with their structural explanation, it would be possible to redefine this major concept of hermeneutics at the end of a lecture which has touched on discourse, literary genre, style, structure, sense and reference in discussing a work. Then, and only then the hermeneutical concept par excellence, *appropriation*, would appear as the dialectical counterpart of distanciation which ought to remain the first and the last word of this lecture.*

---

* This essay first appeared in *Philosophy Today*, 7 (1973), 129-141, translated by David Pellauer, St. Olaf's College, Northfield, Minnesota 55057. It is reprinted by kind permission of the publisher.

NOTES

1. Only the first two categories will be fully developed here. The remaining two received a more complete treatment in connection with the epistemological debate which a third of my Princeton Warfield Lectures dealt with. I have tried to give at least a hint, here, however, of what is at stake in the third and fourth categories in order to preserve the unity of the theory of the text.

2. The example of the "parable" in Lecture V will offer an appropriate occasion to show how the fixed rules of an inherited form of discourse serve as a vehicle to produce a certain kind of discourse--the parabolic discourse. The identification of the genre, on the part of the reader, implies the same competence, i.e., the aptitude to interpret a certain category of sayings along the rules of a traditional type of interpretation.

3. Erhardt Güttgemanns, in *Studia Linguistica Neotestamentica*, speaks of a "generative poetics", which would be for the literary genres what a "generative grammar" is to sentences, according to Chomsky. This generative poetics would have to show that the *structures* of a given "genre" are rules of "competence" which make possible the understanding of a text as a narrative, a parable, etc. The ultimate aim of this generative poetics would be to adjust the existential categories of Bultmann to the "textemes", i.e., to the elementary structures which are to texts what lexemes are to elementary sentences. In the case of the parables of Jesus (this example is treated at length by Güttgemanns), the literary genre provides a traditional kind of codification (the Hebrew *maschal*) on the basis of which a unique and a novel message may be conveyed to and interpreted by an audience. The comparison between the generative character of "genres" and "grammar" brings us back unexpectedly to the concept of "grammatical" hermeneutics in Schleiermacher.

4. G. G. Granger defines stylistics as a "meditation on human works" in his *Philosophie du style*. More precisely, he says that its task is "to investigate the most general conditions of the insertion of structures into an individual practice" (p. 12).

PHILOSOPHICAL HERMENEUTICS AND BIBLICAL HERMENEUTICS

by Paul Ricoeur

The present study aims to explore the contribution of philosophical hermeneutics, whose principles have been expounded in the preceding study, to biblical exegesis.

In posing the problem in these terms, we appear to admit that biblical hermeneutics is only one of the possible *applications* of philosophical hermeneutics to a category of texts. That, however, is only half of my working hypothesis. It seems to me rather that there exists a complex relation of mutual inclusion between the two hermeneutics. Certainly, the first movement goes from the philosophical pole to the biblical pole. The same categories of work, of writing, of the world of the text, of distanciation and of appropriation rule the interpretation here as there. In this sense, biblical hermeneutics is a *regional* hermeneutics in relation to philosophical hermeneutics, which constitutes a *general* hermeneutics. It may seem then that we sanction the subordination of biblical hermeneutics to philosophical hermeneutics in treating it as an applied hermeneutics.

But it is precisely in treating theological hermeneutics as a hermeneutics applied to a species of texts--the biblical texts--that we bring to light an opposite relationship between the two hermeneutics. Theological hermeneutics presents qualities so original that the relation progressively reverses itself, theological hermeneutics finally subordinating philosophical hermeneutics as its own *organon*. It is this working of opposite relations that I now propose to decipher, by taking up again the class of hermeneutical categories centered in the notion of the text; nothing will make the "eccentric" character of theology more apparent than the effort to "apply" the general categories of hermeneutics to it.

I. THE "FORMS" OF BIBLICAL DISCOURSE

A hermeneutics centered in the text finds a primary "application" in the use of *structural* categories in biblical exegesis. But, at the same time that this exegesis is performed as a simple "application" in the biblical domain of an analysis valid in principle for the entire text, it develops traits which signal the reversal of the relation between the two hermeneutics which is affirmed when one passes from the "structures" of the text to the "world of the text".

Here again one limits himself to sketching the framework of problems which are considerable in themselves and to delineating it according to the competence of the philosophy of discourse.

The fundamental point on which I wish to concentrate my attention is this: the "confession of faith" which is expressed in the biblical documents is inseparable from the *forms* of discourse, I mean the narrative structure, for example, of the Pentateuch and the Gospels, the oracular structure of the prophets, the parable, the hymn, etc. Not only does each form of discourse raise up a style of confession of faith, but the confrontation of these forms of discourse produce, in the confession of faith itself, tensions, or contrasts which are theologically significant; the difference between narration and prophecy, so fundamental for the understanding of the Old Testament, is perhaps only one of the pairs of structures whose difference contributes to generating the total shape of meaning; one thinks further of other contrasting pairs on the same level of literary "forms". Perhaps it will be necessary to go as far as to consider the closing of the canon as a fundamental structural act which delimits the space of the working of the forms of discourse and determines the finished configuration at the heart of which each form and each pair of forms displays its significant function.

There will then be three problems to consider under the head of forms of biblical discourse: the affinity between a form of discourse and a certain modality of confession of faith--the relationship between such a couple of structures (for example, narration and prophecy) and the corresponding tension in the theological message--finally, the relation between the configuration of the whole of the literary *corpus* and that which we could call, correlatively, the space of interpretation opened for all forms of discourse taken together.

I should say here that I owe above all to Gerhard von Rad the understanding of this relation between form of discourse and theological content; I have found a confirmation of his method of correlation in similar works applied to the New Testament, in particular those of A. N. Wilder: *Early Christian Rhetoric. The Language of the Gospel*, Cambridge, Mass., 1971; and of W. A. Beardslee: *Literary Criticism of the New Testament*, Philadelphia, 1970.

The example of narration is perhaps the most striking, since it is also in the realm of forms and narrative structures that structural analysis has achieved its most brilliant success. This example, systematically developed, no longer permits the construction of theologies of the Old or the New Testament which hold the narrative category as a rhetorical procedure foreign to the content of which it is a vehicle; it appears on the contrary that something specific, or unique, is said about Jahweh and about his relations with Israel, his people, because it is stated in the form of a narration, a story, which retells the events of the deliverance of the past. The same concept of "the theology of the traditions", which gives its title to the first volume of von Rad's *Old Testament Theology*, New York, 1962, expresses the indissoluble solidarity of the confession of faith and the story. Nothing is said about God, about man, or about their relations, which has not first passed through the act of reassembling of legends, of isolated sagas, and of rearranging them in significant sequences, in a manner to constitute a unique story, centered on a core-event which has both a historic importance *and* a kerygmatic dimension. We know how Gerhard von Rad organizes the great narrative stemming from the primitive *Credo* which he reads in Deuteronomy 26. This manner of connecting the narrative dimension and the kerygmatic dimension is of the greatest importance for us.

On the one hand, the taking into consideration of the narrative structure permits an understanding of structural methods in the realm of exegesis; a comparison between von Rad and the structuralists forms in the school of Russian formalism (post-Saussurian semiology) would in this regard be very interesting.

On the other hand, the relation between the two hermeneutics begins to reverse itself when one considers the other aspect of the narrative, to be aware of the confession of faith. But this other dimension remains inseparable from the structure of the narrative; not just any theology could be bound to the narrative form, but only a theology which announces Jahweh as the great Actant in a history of deliverance. It is there without doubt that the great contrast between the God of Israel and that of Greek philosophy lies;

the theology of traditions knows nothing of the concepts of cause, of foundation, of essence; it speaks of God in accord with the historic drama supplied by the acts of deliverance which the story reports. This manner of speaking of God is no less significant than that of the Greeks; it is a theology homogeneous to the narrative structure itself, a theology in the form of *Heilsgeschichte*.

I have chosen to develop somewhat a single example, that of the narrative structure and the theological meanings which correspond to it. The same work could be done with the other literary forms, in order to make apparent, in theological discourse itself, the tensions corresponding to the opposition of structures. The tension between narration and prophecy is exemplary in this regard; the difference of two literary forms--that of the chronicle and that of the oracle--continues in the perception of time which the one consolidates and the other dislocates and in the meaning of the divine which in turn appears to have the reliability of events which were founders of the people's history and to display the threat of the fatal event. With prophecy, the creative dimension can no longer be attained only beyond an abyss of darkness; the God of the Exodus must become the God of the Exile, if he is to remain the God of the future and not only the God of memory.

I will not speak more of this in the limited framework of this essay. It would, in fact, be necessary to explore other forms of discourse and perhaps also other significant contrasts, for example, those of legislation and wisdom, or further those of the hymn and the proverb. Through all these discourses, God appears differently each time: sometimes He appears as the Hero of the Action of salvation, sometimes as the God of Anger and of Compassion, or as the One whom one addresses in an I-Thou relation, or as the One whom one meets only in a cosmic order which is unacquainted with me.

Perhaps an exhaustive inquiry, if it were possible, would reveal that all the forms of discourse together constitute a circular system, and that the theological content of each among them receives its significance from the total constellation of the forms of discourse. Religious language, then, would appear to be a polyphonic language sustained by a circularity of forms. But perhaps this hypothesis is unverifiable and confers on the closing of the canon a sort of necessity which does not allow what should perchance remain an accident of the history of the text. At least this hypothesis is coherent with the central theme of the present analysis, in knowing that the finished work which we call the Bible is a limited space for interpretation, in which the theological significations are correlatives of the *forms of discourse*. Hence, it is not possible to interpret the *significations* without making the long circuit of a structual explanation of *forms*.

II. THE WORD AND THE SCRIPTURE

The second "application" of general hermeneutics to exegesis concerns the pair of the word and the writing. More precisely, biblical hermeneutics receives from philosophical hermeneutics an important warning: do not too quickly construct a theology of the Word which does not include, initially and in principle, the transition from word to writing. This warning is proper, in so far as theology has been answerable for raising the Word above the Scriptures. It does not do this without good reasons: does not a word [*une parole*] precede all writing [*écriture*]? The story-telling word [*parole*] of *sagas*, the word [*parole*] of the prophet, the word [*parole*] of the rabbi, the word of the preacher? Was not Jesus, as Socrates, a preacher and not a writer? Did not primitive Christianity see in Him the word [*parole*] made flesh? And did his witnesses not announce the Gospel as the word [*parole*] of God? It is thus that Christian theology willingly calls itself the "theology of the word [*parole*]", uniting under this term the origin of its faith, the object of its faith, the expression of its faith, all these aspects of the word [*parole*] becoming a unique Word-Event (*Wort-Geschehen*).

One would, therefore, miss what constituted the primary hermeneutic situation of Christian preaching, if one did not place the word-writing relation at the very beginning of the whole problem of interpretation. At every stage the word maintained a relation to writing; from the first it related itself to an earlier writing which it interpreted; Jesus himself interpreted the *Torah*; St. Paul and the author of the Epistle to the Hebrews interpreted the Christian event in the light of the prophecies and institutions of the old covenant; in a general manner, a hermeneutics of the Old Testament, in so far as it is a writing datum, is implied in the proclamation that Jesus is the Christ; all the "titles" which the exegetes call Christological titles proceed from a reinterpretation of the symbols gathered from written Hebraic culture and from Hellenistic culture: King, Messiah, High Priest, Suffering Servant, and Logos. It seems, then, that writing should precede the word, if the word is not to remain a *cry*; indeed, the novelty of the event demands a transmission by the means of an interpretation of previous significations--already written--and disposable in the community of culture. In this sense, Christianity is, from the very beginning, an exegesis (what is called the role of "symbols" and of "types" on the part of Paul). But this is not all: the new preaching, in its turn, is not only bound back to an earlier writing which it interprets. It becomes in its turn a new writing: the letters written to the Romans become letters for all of Christianity; Mark, followed by Matthew and Luke, then John, wrote a Gospel; new documents are added; and, one day, the Church closed the canon, constituting a complete Scripture and closing the *corpus* of witnesses; henceforth all preaching which takes the Scriptures as a guide to its word will be called Christian; it will not be facing *one* scripture--the Hebrew Bible--but *two* Scriptures, the Old and the New Testaments.

Thus was created a hermeneutic situation which has not been immediately recognized as such. But if the formulation of the problem is modern, the problem itself was subjacent to Christian existence itself. From the beginning preaching rested on the testimonies interpreted by the primitive community. Testimony and the interpretation of testimony already contained the element of *distanciation* which made Scripture possible. If one adds that from the beginning a certain variation in the testimony was a part *of* the testimony of the Church, it appears indeed that to this entirely primitive hermeneutic situation belonged also a certain hermeneutic liberty which the insurmountable difference between the four Gospels clearly attests.

It is clear from this reflection on the hermeneutical situation of Christianity that the word-scripture relation is constitutive of what we call proclamation, kerygma, and preaching. What appears first is the chain word-scripture-word, or indeed scripture-word-scripture, in which sometimes the word mediatizes two Scriptures, as the word of Jesus does between the two Testaments, sometimes the Scripture mediatizes two words, as the gospel does between the preaching of the early Church and all contemporary preaching. This chain makes possible a tradition, in the fundamental meaning of the transmission of a message; before being added to the Scripture as a supplementary source, the tradition is the historical dimension of the process which binds the word and the scripture--the scripture and the word to one another. What the scripture brings is the *distanciation* which detaches the message from its speaker, from its initial situation and its original receiver. Thanks to Scripture, the word reaches us and we gain "meaning" by it and by the "thing" with which it deals and no longer by the "voice" of its proclaimer.

We will be asked what makes the specificity of the word and of the biblical writings among other words and other writings. We reply: nothing more than holds true of the relation of the word and of the writing in them. It is in the "thing" of the text that its originality consists.

III. THE NEW BEING AND THE THING OF THE TEXT

Taking always as a guide the categories of general hermeneutics elaborated above, I now come to the third of these categories which I have called the "thing of the text" or the "world of the text". I can say that this is the central category, for philosophical hermeneutics as well as for biblical hermeneutics. All the other categories are articulated in it: the objectification by structure, the distanciation by writing, are only the preliminary condition by which the text says something which should be the "thing" of the text; as to the fourth category--comprehension itself--we have spoken of how it supports itself in the world of the text in order to issue in language. The "thing" of the text, that is the object of hermeneutics. Now the thing of the text is the world which it spreads out before it. And this world, we would add in thinking especially of poetic "literature" and of fiction, takes *distance* with respect to the daily reality toward which ordinary discourse points.

It is in applying these considerations to biblical exegesis that we also make apparent its veritable finality. Even more, it is in applying them to the Bible, as one category of texts among others, that we make possible the reversal which makes general hermeneutics the *organon* of biblical hermeneutics.

Let us follow, then, the way of a simple "application" of the general theme to the text of which we are proceeding to emphasize the internal structure.

This "application", far from submitting biblical hermeneutics to a foreign law, returns it to itself and delivers it from several illusions. First, it delivers it from the temptation to introduce prematurely existential categories or existentials of comprehension, in order to counterbalance the possible excess of structural analysis. Our general hermeneutics bids us to say that the necessary stage between structural explanation and comprehension itself is the unfolding of the world of the text; it is that which finally forms and transforms according to its intention the being-itself of the reader. The theological implication of this is considerable: the first task of hermeneutics is not to arouse a decision on the part of the reader, but first to allow the unfolding of the world of being which is the "thing" of the biblical text. Thus is placed above the feelings, the dispositions, of belief or unbelief, the offer of the world which, in the language of the Bible is called the new world, the new covenant, the kingdom of God, the new birth. These are there as realities spread before the text, for us certainly, but stemming from the text. This is what may be called the "objectivity" of the new being contemplated by the text.

A second implication: to place above everything else the "thing" of the text, is to cease posing the problem of the inspiration of the Scriptures in the psychologizing terms of the insufflation of meaning on an author which is projected into the text, into the author and his production; if the Bible may be called revealed, this should be said of the "thing" which it speaks, of the new being which it discloses. I would dare to say that the Bible is revealed to the extent to which the new being of which it speaks is itself *revealing*, for the consideration of the world, of the totality of reality, including there my existence and my history. Said otherwise, revelation, if the expression is to have any meaning, is a mark of the biblical *world*.

Now this world is not brought forth immediately by psychological designs, but mediately by the structures of the work; all that we have said above of the relations, for example, between the form of the narrative and the signification of Jahweh as the great Actant of action, or on the relations of the form of prophecy with the signification of the Lord as threat and as promise beyond destruction, constitutes the only possible introduction to what we now call the biblical world. The mightiest power of revelation arises from the contrast and the convergence of all the forms of discourse taken together.

A third theological application of the category of the world of the text: because it involves a world, in the sense of a global horizon, a totality of significations, there is no immunity from the law for a teaching which is addressed to an individual person, and in general no license for the personalistic aspects, of the I-Thou form, in the relation of man to God. The biblical world has cosmic dimensions--it is a creation--members of a community--it involves a people--historico-cultural phenomena--it is a question of Israel, of the kingdom of God--and personal elements. Man is traced according to his multiple dimensions which are cosmological, historical-world-wide, as much as anthropological, ethical and personalist.

A fourth theological application of the category of the world of the text: we have said that the world of the "literary" text is a purposed world and one which is poetically removed from daily reality; is this not true par excellence of the new being planned and offered by the Bible? Will not this new being make a way through the world of ordinary experience despite the blockade of this experience? Is not the power of projection of this world a power of breaking and opening? And if it is thus, is it not necessary to grant to this projection of the world the *poetic* dimension, in the strong sense of that word, which we have recognized in the thing of the text?

Going to the end, and drawing the most ultimate conclusions, is it not necessary to say that what is thus opened in the daily reality is another reality, the reality of the *possible*? Let us remember one of the most valuable remarks of Heidegger on *Verstehen*; for Heidegger, *Verstehen* is diametrically opposed to *Befindlichkeit*, to the degree where the *Verstehen* is addressed to the possibilities the most our own and deciphers them in a situation which cannot be projected, because we are already thrown there. In theological language, this means to say: "the Kingdom of God is come", that is to say, that it makes appeal to the possibilities the most our own starting from the meaning of this kingdom which does not come from us. But this remark has implications of which it will be necessary to speak further when we take up the concept of *faith* in the light of our fourth hermeneutical category, that of "understanding oneself before the text".

The path which I have followed was that of the "application" of a general hermeneutical category to biblical hermeneutics treated as a regional hermeneutics. My thesis is that this way is the only one at the end of which the specificity of the biblical "thing" can at the same time be recognized. In this Ebeling is right: it is by going to the end of listening to this book, as one book among others, that one can meet it as the word of God. But, once more, this recognition does not make an appeal to a psychological concept of inspiration, as if the authors repeated a word which had been whispered in their ears. This recogniton speaks to the quality of the new being, such as it announces itself.

One of the marks which make up the specificity of the biblical discourse is, as we know, the central place which the referent, God, holds there. It is not a question of denying, but of understanding this place and this role. The earlier analysis shows that the signification of this referent of biblical discourse is implied, in a special manner of which it yet remains to speak, in the multiple solidary significations of the literary forms of narration, of prophecy, of the hymn, of wisdom, etc. The "God-Talk"--to take up McQuarrie's expression[1]--procedes from the concurrence and the convergence of these partial discourses. The referent, God, is at the same time the coordinator of these diverse discourses, and the point of escape, the index of incompleteness, of these partial discourses.

In this sense, the word God does not function as a philosophical concept, such as that of being, whether it be taken in the medieval sense or in the Heideggerian sense; even if one is tempted to say--in the theological metalanguage of all these pre-theological languages--that God is the religious name of being, the word God says more: it presupposes the total context constituted by the entire gravitation space of stories, prophecies, legislations, hymns, etc.; to understand the word God is to follow the arrow of the meaning of the word. By the arrow of meaning, I mean its double power: to reassemble all the significations issuing from the partial discourses, and to open a horizon which breaks out of the enclosure of the discourse.

I will say the same thing of the word Christ. To the double function of the word God which I have pointed out, it adds the power of incarnating all the religious significations in a fundamental symbol: the symbol of sacrificial love, of a love stronger than death. It is the function of the preaching of the Cross and the Resurrection to give to the word God a *density* which the word being does not harbour. Its signification contains the notion of *his* relation to us as "ultimately concerned" and fully "grateful".

It would, then, be the task of a biblical hermeneutics to unfold all the implications of this constitution and of this articulation of *God-Talk*.

We see now in what sense this biblical hermeneutics is at the same time a particular instance of the sort of general hermeneutics described earlier, and a unique affair. It is a particular case, because the new being of which the Bible speaks is not to be sought elsewhere than in the world of this text which is one text among others. It is a unique case, because all the partial discourses are referred to one Name, which is the intersection point and the index of the incompleteness of all our discourse about God, and because this Name has become solidaric with the *meaning-event* preached as Resurrection. But biblical hermeneutics can claim to say something unique only if this unique thing speaks as the world of the text. It is this essential point on which I wish to insist in placing theological hermeneutics under the third category of general hermeneutics, to know the world of the work.

IV. THE HERMENEUTICAL CONSTITUTION OF THE BIBLICAL FAITH

I reach the end of my essay in inquiring about the theological implications of the fourth category of our hermeneutics centered on the text. This is, we remember, the existential category par excellence, that of *appropriation*.

I wish to underline three consequences for biblical hermeneutics of the relation which we have laid down between the world of the work and the understanding which the reader assumes of himself before the text.

First, what, in theological language, is called faith, is constituted in the strongest sense of the term, by the new being which is the "thing" of the text. In thus recognizing the hermeneutical constitution of the biblical faith, we resist as much as possible all psychologizing reduction of the faith. This is not to say that the faith should not be authentically an *act* irreducible to all linguistic treatment; in this sense, the limit of all hermeneutics is indeed reached, at the same time as the non-hermeneutical origin of all interpretation; the limitless progress of interpretation begins and ends in the risk of a response which no commentary can either engender or exhaust. It is to take account of this pre-linguistic or hyper-linguistic character that men have been able to call the "ultimate concern", in order to say that the seizure of the only needful thing begins from what I ascertain to be my position in all my choices; this has been called a "feeling of absolute dependence", to underline that it responds to an initiative which always precedes me; it has again been called "unconditional trust", in order to say that it is inseparable from a progress of hope which opens the way in spite of the contradictions of experience, and which transforms reasons for despair into reasons for hope, according to the paradoxical laws of a logic of superabundance. By all these traits, the thematics of the faith escapes a hermeneutics and attests that this is neither the first, nor the last word.

But what hermeneutics reminds us is this: the biblical faith cannot be separated from a progress of interpretation which raises it to language. The "ultimate concern" remains *mute* if it does not receive power from the word of an interpretation ceaselessly recommencing from the signs and symbols which have, if I may say so, educated and formed this concern in the heart of the centuries. The feeling of absolute dependence remains a weak and inarticulate sentiment if it is not the response to the offer of a new being which opens for me new possibilities of existence; hope, unconditional trust, would be empty if it were not supported by an interpretation constantly renewed from the sign-events reported by the Scriptures, such as the *Exodus* in the Old Testament, and the *Resurrection* in the New Testament. These are events of deliverance which open and uncover the most personal possibility of my own liberty and thus become for me the word of God. Such is the properly hermeneutic constitution of the faith itself. Such also is the primary theological consequence of the indissoluble correlation which we have uncovered between the world of the text and appropriation.

A second consequence results from the kind of distanciation which hermeneutical reflection brings to light at the heart of the understanding of oneself, when this understanding is a "self-understanding before the text". From the time one submits the understanding of self to the *Selbstdarstellung* of the "thing" of the text, a *critique* of illusions on the subject appears included in the act of "self-understanding before the text". Precisely because the subject brings himself into the text and because the "structure of comprehension", of which Heidegger speaks, cannot be eliminated from the comprehension which desires to allow the text to speak, for this reason the criticism of oneself becomes an integrating part of the understanding of oneself before the text.

It is here that I perceive an essential articulation between the criticism of religion in the fashion of Marx, Neitzsche and Freud, and the self-understanding of faith. This criticism of religion, rightly understood, is constituted wholly outside of hermeneutics, as a criticism of ideologies, as a criticism of reactionary worlds, as a criticism of illusions. But, for a hermeneutical understanding centered on the text, this criticism can at the same time remain the recognition of the adversary from *without*, which one is not tempted to retrieve and baptize by force, and become the instrument of an *inner* criticism, which properly belongs to the work of distanciation which all comprehension of oneself before the text requires. I, myself, have begun to do this work in my book of Freud;[2] I have pushed it a little further in *The Conflict of Interpretations*;[3] a "hermeneutics of suspicion" today is an integral part of all appropriation of meaning. Along with it goes the "demolishing" of prejudices which hinder the untrammeled existence of the world of the text.

The third and last consequence which I should like to draw from the hermeneutics of appropriation concerns the positive aspect of distanciation itself which I see implied by all comprehension of oneself before the text; the demolishing of the illusions of the subject is only the negative aspect of what it is rightly necessary to call "the imagination".

I am venturing to speak for the first time of the *creative* dimension of distanciation, in using an expression borrowed from Husserl; I have spoken of "imaginative variations" on my ego, to describe this opening of new possibilities which is the work in me of the "thing" of the text; one could have recourse to another analogy which Gadamer himself loved to develop, the analogy of "play" [*jeu*];[4] just as play sets free, in the vision of reality, new possibilities held prisoner by the spirit of "seriousness", play also opens within subjectivity the possibilities of a *metamorphosis* which a purely *moral* vision of subjectivity does not permit to be seen. Imaginative variations, play, metamorphosis--all these expressions seek to encircle a fundamental phenomenon, to know what it is in the *imagination* which first forms the new being in me. I rightly say the imagination and not the will. For the power of allowing oneself to be seized by new possibilities precedes the power of deciding and of choosing. The imagination is that dimension of subjectivity which responds to the text as a *Poem*. When the distanciation of the imagination responds to the distanciation which the "thing" of the text digs out at the heart of reality, a poetics of existence responds to the poetics of discourse.

This last consequence of a hermeneutics which puts the "thing" of the text above the comprehension of oneself is perhaps the most important, if one considers the most general tendency of existential hermeneutics to accent the moment of decision before the text; I will say, for my part, in line with a hermeneutics starting with the text and with the "thing" of the text, that it is first to my imagination that the text speaks, in offering to it the "symbolics" of my liberation.

NOTES

1. J. McQuarrie, *God-Talk. An Examination of the Language and Logic of Theology*, London, 1967.

2. P. Ricoeur, *Freud and Philosophy; An Essay in Interpretation*, New Haven, 1970.

3. P. Ricoeur, *The Conflict of Interpretations*, Evanston, 1974.

4. H. G. Gadamer, *Truth and Method*, New York, 1975, p. 91ff.

PART FOUR

A Look at the Exegesis of the Fathers

GRÉGOIRE ROUILLER

Augustine of Hippo Reads Genesis 22:1-19

YVES TISSOT

Patristic Allegories of the Lukan
Parable of the Two Sons

Luke 15:11-32

AUGUSTINE OF HIPPO READS GENESIS 22:1-19

by Grégoire Rouiller

This should not surprise us: we do not find on the part of Augustine a literal commentary on Genesis 22 comparable to that of H. Gunkel. Nevertheless, we will ascertain to what degree this page of the Old Testament remained vital throughout the work of the Bishop of Hippo. It is mentioned in relation to varied situations and interpreted according to various literary genres.

We can examine here only some of the principal texts:[1]

a homily probably delivered in A.D. 391, Sermon II;

a fragment of an exegetical treatise, taken from the *Enarrationes* on Psalm 30, dated from the years A.D. 394-396, second sermon, numbers 9-10;

finally, a passage from the major work, the *City of God*, written probably between the years A.D. 410-413, the 32nd chapter of Book XVI.

I. SERMON II: "*De Abraham ubi temptatus a Deo*"

After the anquish to which the scene in the garden at Milan testifies,[2] Augustine received baptism in A.D. 387. In continuity with what he had just experienced, he desired to retire in company with some friends (some "servi Dei") to a philosophical-theological retreat where prayer, fraternal communion, and the intellectual quest should hold the chief place. The experience which has been called the "ecstasy of Ostia" appears to me revelatory of his state of mind during the years which followed his baptism. Lasting echoes of it are also to be found not only in the *Confessions* but in his biblical commentaries.[3]

We know how his initial project was denied by the mission which the Church of Hippo entrusted to him:

> I, in whom you see your bishop by the grace of God, was still a young man when I arrived in this city, as many of you know. I was looking for a place to establish a monastery to live with my brothers....I feared so much the episcopal charge that, when my reputation had begun to reckon me among the servants of God, I took care not to go where they were on the lookout for a bishop, I attentively saw to this and did my utmost to seek salvation in a humble position rather than to risk perishing in an elevated rank. But, as I have said, a servant cannot be opposed to his master. I came into this city to see a friend whom I thought I could win to God and to invite him to take part in our life in the monastery. I was peaceful since Hippo had settled on a bishop. I was seized, made a priest, and that led me finally to the episcopate (*Sermo* 355. I).

The first priest to support Valerius, the Greek bishop who spoke Latin poorly and did not know Punic, was established, against custom, in A.D. 395, as bishop-coadjutor with Valerius.

It is at Hippo that he preached our sermon. The task of Augustine was not simple in this city of around 40,000 inhabitants, where the "catholic" church found itself very much in a minority position faced with a Donatist Church supported by the landed proprietaries and holding the levers of economic life as well as the administration.[4] For a long time he had to reckon with the influence of a Donatist exegete as renowned as Tyconius[5] and, even in the city of Hippo, with a strong portion of Manichaeans grouped around Fortunatus.[6]

The Arrangement of the Sermon

It unfolds itself with much flexibility by a concatenation sometimes verbal--one predicts the ancient rhetorician--and sometimes doctrinal. In spite of its incontestable unity, it presents itself as a series of replies to some precise questions. Let us go over the principal steps.

Lines 1-9a. At the outset Augustine places us before a striking example of *pietas* and of *fides*: the scene is presented afresh.

Lines 9b-41a. The two major moments in the life of Abraham are brought together in an evocative parallel: that of the promise (Gen. 15) and that of the sacrifice (Gen. 22). In both cases, the *religio* of Abraham was identical:

> His arm was chosen for the sacrifice which could lead Isaac to death as his heart had been elected for the faith which could permit his birth. Abraham had no hesitation in his faith when the birth of Isaac was announced to him; he did not hesitate the more to offer him when that was demanded of him.

He did not at all question himself over the apparent contradiction between the two interventions of God. His trust towers over all.

Lines 41b-129. Augustine must then inquire about the temptation itself. He proceeds by stages:

Lines 41b-54a. He first clothes his thought in a very compact sentence. God tempts, yes, but "ut ipse homo se inveniat", "in order that man may discover himself".

Lines 54b-96. Then, before developing the meaning of this sentence, he must refute an otherwise radical objection: is it not necessary to reject the God of the law and of the Old Testament? Does not the fact that he tempts furnish proof of his cruelty?

Lines 97-116. The objection of the Manichaeans resolved, he can ask: how is man able to discover himself by temptation? By responding to the interrogation of the teacher, he says, since temptation is an examination. In fact, "if God should cease to tempt, the teacher would cease to teach".[7]

Lines 117-129. The theme of instruction continues. Even if Abraham had no need of it, we could not say as much. Also the message of his example ought to be heard.

Lines 130-258. To this point Augustine has sought the meaning of the *rerum gestarum*. He proceeds to penetrate the *sacramentum* of it.

Lines 130-168. This *sacramentum* is so elevated that a long preparation of spirit is necessary. The mystery opens itself only to the eyes and the ears of the believing heart.

Lines 169-218. The prophetic aspect is illuminated. The person of Isaac, the actions of Abraham, the presence and the immolation of the ram, all point us toward what was accomplished in Jesus Christ. The promises made to Abraham are themselves fulfilled in the people "who believe without having seen" in the crucified.

Lines 219-253. By way of inclusion and of homiletic conclusion Augustine finally admires in Genesis 22 the *magna fides* and the *magnum opus*, "faith working through love".[8]

We may then schematize this compact arrangement:

1. *An exemplary conduct:* lines 1-41a
   --introduction: lines 1-9a;
   --the trial resulting from faith: lines 9b-41a.

2. *The human meaning of this trial:* lines 41b-129
   --as ground of freedom: lines 41b-54a; 97-116;
   --compatible with the love of God: lines 54b-96;
   --educator of a lineage: lines 117-129.

3. *The prophetic meaning of this trial:* lines 130-253
   --*sacramentum* to accept humbly: lines 130-168;
   --*sacramentum* realized in Jesus Christ and in the believing people: lines 169-218;
   --conclusion: lines 219-253.

Annotations on the Reading

We could not think of giving a literal commentary on this sermon. Nevertheless, let us underline some of its important aspects.

Lines 1-9a. The introduction permits us to divine the aesthetic sense of Augustine. He has perceived that the narrative of Genesis 22 was of such an art that its reading has the character of a memorial. The reader reconstitutes the event with its original feeling, as if temporal distance were abolished.[9]

The attitude of Abraham is characterized as *pietas*. The French term piety does not capture the richness of this Latin word. It involves a complex and total attitude which corresponds precisely with the reverence and the kindness called forth by the Hebrew חסד. In any case we are not far from what Genesis 22 calls "the fear of God".

Lines 9b-41a. Augustine is too sensitive to the teaching of Saint Paul to insist, as a certain Jewish theology does, on the merit of Abraham and of Isaac. By instinct he senses that one arch joins the main centers of Abraham's life (the promise and the sacrifice), that in the one case as in the other the Word of God (promising or ordering) had encountered the same faith on the part of the patriarch. Thus, for Augustine, Genesis 15:6, which he explicitly cites, overhangs the entire behaviour of Abraham as the last redactor of Genesis wished to transmit it to us.

It is for this reason that the faith of Abraham is presented to us in the light of Romans 4 and Galatians 4. It is a faith which conquers contradictory appearances, according an unlimited credibility to the word of a God whose kindness it has experienced. For Augustine the confidence of Abraham in the wisdom[10] of the creator God is such that at no instant could it be touched with the thought of a contradiction between the will of the creator God and the will of the Saviour who demanded such a sacrifice of him. This unlimited confidence in the goodness of God cleanses even Abraham from all suspicion of cruelty. He was, said Augustine: "ubique fidelis, nusquam crudelis".

Lines 54b-96. Why did God tempt him? Before studying Augustine's reply, we must recall his vigorous reaction to the Manichaean objections. Temptation is not fitting for God, said the Manichaeans.[11] Does it not lift up again the God of the Law, who is cruel and evil?[12] Augustine, because he had lived for nine years as an auditor among the Manichaeans, was well acquainted with their doctrines. He also had been tormented by the question of the origin of evil; he also had thought to find the elements of a solution in the radical dualism of the Manichaeans, an appeasement in their quest for liberation.[13] To the precise question which is posed here, he replied according to the procedure which he utilized several times: "If you wish to reject the God of Abraham because he tempts, you must also reject the Christ since he likewise tempts, as is proved by the word which the Gospel of John relates to us (6.6)."[14] On this point we might be tempted to say that Augustine's reply is no more profound than the objection which was made to him.[15] On the contrary, the end of the paragraph reveals to us his competence as a polemicist. The Manichaeans reproached God for tempting. Augustine returned the accusation, by a verbal game, and showed that the true temptor, and that in the most pejorative sense possible, is the Manichaean himself: "It must be acknowledged: Christ tempts; God tempts; but let the heretical tempter be confounded. Indeed, the heretic does not tempt in the same manner as God. God tempts to open the door to man, the heretic to close himself to God's revelation."[16]

Lines 41b-54a; 97-116. We have observed: Augustine first gives a weighty reply (God tempts "ut ipse homo inveniat"), then, once the basic objection is resolved, he brings forward the explanations. We especially wish to note the course of these.

Without temptation, man would never attain his stature. Temptation is, in fact, nothing other than space offered to freedom. Trial, yes; but a testing which presents itself as a possibility to seize, as a risk to run, as a dignity to receive. There are some very valuable insights here for a theology of freedom. Man is not a prefabricated robot. Without prejudice for the knowledge of God nor for the necessity of his grace, the free choice of man is set in full light. No one can substitute himself for man in the face of *his* temptation, not even God. This solitude in the face of essential choice constitutes the grandeur of a free being. If God tempts it is because there is for man no other way toward fulfillment.[17]

Beginning with line 97, the forms and the meaning of this testing of man are stated precisely in categories with a neo-Platonic coloring. Temptation is an interrogation ("illo temptante, id est, interrogante"). This interrogation itself is nothing other than an instruction, that which leads man to the discovery of his true self.[18] If God should cease tempting, the teacher would cease teaching. One could follow the numerous resonances of this trilogy in Augustine's work:

temptation, interrogation, teaching, the three gravitating around the idea of the inner teacher.

There is, as it were, a hesitation by Augustine in line 117. Perhaps Abraham, by reason of his dignity as patriarch, had no need of this trial in order to know himself and to realize himself? In the face of this possibility Augustine reveals himself as pastor and preacher. Even if, in the precise case of Abraham, his interpretation proved to be erroneous, the trial to which Abraham submitted retains all its importance in the face of its exemplary value. It is a valuable lesson for us. We believe that Augustine here reached one of the summits of his interpretation. Everything is cancelled from the walk of Abraham, and that of Isaac, and from the preparation and execution of the sacrifice which would confine it within a too narrow context. The story is decontextualized, in order that nothing may do injury to its universal importance. Then it lives for us as pure invitation, axial to our freedom, a lesson which can be transformed into a rule of life. "What does Abraham teach us? I will say it briefly (note how this *brevity* announces the importance and the decisive imprint of the formula which follows!): he teaches us not to prefer the gifts of God to God."[19] Thus reflection on the events recounted (the *littera rerum gestarum*) is not disregarded. We learn there who man is: a free being summoned to the dignity of responding. We discover a new aspect of God: that of a pedagogue who takes seriously the man whom he has created. We know finally that the true destiny of man resides in a perpetual self-effacement which forbids all improper and idolatrous worship of that which God has given him, be it an only son. If man follows this teaching which the example of Abraham brings to him, sin will no longer dwell in his life. For is not an excellent definition of sin to prefer "that which God gives to God"? Or positively, "what sweeter recompense could come to us from God, than God himself?"[20]

Lines 130-253. The first part of the sermon has developed what we could call the anthropological comprehension of the sacrifice of Abraham. It must now aim higher and put on the alert the inner senses of his hearers, the eyes and the ears of the heart.[21] For it is a question of searching closely into the grand *sacramentum* contained in the strange order to sacrifice the son of the promise. Some important points, it seems to us, should be underlined in this second part of the sermon:

First, the advice given by Augustine. It is of, not to take refuge too quickly, and before a serious examination of the events recounted, in spiritual speculations "for fear," he observes, "that having neglected the foundation set in the event itself, you should try to construct it in the air".[22]

Augustine has previously brought this realistic view to the sacrifice of Abraham. That is why he can in the future, without temerity, search closely into it for the prophetic aspect, for, as often happens in the Old Testament, "that which is written on the subject of Abraham is both the narration of an event and a prophecy",[23] as the authority of St. Paul, whom Augustine invokes, confirms. To search deeply into these figures for the realities to come in Jesus Christ was always one of the great tasks of Augustine as a reader of the Old Testament.

Also, according to him, what the story of Genesis 22 foretells and what the Christian contemplates as realized is magnificent: it is the accomplishment of all the prophecies of salvation in the slain Jesus, the realization of the blessings in the multitude of believers.[24] What is striking here is the sobriety of his typological reading and the feeling which obtains in the quasi-liturgical enumeration of symbolic acts which find their full justification when the Christ can apply to Himself the word of the Psalmist: "they have pierced my hands and feet".[25]

II. A FRAGMENT OF THE ENARRATION ON PSALM 30

This commentary on Psalm 30 belongs to the Carthaginian period. We know that by reason of the events which troubled the Christians of Africa, Augustine was particularly sensible in his *Enerrationes* to the mystery of the Church. He read in the Psalms all the vicissitudes of the Church in history. He interpreted all of them in the single light of Jesus Christ foretold, incarnated, and continuing in His members. The city of which the Psalms speak is established in Jesus Christ. It is of Him as Husband that we speak when we call forth the image of the Spouse. The voice which is heard in the Psalms is always that of Christ, sometimes as head of the body, sometimes as a member.

Likewise, the commentary on our Psalm is strongly marked by the Donatist crisis. Augustine sees the misfortunes of the Church of his time foretold and described in it. When he meets the words of the Psalm: "those who see me in the street flee from me", he compares the situation of those who are born among the Donatists to that of those who read the Scriptures and preach in this Church. These last appear impardonable to him. How have they not ascertained that the Church is clearly foreseen as universal, that it is called to embrace the entire universe?[26] Besides, the prophets, who have predicted the coming of Christ in a veiled fashion, have, on the contrary, spoken clearly of the Church. Genesis 22, according to Augustine, furnishes a beautiful example of this double attitude of the prophets. He also insists on three points.

First, on the obedience of Abraham, over which he lingers to relate the evidence in detail. He was "always obedient," he says, "and never timorous." Here again we meet, with the insistence on the part of Augustine on the events, the *res gestae*.

Further, Genesis 22 prophetically foresees the Christ and His Cross. To speak of it he introduces the term *figura* which is not found in Sermon II. The whole scene is read as "a figure of Christ enveloped in mysteries",[27] as a chain of symbols which call for interpretation.[28] It is necessary to recognize that, without doing it in excessive fashion, the exegesis of Augustine is here plainly more allegorical than in the sermon.[29]

Finally, the Church is foreseen, but without any figure: "The head having been foretold, immediately the body must be foretold"; "the Spirit foretold the Christ in figure, but he predicts the Church openly."[30] Augustine thus stresses Genesis 22:15-18, because these verses admirably serve his purpose.

III. THE SACRIFICE OF ABRAHAM IN THE CITY OF GOD

"Great work is difficult," said Augustine. We know that the *City of God* was undertaken and written after the event which most men held as inconceivable: the taking of Rome by the Goths of Alaric, in August, A.D. 410. In Africa, as a consequence of the influx of well-to-do intellectuals and disillusioned men, we witness a sort of small literary "Renaissance" devoted to the cult of pagan Antiquity. The *Saturnales* of Macrobius are a good example of this. Once more

Augustine wishes to respond to the questions of his time. During thirteen years he worked, in the midst of numerous difficulties and temptations, on this work which will endure as a testimony to his erudition and his faith.

Abraham and his sacrifice find their place in the vast fresco which describes the outlines of the City of God in the Old Testament. Let us recall the following points:

One senses in the language and in the thought of Augustine a great assurance. The beginning of the chapter recapitulates, in a very spirited style, what the sermon had detailed:

> Abraham was tempted to prove his devout obedience, and so make it known to the world, not to God. For trial is not intended to blame in every case: inasmuch as it becomes a confirmation, it must be seen as felicitous. Generally the human spirit cannot come to self-knowledge except in the response it makes to the trial which tests its powers, not verbally but experimentally; if it recognizes it as a gift of God, then it is pious and is strengthened in the power of grace rather than being puffed up by vainglory.[31]

All the earlier elements are restated here but softened and clarified by a more conscious contrast between a response "in word" (*verbo*) and a response "in act" (*experimento*).

The exegesis of Augustine is also more under the influence of St. Paul, exalting grace and distrusting all vainglory.[32] It is also very strongly inspired by the Epistle to the Hebrews: Abraham believed greatly in God who is capable of resurrecting the dead.[33]

The sacrifice, he notes anew, presents to us symbolically the death of Christ,[34] but above all--and this trait agrees well with the purpose of the *City of God*--Augustine exalts the blessings and promises which foretell the calling of the Gentiles.[35] The promise of universality for the Church emphasized in the *Enarrationes* on Psalm 30 here becomes the *vocatio gentium* foretold and sanctioned by an oath.

In the three principal texts dealt with, we verify both the strength and the flexibility of Augustine. Three centers of interest meet again with an astonishing persistence: the anthropological importance of the temptation, the symbolic foretelling of the Cross of Jesus, the undisguised preaching of the gathering of the nations in the redeemed City. This does not prevent us from rereading the text in situations as different as the anti-Manichaean polemic, the anti-Donatist battle or the profound troubles consequent to the fall of Rome. A complete study of Augustine's exegesis of this chapter of Genesis should take account of other passages of his work.[36] These three, however, permit us to draw some lessons in method.

IV. REMARKS AND CONCLUSIONS

1. Augustine's reading may be characterized as at once theological and timely. It unfolded under the light of the faith formulated at Nicea, it moved forward on dogmatic evidences (concerning, for example, the Christ, the Cross and the Church) never brought into question. In spite of that, and this seems to me very interesting from the hermeneutical point of view, it is an exegesis which is not willing to be atemporal. It means to respond to the interrogations and the difficulties of its time.

2. For him, all Scripture constitutes a coherent *corpus* without possible contradiction. The Spirit is good and He is unique. It is He who presided at the drawing up, as it is He who ought to preside at the interpretation of the entire Scrip-

tures. The obscurities of Scripture should not astonish us since it, of necessity, introduces us to mystery; but everything should be clarified by recourse to Scripture itself. The verb "tempt" in Genesis 22 should thus be related to the verb "tempt" in John 6:5, etc.

3. There is not in our texts, nor in the rest of Augustine's work, a firm theory of the meaning of Scripture such as those formulated later.[37] With him there is a prolixity of terms and a multiplicity of points of view in speaking of the meaning of Scripture. Nevertheless, by aesthetic sensibility and by neo-Platonic formation, he was at the same time drawn toward concrete detail and toward the quest for strongly spiritual hidden meanings. As E. Gilson has well seen, there was within Augustine a poet who delighted in digression. But in other respects there is in him an ardent reader of parables, always sensing a surplus of meaning, a further meaning. That is why the terms *velatio*, *mysterium*, and especially *sacramentum* hold such a place for him.[38] It is necessary to value the fruitfulness of this permanent interrogation of the "letter" in order to make the "spirit" burst forth, this refusal to lock up Scripture in a definitively formulated interpretation.[39]

4. The passing from "figures" to the reality which they evoke is above all effected according to a chronological axis, that of the harmony between the two Testaments. Augustine loves to speak of the "passing to Christ" and the term *transitus* is likewise revealing. Thus the entire Old Testament becomes a figure to interpret,[40] with the presence of Christ as the unique key of interpretation.[41]

5. Finally, one must ask himself whether, when dealing with a text like Genesis 22 which, manifestly, is not the register of an event but the fruit of a very conscious theological composition, the method championed by Augustine of

believing interrogation of the *rerum gestarum*, then the listening to the *sacramentum*, is not scientifically more justified than that which delights in a documentary dissection turned towards the past and ignores the final stages of the writing. In any case, we think that Augustine would not be far from subscribing to certain remarks made by E. Auerbach concerning Genesis 22:

For the narratives of Scripture

> are not like Homer's simply narrated 'reality'. Doctrine and promise are incarnate in them and inseparable from them; for that very reason they are fraught with 'background' and mysterious, containing a second, concealed meaning. In the story of Isaac, it is not only God's intervention at the beginning and the end, but even the factual and psychological elements which come between, that are mysterious, merely touched upon, fraught with background; and therefore they require subtle investigations and interpretations, they demand them....The text is charged with a content so rich, it carries so many indications on the being of God and on the conduct of pious men, that the believer must ceaselessly plunge into it, he must search in the details of the story for an elucidation which could have escaped him. Since so much in the story is dark and incomplete, and since the reader knows that God is a hidden God, his effort to interpret it constantly finds something new to feed upon. Doctrine and the search for enlightenment are inextricably connected with the physical side of the narrative--the latter being more than simple 'reality', indeed they are in constant danger of losing their own reality, as very soon happened when interpretation reached such proportions that the real vanished.[42]

NOTES

1. We cite the texts from the edition *Corpus Christianorum*, Latin Series, Leiden (beginning from 1958), the French translation of Sermon II by A. Rouiller: "Saint Augustin: La tentation d'Abraham (Genèse 22)," *Echos de Saint-Maurice* 4 (1974), pp. 51-58.

2. Cf. *Confessions*, VIII, 12.

3. For example, in the *Enarration* on Psalm 41, nums. 7-10.

4. Cf. C. *Litt. Pet.* LXXXIII, 184: "Nonne apud Hipponem, ubi ego sum, non desunt qui meminerint Faustinum uestrum regni sui tempore praecepisse, quoniam catholicorum ibi paucitas erat, ut nullus eis panem coqueret."

5. Cf. P. Brown, *La vie de saint Augustin*, Paris, 1971, p. 323.

6. It was on August 28, 392 that he had a decisive confrontation with Fortunatus. Vanquished, this one had to leave the city; cf. *C. Fortun.* I.

7. "Si Deus cessat temptare, magister cessat docere", lines 106-107. "...illo temptante, id est, interrogante, quod est in homine occultum prodatur", lines 99-100.

8. He supported himself by the interpretation already suggested of Romans 4 and Galatians 4.

9. "Verumtamen nescio quomodo, quotiescumque legitur, *quasi tunc fiat*, ita afficit mentes audientium", lines 5-7.

10. On his part, this was connected with a very firm vision of the world. Read on this point: G. Madec, "Sur la vision augustinienne du monde," *Revue des études augustiniennes* 9 (1963), pp. 139-146.

11. Perhaps he even had some Manichean hearers. He spoke then "propter hos ergo tales, ne qui forte hic lateant, aut et si hic non sunt, habeant qui adsunt quid talibus respondeant", lines 62-64.

12. We find numerous references in the following work: M. Pontet, *L'exégèse de S. Augustin prédicateur*, Paris, 1944, p. 234ff.

13. Cf. this declaration of the Manichaean catechism: "The first thing which a man ought to do is to distinguish the two Principles. Whoever wishes to adhere to our religion must know that the two Principles of Light and of Darkness have absolutely distinct natures: if he does not discern that, how can he put the doctrine into practice?" Cited by P. Brown, *op. cit.*, p. 53.

14. The Manicheans placed in contradiction several texts from the Old and the New Testament, for example, Gen. 1:1 and John 1:1; or again, Psalm 35:7 and I Cor. 9:9.

15. Elsewhere, in *Question. in Heptam.* I, 57, PL 34, 562-563, he discusses from the passage in the Epistle of James: "Quaeri solet quomodo hoc verum sit, cum dicat in epistula sua Jacobus, quod Deus neminem tentat; nisi quia locutione Scripturarum solet dici: tentat, pro eo quod est probat."

16. "Agnoscitur temptator Christus, agnoscitur temptator Deus, corrigatur temptator haereticus. Non enim sic temptat haereticus, quomodo temptat Deus. Deus enim temptat *ut aperiat homini*, haereticus temptat *ut Deum sibi claudat*", lines 92-96.

17. It is difficult to translate the verb "inveniat" in the pregnant formula: God tempts "ut ipse homo se *inveniat*", line 54.

18. "Quia nescit se homo, nisi in temptatione discat se", lines 114-115.

19. "Quid ergo nos docet Abraham? Ut breviter dicam: ut Deo non praeponamus quod dat Deus", lines 121-122.

20. "Quod enim dulcius a Deo praemium, quam ipse Deus?", lines 128-129.

21. E. Gilson, *Introduction à l'étude de S. Augustin*, Paris, 1943[2]. The idea of inner meaning is here studied at length. One will note the completeness of the phrase: "Patente aure cordis audite magnum sacramentum", line 159.

22. "...admonemus...ut quando auditis exponi sacramentum scripturae narrantis quae gesta sunt, prius illud quod lectum

est credatis sic gestum, quomodo lectum est, ne subtracto fundamento rei gestae, quasi in aere quaeratis aedificare", lines 170-174. One could consult on this important point the work of H. De Lubac, *Exégèse médiévale*, II, Paris, 1959, p. 435ff.

23. "Quidquid scriptum est de Abraham, et factum est, et prophetia est", lines 192-193. Further, lines 197-198: "...quia Isaac et natus est Abrahae, et aliquid significavit."

24. He cites implicitly John 20:29: "Felices gentes, quae illud non audierunt, et nunc legentes crediderunt quod credidit ille qui audivit", lines 221-223.

25. Psalm 22:16.

26. On the Donatist Church as the pure Church, on the defensive, consult P. Brown, *op. cit.*, pp. 249-265.

27. "...figura est Christi inuoluta sacramentis", line 15.

28. "Denique ut videatur discutitur, ut videatur pertractatur, ut quod inuolutum est euoluatur", lines 15-16.

29. For example, as line 20: "Quid est enim haerere cornibus, nisi quodam modo crucifigi?"

30. "Et paene ubique Christus aliquo inuolucro sacramenti praedicatus est a prophetis, ecclesia aperte", lines 29-30. Or again, "Christum figurate praedicabat, ecclesiam aperte praedicavit", lines 24-25.

31. "...temptatur Abraham de immolando dilectissimo filio ipso Isaac, ut pia ejus oboedientia probaretur, saeculis in notitiam proferenda, non Deo. Neque enim omnis est culpanda temptatio, quia et gratulanda est, qua fit probatio. Et plerumque, aliter animus humanus sibi ipsi innotescere non potest, nisi uires suas sibi non uerbo, sed experimento temptatione quodam modo interrogante respondeat; ubi si Dei munus agnouerit, tunc pius est, tunc solidatur firmitate gratiae, non inflatur inanitate jactantiae", lines 2-10.

32. In the same chapter, he cites Gal. 4:26; Rom. 9:8; Rom. 8:32.

33. Hebrews 11:17f.

34. This sacrifice is presented with many details. Nevertheless, we may measure the Augustinian sobriety when it is a

question of allegory, if we read in comparison with this page that of Ambrose, *De Abraham II, 8.*

35. "Hoc modo est illa de uocatione gentium in semine Abraham post holocaustum, quo significatus est Christus, etiam juratione Dei firmata promissio", lines 64-67.

36. For example, *De Trinitate*, III, 11 where he examines himself on a precise question, that of the relations between God and the angel who called in Genesis 22:11, 12, 15, etc.

37. On this whole question, read the great work of H. de Lubac, *Exégèse médiévale*, Paris, 1959, 4 vols.

38. The statement of C. Couturier numbered 2279 employs the terms "mysterium" and "sacramentum". His entire study is: C. Couturier, "'Sacramentum' et 'mysterium' dans l'oeuvre de saint Augustin," in: *Etudes augustiniennes*, Paris, 1953, pp. 161-332.

39. M. Pontet, *op. cit.*, pp. 167-170, points out numerous references illustrating this opposition between the letter and the spirit.

40. "Solent divini veteres libri, non solum rei gestae fidem, sed etiam futurae insinuare mysterium", PL 38, 92.

41. "Christum in divinis libris videris", PL 38, 92.

42. E. Auerbach, *Mimésis*, Princeton, 1953, p. 12. As an example of very independent reading, the entire chapter is suggestive.

PATRISTIC ALLEGORIES OF THE LUKAN PARABLE OF THE TWO SONS (LUKE 15:11-32)

by Yves Tissot

"Non est levior transgressio in interpretatione quam in conversatione (Tertullian, *De pudicitia*, 9, 22).

Patristic allegory is a type of exegesis no longer used, but rather disparaged.[1] Under the pretext that it will produce a misinterpretation of the text, critical exegetes have trampled it mercilessly. To those who believe this, the text of the allegorists would be only a pretext, and I fear that the commentary which Ambrose of Milan devoted to the Lukan parable of the two sons (Luke 15:11-32)[2] offers little evidence to the contrary on this point.

Moreover, the allegorical approach has been contested from Antiquity: the exegetes of the Antiochian tradition, indeed, vigorously reproached the Alexandrian allegorists for sacrificing history by mythifying it. In spite of the malevolence of this grievance, it remains quite true that the latter insisted on the spiritual meaning to the detriment of the historical meaning. But the Antiochian philologists have been accused in return for Judaizing by viewing the spiritual meaning as adventitious.[3] In reality, this conflict revolved around the hermeneutics of the Jewish Scriptures rather than exegesis itself, for the Antiochians no more denied the polysemy of the text and hence the spiritual meaning, than the Alexandrians denied the reality of history and hence the historical meaning.[4] But it was the articulation of the historical and spiritual meanings, and finally even the conception, which was contested. It would have been interesting, therefore, to consider the methodological relationship of the Alexandrian and Antiochian exegeses by taking as a point of reference a New Testament text which involved this hermeneutical question and, what is more, a parable. Indeed, by its nature a parable requires an allegorical interpretation, for it *speaks of another thing*.[5]

The exegetical writings of the fathers, however, scarcely permit such confrontations.[6] Frequently, indeed, their commentaries have been lost, or the extant odds and ends prohibit any significant analysis. In the case of the Lukan parable of the two sons, this confrontation appears likewise impossible. The commentaries on Luke by Diodore of Tarsus and Theodore of Mopsuestia[7] have not been preserved, because of the Nestorianism imputed to their authors. From the Alexandrian side, the situation is hardly enviable: just as the *Hypotyposes* of Clement, so the five volumes of Origen on Luke are lost, and his homilies partially preserved in Latin end with Luke 4:27.[8] Of the works of Pierias, there remains only one title: Εἰς τὸ κατὰ Λουκᾶν. As to the series of fragments (sometimes doubtful) attributed to Cyril, they originate in different writings, which renders their treatment difficult.[9]

In short, the choice of Luke 15:11-32 as a text of reference for our study excludes the greatest exegetes of the Greek Orient. Therefore our sources will be chiefly Latin.

On the subject of exegetical history, the establishment of a patristic group of documents remains quite empirical. Fortunately, the pre-Nicean texts relative to the parable of the two sons are examined in two recent studies of P. Siniscalco and A. Orbe;[10] as to subsequent texts, several have been listed by A. Adam,[11] so well that I can only indicate here those which have escaped him:

a) Among the Greeks:

Constitutions Apostoliques, II 41:1-3 (ed. F. X. Funk, I, Paderborn 1905, 129f.--without corresponding in the *Didascalie syriaque*).

John Chrysostom, *Hom.* I *de paenitentia*, 4 (*PG* 49, 282f.).

Asterius of Amasia, ὁμιλία εἰς τοὺς δύο υἱοὺς τοὺς παρὰ τῷ Λουκᾷ (ed. A. Bretz, TU 40/I, 107-115).[12]

b) Among the Latins:

Ambrose of Milan, *De paenitentia*, II 3. 13-19 (*SC* 179, 140-146).

Pseudo-Jerome, *Epistola* 35 *seu homilia de duobus filiis, frugi et luxurioso* (*PL* 30, 248-254).[13]

Pseudo-Jerome, *Expositio quatuor Evangeliorum. Lucas* (*PL* 30, 574f.).

Augustine, *Sermo* Caillau-Saint-Yves II, 11 (*PLS* 2, 427-435).

Caesarius of Arles, *Sermo* 163 (ed. G. Morin, Ib, 631-635).

Latin Epiphanius, *Interpretatio Evangeliorum*, 37 (*PLS* 3, 894-898).

Arnobius the Younger, *Annotationes ad quaedam Evangeliorum loca*, 8 (*PLS* 3, 218).

Pseudo-Theophilus, *Commentarius in quattuor Evangelia*, III 10 (*PLS* 3, 1317f.).

Isidore de Seville, *Allegoriae quaedam sacrae Scripturae*, 216 (*PLS* 83, 126).[14]

Among the patristic texts, I have withheld the resolutely allegorical commentary which Ambrose of Milan has done in his *Expositio evangelii secundum Lucam*, VII 212-244.[15] This passage offers us one of the oldest popular exegeses of the parable, which enhances its interest for us. In an allusion in his prologue to the translation of the homilies of Origen on Luke, Jerome does not refrain from disparaging Ambrose by comparing him to a *corvus crocitans* dressed out in a variegation of other birds.[16] Ambrose would thus be only a plagiarist, a fact which is revealed in his commentary by numerous veiled borrowings, notably from Origen, Eusebius, and Hilary.[17] There are good grounds, then, for believing that the Ambrosian exegesis of the parable of the two sons (Luke 15:11-32) is not original, but corresponds to a tradition--and a tradition which without doubt owes much to Origen[18] of whose homilies Ambrose would have known in an edition much longer than that known by Jerome.[19] But it is at once necessary to indicate that Ambrose had neither the richness, nor the depth, nor the fullness of Origen. In reading him, one is struck by the rush of ideas which could be taken for an incapacity for their development. In reality, this defect is due in part to the form of composition in the work. Certain parts betray a homiletic style which suggests that in the commentary "we have a case of regrouping, of a rehandling worked out by Ambrose to make of his discourse a relatively complete whole: here and there, this or that introduction, this or that conclusion, this or that bringing together has been the object of an editing".[20] The rush of ideas is consequently accounted for if one recognizes that the homilies are the primary material of the commentary or, more precisely, "some personal notes [and] simple summaries, put rapidly on paper in the course of lectures, sufficient to recall to the mind of the speaker the developments encountered on the part of other authors or already given by him in preceding works".[21]

I. THE DIVERSE TRADITIONAL HERMENEUTICAL TYPES OF THE PARABLE OF THE TWO SONS (LUKE 15:11-32)

We have seen that the Ambrosian exegesis of the parable is not original, since it corresponds to a tradition. It would be more valid to speak of *traditions*. We shall see, in fact, that in his commentary Ambrose mixes several hermeneutical lines in a sometimes confusing manner. It is fitting, then, in order to grasp his exegesis, first to define and to characterize the hermeneutical types attested in the patristic tradition. These are four in number. Although it will not always be easy to distinguish them *in textu* by reason of their intermingling, the allegorical equivalences proposed for the two sons lead to the following theoretical division:

1. For a *gnosticizing* interpretation, the older son symbolizes the angels and the younger son humanity.
2. In the *ethical* interpretation, the two brothers become types of the righteous and the sinners.
3. At the *ethnic* level, they are Israel and the heathen.
4. Finally, in a *penitential* perspective, the older brother represents the Christian rigorist who is opposed to a reconciliation with his bankrupt brother, represented by the dissolute son.[22]

1. The *gnosticizing* interpretation is indirectly attested by Epistle 35 of Pseudo-Jerome and by a scattered fragment of Cyril of Alexandria.[23] It appears to me to originate in a Gnostic exegesis of the parable of the lost sheep (Luke 15:4-7, cf. Matthew 18:12-14), where the Valentinians again find their myth of Wisdom, fallen into the world and reintegrated by the Savior into the Pleroma.[24] It seems indeed that in comparing the hundred sheep to the κόσμος νοητός attained by the fall of man, then reestablished by his return among the angels thanks to the coming of Christ, Origen was proposing to reinterpret this Valentinian exegesis, destined from that time onwards to a great publicity.[25] Now Siniscalco has observed that often, in spite of their divergent structures, the exe-

gesis of the parable of the two sons reveals an exegesis *established earlier* from the parable of the strayed sheep.[26] There is, then, good reason to think that the Gnostic interpretation of Luke 15:11-32 is definitively derived from the Gnostic exegesis of Luke 15:4-7, perhaps by the expedient of Origen. Certainly, Origen's fragment 217 on Luke which sees in the confession of the son in verse 18 (πάτερ, ἥμαρτον εἰς τὸν οὐρανόν...; cf. vs. 21) an indication of the celestial origin of man, is inauthentic and must be restored to Gregory of Nyssa.[27] But precisely, was not Gregory here, as often elsewhere, tributary to Origen? However that may be, the Gnosticizing exegesis of the parable appears to be badly acclimated to orthodox terrain and those who are the witnesses to it are not sparing in their criticism of it![28]

The two following interpretations, ethical and ethnic, present many analogies, although each one follows its own tendency: individualistic for the first, which recognizes in the return of the younger son the conversion of each sinner become Christian, and collectively for the second, according to which the parable speaks *de vocatione gentium*.[29] But it is evident that the equivalences of an ethical exegesis often incline toward those of an ethnic exegesis by the fact that the heathen are, according to the Pauline expression in Galatians 2:15, ἐξ ἐθνῶν ἁμαρτωλοί. It is possible, moreover, that this exegesis is derived from an ancient "pre-ethical" interpretation confined to verses 11-24 (significantly, the interest of Irenaeus, which nevertheless gives to the parable the title of *parabola duorum filiorum*,[30] is focused on the return of the younger son as a figure of the salvation of men insofar as the πλάσμα θεοῦ[31] is concerned) and that it should be one step removed from identifying the older brother with the Jews. Methodologically, however, it is fitting to distinguish two exegetical traditions:

2. The *ethical* interpretation represented by Titus of Bostra,[32] Jerome,[33] *Epistle* 35 of Pseudo-Jerome,[34] and Cyril of Alexandria[35] continued the exegesis of Irenaeus, but with the difference that Irenaeus insisted more on the "extensive" aspect of salvation. His general line of thought is the following: God accords to man the freedom to serve him,[36] but man misuses this and forgets his creator. He falls into debauchery and dedicates himself to demons. But at the depth of his misery, should he acknowledge his creator, God will come to his aid. He will restore to him his lost dignity and forearm him against the devil,[37] and will welcome him to the eucharist. But the ethical exegesis appears to falter in that it attempts to include the older brother by assimilating him with the righteous or the saints. In reality, Jerome proceeds to an ethnic interpretation in verses 25-32.[38] The fragment of Titus on verses 25ff. is content to interpret positively the fact that the righteous return ἐκ τοῦ ἀγροῦ, seeing signified in that the cultivation of virtues.[39] At halfway, Pseudo-Jerome inclines toward an ethnic exegesis by explaining that the older brother returned to the works of the law.[40] This uncertainty in the tradition tends to prove that originally the ethical interpretation omitted the end of the parable, and that in its development the inevitable recognition of the righteous man in the elder brother would underline an unforeseen difficulty. Indeed, how can we believe that a righteous man could be grieved "de salute alterius et fratris maxime"?[41]

3. Like the ethical exegesis, the *ethnic* exegesis attested especially among the Latins,[42] appears to go back to Irenaeus who draws from the parable of the prodigal son an antidualist argument: "...sed et per parabolam duorum diliorum minor luxuriose consumpsit substantiam vivens cum fornicariis *unum et eundem* docuit *patrem*, maiori quidem filio ne

haedum quidem indulgentem, propter eum autem qui perierat minorem filium suum iubentem occidi vitulum saginatum et primam ei stolam donantem."[43] It seems that the declaration of verse 11b: ἄνθρωπός τις ἔιχεν δύο υἱούς, was determinative in the emergence of this hermeneutical line, for it animated the entire Old Testament typology of the two sons designating, according to the model, Israel and the *Gentile*-Christian Church.[44] Meanwhile the historical tension inherent in this typology often changes into actual antagonism in the ethnic exegesis of the parable, which demonstrates that the Churches at that time were always confronting Judaism. As we have said earlier, ethnic exegesis frequently recovers the allegories of ethical interpretation, save that the sin of the younger son is more specific: it is in the idolatry into which the pagan falls.[45] Moreover, the end of the parable receives a stronger interpretation, but one finds himself in the presence of two traditions. The oldest is of anti-Jewish inspiration: the Jew in the fields would be occupied with worldly affairs, his protestation of fidelity in verse 29 is called a shameless falsehood. As to the kid which he covets, this would be nothing less than the Antichrist![46] The second tradition, which is philo-Semitic, goes back to Augustine who sees in the *ager patris* a designation of the law. The faithfully observed commandment concerns only monotheism, and the mention of the kid indicates the error of the Jews blind to the worth of Christ. Moreover, the invitation of the father to his son foretells the final welcome of Israel.[47]

4. As for the *penitential* interpretation,[48] it is close to the ethical interpretation at the level of allegory, but its temporal structure is different. Indeed, it no longer holds the threefold present of verse 22 to be a baptismal symbol. It is rather a question of baptism in the *portio substantiae* in verse 12,[49] so that the younger son no longer

represents the worldly sinner, but rather the Christian who sins against his baptism and who is reconciled by penitence. The first traces of this interpretation arise in Tertullian and Clement of Alexandria.[50] Both, however, leave the end of the parable in the background, and the Novatian crisis[51] will be necessary for the older son to take form as a type of the rigorist Christians hostile to the penitence of the baptized. As much as the taking of the older son into consideration troubled the ethical interpretation, by so much it appears to confirm the penitential exegesis, so much so the *Apostolic Constitutions* can give to the reconciling bishops this naive counsel: κἄν τις τῶν μὴ σεσαλευμένων ἀδελφῶν αὐτοῦ (sc. τοῦ ἐπιστραφέντος) ἐπεγκαλέσῃ σοι, ὅτι δὴ κατηλλάγης αὐτῷ, εἰπὲ πρὸς αὐτόν· Σὺ πάντοτε μετ' ἐμοῦ εἶ, κτλ (cf. vs. 31-32).[52]

II. AMBROSE'S EXEGESIS OF THE PARABLE OF THE TWO SONS

Far from being debarred, the exegetical traditions which we have mentioned are often accepted and even contaminated. For his part, Ambrose knew three of them.

Thus, after having presented a penitential interpretation, he takes up in an appendix the existence of an ethnic interpretation: "Nec invidemus si qui duos fratres istos velit referre ad populos duos, ut sit adulescentior populus ex gentibus tamquam Israhel, cui frater maior beneficium paternae benedictionis invidit."[53] But also in the full commentary he suddenly changed the register at the price of flagrant contradictions with the penitential context. These hermeneutical leaps are neither always signaled nor always disclosed by internal criticism alone, and only a comparative analysis of patristic exegesis permits them to be located.

Ambrose always stresses particularly the penitential importance of the parable. In fact, from the demand of the younger son to the father (cf. vs. 12), he draws an argument in favor of padobaptism: "Nulla dei regno infirma aetas, nec fides gravatur annis."[54] The lost son, then, is a Christian, and his departure is presented as a withdrawal from the church.[55] With respect to his confession in verse 21, Ambrose succinctly evokes the public confession of the penitent: "Confitere magis, ut...roget pro te ecclesia, inlacrimet populus."[56] He hastens to note that one is "filius per lavacrum",[59] when the younger son acknowledges that he is no longer worthy of the name of a son.

Consequently, several ambiguous expressions of the commentary are clarified: the *spiritalis patrimonium dignitatis*[58] which the father gives to his children, just as the *caelestia dona spiritus*[59] compromised by the sin "against heaven" (cf. vss. 18, 21), are baptismal gifts--and particularly faith. The departure of the younger son for a far country (cf. vs. 13) marks the going back of the baptized into the sinful world. The threefold gift of the father in verse 22 conceals some sacramental symbols: it depicts the return to baptismal innocence which permits access to the eucharist represented by the fatted calf.[60] The "symphony" which made the older son indignant designates the antiphony of the psalms and the response of the Amen--the entire liturgical life with which the reconciled penitent is renewed.[61] In his anti-Novatian treatise *De paenitentia*, the parable is seen in the same penitential perspective, but there Ambrose discovers more sacramental features: thus, the younger son is removed *a sacris altaribus*, as a foreigner he hungers for the *divinum alimentum*, and the kiss of the running father at meeting him becomes the *insigne sacrae pacis*.[62]

There are at the same time some traits in the commentary which strongly contrast with this interpretation and denote another hermeneutical direction. Thus, in VII 214 we notice a marked tension between the initial affirmation according to which the Christian sinner, separated from Christ, no longer belongs to the Church, and the final remark according to which the Christians, estranged as they are, *themselves also* have been brought near by the blood of Christ (cf. Eph. 2:13), in a fashion that they should not give black looks to those who return from the far country, from the shadow of death (cf. Isa. 9:1). Manifestly, Ambrose presupposes here that *all* have experienced this return, which excludes an anti-Novatian attack, all the more as public penitence remained at that time an exceptional procedure.[63] Ambrose elsewhere precisely states that the younger son has squandered all the *ornamenta naturae* and that he had deformed the *imago dei* in giving himself to idolatry.[64] This last theme is found again in VII 234, in a confused discussion on the exegetical implication of the verb *perierat* (vs. 24): scarcely has Ambrose justified his penitential interpretation by making it say that "ille perit qui fuit",[65] when he recognized the validity of another interpretation which would make the younger son a figure of men and, what is more, of pagan men.[66] This contradiction evidently springs from the fact that he has inserted into his commentary a nonpenitential theme, descended from the tradition reported in line 214. As to the expression *ornamenta naturae*, it finds its counterpart in line 225 where Ambrose remarks, with regard to the confession of the younger son to his father (cf. vs. 21): "Haec est prima confessio aput *auctorem naturae*." Now similar terminology has nothing of the penitential![67]

We might think that the rival tradition thus disclosed sets up an ethnic hermeneutics, since in line 234 the *popu-*

lus Iudaeorum is explicitly put in opposition to the *populus gentium*, and that Ambrose devoted an appendix of his commentary on the parable to an ethnic exegesis of verses 25-32, set forth in its anti-Jewish interpretation.[68] A hasty comparative analysis could confirm this since the ethnic exegetes insist on the idolatry of the younger son and speak, when occasion permits, of *naturalia bona*,[69] etc. However, the interaction of ethical and ethnic interpretations of verses 11-24 attenuates the importance of such remarks. It is my judgment that the second interpretation in VII 212-235 is of an ethical type. An indication on line 242 could, in fact, show that Ambrose knew this interpretation, which he had just sketched out in lines 239ff., to be more than an ethnic interpretation. He notes in relation to verse 31: "Sed bonus pater etiam hunc (sc. fratrem maiorem) salvare cupiebat dicens: 'tu mecum semper fuisti', vel quasi *Iudaeus* in lege, vel quasi *iustus* in communione."[70] The literary and thematic affinities of Ambrose with the ethical tradition are decisive: the citing of Ephesians 2:13 found also in Pseudo-Jerome, *Ep*. 35:7,[71] and that of Isaiah 9:1 by Jerome, *Ep*. 21:10,[72] in identical contexts. But above all the surprising themes of the *auctor* and *natura* are developed with persistence by Titus who speaks of πλάσας, of πλάσις and of φύσις.[73] Is there not here a reminiscence of the πλάσμα θεοῦ of Irenaeus? In any case, when in relation to the vocative πάτερ in verse 18, Titus notes that ἐγνώρισεν ἡ θύσις τὸν πλάσαντα,[74] the convergence with Ambrose, VII 225, is evident. Certainly the ethical exegesis does not compare the debauchery of the younger son to idolatry as much as the ethnic exegesis; it sees there sin in itself (including idolatry!). But it must be pointed out that in VII 214, the brief passage on idolatry is closely bound to the theme of the *imago dei* which, very paradoxically, is not employed by any of the allegorical exegeses of the parable.[75] Thus, one could see here a specifically ethnic influence. The statement of the defense against idolatry, moreover, requires an explicit relation to the ethical tradition: "*Opus dei* es, noli ligno dicere: 'pater meus es tu'...."[76] So then, the ethnic interpretation of VII 239-243 does not prolong the second exegesis which emerges here and there in lines 212-235, and Ambrose confirms by his style that the ethical interpretation is attached to verses 11-24, but that an ethnic reading prevails as soon as one includes verses 25-32 in the exegesis.

III. SOME OBSERVATIONS ON ALLEGORICAL EXEGESIS

The fact that in his commentary on the parable Ambrose can intermingle allegories arising from distinct hermeneutical types shows that there is a very loose bond between the determination of the meaning of the parable and the search for allegorical equivalences, but still more that the fathers were infatuated with allegory to the point of neglecting coherence of meaning. This flaw is particularly acute in Ambrose, partly for the reasons that we have mentioned.[77] But it would be shabby to make this hermeneutical incoherence a constitutive mark of allegory! The exegesis of Origen is decisive in this regard. It suffices to go through his homilies to be convinced that the polysemy of the text does not induce hermeneutical confusion: the various meanings are so clearly distinguished that at each level of reading Origen succeeds in releasing a coherent interpretation, even when his allegories contradict the corresponding allegories of another meaning. All the weaknesses embodied in his Epigones take nothing away from this truth, and there would be grounds for asking ourselves whether the frequent confusions in these do not arise from the fact that the allegorical tradition of their time was already nothing more than a decadent movement, living on its momentum. The precedence accorded to allegories to the detriment of fixity of purpose and of hermeneutical coherence would be a symptom of this decline, and throws light on why Jerome, in his prologue to the translation of the homilies of Origen on Luke, could deride the commentary of Ambrose which "in verbis luderet, in sententiis dormitaret"![78]

The verbal games of allegory are sometimes disconcerting, and although Jerome would be the first to permit himself to take them up, one readily assents to his criticism. For example, the semantic enrichment of a text by intertextual contributions appears to us to involve a pun rather than serious exegesis. Meanwhile stylistic research, however, perhaps permits us to appreciate more than in the past the effort undertaken by the fathers to explain the allegories from the Scriptures considered in their unity.[79] Origen, moreover, believed that the principle of this intertextual reading was to be found in I Corinthians 2:13:

> ...πνευματικὰ πνευματικοῖς εὐκαίρως συγκρίνωμεν, οὐ τὰ ἀσύγκριτα πρὸς ἄλληλα συγκρίνοντες, ἀλλὰ συγκριτὰ καὶ ὁμοιότητά τινα ἔχοντα, λέξεως ταὐτὸν σημαινούσης καὶ νοημάτων καὶ δογμάτων, ἵν' ἐπὶ στόματος δύο ἢ τριῶν ἢ καὶ πλειόνων μαρτύρων τῶν ἀπὸ τῆς γραφῆς στήσωμεν καὶ βεβαιώσωμεν πᾶν ῥῆμα τοῦ θεοῦ.[80]

This hermeneutical attitude explains the numerous flights toward other texts, and notably toward other parables, which is taken up in Ambrose's exegesis of the parable of the two sons. Thus, the remembrance of the father's workers (cf. vs. 17) evokes by antithesis the parable of the workers sent into the vineyard (Matt. 20:1-16).[81] With Ambrose, the bond is especially verbal: the μισθώσασθαι of Matthew 20:1 answers to Luke's μίσθιοι. The workers of the father, in fact, represent the Jews "qui ad mercedem serviunt", seeking for "saecularis mercedis lucella". The workers in the vineyard are by contrast good workers who merit "aequalem mercedem vitae".[82] Then, in a historicizing digression, Ambrose identifies the workers engaged at the ninth hour with the righteous, with the patriarchs and the prophets.[83] Titus of Bostra presents a similar development and, in agreement with codex P, also omits the case of the last workers employed.[84] But the function of bringing passages together in this fashion appears clearly on the part of Jerome, who introduces the Matthean parable into his ethical exegesis of verses 28-30 to explain that the salvation of the sinner could fill a righteous man with *invidia*: such, in fact, had been the reaction of the workers when they saw that even the last employed received their denarius.[85] The verbal bond between the two parables, then, is doubly strengthened by a thematic relationship which forces their union. But we understand clearly why, engaged in an antithetical comparison between *mercennarii*, Ambrose renounced any consideration of the end of the Matthean parable which would have led him to affirm that the patriarchs and the prophets--and no longer only the Jewish people--were indignant at the salvation of the pagans called at the time of the *adventus* of the Lord!

The same is true for the parable of the marriage feast (Matt. 22:2-14; cf. Luke 14:16-24). Ambrose establishes a bond between the field where the devil sent the sinner (Luke 15:15) and the field acquired by the one who declined the invitation of the master (Luke 14:18; cf. Matt. 22:5).[86] Bordering on the same sense, Jerome cites Luke 14:18-20 to describe the elder brother laboring in the field (Luke 15:25) as the Jews labor at the law, "longe a gratia spiritus sancti".[87] The theme of absence would then be common to the two parables, and it has resulted from some verbal vibrations reinforced by some terminological collisions. The μόσχος σιτευτός sacrificed by the father (cf. Luke 15:23, 30) recalls, in fact, the σιτιστά prepared by the king (cf. Matt. 22:4), and especially the στολὴ πρώτη offered to the younger son (cf. Luke 15:22) is equivalent to the precise ἔνδυμα γάμου of those invited to the marriage (cf. Matt. 22:11f.). This explains the somewhat surprising irruption of the nuptial theme into the exegesis of the threefold gift of verse 22. Ambrose, like Jerome, indeed identifies the *stola* with the "vestis nuptialis quam si qui non habuerit a convivio nuptiali excluditur".[88] Following this line, others make of the ring a *sponsalium signum*,[89] and Maximus of Turin even risks giving a nuptial interpretation of the shoes: "Calceamenta in pedibus, et hoc ad signum est nuptiarum quoniam sponsae Christi calceantur pedes in praeparationem evangelii pacis"![90]

The presence of the nuptial theme in the exegesis of verse 22 discloses another aspect of patristic allegory: its relish for a symbolic of biblical inspiration which likewise permits it to enrich the meaning of texts. In the exegesis of the Lukan parable of the two sons, this symbolic investment is striking in verse 22 precisely, which the Fathers always referred to baptism[91]--or, in the penitential interpretation to the restoration of baptismal grace. The robe and the ring have thus been related to the rites of investiture of the baptized and to the sign of the Cross over them,[92] their signation, so that the sacramental theology attested in the patristic catecheses is refracted in the exegesis of verse 22. Ambrose describes the robe, for example, as an *amictus sapientiae*, a *spiritale indumentum*, or again a *vestimentum nuptiale*.[93] If the wisdom theme seems to be isolated, the other two are found again frequently in the baptismal theology of the Fathers.[94] The same is true for the expressions τὸ τῆς ἀφθαρσίας ἱμάτιον,[95] στολὴ τοῦ φωτός,[96] *stola immortalitatis*,[97] *ornamentum redemtionis*,[98] to which other authors resort. Elsewhere, the theme of the return to the primitive integrity lost by Adam, which often stamped the rite of postbaptismal revesting, is so much more easily slipped into the exegesis of the parable so that it is not a question of just any στολή, but of the στολὴ πρώτη. Now by giving a temporal value to the adjective, Tertullian can write: "Vestem *pristinam* recipit, statum scilicet eum quem Adam transgressus amiserat."[99] It is possible, furthermore, that this interpretation, referring to the haggadic theme of the glory lost by Adam, is original.[100]

The symbolism of the ring is also very rich. Ambrose sees in it a *fidei signaculum*[101] and Titus even specifies, in following a catechetical tradition which delights in emphasizing how much the baptismal sign is dreaded by demons: σημεῖον τῆς πίστεως τὸ κατὰ τοῦ διαβόλου.[107] Elsewhere, Ambrose recognizes in the ring a trinitarian stamp, "quia signavit deus, cuius imago Christus, et dedit pignus spiritum in cordibus nostris".[103] To understand this complex of ideas, it must be recalled that rings were related to seals, making it possible to pass from the term δακτύλιον to the idea of σφραγίς[104] which, as far back as the New Testament, has a baptismal resonance. Christians are, indeed, "signati spiritu sancto" (cf. Eph. 1:13[105]). Since they are marked with a frontal sign, one could then write, in spite of the mention of the hand in Luke 15:22: "Annulum, id est crux in fronte."[106] In addition, the notion of σφραγίς implies the extremely fecund idea of εἰκών, which allows the rejoining of the adamic theme already elaborated on the subject of the robe: the baptized receives not only a "signaculum similitudinis Christi",[107] but he likewise receives the original κατ' εἰκόνα.[108]

These symbolisms of the robe and the ring, nurtured by

biblical reminiscences, could be seen as verbose, but I should like to recall that it was otherwise in past times when one passed through a baptismal initiation requiring the ritual investiture with the white alb and the signation of the oil. Allegory here corresponds to life. That is why I ask myself if, here and there, one must not end up by seeing a re-covering of the feet which followed the pre-baptismal penitential rite in the course of which the candidate stood with bare feet,[109] a meaning conforming to that which we find in the exegesis of the shoes in Luke 15:22. Ambrose, in fact, sees in that a triple symbol of protection, of *praeparatio evangelii* (cf. Eph. 6:15) and of walking *in spiritu*,[110] and in his *De paenitentia* he establishes in addition to this a bond with Easter, a eucharistic model celebrated with "sandals on the feet" (Exod. 12:11).[111]

The exuberance of allegory, however, should not hide the fact that the fathers bound themselves to a pressing hermeneutical research and that their exegetical niceties were first subjected to meaning. Certainly, they often were wanting in the balanced principle expressed by Chrysostom: οὐδὲ χρὴ πάντα τὰ ἐν ταῖς παραβολαῖς κατὰ λέξιν περιεργάζεσθαι, ἀλλὰ τὸν σκοπὸν μαθόντας δι΄ ὅν συνετέθη τοῦτον δρέπεσθαι καὶ μηδὲν πολυπραγμονεῖν περαιτέρω.[112] Again it must be remembered that in no longer conceiving the parable as a succession of metaphors, we are more quickly annoyed by these niceties than were the Fathers. Do we find an ally in Tertullian who asks, ironically, on the subject of the parable of the lost coin: "...et quae illae scopae?"[113] (cf. Luke 15:8), to answer immediately that certain narrative traits are required by the structure of the story without having the least semantic value, since on the occasion "necesse erat ut habitus requirentis drachmam in domo tam scoparum quam lucernae adminiculo adcommodaretus"?[114]

This would be to forget that he himself, if he did not allegorize the broom, nevertheless sees in the *lucerna* necessary to the story the sign of the grace of God.[115] It is enough for him that this supplementary allegory conforms to the meaning of the text, determined beforehand. Ambrose, it is true, lays little stress on this pre-allegorical determination of the meaning, for insofar as his epigones is concerned, he can build a foundation on the recognized and tested exegetical traditions. We have seen, however, that he shows some signs in favor of a penitential interpretation of the parable of the two sons: the term *filius* implies the faith of the younger son, looking forward to his becoming *filius per lavacrum*, and elsewhere the verb *perierat* in verse 24 excludes, in one sense at least, that it should be a question of a pagan, since the latter *semper est mortuus*.[116] But ordinarily, the passages which have shown the heuristic procedure of the Fathers are very decisive: they are the historic introduction in Luke 15: 1-2, and the closing part of the parable, where the *invidia* of the older brother, his protestation of fidelity in verse 29 and the reply of the father assuring him, in verse 31, of his continuing presence, have often contradicted their exegesis, just as we observed with respect to the ethical interpretation.[117]

This is not to contradict Tertullian who has labored the most for the prior determination of the meaning of the parable. In the name of his long antiheretical polemic, in fact, he was always lying in wait for errors transmitted under the cover of allegory. The refutation of heretics doubtless revealed to him how much their exegesis was motivated by their faith. Besides, his adherence to Montanism confirmed for him the necessity of recourse to the *regula veritatis* in exegesis.[118]

Save for one allusion in *De patientia*,[119] Tertullian refers only twice to the parable of the two sons: in *De paenitentia*, 8, 6-9,[120] and in *De pudicitia*, 8-9.[121] Curiously, he does not breathe a word about it in Book IV of the *Adversus Marcionem* where he occupies himself by combatting Marcion on his own terrain, that is to say, by an argument drawn from his expurgated edition of Luke. He did not render a grievance against the heretic for having censured this pericope,[122] nor did he draw any advantage from this, although he could have demonstrated, following Irenaeus, that God is the one father of both Jews and pagans.

After having treated of baptismal penitence, Tertullian consecrates the end of his *De paenitentia* to presenting, not without apprehension, the unique *paenitentia secunda* which is offered to those who have failed in their baptismal engagements. The Lukan parable of the two sons is then recalled, among other texts, as an example of post-baptismal penitence. But at the time of the *De pudicitia*, Tertullian had gone over to Montanism, according to which mortal sins are irremissible, which imposed a revision of his earlier exegesis of the parable. That is why he grapples with some "psychic"[123] exegetes who give the parable a hybrid interpretation in which the older brother represents the Jews envying the *secunda restitutio* of Christians, and in order to do this, he points out that such an exegesis lacks evidence since the Jews know nothing of the reconciliation internal to the church.[124] But his essential criticism bears on the Jewish identity of the older brother: "Porro si Iudaicum ostendero deficere a comparatione filii maioris, consequenter utique nec Christianus admittetur de configuratione filii minoris."[125] Also, we are not a little surprised to see him afterwards propose an ethnic interpretation conformed to Montanism no doubt, but preserving the Jewish identity of the older brother![126] However that may be, what is important to us is to mark the hermeneutical effort of Tertullian, who proceeds moreover by elimination rather than by specification. To discard the hybrid interpretation of the "psychics", Tertullian begins by pointing out that the protestation of fidelity by the older brother in verse 29 is as little suited to the apostate Jews as the reply of the father in saying: "Tu semper mecum es et omnia mea tua sunt" (vs. 31). On the contrary, the history of the Jews evokes the lot of the younger son since, having dissipated the inheritance of God, they serve the princes of this world in the diaspora![127] There is no doubt that in the last part of the parable, the brief dialogue between the father and the son has embarrassed the ethnic exegesis by which Tertullian's adversaries assumed the identity of the older brother. Cyril, in fact, refuses to recognize in him Israel κατὰ σάρκα, by setting him off as τὸ κατ᾽ οὐδένα τρόπον ἁρμόσαι τῷ Ισραὴλ τὸ ἀκαταψέκτως ἐλέσθαι βιοῦν.[128] On their part, when they do not very simply accuse the Jew of falsehood,[129] the ethnic exegetes are constrained to resort to a subtle explanation of the ἐντολή observed (cf. vs. 29), which only covers the monotheistic faith.[130] As to the presence of the Jews close to God, which is affirmed in verse 31, this would be guaranteed by the ancient righteous, by the law, and indeed even by the divine anger![131] It must be noted, however, that in the finale, the envious and disappointed reaction of the older brother favors the ethnic interpretation which recognizes there the irritation of the Jews faced with the calling of the Gentiles, even though it is troubling to the ethical exegesis where the salvation of sinners provokes the spite of the saints.[132] It would seem, then, that after the Montanist controversy and especially the Novatian quarrel where the rigorists rose against the reconciling bishops, all these exegetical difficulties would have been easily resolved in the penitential interpretation. But Tertullian precisely denied it here by arguing from criteria external to the parable, and it is here that the investigation of the introductory observation of Luke 15:1-2 is interposed. It, in fact, sets up the following exegetical prescription: "Ea semper responderi quae provocantur."[133] It is necessary, then, that the proposed interpretation be conformed to the *materia* of the parables, that is to say, to the concrete situation which has produced them.[134] Now Luke indicates that the parable of the two sons is aimed at the Pharisees who are angered by seeing Jesus associate with publicans and sinners, in whom Tertullian sees the heathen, considering that, according to Deuteronomy 23:19, the Jews could not be publicans and that the Pharisees would not be offended by a table fellowship with other Jews.[135] Criticized by Jerome,[136] this opinion of Tertullian moves on through the exegetes of the ethnic tradition cited by Ambrose.[137] It allows a Montanist to set aside the "psychic" exegesis which identifies the younger son with a fallen Christian in order to substitute an ethnic interpretation. Although Tertullian was deceived in the identification of the publicans, and consequently, of the younger son, it is evident that he defines here an essential exegetical principle, and that this principle implies the subordination of allegories to the *materia* of the texts. An exegesis which reckons with all the elements of a parable would be no less false if it violates its *materia*.[188] Also Tertullian made little effort to give a detailed explanation of the parable of Luke 15:11-32 in an ethnic perspective.[139] Moreover, he insists on the historical reference included in the notion of *materia* to assure that in his parables the Lord could not be concerned "[*de*] Christiano qui adhuc nemo".[140]

Nevertheless, it would be false to see in Tertullian an exegete mistrustful of allegory.[141] He had recourse to it himself without false shame. Certainly, his reserve and his taste for *simplicitas*[142] contrast with the exuberance of Alexandrian allegory, but it is worthwhile to point out again that the African did not have a grudge against a too sophisticated allegorizing, but rather a heretical allegorizing that gives to the bear texts a false meaning.[143] His anti-allegorical criticisms, then, bear less on exegesis than on hermeneutics, and his example shows us a fact which is often forgotten, that the allegorical movement wholly presupposed a hermeneutical self-restraint. We are not surprised that the movement carried away Ambrose who, differently from Tertullian, worked on the basis of tested exegetical traditions. And moreover, what would we accurately know of this pre-allegorical research if Tertullian had not been obliged, especially by his adherence to Montanism, to revise some of his earlier exegetical positions?

We thus reach the conclusion that allegory is not as arbitrary as it appears. It is not just a method of construing the texts by the expedient of farfetched analogies![144] Certainly some controvertible allegories exist, and the desire to explain everything has ended in discrediting patristic allegory. But its excesses imply no more than that it was corrupted in its principle, especially when it was applied to a *parable*, of which it sought to explain the paradigmatic resonances. The simple statement of Luke 15:11b: ἄνθρωπος τις ἔιχεν δύο υἱούς, evoked for a Christian of the patristic age all the typology of the two sons symbolizing Israel and the Church,[145] but this typology is not related by force to the parable, since it derives in its turn from a Jewish theme, original in the parable, likening the elect younger son to the *verus Israel*.[146] Even so, to return to verse 22, is it not evident that in spite of his denial of allegorizing the parables,[147] J. Jeremias makes the whole Jewish theme of vestment vibrate by underlining the symbolic importance of the robe, "Sinnbild der Heilszeit"?[148] Consequently, was it not inevitable that the nuptial, spiritual, and eschatological reverberations of the Jewish concept of ἔνδυμα[149] should resonate with the στολή of the parable, which justifies its baptismal allegorization by the Fathers, since baptism, which consists in a χριστὸν ἐνδύεσθαι (cf. Gal. 3:27), harbors essentially the same paradigms as the vestment?[150] The arbitrariness of allegory is then reduced if, instead of considering it as an anachronism on the basis of our cold exegesis, we take account of its rootage in the Jewish midrashic tradition,[151] and of its growth in the bosom of the church whose theology and life it reflects.

NOTES

1. It is striking to see that the current attempts to rescue typology are made to the detriment of allegory, which is judged as essentially unhistorical. S. Amsler, *L'Ancien Testament dans l'Eglise. Essai d'herméneutique chrétienne*, Neuchâtel, 1960, p. 58, note 2, resents the expression "historical allegorism" as a contradiction in terms. But J. Barr, *Old and New in Interpretation. A Study of the Two Testaments*, London, 1966, pp. 103ff., rightly protests this prejudice, in giving worth particularly to the historical allegorization of the parables on the part of the Fathers. For an appreciation nuancing the distinction between allegory and typology, cf. H. Crouzel, "La distinction de la 'typologie' et de l' 'allégorie'," *BLE* 65 (1964), pp. 161-174.

2. *Traité sur l'Evangile de S. Luc*, VII, 212-244 (*SC* 52, 88-98), henceforth cited without mention of title and pagination.

3. On this conflict, cf., for example, R. M. Grant, *The Bible in the Church*, New York, 1948, pp. 60-84.--Whatever the Fathers claimed about their own exegesis and that of their rivals, the essential difference is this: for the Alexandrians, Christ is present in history (assimilable to his Scriptural relation, cf. S. Amsler, *op. cit.*, pp. 169f.) before his incarnation, although this presence was fully revealed only by the incarnation. For the Antiochians, on the contrary, it is precisely this retroactive revelation which is important and which gives a surplus of meaning to the Jewish Scriptures; cf. on this subject the texts cited by M. Aubineau, "Dossier patristique sur Jean XIX, 23-24: La tunique sans couture du Christ," in *La Bible et les pères*, *Colloque de Strasbourg* (1-3. 10. 1969) Paris, 1971, pp. 13-15.

4. Insofar, to be sure, as the literal meaning would be possible, cf. J. Pepin, "A propos de l'histoire de l'exégèse allégorique: l'absurdité signe de l'allégorie," in *Studia Patristica* I, Berlin, 1957, pp. 395-413. And yet it must be remembered that the allegorists were more sensible than we to the asperities of the text, and hence to its "absurdities".

5. Cf. H. Clavier, "L'ironie dans l'enseignement de Jésus," *NT* I (1956), p. 15: "The parable...consists in throwing alongside (παρὰ βάλλειν) of the idea which one wishes to

inculcate an image more accessible and taken from elementary experience. The hearer is enticed, perhaps without being aware of it, onto a road which conducts him to the truth of which the theoretical aspect alone would have been immediately rejected. The parable, then, in this regard, is a feigned word; it is spoken otherwise (ἄλλως ἀγορεύω) than in habitual language." Cf. the remark made concerning Luke 15:22f. by Asterius of Amasia, *hom.* I (ed. A. Bretz, *TU* 40/1, pp. 107-115), p. 113: ταῦτα δὲ πάντα οὐχ ὡς διήγημα ἐν τῷ κοινῷ ἀνεγράφη, ἀλλ' ἕκαστος λόγος γέμει μυστήρια κεκρυμμένης ἀλληγορίας· παραβολὴ γάρ ἐστιν, ὡς ἴστε· πᾶς δὲ παραβολικὸς λόγος ἐξ ἄλλων τῶν φαινομένων πρὸς ἕτερα μυσταγωγεῖ τὰ νοούμενα.

6. Cf. J. Guillet, "Les exégèses d'Alexandrie et d'Antioche. Conflit ou malentendu?," *RechSR* 34 (1947), pp. 257-302, particularly p. 260.

7. Cf., however, Th. Zahn, *Das Evangelium des Lucas*, Leipzig, 1913, pp. 565f., note 72: Ishodad represented the interpretation of Theodore, "welche im engeren Anschluss an die Veranlassung der drei Parabeln (*sc.* Lc 15, 4-32) in den beiden Söhnen ganz allgemein die beiden Klassen der Sünder und der Gerechten, der noch nicht getauften Heiden und der Kirchenglieder abgebildet findet."

8. Origen, *Homélies sur S. Luc* (*SC* 87). The last homilies (34-39) deal with isolated pericopes.

9. Cyril of Alexandria, *Explanatio in Lucae Evangelium* (*PG* 72, pp. 801-807).--It is not unimportant that a biblical citation comes from a commentary or another writing. In the first case, in fact, the interpreted text has an exegetical importance of which the simple Scriptural instance is sometimes destitute.

10. P. Siniscalco, *Mito e storia della salvezza. Ricerche sulle più antiche interpretazioni di alcune parabole evangeliche*, Turin, 1971; A. Orbe, *Parabolas evangelicas en san Ireneo*, I, Madrid, 1972, pp. 154-204; cf. also H. Smith, *Ante-Nicene Exegesis of the Gospel*, IV, London, 1928, pp. 132-138.

11. A. Adam, "Gnostische Züge in der patristischen Exegese von Luk. 15," *Studia Evangelica* III, Berlin, 1964, pp. 299-305.--A deceptive study: Adam estimates that the patristic exegesis of the parables of the lost sheep and the lost coin follow a "wisdom" line which has a savior intervene in

redemption, while the exegesis of the Lucan parable of the two sons expresses a Gnostic conception in which salvation derives from an ἀνάμνησις of the celestial origin. Adam would certainly have been right in writing "ein Erretter tritt nicht auf" (p. 304), if it were a question of the exegesis of Luke 15:11-32. But this assertion must be modified when one approaches the history of exegesis, for if the theme of the ἀνάμνησις agrees well with Gregory of Nyssa, *De oratione dominica*, II (*PG* 44, 1144f.), who brings together the confession of the dissolute son: πάτερ, ἥμαρτον εἰς τὸν οὐρανόν καὶ ἐνώπιόν σου, with the beginning of the Lord's Prayer: πάτερ ἡμῶν ὁ ἐν τοῖς οὐρανοῖς, the fathers did not elsewhere fail to see a *Christological* allegory in the embrace of the father in Luke 15:20. Thus Augustine, *sermo* Caillau 11, 6: "Incubuit in illum occurrens: id est, super collum eius posuit brachium suum. Brachium patris, filius est" (*PLS* 2, 430), cf. Caesarius of Arles, *sermo* 163.2 (Morin, Ib 633, with citation of Isa. 53:1); Jerome, *epist.* 21:19: "...ad eius praecurrit adventum et per verbum suum quod carnem sumpsit ex virgine reditum filii iunioris anticipat" (Labourt, I 96); Peter Chrysologus, *sermo* 5: "Cedidit super collum eius: cecidit cum per Christum divinitas tota nostra decumbit et incumbit in carne" (*PL* 52, 200); Ambrose, VII, 230: "Cadit in collum tuum Christus..."

12. Cf. the paraphrased fragments published by A. Mai, *Scriptorum veterum nova collectio*, IX, Rome, 1837, pp. 695-697.

13. The attribution of this "homily" to Pelagius is rejected by G. de Plinval, *Pélage, ses écrits, sa vie et sa réforme*, Lausanne, 1943, p. 44, who finds it "prolix and banal".

14. Cf. in addition the following allusions: the prayer of the penitents in *Const. Apost.*, VIII, 9, 9 (Funk, I, 486); John Chrysostom, *hom.* 64 (65) on Matt., 3 (*PG* 58, 613); Hilary, *Tract. myst.*, 22 (*SC* 19.112f.); Pacianus, *Paraen.*, 12 (*PL* 13.1090); Ambrose, *De paen.*, II 7.65 (*SC* 179, 174); *In Ps* 37 *expl.*, 10 (*CSEL* Amb. VI 144); *In Ps* 118 *expos.* 15. 34 (*CSEL* Amb. V 348f.); Jerome, *com. Jon.* 4 (*PL* 35, 1151); *Brev. in Ps* 107 (*PL* 26, 1221); Augustine, *Enarr. in Ps* 138.5 *de epiphania* II (*PLS* 3, 560); Gregory of Nyssa, *De orat. domin.* V (*PG* 44, 1181).--Among the Ante-Nicene Fathers, I have picked up only one allusion which has escaped such as P. Siniscalo and A. Orbe: Origen, *com. in Rm.* 2.8 (*PG* 14, 891).

15. Cf. *supra*, n. 2, p. 386.

16. Cf. *Praefatio beati Hieronymi presbyteri in omelias Origenis super Lucam evangelistam* (*SC* 87, 94). On the identification with Ambrose, cf. the Introduction II of F. Fournier, *ibid.*, pp. 70ff.

17. Cf. the Introduction of G. Tissot to the commentary of Ambrose, in *SC* 45, 15-18.

18. Cf. F. Fournier, in *SC* 87, 73. The exegesis of Origen is known only by some allusions which do not all have exegetical value (cf. *supra*, note 9, p. 387). A. Orbe, *op. cit.*, I 177 believes it possible to rediscover his exegesis and sends us back to P. Courcelle, *Recherches sur les Confessions de S. Augustin*, Paris, 1968[2], pp. 424ff. But the study of Courcelle is supported only by a detail: the joining of the neo-Platonic theme of the *regio dissimilitudinis* with the χώρα μακρά of Luke 15:13. P. Siniscalco is alas! within the truth when he writes that "ricostruire l'esegesi origeniana delle nostre parabole non è impresa facile" (*op. cit.*, p. 159). I, nevertheless, have the clear impression that certain themes of Ambrose have their origin in Origen. Thus, the designation of the sinner as κοσμοπολίτης (cf. Ambrose, VII 214: *civis mundi*), the theme of the nothingness of the pagans (cf. Ambrose, VII 219, on Luke 15:16b: "Nemo illi debat: erat enim in regione illius qui neminem habet, quia eos qui sunt non habet"; 234, on Luke 15:24. Compare *In Ps* 37 *expl.*, 10 with Jer. 31:15: "...ergo ecclesia domini in Iudaeis consolari noluit, quia non sunt; in Christianis autem qui ex nationibus congregati sunt, *epularetur et gaudet*, quoniam coeperunt esse qui non erant" (*CSEL* Amb. VI 144); on the theme of the non-existence of sinners on the part of Origen, cf. H. Crouzel, *Origène et la "connaissance mystique"*, Paris-Bruges, 1961, p. 518; and *Théologie de l'image de Dieu chez Origène*, Paris, 1956, p. 162.

19. Cf. F. Fournier, in *SC* 87, 82.

20. G. Tissot, in *SC* 45, 10f.

21. G. Tissot, *ibid.*, 12f.

22. This classification takes into consideration neither the mixed types, such as the "psychic" interpretation criticized by Tertullian, *De pud.*, 8f., cf. *infra*, pp. 380f.; nor the hypothetical types, such as the inverted ethnic interpretation of Tertullian, *ibid.*, 8, 7-9, cf. *infra*, note 44, p. 394, nor his martyrological interpretation, *ibid.*, 9, 21; nor finally, the dubious types, such as the Adamic interpretation

of Pseudo-Theophilus, *Commentarius*, III 10, who wrote on Luke 15:11f.: "Hic autem Adam et Christus est intelligendus" (*PLS* 3, 1317; cf. Arnobius the Younger, *Annotationes*, 8: "Nam duo filii, Adam et Christus intelliguntur"!): taken literally, this phrase proposes to identify the younger son with Adam and with Christ, stated otherwise, a heathen lost in Adam and saved in Christ, which is not without a recollection of Irenaeus, *Adversus haereses*, III 19, 3 (*SC* 34, 336), where Christ, in his ascension, is said "offerentem et commendantem patri *eum hominem qui fuerat inventus*" (cf. Luke 15:24), namely: presenting to God the *homo assumptus* is here likened to the younger son of the parable.--Moreover, the classification proposed neglects an important fact: at an early stage, the ethical and penitential interpretations seem to have considered only the person of the younger son (Luke 15:11-24), while leaving aside the second act of the parable relating the irritation of the older son faced with the clemency of his father (Luke 15:25-32), cf. *infra*, pp. 367f. and 369f.

23. Pseudo-Jerome, *ep*. 35, 3 (*PL* 30, 249) and Cyril, *Expl. in Lucae Evang., ad* 15.11ff. (*PG* 72, 804 and 805; cf. J. A. Cramer, *Catenae Graecorum Patrum in Novum Testamentum*, II, Hildesheim 1967, p. 120f.).

24. Cf. P. Siniscalco, *op. cit.*, pp. 47-52 and A. Orbe, *op. cit.*, II, pp. 130-133.

25. Cf. P. Siniscalco, *op. cit.*, pp. 160-168 and A. Orbe, *op. cit.*, II, pp. 153-160.

26. Cf. for example, *op. cit.*, pp. 98f. (concerning Irenaeus). Tertullian writes thus in *De pud.* 9,4 (*CC* 2, 1297): "Et duo utique filii illuc spectabunt, quo et drachma et ovis." But it does not appear that the 2nd century Gnostics had proposed an interpretation of the parable of the prodigal son, whether or not it was derived from their exegesis of Luke 15: 4-7, cf. P. Siniscalco, *ibid.*, 67, n. *. What Origen says in his *Comment. in Jon.,* XIII 20, 119ff. (*GCS* Orig. IV 244) concerning fragment 23 of Heraclus seems to me to indicate that the latter did not interpret the parable of the two sons, and on this point I dissociate myself from A. Orbe who writes: "Conocía las parábolas del hijo pródigo y de la oveija perdita. Es muy creíble representasen para él lo mismo: la trayectoria de la naturaleza espiritual por el mundo de la materia" (*op. cit.*, I, p. 176).

27. Fragment 217 (72), (*GCS* Orig. IX 321) = Gregory of Nyssa, *De orat. domin.*, II (*PG* 44, 1144 CD): τῆν ἀνθρωπίνην

ἀθλιότητα--καὶ φιλήματι τὸν τράχηλον δεξιώσασθαι, with some slight differences. The fragment says particularly ἀτοπίαν where Gregory writes ἀσωτίαν (cf. ζῶν ἀσώτως, Luke 15:13). One could, however, ask himself if Gregory did not take up into his work a comment of Origen's; cf. the remarks of F. Fournier concerning the Greek fragments on Luke attributed to Origen, in *SC* 87, 462.

28. Is it not significant that Cyril placed those who hold this exegesis in opposition to those of an ethnic interpretation (which he equally rejected), in styling the first as τῶν ἐν ἡμῖν τινες, while reserving to the latter a simple τινες (*PG* 72, 804 A)? Wholly in agreement with him, Pseudo-Jerome points out that the jealousy attributed to the angels in the gnostical interpretation contradicts the word of the Lord who, on the contrary, describes their joy at the penitence of sinners, and both of them present to this effect a confluent reading of Luke 15:7 and 15:10: χαρᾶν εἶναι...ἐν οὐρανοῖς ἐνώπιον τῶν ἁγίων ἀγγέλων (*PG* 72, 804 B), and: *laetitiam esse in caelo apud angelos* (*PL* 30, 249 D). Pseudo-Jerome observes, besides: "Sed hic sensus pius quidem videtur, nescio tamen si verus sit. Dicit aliquis: quare? Quia minor filius et iunior ad paenitentiam venit sua sponte, recordatus praeteritae abundantiae patris sui, sicut habet series lectionis" (249 C), whereas the sheep is recovered "errantem et non sapientem" (*ep.* 35, 5, col. 250 D). For a similar idea, cf. Ambrose, VII 208 who, with the aid of Psalm 36/35:7 and Jer. 31:27, develops an idea dear to Origen (cf. H. Crouzel, *Theologie de l'image de Dieu chez Origene*, Paris, 1956, p. 201), in concluding a comparison of the two parables of the lost sheep and the lost son with these terms: "Malo ergo filius esse quam ovis; ovis enim a pastore repperitur, a patre filius honoratur."

29. Cf. Ambrose, VII 241; Jerome, *ep.* 21, 28 (Labourt, I 99); Augustine, *sermo* Caillau 11. 10 (*PLS* 2. 432).

30. The earliest attested titles among the fathers and the one most frequently utilized mentions the two sons, cf. Irenaeus, *Adversus haereses*, IV 36, 7 (*SC* 100**, 910); Clement of Alexandria, *Stromates*, IV 30, 1: ἡ τῶν δυεῖν ἀδελφῶν παραβολή (*GCS* Clem. II 261); Tertullian, *De pud.*, 8.2: *filiorum duorum parabola* (*CC* 2, 1295), etc. One of the oldest attestations of the title referring to the younger son alone could be found in a fragment of a catena attributed to a certain Macarius: ἡ περὶ τοῦ νέου υἱοῦ παραβολή (A. Mai, *Scriptorum veterum nova collectio*, IX, 696).

31. On the exegesis of Irenaeus, cf. P. Siniscalco, *op. cit.*, pp. 81-97, and A. Orbe, *op. cit.*, I, pp. 185-199.

32. Titus of Bostra, *Lukasscholien* (ed. J. Sickenberger, *TU* 21/1, 214-224), on 15:11f.: εἵς πατήρ δύο ἀδελφῶν. τίνων τούτων; δικαίων καὶ ἀδίκων, ἁμαρτωλῶν καὶ εὐλαβῶν (p. 214); his "notes" have been done over again in the Cramer *Catena* on Luke (II 117ff.) and by the Pseudo-Chrysostom homily Εἰς τὴν παραβολὴν περὶ τοῦ ασώτου (*PG* 59, 515ff.).--Cf. also Pseudo-Athanasius, *Dicta et interpretationes parabolarum Evangelii*, II (*PG* 28, 713): οἱ δύο υἱοί; οἱ δίκαιοι καὶ οἱ ἁμαρτωλοί.

33. Jerome, *ep.* 21 *ad Damasum*, 3: "...in publicanis (cf. Lc 15, 1) non tam gentilium quam generaliter omnium peccatorum, id est qui erant et de gentilibus et de Iudaeis, accipi posse personas" (Labourt, I 88; the remark is aimed at Tertullian, cf. *infra*, p. 383); and 39: "...vidaemus autem quomodo super sancto generaliter et peccatore parabola ista possit intellegi" (106; this is said after an ethnic exegesis of Luke 15:25-32, cf. *infra*, p. 368).

34. *Ep.* 35, 6, on Luke 15:12: "Dat autem hic pater divitias suas ex aequo. Non enim quisquam aut iustus aut peccator nascitur. Sed quae ex deo est, in prima nativitate hominis portio substantiae rationalis, aequaliter cunctis nascentibus datur..." (*PL* 30, 251 A).

35. Cyril, *Expl. in Lucae Evang.*, on 15:11ff. (*PG* 72, 805 D and 808 A). With Cyril, the righteous is compared to the Christian who is indignant at the pardon accorded to the sinner converted at a late hour (cf. col. 808 AB). Such was also the exegesis of Theodore of Mopsuestia, cf. *supra*, n. 7, p. 387.

36. It must be pointed out that the demand of the younger son is always considered favorably by the Fathers. With them, one is very far from the childish paraphrase of a K. Munk, *Histoires de Jésus racontées aux enfants* (French adaptation of G. Cavin), Geneva 1949, p. 22: "A man had two sons. The younger said to him one day: 'Really, what should I inherit from you? I wish that you gave it to me now!' This was a hard blow for this affectionate father to hear such a thing. Fancy that he said nothing. It is thus that he dealt with his sons." For the Fathers, in fact, the younger son did not covet the property of his father, but allegorically asked to be able to serve him freely. This is why Jerome is easily enough satisfied by the Latin translation of verse 12b, which

he therefore preserves in the Vulgate: "Qui divisit eis substantiam", while remarking this: "Significantius in Graeco legitur διεῖλεν ἀυτοῖς τὸν βίον, id est dedit *liberum arbitrium*, dedit mentis propriae voluntatem, ut viveret unusquisque non ex imperio dei, sed ex obsequio suo, id est non ex necessitate, sed ex voluntate..." (*ep.* 21, 6, Labourt, I 89). For his part, Titus cleverly glossed the term οὐσία of vs. 12a by ἐξουσία: προσῆλθεν οὖν ὁ νεώτερος αἰτῶν τῆς ἰδίας οὐσίας τὸ μέρος, τουτέστιν τῆς ἰδίας ἐξουσίας (*Lukasscholien*, on 15:12, Sickenberger, 216). It is necessary to await the "historical", that is to say, literal exegesis of a Peter Petrologus in the 5th century to see the behavior of the younger son criticized: "quantum pius pater, tantum haeres impatiens qui patris fatigatur ad vitam..." (*sermo* I, *PL* 52, 183f.). But in his "mystical" exegesis, allegory of the ethnic type, Chrysologus follows the tradition which found a praiseworthy act in it (cf. *sermo* 5, col. 197f.).

37. The ethical exegetes seem to insist by design on this aspect in their allegories of the triple gift of Luke 15:22. Titus sees in the ring a σημεῖον τῆς πίστεως τὸ κατά τοῦ διαβάλου (*Lukasscholien*, on 15:22[3], Sickenberger, 223; cf. *infra*, p. 378), and like Jerome, *ep.* 21, 25 (Labourt, I 98), he recognizes in the shoes a sign of protection against serpents and scorpians (cf. Luke 10:19). Cf. also Ambrose, *De paen.*, II 18 (*SC* 179, 144).

38. Jerome, *ep.* 21, 28-38 (Labourt, I 99-106): "Erat autem filius illius senior in agro (Luke 15:25). Hucusque de persona iunioris filii disputatum est, quem *secundum praesentem parabolam* in publicanis et peccatoribus (cf. Luke 15:1) qui a domino ad paenitentiam provocabantur debemus accipere, *secundum mysticos* autem *intellectus* de futura quoque vocatione gentium prophetari..." (28, pp. 99f.).--The expression *praesens parabola* refers to the obvious meaning of the parable, which is in itself allegorical (cf. *supra*, note 5, p. 386), to distinguish it from a derived meaning, that is to say, allegorical in the second degree. We find this again from the pen of Ambrose at the moment when he adds to his penitential interpretation a complement on the ethnic exegesis of Luke 15:25-32: "Haec de parabola praesenti putavimus esse tractanda. Nec invidemus si qui duos fratres istos velit referre ad populos duos..." (Ambrose, VII 238f.).

39. Titus, *Lukasscholien*, on 15:25ff. (Sickenberger, 223f.).

40. Pseudo-Jerome, *ep*. 35, 13: "Quid enim est quod de agro veniens dicit, nisi significans de legis operibus venientem et in his gloriantem et quasi diuturnos labores imputantem" (cf. Matt. 20:12; on this allusion, cf. *infra*, p.) (*PL* 30, 253).

41. Damasus, in Jerome, *ep*. 21, 1 (Labourt, I 84). Jerome expressed the difficulty raised by the jealousy which an ethical interpretation is obliged to attribute to the saints, by explaining: "Omnem mundi istius iustitiam ad dei comparationem non esse iustitiam" (*ep*. 21, 39, p. 106).

42. Cf. Maximus of Turin, *Expositiones de capitulis Evangeliorum*, 18 (*PL* 57, 824f.): "Isti duo fratres, ut exiguitati meae videtur, carissimi, duorum populorum significantiam gerunt" (825 A); Augustine, *sermo* Caillau 11 (*PLS* 2, 427-435): "Homo habens duos filios, deus est habens duos populos" (11. 2, col. 427); *Quaestionum Evangeliorum liber* II 33 (*PL* 35, 1344-1348); and in dependence on him, Caesarius of Arles (cf. *supra*, p. 364); Peter Chrysologus, *sermo* 5 (*PL* 52, 197-201); Pseudo-Jerome, *Expositio*; latin Epiphanius, *Interpretatio*; Isidore, *Allegoriae*, 216 (cf. *supra*, p. 364). --For the exegesis of Tertullian, cf. *infra*, p. 380.

43. Irenaeus, *Adversus haereses*, IV 36, 7 (*SC* 100**, 910).--We note that here, as in IV 14, 2, Irenaeus is brought, by insisting on the intensive aspect of salvation, to reverse the order of vss. 22 and 23 and to mention the Christological type of the calf sacrificed before the baptismal symbol of the robe, cf. A. Orbe, *op. cit.*, I 194 and 198f. Error excepted, this reversal is found again only on the part of Isidore, *Allegoriae*, 216: "...et pro conversione eius sub vituli typo immolat filium unicum, tribuit etiam annulum fidei et stola immortalitatis induit eum" (*PL* 83, 126 B).

44. Jerome's reaction with regard to vs. 11b is revealing. He has hardly determined the ethical character of the parable, when he writes: "Quod autem ait 'duos filios', omnes paene scripturae de duorum vocatione populorum plenae sunt sacramentis" (*ep*. 21, 4, Labourt, I 89). We have already indicated that he passed to an ethnic interpretation from the time the second son intervenes (Luke 15:25-32, cf. *supra*, p. 368). For his part, Tertullian, while estimating in his *De pud.*, 8, 8, that the destiny of the Jews who live in his time *in aliena regione* and serve foreign *principes* (cf. Luke 15:13 and 15, where εἷς τῶν πολιτῶν is often interpreted in this fashion: Origen, *hom. Num.*, 18, 4, *GCS* Orig. VII 176, speak of a *primarius civitatis*; Ambrose, VII

216, of *princeps istius mundi*, etc.) calls forth the destiny of the younger son rather than that of the older brother, refuses to propose an inverted ethnic interpretation where the younger son will be Jewish and the older brother Christian, and this because of the "ordo utriusque populi ab utero Rebeccae designatus" (*De pud.*, 8, 8, *CC* 2, 1295f.; cf. also Justin, *Dial.* 134, 2). It may be said in passing, it is to rediscover this *ordo* that the other parable of the two sons (Matt. 21:28-32) has frequently been reworked to give it the form attested by the Ms. B, cf. J. Jeremias, *The Parables of Jesus*, London, 1972, p. 125, n. 43.

45. Cf. Augustine, *Quaest. Evang.*, II 33: "Homo habens duos filios, deus ad duos populos intelligitur, tanquam stirpes duas generis humani: unam eorum qui permanserunt in unius dei cultu, alteram eorum qui usque ad colenda idola deseruerunt deum" (*PL* 35, 1344); Caesarius of Arles, *sermo* 163, I; Peter Chrysologus, *sermo* 5 (*PL* 52, 197); Isidore, *Allegoriae*, 216.--Jerome, *ep.* 21, 13, and Ambrose, VII 217f., presenting a double interpretation of the carob pods of Luke 15:16, liken them first to vices, then to vain philosophy (on this equivalence, cf. B. Blumenkranz, "Siliquae porcorum (cf. Luc. XV, 16). L'exégèse médiévale et les sciences profanes," *Mélanges Louis Halphen*, Paris, 1951, pp. 11-17). There would be grounds for asking if this last interpretation did not spring from the ethnic exegesis of the parable.

46. Cf. especially Jerome, *ep.* 21, 28-38, and Ambrose, VII, 239-243.

47. Cf. Augustine, *Quaest. Evang.*, II 33 (*PL* 35, 1346ff.), and in his progeny Caesarius, *sermo* 163, 3.--On the philo-Semitism of Augustine, cf. K. Thieme, "Augustinus und der 'ältere Bruder'. Zur patristischen Auslegung von Lk 15, 25-32," *Universitas*, *Festschrift Alber Stohr*, Mayence, 1960, pp. 79-85.

48. Cf. *Const. Apost.*, II 41, 3 (Funk, 131); John Chrysostom, *hom.* I *de paen.*, 4 (*PG* 49, 282f.); Asterius of Amasia, *hom.* I (cf. *supra*, p. 364); Pseudo-Clement, *fragm. Macar. Chrysoceph.* (*PG* 9, 757-765); Pacianus (cf. *supra*, p. 388, n. 14); and Ambrose, cf. *infra*, p. 370f. Cf. also Arnobius the Younger, *Annotationes*, 8: "duo filii quos dicit, fidelium et paenitentium inducit parabolam" (*PLS* 3, 218).

49. Cf. Asterius, *hom.* I: οἱ πολλοὶ τῶν ἀνθρώπων τὴν τοῦ βαπτίσματος μετουσίαν καὶ τὴν τῶν μυστηρίων ἀπόλαυσιν ὡς ἐπιβάλλουσαν κληρονομίαν παρὰ τοῦ θεοῦ ἀπαιτοῦσιν (Bretz, 109); etc.

50. Tertullian, *De paen.*, 8, 6-8 (*CC* I, 335f.); Clement of Alexandria, *Quis dives salvetur?* 39, 2 (*GCS* Clem. III 185).

51. With the exception of the anti-Novatian *De paen.* of Ambrose, the name of Novatian is nevertheless cited only by Pseudo-Clement, *fragm.* 7: ἀλλ' οὓς εὑρίσκει Χριστὸς ἀπολωλότας μετὰ τὴν ἁμαρτίαν τὴν εἰς βάπτισμα, τούτους ὁ θεομάχος Ναυάτος ἀπόλλυσι (*PG* 9, 765 A). On the confusion of names of Novatian and of Novat, cf. P. Nautin, *Lettres et écrivains chrétiens des IIe et IIIe siècles*, Paris, 1961, pp. 149f.

52. II 41, 3 (Funk, 131).

53. Ambrose, VII 239. Likewise, after having identified the swine of Luke 15:15f. with debauchees repulsed by their vices following a rather ethical exegesis, he mentions another exegesis which seems to originate from an ethnic tradition (cf. *supra*, n. 45, p. 395): "Sunt qui porcos accipiant pro gregibus daemonum, siliquas pro exili virtute inanium hominum sermonumque iactantia, qui nihil prodesse possunt, inani quadam philosophiae seductione et quodam sonorum facundiae plausu pompam magis quam utilitatem aliquam demonstrantes" (VII 218).

54. Ambrose, VII 213. On the reference to baptism (and to penitence), cf. also VII 221.

55. Cf. *ibid.*, 213: "Merito ergo prodegit patrimonium, qui recessit *ab ecclesia*." Cf. also Asterius, who styles the older brother as οὐδαμοῦ τῆς ἐκκλησίας ἀφηνιάσας (*hom.* I, Bretz, 108).

56. Ambrose, VII 225.

57. *Ibid.*, 228. Similar arguments are made by Chrysostom, *hom.* I *de paen.*, 4: οὐδεὶς δὲ υἱὸς βαπρίσματος ἂν κληθείη χωρίς (*PG* 49, 282 fin.), and by Pseudo-Clement, *fragm.*, 6: ὅτι οὗτος ὁ υἱός μου (Luke 15:24). ἄκρας οἰκειότητος ὄνομα καὶ μηνυτικὸν τοῖς πιστοῖς δεδομένου (*PG* 9, 764 D).

58. Ambrose, VII 212; cf. 213: *divinum patrimonium*.--The substitution of *patrimonium* for the primitive *substantia* (οὐσία) is frequent, cf. Luke 15:11 e: *pater, da mihi partem patrimonii mei quae me tangit*, a reading followed by Pseudo-Theophilus, *Commentarius*, III 10 (read *partem*, and not *patrem*!) and by Arnobius the Younger, *Annotationes*, 8. Likewise, on the part of the Greeks: Titus, *Lukasscholien*, on 15:12: δός μοι τὸ ἐπιβάλλον μέρος τῆς κληρονομίας (Sickenberger, 215); Asterius (cf. *supra*, n. 49, p. 395).

59. Ambrose, VII 226. One will note in this regard the use of terms prefixed by *re-* when it is a question of the triple gift (and not only of the *stola prima*, cf. *infra*, n. 91, p. 401) and of the calf: "Stolam anulum calciamenta proferri iubebit. Tu adhuc iniuriam metuis, ille *restituit* dignitatem" (VII 212): "mysteriorum consortio *restitutus*", and: "Nemo enim...nisi signaculum spiritale vel custodierit vel *receperit*...sacramentis debet interesse caelestibus" (VII 232). Cf. *Const. Apost.*, II 41, I: καὶ τὴν ἀρχαίαν στολὴν καὶ τὸν δακτύλιον καὶ τὰ ὑποδήματα ἀποδούς (Funk, I 131), and 4: οὐ μόνον προσδέχεται ὁ θεὸς τοὺς μετανοοῦντας, ἀλλὰ καὶ εἰς τὴν προτέραν ἀξίαν ἀποκαθίστησιν (*ibid.*); Asterius, *hom.* I: στολὴν τὴν πρώτην κομίσαι καὶ δακτύλιον καὶ ὑποδήματα, ἀποδοῦναι δὲ αὐτῷ τῆς προτέρας τιμῆς τὴν ἀξίαν (Bretz, 113), and: ἐδόθη καὶ ὁ δακτύλιος τῷ νεανίσκῳ, σύμβολον τῆς νοητῆς δωρεᾶς εἰς ἣν ἀποκαθίσταται (114), etc.

60. Cf. Ambrose, VII 231f.

61. Cf. Ambrose, VII 238.

62. Cf. *De paen.*, II 3, 13-19 (*SC* 179, 140-146).

63. At Milan, in fact, public penitence could not be renewed, cf. Ambrose, *De paen.*, II 95: "Repperiuntur qui saepius agendam paenitentiam putant. Qui 'luxuriantur in Christo' (cf. I Tim. 5:11). Nam si vere agerent paenitentiam, iterandam postea non putarent, quia sicut 'unum baptisma' (Eph. 4:5), ita una paenitentia, quae tamen publice agitur; nam cottidie nos debet paenitere, sed haec delictorum, leviorum, illa graviorum" (*SC* 179, 192).

64. Ambrose, VII 214.

65. The Christian is, the sinner is not, cf. *supra*, n. 18, p. 389.

66. Ambrose, VII 234f.: "Laetatur autem pater, quia filius perierat et inventus est, mortuus fuerat et revixit (Lk. 15:24). Ille perit qui fuit; non enim potest perire qui non fuit. Itaque gentes non sunt, Christianus est iuxta quod supra dictum est (cf. VII 219, cited *supra*, n. 18, p. 389) quia elegit deus quae non sunt, ut quae sunt destrueret (I Cor. 1:28). *Potest tamen* et hic in uno species accipi generis humani. Fuit Adam et in illo fuimus omnes: periit Adam et in illo omnes perierunt. Homo igitur et in illo homine qui perierat reformatur et ille ad similitudinem dei factus et imaginem divina patientia et magnimitate re-

paratur. Quid est ergo: elegit deus quae non sunt, ut quae sunt destrueret? Id est: elegit populum gentium qui non erat ut destrueret populum Iudaeorum. (235) *Potest* et de agente paenitentiam dictum videri, quia non moritur nisi qui aliquando vixit. Et ideo gentes non moriuntur, sed mortui sunt; etenim qui in Christum non credidit, semper est mortuus. Et gentes quidem cum crediderint per gratiam vivificantur, quo vero lapsus fuerit per paenitentiam revivescit." --Concerning this distinction between the *vivificari* of the pagan and the *reviviscere* of the Christian, one could ask himself if the ethnic interpretation of Luke 15:25-32 which rests on the ethical interpretation of the beginning of the parable by Jerome (cf. *supra*, n. 38, p. 393) and which doubles the penitential exegesis of Ambrose (cf. *supra*, p. 370) is not imposed by the fact that at vs. 32 ἔζησεν (א* BL) is said of the lost son and no longer ἀνέζησεν as in vs. 24 (א AD). This hypothesis, which would not be unlikely given the attention that the allegorists gave to the least detail of the text, should nevertheless be forsaken, for none of the patristic citations of Lk. 15:32 in an exegetical context carry the simple verb. All have conformed to the ἀνέζησεν or the *revixit* of vs. 24.

67. The fact that Ambrose speaks readily of God in terms of the *auctor* does not deprive this remark of its accuracy. Cf. Leon the Great (cf. *supra*, n. , p.): "...pen incarnationem Verbi potestas data est, ut de longinquo (cf. vs. 13) ad tuum revertaris *auctorem*."

68. Cf. Ambrose, VII 239-243. Ambrose becomes particularly violent in speaking of the goat: "Iudaeus haedum requirit, Christianus agnum, et ideo illis Barabbas solvitur, nobis agnus immolatur....Qui haedum quaerit exspectat antichristum" (VII 239).

69. Augustine, *Quaest, Evang.*, II 33 (*PL* 35, 1344).

70. Ambrose, VII 242. But perhaps this passage should be understood otherwise if *iustus* is parallel to *baptizatus* in VII 243: "Sed et, si desinas invidere, et omnia mea tua sunt (Lk. 15:31), vel Iudaeus sacramenta veteris testamenti, vel baptizatus etiam novi possidens" (VII 242f.). The Jew who is with the father *in lege*, will be in addition with him *in communione* inasmuch as he is a Christian.

71. "Hac ergo peregrinatione per magnam ignorantiam peregrinatos fuisse nos sciens beatissimus Paulus dicit: Vos qui aliquando longe fuistis, nunc autem facti estis prope" (*PL* 30,

251 CD); cf. Ambrose, VII 214: "Sed nos non sumus advenae atque peregrini, sed sumus cives sanctorum et domestici dei (cf. Eph. 2:19), qui enim eramus longe facti sumus prope in sanguine Christi."

72. "Famis autem μετὰ ἐκτάσεως validae haec est regio, de qua dicitur per prophetam: Qui habitatis in regione umbrae mortis, lux fulgebit super vos" (Labourt, I 91); cf. Ambrose, VII 214: "Non invideamus de longinqua regione remeantibus, quia et nos fuimus in regione longinqua, sicut Esaias docet. Sic habes: Qui sedebant in regione umbrae mortis, lux orta est illis."--One will notice that Ambrose in the course of time sets in contrast to the shadow of Isa. 9:2 the shadow of Christ in Lam. 4:20 and Song of Solomon 2:3, and that this complex of citations is found again in Origen, *hom. in Cant.*, 2, 6 (*SC* 37, 90f.).

73. Cf. *Lukasscholien*, on 15:11f.: πλάσμα θεοῦ (Sickenberger, 215); on 15:13[1]: μακρὰν τοῦ πλάσαντος (216); on 15:13[2]: τὴν αἴσθησιν τῆς πλάσεως (217); on 15:17: θεοῦ πλάσμα (219); etc.

74. *Ibid.*, on 15:18[1] (220). For the text of Ambrose, VII 225, cf. *supra*, p. 372.

75. With the exception of the allegories on the ring in Lk. 15:22, cf. *infra*, p. 378.--For this reason, I ask myself if the eagerness of P. Siniscalco, *op. cit.*, pp. 90ff., to identify on the part of Irenaeus the restitution of the *stola prima* with the recovery of the ὁμοίωσις is fully justified.

76. Ambrose, VII 214, with the citation of Jer. 2:27.

77. Cf. *supra*, p. 365.

78. *Praefatio* (*SC* 87, 94). Cf. G. Tissot, in *SC* 45, 33f.

79. Dealing with the sterility of Hannah and the fecundity of Peninnah, Origen declares, for example: "Similia invenies etiam in Genesi; cognata quippe sibi est scripta divina (*hom. in I Reg.*, I, 5, *GCS* Orig. VIII 8).

80. Origen, *Com. in Mat.*, X 15 (*SC* 162, 204), on Matt. 13:52, with citation of Deut. 19:15 (cf. II Cor. 13:1). In I Cor. 2:13, Origen understands πνευματικὰ πνευματικῶν as a double neuter, just as that comes out from the context.

81. Cf. Ambrose, VII 220-223.

82. *Ibid.*, 220.

83. Cf., *ibid.*, 223.

84. Cf. *Lukasscholien*, on 15:17: ἐπὶ μισθῷ γὰρ ἡ κλῆσις...(Sickenberger, 220; the theme of the κλῆσις is equally highlighted, apropos of Lk. 15:11ff., by Clement of Alexandria, *Exc. Theod.*, 9,2). The text of P is interesting to the degree that, like Ambrose, it avoids speaking of the workers of the eleventh hour: καὶ εἰσάγει ἐν παραβολῆς τύπῳ ὅτι μισθοῦται θεός· ἐξῆλθε γάρ, φησι, μισθώσασθαι ἐργάτας τρίτην καὶ ἕκτην ὥραν καὶ τὰ ἑξῆς. ἐπὶ μισθῷ γὰρ ἡ κλῆσις τῶν πολλῶν. δηνάριόν ἐστιν ἡ βασιλεία τῶν οὐρανῶν· οὕτω δὲ καλεῖται διὰ τὸν χαρακτῆρα τοῦ βασιλέως (*ibid.*).

85. Cf. Jerome, *ep.* 21, 40: "Solus deus est, in quo peccatum non cadit; caetera, cum sint liberi arbitrii, iuxta quod et homo ad imaginem et similitudinem dei factus est, in utramque partem possunt suam flectere voluntatem. Quodsi hac sententia non adduceris, saltem illius auctoritate parabolae commovere, in qua per totam diem operarii mittuntur ad vineam..." (Labourt, I 108). Cf. also Pseudo-Jerome, *ep.* 35, 12 (*PL* 30, 253), who speaks of workers recruited "ad duodecimam horam"! Asterius, *hom.* I (Bretz, 114).--Matt. 20:1-16 is found equally paired with Lk. 15:11-32 by Irenaeus, *Adversus haereses*, IV 36, 7 (*SC* 100**, 110f.), who discovers there a similar antidualist teaching: Luke has "unus et idem pater", Matthew εἷς καὶ ὁ αὐτὸς οἰκοδεσπότης.--It does not seem to me that the Matthean parable of the two sons sent *to the vineyard* (Matt. 21:28-32) has occasioned the studied relationship. The allusion to Matt. 21:28 attested by a late pseudo-Chrysostom homily (ποίησόν με ὡς ἕνα τῶν μισθίων σου· ἐργάσομαι κἀγὼ εἰς τὸν ἀμπελῶνά σου, *PG* 61, 782) results rather from the tradition uniting the younger son to the day-laborers from which Ambrose and Titus had borrowed.

86. Cf. VII 216: "Denique ad villam eius (= civis) mittitur, quam emit qui excusat a regno."

87. Cf. *ep.* 21, 28 (Labourt, I 100).--For his part, Clement of Alexandria, *Exc. Theod.*, 9, 2, joins the passers-by *called* to the marriage feast (cf. Matt. 22:9) with the returned son who symbolizes the κλῆσις (cf. *supra*, n. 84).

88. Ambrose, *De paen.*, II 18 (*SC* 179, 144). Cf. also *Expos. sec. Luc.*, VII 231: "Ergo stola spiritale indumentum et vestimentum est nuptiale": Jerome, *ep.* 21, 23: "Stolam quae in alia parabola indumentum dicitur nuptiale, id est

vestem spiritus sancti, quam qui non habuerit non potest, regis interesse convivio" (Labourt, I 97f.); Tertullian, *De pud.*, 9, 11: "Recuperabit igitur et apostata vestem priorem, indumentum spiritus sancti...et recumbet eo in toro, de quo indigne vestiti a tortoribus solent tolli et abici in tenebras, nedum spoliati" (*CC* 2, 1298).--On the nuptial significance of the στολὴ ἡ πρώτη cf. *Joseph et Aséneth*, 15:10: καὶ ἔνδυσαι στολὴν γάμου, τὴν στολὴν τὴν ἀρχαίαν τὴν πρώτην (ed. M. Philonenko, 184; cf. also 18, 2, p. 192 and 20, 5, p. 194.--The editor, in his note on 15:10, is astonished that converted Aséneth again puts on the robe which symbolizes paganism in 3:9; but the said robe having been thrown to the mendicants according to 10:12, he can only act in the sequel with another robe). However it may be with the question of a Christian rehandling of the work, it appears to exclude the view that the author of the romance makes allusion to Lk. 15:22.

89. Maximus of Turin, *Expos.*, 18 (*PL* 57, 825 B); cf. Caesarius of Arles, *sermo* 163, 2 (Morin Ib 633f.); Peter Chrysologus, *sermo* 5 (*PL* 52, 200 B). All three cite on this subject II Cor. 11:2, but they do not place the shoes in relation to the bruising of the serpent (cf. *infra*, n. 110, p. 403) as vs. 3 could have suggested to them.

90. *Ibid.* (825 B).

91. Considered as a return to paradise, especially because of the restitution of the robe (cf. *infra*, p. 377). But although only the robe can be restored, the Fathers have sometimes spoken of the restitution of the ring, as if Luke had spoken of the δακτύλιος πρῶτος, cf. Gregory of Nyssa, *De orat. domin.*, II: ὅ τε περὶ τὴν χεῖρα δακτύλιος, διὰ τῆς ἐν τῇ σφενδόνῃ γλυφῆς, τὴν τῆς εἰκόνος ἐπανάληψιν ὑποσημαίνει (*PG* 44, 1144f.): and, implicitly, Pseudo-Theophilus, *Comment.*, III 10 (*PLS* 3, 1317); latin Epiphanius, *Interpr.*, 37 (*PLS* 3, 897). For their part, the penitential exegetes of the parable speak logically of a restoration of the robe as much as of the ring and the shoes, since the reconciliation adds nothing to baptism (for the texts, cf. *supra*, n. 59, p. 397). Since this was also the interpretation of his adversaries (cf. Tertullian, *De pud.*, 9, 11: "*Recuperabit* igitur et apostata vestem priorem, indumentum spiritus sancti, et anulum *denuo*, signaculum lavacri...," *CC* 2, 1298), we understand why Tertullian, more than all the others, insisted on the difference between the restored robe and the given ring: "Vestem pristinam *recipit*, statum scilicet eum quem Adam transgressus amiserat. Anulum quoque accipit *tunc primum*,

quo fidei pactionem interrogatus obsignat..." (*ibid.*, 9, 16, p. 1298).

92. Cf. J. Daniélou, *Bible et liturgie*, Paris, 1958[2], pp. 69-96; P. Th. Camelot, *Spiritualité du baptême*, Paris, 1963[3], pp. 224-235.

93. Ambrose, VII 231.

94. He has not insisted on the spiritual theme. For the nuptial theme, cf. J. Daniélou, *op. cit.*, pp. 260ff. and 278ff.; P. Th. Camelot, *op. cit.*, pp. 164ff.

95. Astérius, *hom.* I (Bretz, 113).

96. Macarius, *fragm.* on Lk. 15:22, in A. Mai, *Scriptorum veterum nova collectio*, IX 696.

97. Latin Epiphanius, *Interpr.*, 37 (*PLS* 3, 897); Isidore, *Alleg.*, 216 (*PL* 8, 213, 126); etc.

98. Maximus of Turin, *Expos.*, 18 (*PL* 57, 825).

99. Tertullian, *De pud.*, 9, 16 (*CC* 2, 1298); cf. *vestem priorem, ibid.*, 9, 11; *stolam priorem*, Jerome, *ep.* 21, 23, and ms. *a*; τὴν ἀρχαίαν στολήν, *Const. Apost.*, II 41, 1 (Funk, I 131).--The adamic interpretation of the robe is dominant with the Fathers, but Ambrose only alludes to it in VII 231, where he likens the robe to the wisdom with which the apostles covered the *nuda corporis* (cf. Gen. 3:7).

100. Cf. J. D. M. Derrett, "The Parable of the Prodigal Son: Patristic Allegories and Jewish Midrashim," *Studia Patristica* X, Berlin, 1970, pp. 219-224.

101. Ambrose, VII 231.

102. *Lukasscholien*, on 15:22[3] (Sickenberger, 223); cf. σφραγὶς κατὰ τοῦ διαβόλου on 15:32 (224). On this tradition, cf. J. Daniélou, *op. cit.*, pp. 83ff.; and *Les symboles chrétiens primitifs*, Paris, 1961, pp. 144f.

103. Ambrose, VII 232, with an allusion to II Cor. 1:22. We note the kinship of this text with *De myst.*, 7, 42: "Signavit te deus pater, confirmavit te Christus dominus et dedit pignus spiritum in cordibus tuis, sicut apostolica lectione didicisti" (*SC* 25 twice, 178); cf. also *De sacram.* 6, 2, 6 (*ibid.*, 140). After having evoked the baptismal consignation,

Ambrose comes to the eucharist (cf. *De myst.*., 8, 43 and *De sacram.*, 3, 2, 11), following a movement which is found again in his exegesis of Lk. 15:22f., where the calf becomes a eucharistic type: "Occiditur et vitulus saginatus, ut carnem domini spiritali opimam virtute per gratiam sacramenti mysteriorum consortio restitutus epuletur" (VII 232; cf. *De paen.*, II 18).

104. Cf. J. Daniélou, *Bible et liturgie*, pp. 76-96; and especially *Les symboles*, pp. 143-152, where the author concludes: "It may be considered as certain that the sign of the cross with which the early Christians were marked designated for them the name of the Lord" (p. 149); P. Th. Camelot, *op. cit.*, pp. 224-235.

105. Cited by Ambrose, VII 232; Jerome, *ep.* 21, 24.

106. Pseudo-Jerome, *Expositio* (*PL* 30, 574 D); cf. Jerome, *ep.* 21, 24, citing Ezek. 9:4.

107. Jerome, *ep.* 21, 24 (Labourt, I 98).

108. Origen, *fragm.* 14 *in Ier.* 22, 24ff.: σφραγὶς δὲ ἤτοι σφενδόνη ἐν τῇ δεξιᾷ τοῦ θεοῦ γίνεται πᾶς ὁ τὸ κατ᾽ εἰκόνα διὰ μετανοίας ἀναλαμβάνων...ἥν δὴ σφραγῖδα τῷ ἀσώτῳ υἱῷ δέδωκεν ὁ πατὴρ ἐπιστρέψαντι (*GCS* Orig. III 204f.). For a parallel text of Gregory of Nyssa, cf. *supra*, n. 91, p. 401.--On Origen's theology of κατ᾽ εἰκόνα, cf. H. Crouzel, *Théologie de l'image de Dieu*, pp. 147ff.

109. Cf. J. Daniélou, *Bible et liturgie*, pp. 32f. and 39.

110. Cf. Ambrose, VII 231: "Calciamentum autem evangelii praedicatio est. Et ideo accepit...quoddam munimentum bonae intentionis et cursus, necubi offendat ad lapidem pedem suum (cf. Ps. 91/90:12) et subplantatus a diabolo dominicae praedicationis officium derelinquat. Haec est praeparatio evangelii (cf. Eph. 6:15) ad caelestium cursum dirigens praeparatos, ut non in carne ambulemus, sec in spiritu." One finds again in most of the exegeses of vs. 22 these same symbols confirmed by the same references; to express the idea of protection, the Fathers nevertheless had recourse to Gen. 3:15 and Lk. 10:19 (cf. Ps. 91:13!) in preference to Ps. 91:12. To clarify the theme of life *in spiritu*, cf. particularly Augustine, *Quaest. Evang.*, II 33: "Calceamenta in pedes, praeparation evangelizandi ad non tangenda terrena" (*PL* 35, 1346).

111. Cf. *De paen.*, II 18: "Calciamenta deferri praecipiat--celebraturus enim Pascha domini, epulaturus agnum, tectum debet adversus omnes incursus bestiarum spiritalium morsusque serpentis habere vestigium" (*SC* 179, 144). Cf. also Jerome, *ep.* 21, 25.

112. John Chrysostom, *hom.* 64 (65) *in Mat.*, 3 (*PG* 58. 613--cf. Cramer *Catena* on 15:24, II 120). This exegetical principal is stated with respect to Matt. 20:1-16, and comes a little after an allusion to Lk. 15:11ff.--It is necessary, however, to point out that the ancients approached the texts with more curiosity than we, as is seen by the questions of Damasus, reported by Jerome, *ep.* 21, 1: "Quis est iste in evangelio pater, qui duobus filiis substantiam dividit? qui duo filii? qui maior quive minor? quomodo iunior acceptam substantiam cum meretricibus dissipat, fame facta a principe regionis praeponitur porcis, siliquas comedit, ad patrem redit, accipit anulum, stolam et immolatur ei vitulus saginatus? qui sit maior frater, et quomodo de agro veniens susceptioni fratis invideat? et caetera, quae in evangelio plenius explicantur" (Labourt, I 84). This approach to the parables no longer satisfies us, and it is to be conceded that "the error is to explain allegorically the elements of a parable which are refractory to allegorical explanation, because a parable is not an allegory" (Ch. Masson, *Les paraboles de Marc IV*, Neuchâtel, Paris, 1945, p. 37). But do we do injury to the Fathers on this, since this type of interpretation was suggested to them by the Gospels, which, programmatically, allegorize the first parable of Jesus, that of the sower (cf. Mk. 4:1-20)?

113. *De pud.*, 9, 2 (*CC* 2, 1296).

114. *Ibid.*

115. Cf. *ibid.*, 7, 11. Tertullian sets grace illuminating the world (= house) over against the *dei verbum* enlightening the Church in the penitential interpretation of the Catholics.

116. Cf. *supra*, n. 66, p. 397.

117. Cf. *supra*, p. 368.

118. Cf. *De pud.*, 8, 12. To speak truly, Tertullian was already, in so much as he was a Catholic, convinced of the necessity of the *regula* in exegesis, although the Scriptures themselves should be a *regula*, cf. H. Karpp, *Schrift und*

Geist bei Tertullian, Gütersloh, 1955, pp. 38-42, and T. P. O'Malley, *Tertullian and the Bible. Language--Imagery--Exegesis*, Nimègue, Utrecht, 1967, p. 133. But what is without doubt new in his Montanist period is the appeal to the *regula* in disciplinary problems.

119. *De pat.*, 12, 7: "Illum quoque prodigum filium patientia patris recipit et vestit et pascit et apud inpatientiam irati fratris excusat. Salvus est igitur qui perierat quia paenitentiam iniit, paenitentia non perit quia patientiam invenit" (*CC* I, 313).

120. *CC* I, 335f.

121. *CC* 2, 1294-1299.

122. Epiphanius accused him of it nevertheless, cf. A. Orbe, *op. cit.*, I 157. Following Zahn, Orbe, *ibid.*, 158 (cf. II 474), deems that Marcion eliminated the parable because of his ethnic interpretation, involving the unity of God and the faithfulness of Israel (cf. Lk. 15:11 and 29). As for myself, I would be more reserved, for this interpretation, which is undoubtedly progressively distinguished from the ethical interpretation once the older son was likened to the Jewish people, does not appear to me so old that Marcion would have taken it into account. Besides, in the second century exegesis was interested in the lost son more than in his envious brother, as Irenaeus, Clement, and Tertullian show (cf. *supra*, pp. 367 and 370). And even if one concedes to Orbe that the ethnic allegory is "muy general desde antiguo", does it follow that its implications relative to the unity of God and the faithfulness of Israel had been set out before the year 140? Does not the antidualist argument of an Irenaeus (cf. *supra*, p. 369) postulate Marcionism? But above all, it seems likely that the faithfulness of Israel did not receive a positive interpretation before St. Augustine (cf. *supra*, p. 368)!

123. That is to say, Catholics. In spite of a tenacious opinion, it is not a question here of a nickname created by Tertullian, since Clement also knew it (cf. *Strom.*, IV 93, 1).

124. Cf. *De pud.*, 9, 19 (*CC* 2, 1299). Tertullian, then, had in view a penitential exegesis contaminated by an ethnic interpretation.

125. *Ibid.*, 8, 4 (1295).

126. Cf. *ibid.*, 9, 18 (1298f.).--At the end of the parable, Tertullian bespeaks only the jealousy of the older brother, which could avail itself of the principle stated in 9, 3: "Huiusmodi enim curiositates et suspecta faciunt quaedam et coactarum expositionum subtilitate plerumque deducunt a veritate. Sunt autem quae et simpliciter posita sunt ad struendam et disponendam et texendam parabolam, ut illuc perducantur, cui exemplum procuratur" (1296f.).

127. Cf. *ibid.*, 8, 4-7 (1295).

128. Cyril, *Explanatio*, on 15:11ff. (*PG* 72, 804 D).--Citing Jer. 2:5 and Isa. 29:13 (805 A), Cyril adds that all Scripture testifies to the apostasy of Israel. Besides, the complaint of verse 30 on the subject of the kid appears to him absurd since Christ died not only for the pagans, but also for Israel (cf. 805 C, citing Heb. 13:12).

129. Cf. Latin Epiphanius, *Interpr.*, 37: *hic mentitus est* (*PLS* 3, 897).

130. Cf. especially Augustine, *Quaest. Evang.*, II 33: "Sed de mandato non praetergresso facile illud occurrit, neque de omni mandato dictum esse, sed de uno maxime necessario, quo nullum deum alium praeter unum creatorem omnium colere iussus est; neque iste filius in omnibus Israelitis, sed in his intelligitur habere personam, qui nunquam ab uno deo ad simulacra conversi sunt" (*PL* 35, 1347).

131. Cf. Peter Chrysologus, *sermo* 5 (*PL* 52, 201 B); Jerome, *ep.* 21, 34 (Labourt, I, 103); etc.

132. Cf. *supra*, p. 368.

133. *De pud.*, 7, 2 (*CC* 2, 1292. As Preuschen, Dekkers holds the words "id est ad ea quae provocant" to be a gloss.).

134. Cf. *ibid.*, 7, 10, where Tertullian says on Lk. 15: 8-10: "Perinde drachmae parabolam, ut ex eadem materia provocatam, aeque in ethnicum interpretamur..." (*CC* 2, 1293). This is the same *provocare* which is found in 7, 2, with a reference to Lk. 15:2: "Provocabat, ut opinor, quod pharisaei publicanos et peccatores ethnicos admittentem dominum et cum illis de victu communicantem indignati mussitabant" (1292). As to the term *materia*, it reappears in 8:2 and 10: 9, 20 and 10:1; and in the plural in 8:12 and 9:1. Nevertheless, his meaning is variable, and he can also choose the tenor or even the doctrinal content of a text. It is thus

that in opposing the heretics who err in the matter of exegesis in order to escape from the *regula veritatis*, Tertullian lays down a hermeneutical principle which is disconcerting for a Protestant: "Non ex parabolis materias commentamur, sed ex materiis parabolas interpretamur" (*ibid.*, 9, 1, p. 1296); cf. *De praesc.*, 38, 10: "Valentinus autem pepercit (sc. scripturis) quoniam non ad materiam scripturas, sed materiam ad scripturas excogitavit" (*SC* 46, 141). But the examples of actors (cf. *De pud.*, 8, 11) and of centos (cf. *De praesc.*, 39, 1-5) show clearly the meaning with which this principle was invested by Tertullian: it was not a question of giving a preestablished meaning to a text, but of setting its meaning free necessarily prior to the text which carried it, in order to avoid the misinterpretations of a strictly irregular heretical exegesis. Tertullian observed, in fact, that with the *regula veritatis*, the heretics "parabolas quo volunt tribuunt, non quo debent" (*De pud.*, 8, 12, p. 1296), for with them "everything takes place as if the Scriptures were foreign to the *fides tradita* of which they are the 'documents'" (D. Michaelides, *Foi, Ecritures et tradition. Les "praescriptiones" chez Tertullien*, Paris, 1961, p. 137); their exegesis, elaborated "sine disciplina rationis", rests assuredly on some *verba*, but it neglects the *ratio verborum* (cf. De praesc., 9, 2 and 6, p. 102). Tertullian, especially in his catechetical works, is nevertheless not hostile to all enlargement of the original meaning of texts. In *De cultu fem.*, II 2, 5, he writes, for example: "Nulla enuntiatio spiritus sancti ad praesentem tantum materiam, et non ad omnem utilitatis occasionem dirigi et suscipi debet" (*CC* I, 355; cf. T. P. O'Malley, *op. cit.*, 132). But it is clearly evident that for him the *utilitas* is limited by the *regula veritatis* comprising both the faith and discipline (cf. *De pud.*, 9, 20: "tutela disciplinarum", p. 1299).

135. Cf. *De pud.*, 9, 4-7 (1297), citing Deut. 23:19 under the form: "Non erit vectigal pendens ex filiis Israel."

136. Cf. *ep.* 21, 3 (Labourt, I 87f.).

137. Cf. Ambrose, VII 239: "Quod faciebant Iudaei, cum quereruntur quia Christus *cum gentibus* epularetur..."

138. Cf. especially *De pud.*, 8, 10: "Quamquam, et si omnia ad speculum respondere possint, unum sit praecipuum periculum interpretationum, ne aliorsum temperetur facilitas comparationum, quam quo parabolae cuiusque materia mandavit" (1296).

139. Note especially his very unconstrained manner after the acrimonious criticism of the exegesis of the "psychics" (cf. *De pud.*, 8, 407), in justifying the Jewish identity of the older brother implied by his ethnic interpretation, in 9, 17f.: "Hunc (= ethnicum) et Pharisaei de saeculo ad patris complexus revertentem in publicanis et peccatoribus maerebant. Et ideo ad hoc solum maioris fratris adcommodatus est livor, non quia innocentes et deo obsequentes Iudaei, sed quia invidentes nationibus salutem, plane quos semper apud patrem esse oportuerat" (1298f.).

140. *De pud.*, 7, 3 (1292). One will compare with this passage the very strong affirmations by which Tertullian, *ibid.*, 11, 1-3, forbids the faithful to infer anything, as to Christian discipline, from the fact that Christ pardoned some female sinners, since this discipline "a redemptione carnis, id est domini passione, censetur" (*ibid.*, 11, 3, p. 1302).

141. As R. P. C. Hanson, "Notes on Tertullian's Interpretation of Scripture," *JTS* N.S. 12 (1961 f.), is inclined to believe.

142. Cf. T. P. O'Malley, *op. cit.*, pp. 166-172.

143. This is what must be understood in the exegetical rule set forth in *De pud.*, 9, 22: *sed malumus in scripturis minus, si forte, sapere quam contra* (1299).--On the criticism of heretical allegory, cf. G. Zimmermann, *Die hermeneutischen Prinzipien Tertullian's*, Wurzburg, 1937, pp. 14ff.; T. P. O'Malley, *op. cit.*, pp. 154ff.

144. One thinks of the disparaging definition of E. de Faye, *Clément d'Alexandrie*, Paris, 1926[2], pp. 124f., who sees in allegory "the process which consists in discovering relationships of resemblance between a text and some ideas which are totally foreign to it"!

145. Cf. *supra*, p. 368f.

146. Cf. J. D. M. Derrett, "Law in the New Testament: the Parable of the Prodigal Son," *NTS* 14 (1967f.), pp. 73f.

147. Cf. J. Jeremias, *The Parables of Jesus*, London, 1972, p. 128, who relies on the fact that in the expression εἰς τὸν οὐρανὸν καὶ ἐνώπιόν σου (vss. 18, 21), the metonymy of οὐρανός for God afterwards excludes the identification of the father with God. He recognized, however, that this identification

is suggested by some expressions, among which he precisely points out ἐνώπιόν σου (cf. *ibid.*, 128, n. 65)!

148. *Ibid.*, 130.

149. Cf. *ibid.*, 187ff.; E. Haulotte, *Symbolique du vêtement selon la Bible*, Paris, 1966, pp. 194ff., 225ff., 301ff.

150. Cf. J. Daniélou, *Bible et liturgie*, pp. 60ff. and 259ff.; P. Th. Camelot, *op. cit.*, pp. 179ff.

151. Cf. the remarks of A. Jaubert on the subject of the Philonic identification of the promise of Land with Wisdom, in *La notion d'alliance dans le judaïsme aux abords de l'ère chrétienne*, Paris, 1963, pp. 416ff. and 440ff. Often the dependence of allegorists on midrashic traditions is condemned, a fault of literary affinities, remaining in the realm of hypotheses. But it sometimes happens that a supposed bond verifies itself. Thus J. D. M. Derrett, *art. cit.*, *NTS* 14, 70 and in *Studia Patristica*, X, Berlin, 1970, pp. 220f., suggests, because of the attachments of the parable of Lk. 15:11-32 with the story of Jacob, a bringing together of the στολὴ ἡ πρώτη with the στολή stolen by Rebekah from Esau (cf. Gen. 27:15), which the Rabbis made a priestly vestment, often identified with the lost robe of Adam--for the priestly vestment preserves from death (cf. Ex. 28:43). The preponderance of the Adamic theme in the exegesis of vs. 22 does not permit us to affirm that the Christians had early interpreted the robing of the younger son by the blessing of Jacob at the expense of his older brother, as Derrett is inclined to think (cf. *NTS* 14, 73f.). It does not prevent the robe of the parable being identified by Hilary, *Tract. myst.*, 22, with that of Jacob, under a form which denotes the knowledge of the midrash: "Nam Iacob Esau stola induitur, quae pro immortalitatis veste commemorari solet etiam in evangelio, ubi stolam primam iunior frater et idem acceptis patrimonii decoctor accepit" (*SC* 19, 112f.).

PART FIVE

Second Reading of the Texts of Reference

Genesis 22:1-19

Luke 15:11-32

GRÉGOIRE ROUILLER

The Sacrifice of Isaac

FRANÇOIS BOVON

The Parable of the Prodigal Son

THE SACRIFICE OF ISAAC

by Grégoire Rouiller

SECOND READING

There was so much brilliance in the demeanor, the questions and the results of an exegesis conducted according to the principles of the historical-critical school! Such assurance, however, is indeed gone. Some lament this. Personally, I rejoice in it. Scripture may again find its place. Interpretation may come into its own. Its task is then comparable to that of an organist: one expects from him a new reading, a "creation" which is ignorant neither of the skeleton of the text (not all interpretation is legitimate) nor of the community of culture and of faith to which it belongs and which it wishes to serve. Like the organist, the interpreter (or the reader) is before his console: there are various keys and multiple movements. His art will consist always in a succession of creative choices.

The preceding statements have occasioned some disturbance; the researches, which are so varied, concerning language have opened some skylights; the resources of the human sciences sometimes permit the resolution of a difficulty, but they especially multiply questions. That is why the remarks which follow are confessedly stammering. This is caused by our incompetence, but also by the limits of time and space, and above all by the fullness of the problems as well as the multitude of partisan trails which could be followed.

I. ON SOME OPTIONS

My first remark will be negative. Face to face with Genesis 22, I am not much tempted by a psychoanalytic reading. Assuredly, in recoil before its difficulties; but especially because I have the conviction that if one wishes to go beyond the too facile fascinations of a cheap Freudianism (a father lording it over a son to the point of suppressing him; a son collaborating in his appropriate and radical castration) the materials show the defect of such a reading. For, in spite of the opinion of certain commentators, our text offers little for psychologists to lay hold of, since interpersonal relations scarcely find any place, in spite of the brief dialogue of verses 7-8. Everything was raised by the narrator to the height of a network of essential actions and the theological topics which encompass them.[1] That is also what Augustine seems to have strongly perceived. According to him the obedience of Abraham existed in such a climate of serenity, the bond which united the patriarch to his God was so alive that we can divine as the source of his action neither the pressure of an external law, nor the thrust of a fear or an inner anguish. The question of the cruelty of Abraham, then, is not posed, Augustine affirms. Further, Isaac is to such a degree "patient", he assumes his role as "object" in such perfect harmony with the general tenor of the story, that all psychoanalytical speculation about him strongly risks being purely gratuitous.

On the other hand, a sentence cited by M. Gerald Antoine may serve as a bait for our reflections: "The whole text which engages the attention of the reader by its form is literary, independent or not of its content (cf. *supra*, p. 170). This, we conclude, applies indisputably to Genesis 22--to verses 1-12 antecedently, and to the rest of the story by extension. Working from this evidence we may formulate some options which we have gradually adopted.

1. Never lose sight of the text, considered as a literary creation and giving, as Max Jacob demands for a poem, "the feeling of exclusiveness". The text is a word event. To consider it as such is to refuse an exclusively genetic approach which is content to locate the diachronic stages prior to the final composition and to label its sources or its underlying influences. Let us formulate this in a positive fashion: in Genesis 22 we hail the existence of an autonomous literary text, we recognize the composition of a powerful theologian. The composition of the story has created a discontinuity between such a literary result and all that precedes it (vocabulary, etiological allusions, cultural customs, etc.). It has set up a synchronous novelty irreducible to all the rest.[2]

This yes to the text and its reality allows us to surmount the dismemberment which we have recognized on the part of H. Gunkel, drawn by the quest for the original *Saga* and at the same time fascinated by the perfection of the final story.

This choice in favor of the final text permits us equally to relegate minor questions to their rightful place, the tantalizing questions over the historicity of the act of Abraham and the description of primitive occurrences (Where did they start? How many kilometers can one cover in three days? Were the sacrifices of infants frequent? What rites could be carried out at this ancient sanctuary, assuming that it existed?). We in no wise deny the interest which such questions may assume for other disciplines, but it is important not to allow them to be substituted for the task of a true reading.

Finally, once the text is known, one is authorized to utilize the modern resources of analysis to grasp it better.

For behind this discourse event there is no doubt that a whole network of intratextual correlations exists, affecting most particularly the language pole (schema, province) of this fact of language.

2. To declare one's self for the text, is not to renounce treating it as belonging to an ensemble.[3] Here two extremes are to be avoided. One is a generalized typological reading which easily falls into the excess and the complexity of allegorizing applications. The other is the opposite attitude which advertizes contempt with regard to all intertextuality.[4]

The belonging to an ensemble can be understood in several ways. Genesis 22 could be considered as the unit of a *corpus*, in the sense in which V. Propp works on a precise collection of Russian tales, or again in the sense of A. J. Greimas.[5] But this *corpus* would be difficult to establish, with Genesis 22 representing a considerably formal isolation. Furthermore, we believe the remark by R. Barthes is justified when he recognizes the possibility of working from a single text.[6]

On the other hand, an ensemble in the midst of which Genesis could be situated and establish a multitude of correlations would be perhaps the Elohist tradition.[7] Or again, if one takes into account the relation of the other traditions and of the order established by the final redactor, it might be the totality of texts which constitute the action of Abraham.

Other ensembles are possible. For example, a paradigmatic network of which Genesis 22 would be one of the witnesses. This network could be established on the basis of a canonical *corpus* of the Scriptures, accepted by a decision of faith which manifestly no longer highlights any single criterion of linguistic or literary analysis. Then Genesis

22 would be considered as "an entrance" peculiar to this "stable linguistic space" of which E. Haulotte speaks.[8]

3. We opt equally for a reading of the text which receives it as a *message*,[9] it being understood that we recognize ourselves as the addressees and that we could allow several principles of organization (for example, the norms of the condition of the covenant before God, the carrying out of a liturgical life, the fulfillment of the promises in Jesus Christ[10]). This means also that we thus admit into the text a tension between the "veiled" and "revealed", a tension which, in order to surmount it, demands an activity on the part of the interpreter or reader.[11]

4. Let us mention a final methodological decision: that of being attentive to *the protocol of reading* suggested, in a very implicit manner, it is true, by the text itself.[12] For a true reading should "produce the inaugural structure anew"; that is why it is important to situate oneself axially at the same incline as the message. Let us believe, for example, that in Genesis 22 the notion of pilgrimage, the atmosphere of sacrifice, the adjunction of promises (even if late) constitute valuable signs of protocol.

For, to avail ourselves of a more elaborate notion, we think that Genesis 22 can be considered at one and the same time as a text "in situation" and "out of situation".[13] That it is "in situation" is proved by the numerous questions remaining without a definite answer posed by classical exegesis (places, rites, sacrifice of infants, etc.), but also by the interpretations of the *midrash* and of the Jewish liturgy. It is because of this character that we may not neglect the contribution of ethnology, and the history of religions any more than the contribution of Jewish theology.

But Genesis 22 is a text on the march toward an "out of situation" status. Indeed, some exegetes have been able to treat it as such. The marks of the story which support us in this judgment are not lacking. The characters, especially Abraham, tend to incarnate types. The actions are charged with solemnity and priestly mien. The inductive themes (temptation and fear of God) have the bearing of theological topics. The epic modeling of the figure of Abraham, due to the oral tradition prior to the writing of the story, has without doubt prepared this open and universalist rereading of the sign of the father. Its appropriation of it was thus primed and facilitated.

II. CONSIDERATIONS ABOUT GENESIS 22:1-12

At the heart of the great story of Genesis 22:1-19 and before all extensive analysis, we recognize the existence of a story which is very restricted, and sufficient to itself. Its accessible dimensions and the perfection of its individuality could designate it as a choice text in view of a complete structural analysis. We cannot accomplish that here. Let us, however, take up that which appears to us the most significant and the most compatible with our total plan.

1. *The Cardinal Functions*[14]

According to R. Barthes, a story allows first some *cardinal functions* which detach themselves from all the rest. They are the "nuclei", "the moments of peril in the story". "In order to classify a function as cardinal," he says, "all we need verify is that the action to which it refers opens (or maintains or closes) an alternative directly affecting the continuation of the story, in other words, that it either initiates or resolves an uncertainty."[15]

"God tempted Abraham." According to a functional analysis, there are two ways to regard this sentence. It could be considered equally as opening a process of modification or closing it. The agent (God) was susceptible to modifying the status of a patient (Abraham); he has passed to the act of modification, that is to say here, of temptation; he has succeeded in an enterprise of modification. (The same function or ensemble of functions could be read from the point of view of the patient, Abraham.) Such an analysis could lean on the sometimes strongly stressed aspect of the Hebrew perfect, נסה designating then the present and permanent result of a completed process but one which has known a previous unfolding. And, in this case, our proposition would be condensed into a complete sequence.[16] The proposition "God tempted Abraham" then performs the role of a title, or better still, a resumé, obviously belonging to the metalinguistic code, the referent being less the reality than the story which is to follow.[17]

One could also consider the proposition "God tempted Abraham" as a cardinal function opening a sequence, of which the "now I see" of verse 12 marks the closing. In this case the יאמר which follows is equivalent to לאמר: saying. And the "tempt" could be paraphrased by "wished to tempt". We prefer, however, the first solution. It gives a better account of the perceptible shock in the Hebraic phrase and of the position of the verb in the original text. We will call it a super-cardinal function drawing out a sequence.

Having in a way detached the little phrase "God tempted Abraham" from the story, we could bring to light a sequence articulating the interventions of God: God said, verse 1--the Angel (or God) said, verse 11--now I know, verse 12.

The three kernels jointly comprise the will to intervene, the modification or explanation of the order, finally the establishing of the success of the temptation. It is interesting to note that the sequence of cardinal functions of which God is the agent are situated exclusively in the register of the word [*parole*]. Thus everything which will happen to Abraham will appear a little as the destiny of the word in him.

We have gone through the divine sequence at its summits. Subordinate to the first kernel, "God says", we could identify in verse 2 a quasi-necessary sub-sequence: take your son--go--sacrifice him. We place this sequence beside the cardinal functions although it well plays the role of some aspects of a catalyst.[18]

From the side of the functions where Abraham is the agent, everything is movement and action. Here again we encounter some summits. A primary sequence of cardinal functions articulates the preparation of the sacrifice: rise--saddle--take servants and son--take the wood. A second sequence is opened by "arose and went" in verse 3 and closes with "they came to the place" of verse 9. Finally, a third sequence runs through the acts of obedience on the mountain: build an altar--lay the wood in order--bind Isaac--put forth the hand--take the knife. These three sequences, because of the redundancies which shape their arrangement, could be considered as three super-functions: preparation, pilgrimage, execution.

We thus have hold of the framework of the story. An imperative which shatters a fixed equilibrium, then the restoration of the situation with the declaration that the order has been carried out: so much for the commandment. The preparation, the journey, and the execution: so much for the obedience.

The characteristic feature of the narrative, and this is frequent in the Bible, consists of detaching certain verbs (tempt, say) which are afterwards modules in subordinate functions.

We have not analyzed verse 1 from the point of view of Abraham. This is because the reaction mentioned too obviously discharges what Jacobson calls the "phatic function". One could, nevertheless, do it.

The Catalyses

Some functions of catalysis exist, notes R. Barthes, which necessarily presuppose the existence of cardinal functions. It is remarkable that there were none at the two principal moments of the story: during the preparation for the pilgrimage and on the mountain. At these two summits the cardinal functions weave a compact network which permits, for example, neither farewells to Sarah nor the slightest dialogue between Abraham and Isaac.[19] Everything proceeds in order and tends toward its exact accomplishment.

On the contrary, and this is very instructive, it is the sequence of the pilgrimage, which the reader should properly go through himself with all its intensity, which requires the greatest number of these catalyses. This joins the journey toward the mountain to expectation in a way differing from the denouement in a detective story or a novel of amorous intrigue.

To give orders and to leave the servants, to indicate how the division of the objects to be carried is to be worked out, is not visibly necessary to the unfolding of the story. These functions are no less important in their restraint by giving compactness to the drama which is transpiring, placing in full light the solitude of Abraham and the unanimous obedience of these two beings.

Still, the short dialogue of verses 7-8 constitutes the best example of catalysis.[20] We speak of dialogue in spite of the paucity of communicative credit on the part of Isaac. Besides, here we recognize that the dialogue does not open the door, as is ordinarily the case, to interpersonality. On the other hand, if dialogue "is capable of conveying presentiality", as R. Lapointe notes,[21] that is verified here. It conveys equally a sense of drama. Besides its phatic function, this dialogue fills up the emptiness of the way, delineates the ascension, and postpones the arrival.

The mixture of cardinal functions and of catalytic functions reveal the competence of the narrator. One of the reasons which explain the beauty and the compactness of the story is precisely this sober but judicious use of catalysis.[22]

The Indices and the Informants

We may, finally, note the presence in the story of integrative functions, called by R. Barthes *indices and informants*. In Genesis 22 it is not always easy to distinguish between them. The expression "after these things" is certainly an informant which sends us back to the whole of the Elohist narration. "Take your son", "whom you love", "Isaac", these are so many indications which report the atmosphere of affection between these two beings. "One of the mountains of which I shall tell you" is an informant. Because of the mention of "the third day" and of the adverb "afar", "lifted up his eyes" and "saw the place" constitute at the same time both indices and informants. They are indications of atmosphere and of states of mind. We could underline equally the indicial function of the expression "they went both of them together" (vss. 6 and 8) so skillfully repeated before and after an unfolding of catalysis.

The restricted number of integrative functions is symptomatic. We do not have a psychological story, but the supreme act of the father in its nakedness. Supported by the cardinal functions and their indispensable expansions, the evocation of Abraham and his son is realized on the foundations of barrenness, of solitude and of silence. It is Abraham who especially receives an epic stature from it.

2. *The Actants*[23]

It is known that, simplifying the distribution of functions in zones of actions such as had been established by V. Propp, A. J. Greimas has proposed the term of actant and has established the number of them as three pairs of two: subject and object; sender and receiver; helper and opponent.

With the terms "agent" and "patient" borrowed from Cl. Bremond, we have already infringed upon this classification. It could, however, furnish some valuable indications, particularly if we follow the perspectives opened by the analysis of cardinal functions.

The story may be analyzed from the point of view of God. God, then, assumes the roles of subject and of receiver. His "desire" is to test Abraham (object). Always seen from the side of God, one could hesitate to identify the receiver. Is it God, or, as Augustine claimed, Abraham? The opponent will be represented by all the difficulties of the task, then the faith of Abraham will be the helper. This relates to the story in its divine "version" of temptation. But the articulation of the actants could be made on the role of Abraham considered as subject. We then get the following distribution:

Subject:	Abraham
Object:	Isaac
Sender:	God
Receiver:	Abraham
Helper:	Faith
Opponent:	Difficulties of the sacrifice

We are even tempted to unify the two distributions and to construct the following schema:

Subject:	God -- Abraham
Object:	Isaac
Sender:	God
Receiver:	Abraham
Helper:	Faith and piety
Opponent:	Obstacles and difficulties of faith

The same zone of action could be named temptation or execution, in a word, test. This could then have a double subject: God and Abraham. P. Ricoeur has already noted that the hierarchy of actants, situating themselves on different levels, could well clarify some passages of Scripture.[24] We would have here a good example of the communion in the action between God and man.

We conclude this section with two remarks. Isaac could not at any moment hold the role of subject. His participation in the journey with Abraham and his initiation of activity in the dialogue of verses 7 and 8 would confer on him no role save that of an object. It is by a mutation of the story and the assimilation of it with the character of Abraham that Jewish exegesis could transform him into the subject of the sacrifice.

Besides, we ask ourselves if a distribution of roles more conformed to the model proposed by C. Bremond would not be nearer to the structure of the story. For the linearity of the text lends itself to that. In particular, the sequences concerning the order could be run through with two successive entries: God and Abraham; that of the journey or of the execution with other entries; Abraham and Isaac; etc.

3. *The Flavor of Words*

In my opinion, the moment will come, after having established the functional and actantial correlations, to practice exegesis in detail and to savor the letter of the text. I think, indeed, that once their structural status is recognized, the words deliver their message more easily. Many an acquisition of classical exegesis would thereby receive a surplus of light and a more solid foundation. Without taking up again what we have said above, we will hold ourselves to the examination of several points.

Thus, if in "God tempts" we have recognized the cardinal function par excellence, or better, the causal sequence of the whole story, we will no longer interpret the term "tempt", as is too often done, as a mere stage in a genealogy of the theme. For everything which takes place with the patient Abraham (become agent in his turn) will be revealing. When Abraham acts it is still God who is the principal agent.

Likewise, the notion of the "fear of God", which functionally closes the divine sequence of the order by an establishment of the outcome and which, on the other hand, is situated at the crowning of all the sequences where Abraham appears as agent, takes, thanks to such an analysis, the relief which is fitting to it.

Furthermore, if the reciprocal and solidary position of the two terms ("tempt" and "fear God") is rightly perceived, the meanings with which they are invested and the connotations they suggest will be so much more readable. To tempt will then connote the aspects of call, of trust, of pedagogy, of taking man seriously, and of liturgical invitation. On the other hand, because of its structural position, some possible meanings will be robbed of effect in the sense of dissimulating, of playing games, and of making pretense. To be recognized as one "fearing God" is to be enriched also by the whole "desire" of God, if it is towards that which the order given is opened. As a consequence of the intertextual tensions and correlations one will understand as connotations of the term promptitude in obeying, trust without calculation, the liturgy of a response which invests one's being, the faith which recognizes that all is grace.

All the terms of the story could be studied (but especially such words as "son", "take", "mountain", "sacrifice", etc.) by taking into consideration their necessity in the compact texture of the text and their importance in the action and the apportionment of roles. I know few biblical stories as compact as Genesis 22, and as lacking in superfluous elements. Everything is necessary and adequate. The stitches form a faultless fabric. Each function needs all the others. Not one, therefore, raises the voice.

4. *Toward Communication by Discourse*

"The story, as an object, is the stake of a communication."[25] After a literal exegesis, our reading should approach the text as discourse, as narrative communication.

Here again our investigation can only be rapid by dealing with an indissociable pair: narrator--"narratee" [*narrateur --narrataire*].

a) *The Narrator*[26]

The narrator is neither the author whose psychology one could pry into, nor an omniscient presence. It is the story itself which must deliver its own marks of him. T. Todorov rightly describes this:

> The narrator is the agent of the total task of construction which we come to observe,.... it is the narrator who incarnates the principles on which the judgments of meaning are based; it is he who disguises or reveals the thoughts of the characters, enabling us thus to participate in his conception of the "psychology"; it is he who chooses between direct or indirect discourse, between the chronological order and temporal disorder. There is no narrative without a narrator.[27]

In Genesis 22, it must be acknowledged that the marks of the narrator are discreet and wholly inward. How could it be otherwise when the structural frugality of the story is so rigorous and so poor? If he had happened to speak of himself in the first person the communication would have been overturned.

Contrariwise, to examine what T. Todorov called "the points of view of the narrative" can help us to know him better.[28] Here the vision of the narrator is double: it is at the same time "from behind" and "with". "From behind": the work proves it. "After these things", shows that he stands above them and that he is consciously adding an episode to the action of Abraham. It is similar to the proposition "God tempts Abraham" which belongs to the metalanguage of the narrator. He soars overhead, summarizes and already declares a value judgment.

His vision is also "with". As soon as the order is given, the narrator forgets his surplus of knowledge: he changes himself into an expert storyteller. He directs the construction of the story but from the very heart of the action. The tension of waiting is thus fully respected, the realism of the journey maintained and the reading becomes a moving act of accompanying the characters. One could say that the magic which is proper to the theatre has performed in behalf of the narrator. He knows what he is going to relate: the temptation. But when the curtain is raised he is no longer in the room but on the stage.

The vision of the narrator is thus bipolar. It looks over the whole, which confers on him a nobility and a theological mastery along with the fervor of an epic celebrant. It also participates in what happens and thus reveals to us the profundity of the poetry and of his dramatic art. The more he hides himself (we think, for example, of the small dialogue of verses 7-8) the more, at the same time, he betrays himself.

b) *The Narratee [Le narrataire]*[29]

"From the instant that one identifies the narrator... it is necessary to recognize also the existence of his 'partner', the one to whom the discourse is addressed and who is today called the narratee."[30]

As G. Prince states, at the end of his study, his functions are numerous: "he constitutes a relay between narrator and reader, he helps to specify the framework of the narration, he serves to characterize the narrator, he puts certain themes in relief, he makes the plot progress, he becomes the spokesman of the moral of the work."[31]

With a narrator so "solo" (one thinks of the monastic reading "recto tono") how could the narratee not be respected? We ought not, nevertheless, to attribute to him the "zero degree" according to the scale of G. Prince. "After these things" necessitates no explanation: he knows, then, who Abraham and Isaac are, he knows their history. Besides, he is perfectly well informed about the most appropriate liturgical practices, of sacrifice in particular. He is not amazed either before the idea of a pilgrimage or before the concrete conditions of the journey. The fear of God belongs to his theology.

The study of the narrator and the narratee apparently gives meager results. We derive from it, however, a positive illumination. If the narrator had nothing to communicate to the narratee outside of the story, it is because they are brothers in the same faith, celebrants of the same word, hearers of the same message. Is this, then, not the law of a story of universal calling? The nobility of the story, its apparent coldness, the quietness in the poverty of the means utilized, all this make us think of the celebration of a community which ends with catechesis and can devote itself to a memorial. The narrator then becomes the celebrant, the narratee, but also the reader, a concelebrant.

5. *Toward the Meaning*

With the study of narrative communication the structural analysis of the story has completed its task. The reader has not finished his. He has not unraveled the message. For that he must have recourse to some extralinguistic information.

It is time, for example, for us to take into account that this story which is so very individualistic finds a place in the life of Israel.[32] We are then delivered from false questions. If we are sensitive, for example, to the prominence which Abraham takes in this confession of faith, that exempts us from setting up an onerous comparison between the historical Abraham, who is difficult to capture, and the Abraham of the story. It is the latter who speaks, and speaks to us.

What is important, then, is to trace the contours of what P. Ricoeur calls "the world of the text", to make this "referent of the second rank" emerge which unifies all the primary referents. The text, we have noted, is scarcely in a position to do this. Besides, it is possible for us to mitigate this lack of information in extralinguistic ways (history, sociology, history of religions, Jewish liturgy, etc.), which unquestionably favor this and prepare for the appropriation of it.

The "world of the text". The confession of Elijah: "God...before whom I stand" (I Kings 17:1) would be an adequate and condensed formulation of it.

A *God* emerges from the entire text who is truly Lord, who is a God whose promise is realized in Isaac. A God whose purpose unquestionably underlies the destiny of free men. A God who supplies wants because he is the source, and before whom everything, marvelously symbolized by the only son, or oneself, ought to be recognized as a gift, that is to say, offered, sacrificed.

In the presence of this God is *the free man*, who is a respondent whom God takes seriously. He is a being in a radical situation of dialogue, for whom the obedience that knows how to listen is essential, and for whom active submission is the highest form of dignity.

Finally there emerges an *existence* from which doubt and mistrust are excluded, for which man knows himself called; a situation where the risk of liberty can be taken without anguish. It is this existence which is magisterially "represented" through the supreme act of the father who prepares a way. All that is reinforced by the performative character of the story, by the epic modeling of the actions recalled, and by the exemplary stature of the characters.

Some Intertextual Correlations

This "existence in the world" which is that of the father is here called forth with a great power of incarnation. The narrator has fixed its image for us in the supreme act of one who receives everything from God, who appropriates nothing for himself, immovable in the expectation of a response from God.[33]

A novel act, yes. And, therefore, this powerful creation of the narrator begins to live in relation with other texts, and to form a structure with them. It is necessary here to work on the level of isolated themes but also on that of the configuration of the whole. Let us stop for an example or two.

Abraham "believed...and he reckoned it to him as righteousness", we are told in Genesis 15:6. In Genesis 22 Abraham carries out the order (concerning which we have gone over the cardinal functions) and God recognized his conduct as being that of one who fears God. How could the similitude of these two moments be missed? Without doubt, in Genesis 22 the term "faith" is not used, but all the details of the bearing of Abraham (emphasized by the catalytic functions) evoke the attitude of the perfect believer. Likewise, the theme of sacrifice is scarcely apparent in Genesis 15:6, but the "reckoned" (חשב) sends us back to an external recognition of a believer who is brought forward in both cases on the side of God.[34] Finally, "righteousness" (Gen. 15:6) and "fear God" (Gen. 22:12) cohabit harmoniously on a paradigmatic scale whose axis would be "existence before God". This intertextual correlation brings to light the irreplaceable role of an attitude of faith which can even render the sacrificial liturgy, its "visible sacrament", useless.

Let us call upon another example. Once entered into the promised land, the people of God will be loaded with gifts (Josh. 24:13; Deut. 6:10-13). What should then be their attitude? That of Abraham: to obey the voice of the Lord, to serve Him, to live sacrificially, that is to say, to recognize everything which they enjoy as a gift. Then their liturgy will be a blessing, since in the mouth of the believer the blessing is a privileged form of sacrifice.[35]

III. A NEW CONTEXTUALITY: VERSES 13-14

Functional analysis and the narrative prove that the story is complete at verse 12. Also it is revealing that, for verses 13-14, the order of God no longer subtends the action of Abraham. That is brought to a close with the temptation.

"This ram is indeed accidental," acknowledges P. Beauchamp.[36] I am tempted to consider these verses as some expansions, some catalyses. Abraham lives sacrificially, that is to say that everything with him is the dynamism of faith and good activity in view of communing in the presence of God.[37] This sacrificial life is wholly inward. It can, nevertheless, proclaim itself, display itself in the communal space of a liturgical act, here the sacrifice of a ram. Hence, the catalysis of verse 13. Likewise, we know already that Abraham sacrifices on the mountain. This mountain may here be named by an etiological expansion.[38]

These verses confer a new contextuality on the whole. The first twelve verses display in a visible painting what should be the inner faith of the Israelite, in its radicality. The sacrifice of the ram contextualizes this attitude in the framework of a communal profession of faith, nourished and expressed by an institutional liturgy. "Each time that you sacrifice an animal," muses Abraham. If this council of Jewish theology is followed, all danger of ritualism is avoided. Jewish cultic life may be served by Genesis 22 in formulating itself: the sacrificial rite is understood only in an indispensable relation with faith.

Moreover, all liturgy knows a tension between the *materiality* of the acts and the *faith* which ought to precede them, animate them, express itself in them, and be nourished by them. To favor only one of the poles of this duality is to run the danger of rubricist hardening or of disincarnation. To unite them, as Genesis 22:1-14 does, exalts the indispensable genuineness of the obedience of the believer, without forgetting his insertion into a concrete liturgical community, which is what Jewish theology has sometimes happily realized, when it has not hardened the text by insisting too heavily on the merit of Abraham and of Isaac.

IV. IN THE AXIS OF THE PROMISES: VERSES 15-18

With verses 13 and 14, the text finds its place in the liturgical life of the Israelite. The great catalysis of verses 15-18 which unfolds the declaration of verse 12 ("you fear God") opens to it the dimensions of the history of the promise, of the history of an elect people. For a believer, the declaration of verse 12 constitutes the fullness of blessing. It was, nevertheless, possible to make explicit what this entailed as a cascade of blessings when this believer was named Abraham, as his vocation is that of a father. Then the chain of promises, begun a long time before, attains its fullness.[39]

The narrative thus finds its definitive contextuality in the history of the people of the Covenant, with a theology which was slowly formulated to attain its maturity in the Deuteronomist writings. The act of the father will then find its full dimension as an example. It will always invite the people blessed with the promises to renew its confession of faith in the presence of a God who supplies their wants; it will set them free from the shackles of imitation into an atmosphere of blessings.

Also I do not see why Jesus of Nazareth would not have appropriated the text by a living reading which remodeled its initial configuration. I think likewise that his so natural appropriation of it modifies the "world of the text" and promises us a renewed reading of it.

V. FINAL NOTE

In reality, it is only at this landing place of the confession of faith that the protocol of reading suggested by the text appears to me reverent. The story brings to us, then, an astonishing revelation of God-toward-man (theology), a grasp of man-before-God (anthropology), and finally a description of the practice of faith by man-toward-God (ethics). Not all the researches on the subbasements of the text are useless; but its kerygmatic importance is fully verified only in the story considered as an event of the word, a message to interpret.

NOTES

1. Some researchers of the Lacanian school probably do not share our reticence. For them this story likely would constitute a sufficient basis for analysis.

2. Just as the slow preparations which have made possible the unexpected gushing out of a metaphor would not furnish a sufficient explanation, so the catalogue of sources and genealogical elements of a text cannot adequately account for it.

3. Cf. the important article by E. Haulotte, "Lisibilité des Ecritures," in *Langages* 22 (1971), pp. 97-237.

4. Especially when it is a question of later texts. R. Barthes, following J. Kristeva, has thoroughly underlined the interest in intertextual correlations, in *Exégèse et herméneutique*, Paris, 1971, p. 190.

5. Cf. A. J. Greimas, *Sémantique structurale*, Paris, 1966, pp. 141ff.

6. R. Barthes, in *Exégèse et herméneutique*, pp. 246f. "All the grammar which supports a text is found in a single text, if we have the aptitude for choosing it carefully, moreover, we obtain not the individuality of the text in the full sense of the word, but the text with its difference from other texts."

7. With the help of a stylistics of themes, H. W. Wolff emphasizes the ties which unite the Elohist texts founded on the fear of God.

8. E. Haulotte, *art. cit.*, p. 101: "This fixed linguistic space (where all the parts simultaneously exist and where each can serve as a place to begin, e.g. the Old Testament or New Testament, the Gospels or Epistles, etc., but which immediately set into motion a system of very precise correlations and permutations) functions as a work of art in relationship to the superimposed discourse which makes it *legible*." *The New Testament and Structuralism*, p. 194, Pittsburgh, 1976.

9. In the sense held by P. Beauchamp, *Leçons sur l'exégèse*, Lyon, 1971, pp. 18ff.

10. Being understood likely that we rejoin the two principles of organization recognized by P. Beauchamp, to have a knowledge of the Law for the Old Testament, the Kerygma for the New Testament.

11. The idea of message, then, falls in with that of the "figure" set forth by B. Pascal: "Figure carries absence and presence, pleasure and displeasure. Figure has a double meaning. A clear one where it is said that the meaning is hidden." *Pensees*, text of the Brunschwicg edition, Paris, 1951, no. 677, p. 253 (no. 265, Lafume).

12. Cf. E. Haulotte, *art. cit.*, p. 99. "The *protocol* of reading is often indicated at the beginning (a psalm to be chanted with the accompaniment of some musical instrument, the proclamation and address and act of thanks at the beginning of the Epistles, at the end of the Gospels of Matthew and John, the prologue of Luke and the Acts of the Apostles)." *The New Testament and Structuralism*, Pittsburgh, 1976, p. 190.

13. For us to hold to the explanation of L. J. Prieto, we will say that the situation constitutes "the totality of facts known by the receiver at the moment of the semic act and independently of it." Cited by R. Lapointe, "La valeur linguistique du *Sitz im Leben*," *Bib* 52 (1971), pp. 469-487. The article establishes a fruitful dialogue between the *Sitz im Leben* such as H. Gunkel elaborates it and the linguistic ideas of reference, situation and context.

14. We do not follow a critic in an exclusive manner. We are evidently inspired by V. Propp, but, for a story such as ours, more particularly by the views of R. Barthes expressed in "Introduction à l'analyse structurale des récits," in *Communications* 8, Paris, 1966, pp. 1-27 ["An Introduction to the Structural Analysis of Narrative," *New Literary History* 6 (1975), pp. 238-272] and by those of Cl. Bremond who makes the act more logical. This latter, in retrieving the three "times" of a function, by refusing to dissociate them from characters and by appointing them "roles" permits a more exact study.

15. R. Barthes, in *New Literary History* 6, p. 248.

16. R. Barthes, in *New Literary History* 6, p. 253: "A sequence is a logical string of nuclei, linked together by a solidarity relation: the sequence opens when one of its terms is lacking an antecedent of the same kind, and it closes when another of its terms no longer entails any consequent function."

17. Cf. R. Barthes, in *Exégèse et Herméneutique*, pp. 199f.

18. It would be the same with the deployment of vss. 11 and 12. The important thing is that the divine sequence opens on an order and closes on the affirmation that the order is respected.

19. Jewish exegesis in which this is, moreover, an habitual process has precisely introduced during this second moment some functions of catalysis under the form of a dialogue between Abraham and his son.

20. Cf. the recent study of R. Lapointe, *Dialogues bibliques et dialectique interpersonnelle*, Paris, Tournai, Montreal, 1971.

21. R. Lapointe, *op. cit.*, p. 39.

22. The degree of implication of a catalytic function can also vary with regard to the cardinal function. Here it is so heightened that these catalyses accede almost to the "dignity" of cardinals.

23. Cf. A. J. Greimas, *Sémantique structurale*, Paris, 1966, pp. 172-191.

24. "There is a hierarchy of actions but also a hierarchy of actants, and this permits us to clarify some problems which we have underlined a moment ago, in particular the place of Israel in all these stories, because Israel is like the actant of the grand sequence, promise--fulfillment. We have actants which are less important but of almost as great amplitude, like Moses...." P. Ricoeur, *Les incidences théologiques des recherches actuelles concernant le langage*, Paris, n.d., p. 70.

25. R. Barthes, in *Communications* 8, p. 18.

26. We refer particularly to T. Todorov, "Les catégories du récit littéraire," in *Communications* 8, Paris, 1966, pp. 125-151; *Poétique de la prose*, Paris, 1971 [Eng. tr., *The Poetics of Prose*, New York, 1977]; *Qu'est-ce que le structuralisme? 2 Poétique*, Paris, 1968, Points, no. 45, Paris, 1973.

27. T. Todorov, *Poétique de la prose*, p. 64.

28. T. Todorov, in *Communications* 8, p. 141.

29. Read on this point: Gerald Prince, "Introduction à l'étude du narrataire," *Poétique*, 14 (1973), pp. 178-196.

30. T. Todorov, *Poétique de la prose*, p. 67.

31. G. Prince, *art. cit.*, p. 196.

32. Here it would be necessary to examine what the text becomes in its function as a confession of faith of a community. We cannot permit ourselves to do it here. In particular, it would be necessary to examine seriously the idea of its *Sitz im Leben* by utilizing the clarifying niceties of R. Lapointe, *art. cit.*

33. The exegesis of Gen. 22 draws great profit from the contemplation of the painting by Marc Chagall entitled *Le sacrifice d'Isaac*. The painter has sensed that the sequence of the accomplishment on the mountain, before the immolation of the ram, condenses the entire "spectacle". One will admire there the living serenity of an adult Isaac (this in conformity with Jewish exegesis), who is fully consenting. But consenting to what? To death or to life? In any case, between the hands of Abraham, Isaac finds again the position which M. Chagall has given to Adam ready to receive the breath of life in *La création de l'homme*. Abraham, himself is a living sacrifice, he is pure ascension, passionate attention. The use of the knife has not been necessary for the overflowing of sacrificial blood. And, therefore, the intensity of his presence does not conceal that of Sarah and of the ram, it does no harm to the verticality of the tree. At that time, in continuity with the blood-stained path, the carrying of the Cross is already celebrated. Correlation of liberation, ultimate meaning? Secret complicity with the haste of the Messenger with helping hands?

34. The verb also takes on the coloration of the judgment of the priest on a sacrifice offered, for example, in Lev. 7:16-18. Cf. on these comparisons, P. Beauchamp, *Etudes sur la Genèse*, Lyon, 1971, pp. 92ff.

35. P. Beauchamp establishes other intertextual correlations, for example, with I Sam. 15:22ff., or with a type of prophetic preaching, Amos 5:21-25, Hosea 6:6.

36. P. Beauchamp, *op. cit.*, p. 91.

37. I paraphrase the celebrated sentence of Augustine: "Verum sacrificium est omne opus, quod agitur, ut sancta societate inhaereamus Deo, relate scilicet ad illum finem boni, quo veraciter beati esse possimus," *De Civitate Dei*, I, 6. *PL* 41, 283.

38. Without prejudice, in the two cases (that of the ram and that of the mountain), other research relates to such a rite of substitution or such an etiological trace.

39. Cf. Gen. 12:1-7; 14:14-18; 15:1-18; 17; 18:9-16.

THE PARABLE OF THE PRODIGAL SON

by François Bovon

SECOND READING

In the exposition which is to follow, I will first pursue the explanation of the parable of the prodigal son by incorporating certain suggestions of those who were invited to write. Taking up the words of P. Ricoeur, I will search for "the 'meaning', that is to say, the intrinsic design of the discourse".[1]

From this *intratextual* view, I will pass to the *intertextual*: I will compare the principal semantic axes of the parable to the similar articulations of certain biblical traditions. Thus a *vision of the world* will appear, which are characteristic of various definite social milieus.

After explaining the plot of the parable and situating the text in its historic and ideological framework, I will attempt to encircle the text in its specificity: that which makes of our parable an original and living parable; that which goes beyond the operative and accedes to the thematic; that which is beyond the parable as a worldly scheme, and contains a possibility of life, a promise of liberty; that which breaks out of the determinisms of language, the mechanisms of reason and the pressures of society.

It will be fitting, finally, to speak of the *reader*. For less than ever can he remain neutral in this choice concerning the world of the text. Ought he not to advance toward this possible world which is opened to him? Far from moving back romantically toward the psychology of the author, he seeks to *apprehend* the world of the text which makes its way freely across the recurrent mechanisms of the stylistic and the commonplaces of the thematic.

This apprehension will be critical to the extent that the reader can either adhere freely to the text, admit it in its truth, or discard it without constraint as an illusion. However, as the freedom of the text is neither absolute nor obvious, the freedom of the reader must thread its way across the maze of social determinations, of psychological rubble and intellectual prejudices. To the conflict of interpretations is added, then, the struggle of the exegete with his text, a battle from which the reader, like Jacob, risks coming out wounded, but blessed.

I. TO INTERPRET THE TEXT. THE INTRATEXTUAL.

1. 1. Luke introduces the parable with two simple words εἶπεν δέ, "he said" (vs. 11). The reader thinks immediately of the decided difference which P. Ricoeur establishes between the oral and the written.[2] He recalls also the themes of F. Overbeck on the oral character of the early Christian literature.[3] What is striking here is the conjoining of the written and the oral. Luke *writes* what Jesus *says*. In writing, the words "he said" imply that the parable will be read as well as heard. The parable has then a double reference, first to an explicit *historical* context (Luke 15:1-2),[4] then to a *decontextualized situation* which permits a recovery of the meaning today. The author has then contextualized the parable by recalling in it the rule of oral discourse which refers to a concrete situation. He has at the same time decontextualized it in including it in a text which breaks

loose from historical and social conditions just as it does from the intended horizon set by the author. It maintains the advantages of the oral (immediacy, historicity, dialogical character) and gains the qualities of the written (durable and universalized value). The autonomy of the text and its virtues are on a par with the action of the word and its success. To compare the Gospel of Luke with certain Gnostic texts where the detachment, and the decontextualization, is most complete, is to discern a change of Christology, the abandonment of a historical Jesus in favor of a docetic Christ.

2. A second remark touches upon the literary genre of the parable. Two opinions permit me to enter into the subject. For contemporary literary criticism, says G. Antoine, the sin of sins is to dissociate the content from the form.[5] According to Max Black, elsewhere, one cannot translate a metaphor of interaction into direct language without "a loss in cognitive content".[6] Now most commentators, beginning with A. Jülicher, have committed this sin and worked out this translation: "Nicht in irgend einem Formellen," writes Jülicher, "sondern im Inhalt liegt die Domäne des Gottessohns."[7] In my opinion, on the contrary, if Luke had simply written that God pardons a repentant sinner, he would have said less than by narrating our parable.

At least four cognitive elements would have been lost in this transcription: 1) The hearer or reader would no longer have been drawn into a process of active interpretation; faced with a speculative and no longer persuasive language, he would have been constrained to adopt a rational attitude of intellectual adherence. 2) The history of exegesis shows that the parable, as a literary genre, provokes and permits a variety of applications: sinner--righteous; Gentile-Christian--Jewish-Christian; Christian--Jew, etc. Because of its literary genre, the parable possesses a certain extensibility. When J. Wellhausen says that the parable aims at individuals, F. Ch. Baur at social groups, and St. Ambrose at humanity, none is wrong, for each one merely utilizes the potentiality of the parabolic genre. 3) By its same genre, the parable evokes concrete situations and men of flesh and blood. That which could be, or appear to be, exclusively spiritual in a dogmatic declaration is thus avoided. The parable presupposes a psychosomatic conception or rather a comprehensive anthropology of the relationship to God. 4) Finally, in resorting to the parable, our text utilizes a mode of expression by analogy. It witnesses thereby to the inadequacy of all discourse about God. God cannot be enclosed and consequently domesticated by any discursive proposition, even if it is that of Jesus Himself.[8]

3. A third remark concerns narration properly so-called, such as a literary critic could appreciate, whether he be a stylist like G. Antoine or a structuralist like R. Barthes. Our parable is a narrative. It does not begin with the words: "The kingdom of God is like...." The necessity of analogical transfer is then implicit. It is the context and the person of the speaker which demand it. Neither does it end with the words: "Go and do likewise." Neither allegory, nor illustration, it is indeed a parable. More developed than some others, it is shorter and simpler than most tales and myths. Without grace notes nor digressions, it has a classic bearing. If its content cannot be disengaged from its form, neither do the formal redundancies detach themselves from the content.

At the level of the indices, we observe that it is a familial story from which women are curiously absent. The milieu--was it adapted to its first hearers?--is that of a well-to-do country home. They have servants, but no vassals. Some traits (the robé, the ring, the shoes) appear to be in contrast with the decor of the middle class. Is it necessary to see here some royal marks which the current story, a democratic version of a royal original, has not succeeded in sifting out?[9] We may doubt this.

Being unable to make rigourously an *actantial analysis* in the manner of A. J. Greimas, I intuitively notice certain elements. If the father is the *sender*, that is to say here, the one who imparts his goods, the younger son is the *receiver* (the older son is also); he is equally the *subject* of the quest. The question whether the receiver and the subject are incarnated in a single character is banal. What is less banal, it seems to me, is that the *object*, or the stake in the quest, should be poorly defined. The parable hardly tells us, in fact, what the prodigal son looks for and desires. This silence is intriguing. Certainly, he desired his father's goods,[10] but what did he wish to do with them? To spend them, no doubt. That, nevertheless, is still not the final aim of his desire. Could we say that he wished to live, to save himself, not to lose himself? In any case, the imprecision exists, and it is heavy with meaning. The stylistic impression corresponds to the thematic imprecision.

What is striking, also, from the *actantial* point of view, is the appearance of the *opponent*. According to the actantial scheme, the opponent is the traitor or the adversary of the hero. Now what is remarkable in this regard is the late arrival of the opponent: it is evidently a question of the older son. To this too late arrival necessarily corresponds not the hostility which disturbs the quest, but the jealousy which interrupts the joy of the conqueror. As long as the Christian mission is not completed and the Kingdom of God is not established, the joy of believers, the ecclesial communion, is disturbed. There is no theology of the resurrection without a theology of the cross.

Finally, where is the *helper* placed? The father is no doubt the helper, but he is a curious helper. He also arrives very late. The subject, that is to say, the younger son, searches in an evil place, inconsiderately. Instead of finding what he looked for, he not only found nothing and ran into nothingness, but he lost *himself*. This is what makes the helper the father, for a long time impassive and inactive, come in at the crucial moment of the *loss* of that which was in *quest*. The helper role, assumed at the decisive and opportune instant, likewise takes on such an importance that the father, from helper, becomes the subject: by reason of the loss ("I perish", vs. 17) and of the death ("my son was dead", vss. 24 and 32) of the hero. The unexpected gratuity of the object thus responds to the defeat of the quest.

What we established at the level of the actants finds its confirmation at the level of the *functions* or the sequences of the narrative. There is a situation of departure or rather an initial action which opens the narrative: the father gives his goods to his two sons. We observe immediately that this father is a surprising father who, like God, has the power to remain rich while robbing himself.[11] We note, moreover, that this father, as G. Antoine has well seen,[12] gives unity to the parable, since he forms the bridge between the two parts of the story: he is present at the beginning (vss. 11-12); he welcomes the younger son on his return (vss. 20-24); he exhorts the recalcitrant older son at the end (vss. 31-32).

In the sequences of the first part, a chiasma strikes the reader, it is a chiasma which may be presented as follows: loss of having, loss of being, gain of being, gain of having. What does that say if not that the dilapidation of goods is followed by a destitution at the level of being or of life,[13] while in the reconcilation scene the son is first reestablished in his identity, and in his being as a free son, before having anew a part in his father's goods. The communion meal follows the rehabilitation symbolized by the robe, the ring and the shoes, which are signs of filial identity and not of possession.

On this subject there is a remarkable correspondence between the effects of the style and the thematic content.[14] Contrary to Massillon, who extended himself over the vice of the prodigal son,[15] Luke describes the loss of goods in a single sentence. He found color and spice only in portraying the want, the result of the waste, and the filial reinvestiture, the result of the pardon. The son, then, interests Luke not in that he was a squanderer, but because he was lost, then refound.[16]

Another element must be taken up. The squandering of having and the loss of being are the work of the son (who is the grammatical subject of the verbs), while the reconciliation scene shows the father at work. The son remains perfectly passive, while the father, who is promoted to the rank of subject, speaks, intervenes, and gives the order. He also addresses himself to his servants, not to his son. This narrative procedure, which is characteristic of the Bible, expresses the creative designs of God and already betokens their realization.[17]

The exegetes who defend the unity of the parable for philological or literary reasons are right. The two parts of the text respond to each other and depend one upon the other. What is this interdependence? It is not a question of the sum of the opposites. As Ernst Fuchs has well seen, the two sons resemble each other more than it appears.[18] But, for this author, their relationship sums up their state of perdition. Now, in my opinion, it is possible to be more specific about this relationship. The composition of the story, that is to say, the sequential succession, shows us that what the one, the younger brother, *lost* and then *regained*, the other, the older brother, must *discover*. He began to discover it in being informed of the lot of his younger brother, which aroused in him the desire for goods which he enjoyed up till now without knowing it, hence without appreciating them. The words of his father also disclose this to him, by recalling to him who he is and what he has. The grasp of this consciousness, which is now possible for the older son, corresponds, then, to the recovery of the second son.

In my opinion, the parable closes again, if one dare say so, on an opening: Will the older son enter or not into the joy of his father?[19] After P. Beirnaert,[20] I observe also that the participation of the *younger son* in the familial joy is not expressly mentioned. We can see here some indications of persuasive style which combine with a characteristic feature of the Lukan theology of responsibility. By these effects of style and this kerygmatic intention, the parable ends on a question and an invitation: do you wish to come that you may be the younger son or the older brother? Come, for all is ready!

The function of catalysis, finally, that is to say, the conversations which the characters express, holds a primordial place. It fulfills a double mission, *metalinguistic* (discourse on a discourse) and *hermeneutical* (explanation of the narrative). By the conversation of the younger son, we learn that he is lost and by the conversation of the father, we discover that he is saved. Finally, it is by the paternal exhortation that the possibility of salvation offered to the older son is revealed to us. This catalysis in verses 24 and 32 furnish us with the most important hermeneutical key: going beyond *narrative* language, the discourse changes into a *theological* language on perdition and salvation, death and life.

4. A fourth point relates to psychology or psychoanalysis. I will go back to one element of the article of P. Beirnaert,[21] and then add another.

Father Beirnaert has shown us that the three characters are true men and not figures of wax. They are beings of desire and not marionettes. Furthermore, their desire carries them toward that which is elementary: the younger son wants to satisfy his hunger, to keep the money, and to be assured of a sheltering home; the father hopes to be able to count on a minimal affection; the older brother becomes conscious of his desire at the instant when his brother becomes his rival, when jealousy springs up. Through the entire story adult sexual desire appears only once, as a negative element in the criticism which the older brother indirectly addresses to his younger brother: μετὰ πορνῶν (vs. 30). This undoubtedly belongs to a civilization which has already declared the sexual domain taboo.

The omnipresent role of the law appears to me to be more important. The conflicts between desire and its moral repression, consciously or unconsciously, are evident in the text: schematically, we could say that with the older brother submission to the law surpasses desire as long as the younger brother is absent. With the prodigal, we witness a voluntary transgression of the law and of the family order in the name of desire. On the part of the father we observe a novel surpassing of the law.

By that we open a way into the world of the text which claims our further attention: to know the love of God which turns aside deference to the law by the granting of pardon. If psychology opens up this going beyond the schema of action-retribution, stylistics, we may add, also shows it, if one remembers that the rabbis often grafted their parables onto the text of the Torah. Rhetorically, Jesus detaches His teaching from the Mosaic law, as he theologically goes beyond the framework of legalistic observance. Sociology will say nothing more than that it will be sensitive to the social group incarnated by the older brother, which is opposed to the social group represented by the younger son.

5. My fifth point relates precisely to sociology. To speak of it, I will start from the older brother. With the older brother, as Father Beirnaert has shown,[22] aggressiveness irrupts into the story: the older brother becomes angry. For him, moreover, the anger is a positive element, since it leads the way toward a sudden awareness (*felix culpa*, dissipation permits the younger brother access to restoration and salvation). With the older brother, we pass from the personal problem of the younger son to the social repercussions of the drama. The narrator turns to account the fact that the *happiness* related in the first part provokes a temporary *unhappiness* related in the second part. A social conflict, then, is hidden behind the parable. The context (Luke 15:1-2) urges us to discover the pain which the pardon offered to the unrighteous, the tax collectors and the sinners, stimulated in the righteous, the Pharisees. The incompleteness

of the text, or the wound left gaping by the unfinished end of the parable, expresses the conflict attested in the life of Jesus and in the history of early Christianity. If Luke thus relates the incomplete denouement of the parable, it is not only to recall a tension which belongs to the past, the opposition between the disciples of Jesus, not very glorious and often outside the law, and the social body of right-thinking Pharisees. It is to attest a present conflict, which is reported several times in the Book of the Acts, between the new-born Church, the younger brother, who is elect and blessed, and the Synagogue, which is the older brother who wraps himself in his self-justification and his jealousy.

At this point of inquiry, the horizontal, *structural*, analysis leads the reader towards a *genetic* inquiry. The synchronic induces us to listen within to the diachronic. The texture of the story directs attention towards history. The literary analysis of the expression "he said" poses, for example, the problem of the citation of one text in another text, and raises the question of the fidelity to the original text. Likewise, the literary relation which Luke establishes between the parable and Luke 15:1-2 induces the comparison of the two brothers to the Pharisees and the tax collectors. The extensibility of the parable also directs the mind toward the history and the genesis of the text. Psychology and sociology, applied to the parable, pose, finally, the problem of its origin. The tradition-redaction problem is imposed, then, not in spite of structural analysis, but because of it. To go back to the genesis of the text (from the Lukan rereading of the parable of Jesus), to make the detour of historical-critical analysis, is not to engage in a supererogatory exercise, which is finally accessory, but to make the difficult climb to an important stage in the process of interpretation.

Space is lacking for such an analysis in detail. J. Jeremias has shown that the language of Luke 15:11-32 is often non-Lukan,[23] while L. Schottrof has indicated that the soteriology of the parable was typically Lukan. Neglecting the arguments of J. Jeremias, Mme. Schottrof concluded that Luke 15:11-32 teaches us nothing about the historical Jesus: the parable is entirely redactional: it adapts an example of Greco-Roman rhetorical tradition to the Lukan soteriology, that of a father being sympathetic to the attentions paid to the weakest of his sons.[24] This hypothetical construction appears to me unlikely for three reasons, one philological, the other two being thematic. 1) Philologically, the non-Lukan marks are numerous and the inventory of them which J. Jeremias has drawn up is impressive.[25] Thematically, the *exemplum* of the pagan rhetorical tradition is certainly not without some resemblance to our parable. But on certain points, the difference is profound. To single out but one, in stooping to embrace his guilty son (literally, he threw himself on his neck), the father in the parable, in distinction from the father in the rhetorical tradition, neither loses his dignity nor his authority. 3) The relationship between the father in the parable and the God of the Old Testament and of the Gospel, who loves and has dominion at the same time, appears to me much more striking. Other Old Testament roots, which I will point out later, confirm these bonds of kinship.

In my opinion, Luke reinterpreted an original parable of Jesus which already dealt with the older brother. The historical framework (publicans, or Pharisees) into which it is inserted is not necessarily original. It is a question, then, of determining, as expressed by J. Leenhardt,[26] whether Luke followed another *coherence* than that of Jesus; whether, for example, the original parable is for him only a pretext for a soteriological recital. The study of the intertextuality (the most limited being Luke, the most extensive being the Gospel and the Bible) will alone permit us to reply to this question and then to have access to the *world of the text*.

II. INTERTEXTUALITY AND VISION OF THE WORLD

1. Up to the middle of the parable the restoration of the younger son and the unveiling of possible salvation for the older son have appeared. The theme is soteriological, but our text, in itself alone, does not exhaust the Lukan soteriology. It is necessary to call on other stories or discourses to confirm the proposed interpretation or to complete it; in a word, to witness to the soteriological coherence of the vision of the world proper to Luke.

In chapter 14 of the Gospel by Luke, the theme of loss and gain has already appeared: to save *oneself*, it is necessary to lose *oneself*. "If any one comes to me and does not hate his own father and mother and wife and children and brothers and sisters, yes, and even *his own life*, he cannot be my disciple" (Luke 14:26). The loss of the self, at a certain level, permits the gain of the self at another level.

In the same chapter, Luke teaches us that to gain the *blessings* of Christ, one must abandon his own riches: "So therefore, whoever among you does not renounce *all that he has* cannot be my disciple" (Luke 14:33).

In the parable of the cunning steward (Luke 16:1-13), Luke distinguishes the *sons* of light, that is to say, the believers, from the *sons* of darkness. To give direction to the faithful, he shows with the help of an examplary son of darkness how one can again *be restored* after having *squandered everything*.

The pair lost-found appears clearly in the two parables of Luke 15 which precede ours. But to the similarity of situations there is a corresponding inversion of subjects and objects. In the parables of the sheep and the coin, the *lost man* is the *object* of the search undertaken by *God* and by the Savior. In our parable, on the contrary, the *lost salvation* is the object of the search of *men*. This inversion of subjects and objects must be understood in an additive and non-exclusive perspective. Our parable itself urges us to make the addition: man finds salvation when God becomes the subject of the search, that is to say, when the father finds and restores his son.

It is necessary, finally, to recall the story of the disciples on the road to Emmaus, a story which is to a certain extent symmetrical to our parable. The two disciples left Jerusalem, the homestead of the history of salvation, as the prodigal son abandoned the familial dwelling. The confusion and the wandering of Cleopas and his friend correspond to the loss and the failure of the younger son. In both cases, nevertheless, a turning is effected, the return to Jerusalem in one case, to the paternal home in the other. The encounter with the father provokes the one, the encounter with the Risen One provokes the other. In the two stories, the return is accompanied by a rehabilitation. Luke undoubtedly develops these two stories to express the truth that salvation is obtained by conversion to God (Luke 15) and by faith in the Risen One (Luke 24).[27] The exegete ought not to complain about his confusion over the absence of Christology in Luke 15, as if this lack necessarily implies a salvation obtained by the younger son thanks to his own efforts. It is necessary to take account of Luke's entire work to see a coherent soteriology being constructed. That this soteriology proceeds through the return to God and the encounter with the risen Lord is confirmed by the Book of the Acts. Acts sometimes evokes conversion toward God (Acts 14:15; 26:20), and sometimes toward the Lord Christ (Acts 9:35; 11:21). There is, then, a single and identical movement of man toward God and toward Christ: "testifying both to Jews and to Greeks of repentance to God and of faith in our Lord Jesus Christ" (Acts 20:21). The relation between Luke 15 and Luke 25 is further illuminated when we reflect that, without excluding Christ, the message to the Gentiles (the younger son) is centered in Acts on conversion to God, while the preaching to the Jews (the older son) bears first on the person of Christ, obviously without discarding God.

If there is a displacement of accent on Jesus by Luke, it bears not on conversion itself, but on the eschatological or ecclesial context in which it was produced. Beginning from the Church, Luke launches his call to conversion because of the resurrection of Christ (Acts 5:31). Jesus, for his part, rooted in Judaism, invites one to repentance, because of the imminence of the Kingdom of God. In detaching the μετάνοια from a temporal eschatology, Luke has not betrayed it, but has integrated it into an ethical process. Thus the stages of conversion as they are presented at the redactional level of Luke 15:11-32 are explained: 1) to speak to himself; 2) to go to his father.[28]

2. The parable of the prodigal son reflects a vision of the world characteristic of Luke's entire work. We must now inquire whether this Lukan thematic is original, whether it overflows and goes beyond being a mere vehicle or mere artisanship.

In my initial reading of Luke 15:11-32,[29] I pointed out a cluster of semantic axes which cross each other to form the plot of the parable. I will repeat them briefly here.

a) The *journey*, not in the sense that we understand it, but in the ancient sense of separation from the household, of a hazardous departure to a foreign land, followed by an often perilous return to reinstatement of the one refound.

b) The progressive *loss* of goods which leads to penury, to want, which is succeeded by a recovery, a reappropriation of goods.

c) The *fault* which occasions an insolvency of being, therefore a death, which restores pardon, rehabilitation and a new life.

These three primary axes perhaps form only one: a viable equilibrium, which is followed by a pernicious disequilibrium, and then a joyous recovery of stability.

d) The image of the *father* who unites love and authority. This father by turns distributes (gives), reestablishes (pardons) and exhorts (questions).

e) The tense relation between *two brothers* who differ in age, temperament and career; the older brother who is domestic, submissive, utilizing, jealous and exhorted; the younger son who is independent, a traveler, free, joyous, guilty and pardoned.[30]

These main axes of the parable are not original: they are constitutive of the Old Testament. The Old Testament, then, appears to be the dominant text of which our parable is a variant, in the way Massillon's sermon is a homiletic version of Malebranche.[31] In fact, our parable functions conformably to several well-known biblical traditions. This statement is confirmed by the vocabulary: certain expressions of Luke 15:11-32 recall a similar journey (that of Joseph or of Tobias) or a similar pardon (that of Job).

The Church Fathers understood well the biblical rootage of our text and its semantic axes. Behind the embellishments of their allegorical interpretations there is the conviction that the themes set in motion by the parable are biblical themes: the journey as an exile far from God, destitution as the loss of the Edenic glory of Adam, the death wrought by sin which is symbolized by the contact with the swine, the regal rehabilitation and the return to the household of the father as the tension between the recently elected nations and the Jews, the veterans of grace.

The *Wirkung*, the effect of the text on the Fathers, follows a straight line of propulsion which it receives from the major biblical axes mentioned above: the figure of the *father* is appropriate to the Bible to the degree that his love is not prejudiced by his justice, nor does his generosity harm his capital. Bound to his son, that is to say, his people, he hopes for a gesture from him as Yahweh awaits a turning in order to pardon. Having a weakness for Judah, he does not neglect Israel. He elects and restores. He creates, that is to say, he establishes, saves and reinstates.

The *journeys* in the Old Testament have a soteriological connotation. The exodus is a blessed return. The exile, on the other hand, is tied to sin. To be sons of Abraham, the itinerant, is to expect blessings, to hope for a country, then a dwelling, and to anticipate the status of a son, that is to say, of a free man. The younger son is a son of Abraham because he refound all that at the end of the course. Beyond the destiny of the people of God, it is the fate of humanity, as the Bible sees it, which is represented in our parable. The Fathers, then, were not wrong in understanding the best robe in the light of the Jewish exegesis of Genesis 2-3:

the clothing with salvation is the restoration of the Adamic state; it is to be clothed by Christ, to be covered by the Holy Spirit.[32] Emerging from this tunnel, redeemed humanity is more mature than Adam before the fall, for the error (the waste of the younger son and the anger of the older brother) has a constructive effect. Man pardoned, by reason of the culpability which he has surmounted, emerges grown up. He has gone beyond the innocence of the child. Irenaeus was not wrong in associating the *imago* with creation and the *similitudo* with redemption. The final equilibrium surpasses in quality the initial equilibrium.[33]

The rivalry of the *two brothers* is likewise not original. It takes up again and makes contemporary various fraternal rivalries which punctuate the Scriptures since that of Cain and Abel. It is sufficient to read the *First Epistle of Clement of Rome*[34] to see what role the menace of envy and of jealousy played in Jewish and Christian thought. Lists of rival brothers were composed: Cain-Abel, Ishmael-Isaac, Esau-Jacob, Israel-Judah, the Jews and the Gentiles, the Synagogue and the Church, without counting the two witnesses of the Apocalypse, the two staffs of Ezekiel, and the two apostles, Peter and Paul.[35] What regularly provokes the jealousy of the older brother is the favor, apparently inequitable, of a God who elects and cherishes the younger son who is unstable and without scruples.

J. Leenhardt has discovered behind Massillon an eminent contemporary author, Malebranche, whose vision of the world responds to a provisional and transient social and political situation.[36] The vision of the world which the Old Testament develops and which Luke 15:11-32 makes current goes beyond and transcends the living moment completed by its composition. Born without doubt in a precise and temporary socio-economic-political context, this vision of the world--to our surprise --has survived. It has even been considered as a vision of the world which is revealed and inspired.

Nevertheless, corrected *sub specie aeternitatis* or rather *sub specie historiae sacrae*, the Goldmannian conception of the vision of the world appears to be an intellectual tool of primary importance. It is so much more useful today than biblical exegesis, obscured by differences, understood as departments, disclosing a plethora of theological conceptions which no vision of the world succeeds in subsuming.

III. THE WORLD OF THE TEXT

The parable of the prodigal son functions normally, then, at a literary, psychological, and sociological level and even, as we have come to see it, at a theological or ideological level. Is that to say that it is only a product whose birth was foreseeable? Is it only the contingent actualization of a known potentiality? To put it in one word, is our text trite? If the answer is yes, it would have lost all *power* because of P. Ricoeur's statement: "Only authentic metaphors, that is to say, living metaphors, are at the same time 'event' and 'meaning'."[37] If it were trite, our text would only look back toward the known world which it could only repeat. Its symbolic dimension would be exhausted and, far from being a living part of the New, it would merely reiterate the Old Testament.

If our parable has been susceptible to becoming trite in the course of twenty centuries of exegesis, this does not lie within itself. If it is supported by some major semantic axes of the Old Testament, if it coincides in large part with the

Lukan soteriology, yet it has its own specificity, its ultimate significance, which is unique. It must be pointed out, however, that it is by a personal wager that the reader can propound this significance or, better, reconstruct it.

In spite of the references to the Old Testament, our text describes the relation of man to God in a new, evangelical, manner. Let us note, first, that the demand of the younger son is not rebuked. The father does not declare his son's aspiration for life illegitimate. The son was right to wish to leave. God is the God of the living, the God of those who wish to live.

This desire to live--such is the originality of the text--is accompanied by a total absence of arguments to make it valid. The younger son has no trump card to place on the table. There remain to him so few rights that he no longer hopes for anything. Now, it is in this nothingness of the pretension of man, in this placing of all hope between definitive parentheses, that hope arises and the response is heard.

The son expects at best a survival which includes retribution for the trouble, which associates punishment with life. He imagines only a servile existence: "Treat me as one of your hired servants" (Luke 15:19). But he receives more than he hoped for, than he had dared to hope for. He receives not what he merits, but what the father gives, without reckoning, without taking account of the fault. The Christian originality of the relation between the Law and the Gospel appears here. The attitude of the father transcends respect for the Law without depreciating its demand.

When we personally feel the possibility of annihilation, or the menace of death, the two brothers of the parable arise in our consciousness. Like they, we have a longing to live, to survive. But how? A reflex drives us to secure our subsistence ourselves, to carry away with us a little of ourselves, to guarantee a continuity between our life and our survival. We are then tempted to do it by following the refrain of the older son: "Lo, these many years I have served you, and I never disobeyed your command" (Luke 15:29). Or, in believing that we are imitating the attitude of the younger son: in confessing to myself, I save myself. Our future is not there. Neither the rigorist attitude of works, nor the legalist attitude of meritorious confession, even should it be that of faith, saves us. Jesus and Luke have understood this, as has Paul. The prodigal son does not save himself. God makes all things new. The new filial identity which he confers on us we owe to him and to him alone.

IV. THE READER

To awaken the significance which transcends the inherent meaning and functioning of the text, an engagement on the part of the exegete is necessary, that is to say, a wager by the reader.

In the case of a biblical text, this wager is kept and this engagement taken only by an act of faith. But to speak of an act of faith does not signify an individual leap into the irrational and the exclusion of all method. Theology should not be uselessly sacrificed.

The community of faith, with its circle of biblical scholars, should indeed intervene to verify the fruit of the work of the reader, as our effort at interpretation serves as a criticism of the preaching and the existence of the Church. The Church then has a mission to call to our attention all the methods, and all the aids to our faith. The faith of the community brings to our attention the psychological blockages, and the sociological pressures of our Christian engagement: all the soil of the exegete which we carry under the soles of our shoes.

It poses for us in particular the following question: is not recourse to the human sciences in exegesis a temptation? In his commentary on Luke 15:11-32, St. Jerome says that the carob pods could symbolize poetry, rhetoric and philosophy.[38] In reading this allegorical interpretation, I believe that I have discovered a signal alarm-bell. St. Ambrose himself, after a long excursus of a rhetorical type, recovers himself and launches this injunction: "But it is time to return to the father."[39] The faith of the Church puts methods in its place, which is precisely that of a tool, and it permits a participation in the joy of the common discovery of final significance. But if we have played to the younger son in this book, the Church also possesses its older sons: those who do not dare to call upon the human sciences a magical respect for the Scriptures.

Scientific exegesis--such is for me the result of this investigation--does not lead us to the Father. Certainly, to achieve this, it is worth the trouble to go a roundabout way. It is worth the trouble of having yielded to the charm of the secular sciences. We are perhaps cured of it. To be cured does not mean to reject them. That would be to be bad companions to them. To be cured is no longer to be their slaves. As Clement of Alexandria said, concerning the terrestrial goods of our parable, it is neither necessary to reject them nor to abuse them, but to use them.[40] To reject them is to hurry away to fundamentalism. To abuse them is to turn to scientism. To use them is to discover that the significance is beyond the meaning, and that life is beyond, and not on this side, of death.

NOTES

1. P. Ricoeur, "La métaphore et le problème central de l'herméneutique," *Revue philosophique de Louvain* 70 (1972), p. 100.

2. P. Ricoeur, "Evénement et sens," in *La Théologie de l'histoire. Révélation et histoire*, Paris, 1971, p. 18ff.

3. F. Overbeck, "Über die Anfänge der patristischen Literatur," *Historische Zeitschrift* 48 (1882), pp. 417-472, reissued in the form of a book, Basel, n.d.

4. Whether the context which squeezes Jesus between the tax collectors and the Pharisees is historically "true" is not important here. What counts now is that this historic context be narratively "true".

5. "His aim [that of a good stylistic method]--I recall once more--is to grasp that which makes the specificity of a text, forms and content reunited in this mystery of incarnation which is a wholly genuine work of art." (G. Antoine, "Les trois paraboles de la miséricorde. Explication de Luc 15, 1-32," *supra*, p. 183).

6. Cited by P. Ricoeur, "La métaphore et le problème central de l'herméneutique," *Revue philosophique de Louvain* 70 (1972), p. 102 ["Metaphor and the Main Problem of Hermeneutics," *New Literary History*, 6 (1974), p. 102].

7. A. Jülicher, *Die Gleichnisreden Jesu*, I, Freiburg im Breisgau, Leipzig, Tübingen, 1899[2], p. 117, cited by J. M. Robinson, "Les Paraboles comme avènement de Dieu," in *Le Point théologique*, 3, Paris, 1972, p. 42.

8. On the importance of the form of the parables, cf. J. M. Robinson, *art. cit.* in the preceding note, and Eric Fuchs, "Trace de Dieu: la parabole," *Bulletin du Centre protestant d'Etudes*, Genève 25, (1973), no. 4-5, pp. 19-39.

9. This is the thesis of K. H. Rengstorf which rests on a related text, the song of the pearl, of the *Acts of Thomas*, in which the milieu is explicitly royal. Cf. K. H. Rengstorf, *Die Re-Investitur des verlorenen Sohnes in der Gleichniserzählung Jesu Luk. 15, 11-32*, Köln, Opladen, 1967.

10. Did Luke wish to play on the polysemy of the terms βίος and οὐσία which here designate the goods of the father and which evoked more "life" and "being" than the son finally sought? This is unlikely.

11. The Fathers of the Church have felt that the bizarre or shocking elements of a story invite the reader to pass from the literal to the spiritual meaning. Cf. J. Pépin, "A propos de l'histoire de l'exégèse allégorique: l'absurdité signe de l'allégorie," in *Studia Patristica*, I, Berlin, 1957, pp. 395-413.

12. Cf. G. Antoine, "Les trois paraboles de la miséricorde. Explication de Luc 15:1-32," *supra*, p. 185.

13. Loss of having: καὶ ἐκεῖ διεσκόρπιζεν τὴν οὐσιάν αὐτοῦ (vs. 13). Loss of being: ἐγὼ δὲ λιμῷ ἀπόλλυμαι (v. 17).

14. G. Antoine has glimpsed this correspondence apropos of the loss. Cf. G. Antoine, "Les trois paraboles de la miséricorde. Explication de Luc 15, 1-32," *supra*, p. 185.

15. Cf. J. Leenhardt, "Approche sociologique d'un sermon de Massillon sur Luc 15, 11-32," *supra*, p. 217.

16. Verses 24 and 32, which belong to the metalinguistic code, attest this excellently.

17. Cf. Gen. 1:26: "Let us make [note the plural] man in our image...."

18. Ernst Fuchs, "Das Fest der Verlorenen. Existentiale Interpretation des Gleichnisses vom verlorenen Sohn," in *Glaube und Erfahrung. Zum christologischen Problem im Neuen Testament*, Tübingen, 1965, pp. 402-415.

19. With W. Trilling, *L'annonce du Christ dans les Evangiles synoptiques*, Paris, 1971, pp. 105-120, criticized, in my opinion unjustly, by G. Antoine, "Les trois paraboles de la miséricorde. Explication de Luc 15, 1-32," *supra*, p. 190.

20. L. Beirnaert, "La parabole de l'enfant prodigue, luc 15, 11-32, lue par un analyste," *supra*, p. 197.

21. L. Beirnaert, *art. cit.* in preceding note, *supra*, pp. 206-208.

22. L. Beirnaert, *art. cit., supra,* p. 201f.

23. J. Jeremias, "Tradition und Redaktion in Lukas 15," *ZNW* 62 (1971), pp. 172-189.

24. L. Schottrof, "Das Gleichnis vom verlorenen Sohn," *ZThK* 68 (1971), pp. 27-52.

25. J. Jeremias, *art. cit.* in note 23.

26. J. Leenhardt, *art. cit., supra*, p. 228f.

27. G. Lohfink writes in relation to the disciples of Emmaus: "Das Sich-Entfernen von der Stadt, in diesem Fall gleichbedeutend mit der Entfernung von Jesus und der künftigen Gemeinde, wird durch die Erscheinung des Auferstandenen eingeholt und umgekehrt in die Bewegung auf die Stadt hin." G. Lohfink, *Die Himmelfahrt Jesu. Untersuchungen zu den Himmelfahrts- und Erhöhungstexten bei Lukas*, München, 1971, p. 264.

28. Cf. the chapter on the appropriation of salvation in the book which I am preparing on the theology of the Acts of the Apostles.

29. "La parabole de l'enfant prodigue: première lecture," *supra*, pp. 50-59.

30. On older sons and younger sons in the Bible, cf. the pertinent remarks of J. D. M. Derrett, "Law in the New Testament: The Parable of the Prodigal Son," *NTS* 14 (1967-1968), pp. 56-74; reprinted in *Law in the New Testament*, London, 1970, pp. 100-125.

31. Cf. J. Leenhardt, *art. cit., supra*, p. 215f.

32. Cf. the exposition of Y. Tissot, "Allégories patristiques de la parabole lucanienne des deux fils, Luc 15, 11-32," *supra*, pp. 368f. and 371f.

33. Cf. J. Quasten, *Initiation aux Peres de l'Eglise*, I, trans. by J. Laporte, Paris, 1955, pp. 339 and 357f., who cites the texts but does not draw all the consequences from them.

34. Clement of Rome, *Epître aux Corinthiens*, 4, introduction, text and translation by Annie Jaubert, Paris, 1971, pp. 104-106.

35. Acts 11:1ff. and Ezek. 37:15ff.

36. Cf. J. Leenhardt, *art. cit.*, *supra*, p. 215f.

37. P. Ricoeur, "La métaphore et le problème central de l'herméneutique," *Revue philosophique de Louvain* 70 (1972), p. 99.

38. "Ad Damasum, Epistula XXI, 13," in Saint Jérome, *Lettres*, text and translation by J. Labourt, I, Paris, 1949, pp. 92-95.

39. Saint Ambrose, *Sur Saint Luc*, VII, 224, text and translation by G. Tissot, Paris, 1958, p. 93.

40. "We ought not then, as if we were leading a dissipated life in the image of the rich son of the Gospel, to abuse the gifts of the Father, but we should use them, since we have dominion over them, without bowing before them." Clement of Alexandria, *Le Pédagogue*, II, 1, 9, 2, text and translation by C. Mondésert, notes by H. I. Marrou, Paris, 1965, p. 27.

CURRENT METHODOLOGICAL RESEARCH

Select Bibliography

L. Alonso-Schökel, *La Parole inspirée*, Paris, 1964.

L. Alonso-Schökel, art. "Poésie," *DBS* 8 (1967 s), pp. 47-90.

"Les méthodes d'analyse structurale" (articles by M. Bouttier, A. Dumas, A. Gounelle, G. Crespy, Corina Galland, A. Blancy and J. Rouquette), *EThR* 48 (1973), pp. 1-120.

J. Barr, *Semantics of Biblical Language*, Oxford, 1961 (French trans., Paris, 1971).

R. Barthes, P. Beauchamp, H. Bouillard, J. Courtes, E. Haulotte, X. Léon-Dufour, L. Marin, P. Ricoeur, A. Vergotte, *Exégèse et Hermeneutique*, Paris, 1971.

R. Barthes, F. Bovon, F. J. Leenhardt, R. Martin-Achard, J. Starobinski, *Analyse structurale et exégèse biblique, essais d'interprétation*, Neuchâtel, 1971. [Eng. trans., *Structural Analysis and Biblical Exegesis; interpretational essays*. Tr. by Alfred M. Johnson, Jr. Pittsburgh: The Pickwick Press, 1974.]

W. A. Beardslee, *Literary Criticism of the New Testament*, Philadelphia, 1970.

P. Beauchamp, *Leçons sur l'exégèse*, Lyon, 1971.

H. Cazelles, *Ecriture, Parole et Esprit. Trois aspects de l'herméneutique biblique*, Paris, 1971.

C. Chabrol, L. Marin, editors, *Sémiotique narrative: Récits bibliques, Langages*, 22 (1971) (articles by M. De Certeau, C. Chabrol, E. Haulotte, E. R. Leach, L. Marin, G. Vuillod). [Eng. trans., *The New Testament and Structuralism. A Collection of Essays*. Ed. and tr. by Alfred M. Johnson, Jr. Pittsburgh: The Pickwick Press, 1976.]

C. Chabrol and L. Marin, *Le Récit évangélique*, Paris, 1974. [Eng. trans., *The Gospel Narratives*. Tr. by Alfred M. Johnson, Jr. Pittsburgh: The Pickwick Press, 1979.]

D. Gewalt, "Neutestamentliche Exegese und Soziologie," *EvTh* 31 (1971), pp. 87-99.

D. Greenwood, "Rhetorical Criticism and Formgeschichte: Some Methodological Considerations," *JBL* 89 (1970), pp. 418-426.

E. Guettgemanns, *Offene Fragen zur Formgeschichte des Evangeliums. Eine methodologische Skizze der Grundlagenproblematik der Form- und Redaktionsgeschichte*, München, 1970. [Eng. trans., *Candid Questions Concerning Gospel Form Criticism; a methodological sketch of fundamental problematics of form and redaction criticism.* Tr. by William G. Doty. Pittsburgh: The Pickwick Press, 1979.]

E. Guettgemanns, *Studia Linguistica Neotestamentica, Gesammelte Aufsätze zur linguistischen Grundlage einer Neutestamentlichen Theologie*, München, 1971.

F. Hahn, "Probleme historischer Kritik," *ZNW* 63 (1972), pp. 1-17.

H. Harsch, G. Voss, editors, *Versuche mehrdimensionaler Schriftauslegung, Bericht über ein Gespräch*, München, 1972 (articles by W. A. De Pater, H. Harsch, H. Leroy, A. Smitmans, G. Voss).

M. Kessler, "New Directions in Biblical Exegesis," *ScotJTh* 24 (1971), pp. 317-325.

R. Kieffer, *Essais de méthodologie néotestamentaire*, Lund, 1972.

J. D. Kingsburg, "Major Trends in Parable Interpretation," *Concordia Theological Monthly* 42 (1971), pp. 579-596.

K. Koch, *Was ist Formgeschichte? Neue Wege der Bibelexegese*, Neukirchen, 1967[2]. [Eng. trans., *The Growth of the Biblical Tradition; the form-critical method.* Tr. by S. M. Cupitt. London, 1969.]

K. Koch, "Linguistik und Formgeschichte, Nachwort der dritten, verbesserten Auflage" in *Was ist Formgeschichte? Methoden der Bibelexegese*, Neukirchen, 1974[3], pp. 289-342.

K. Koch, "Reichen die formgeschichtlichen Methoden für die Gegenwartsaufgaben der Bibelwissenschaft zu?," *ThLZ* 98 (1973), cols. 801-814.

R. Lapointe, *Les trois dimensions de l'herméneutique*, Paris, 1967.

R. Lapointe, "La valeur linguistique du Sitz im Leben," *Bib* 52 (1971), pp. 469-487.

Linguistica biblica, Interdisziplinäre Zeitschrift für Theologie und Linguistik, editor E. Guettgemanns.

G. Maier, *Das Ende der historisch-kritischen Methode*, Wuppertal, 1974.

L. Marin, *Sémiotique de la Passion, Topiques et figures*, Bruges, Neuchâtel, Paris, 1971. [Eng. trans., *The Semiotics of the Passion Narratives*. Tr. by Alfred M. Johnson, Jr. Pittsburgh, The Pickwick Press, 1979.]

J. M. Pohier, *Au nom du Père. Recherches théologiques et psychanalytiques*, Paris, 1972.

W. Richter, *Exegese als Literaturgeschichte*, Göttingen, 1971.

P. Ricoeur, *Le Conflit des interprétations. Essais d'herméneutique*, Paris, 1969. [Eng. trans., *The Conflict of Interpretations; essays in hermeneutics*. Ed. by Don Ehode. Evanston: Northwestern University Press, 1974.]

P. Ricoeur, *Les incidences théologiques des recherches actuelles concernant le langage*, Paris, n.d.

G. van Riet, "Exégèse et réflexion philosophique," in *Exégèse et Théologie. Les Saintes Ecritures et leur interprétation théologique*, Mélanges J. Coppens, 3, Gembloux, Paris, 1968.

J. Rohde, *Die redaktionsgeschichtliche Methode*, Berlin, 1965.

J. F. A. Sawyer, *Semantics in Biblical Research. New Methods of Defining Hebrew Words for Salvation*, London, 1972.

W. Schenk, "Die Aufgaben der Exegese und die Mittel der Linguistik," *ThLZ* 98 (1973), cols. 881-894.

J. Schreiner, *Einführung in die Methoden der biblischen Exegese*, Würzburg, 1971.

Y. Spiegel, editor, *Psychoanalytische Interpretationen biblischer Texte*, München, 1972.

P. Stuhlmacher, "Neues Testament und Hermeneutik. Versuch einer Bestandsaufnahme," *ZThK* 68 (1971), pp. 121-161.

P. Stuhlmacher, "Thesen zur Methodologie gegenwärtiger Exegese," *ZNW* 63 (1972), pp. 18-26.

G. Thils and R. E. Brown, editors, *Exégèse et Théologie. Les Saintes Ecritures et leur interprétation théologique*, Mélanges J. Coppens, 3, Gembloux, Paris, 1968.

A. N. Wilder, *Early Christian Rhetoric, The Language of the Gospel*, London, 1964.

W. Wink, *The Bible in Human Transformation. Toward a New Paradigm for Biblical Study*, Philadelphia, 1973.